MENNONITES OF AMERICA

The Mennonites of America

C. HENRY SMITH, A. M., Ph. D. (Chicago)
Professor of History in Goshen College

Published by the Author
1909

WIPF & STOCK · Eugene, Oregon

Wipf and Stock Publishers
199 W 8th Ave, Suite 3
Eugene, OR 97401

The Mennonites of America
By Smith, C. Henry
ISBN 13: 978-1-55635-315-4
Publication date 3/2/2007
Previously published by Mennonite Publishing House, 1909

To the memory of my
FATHER
For many years
a bishop in the church
and my
MOTHER
This volume is affectionately
Dedicated.

TABLE OF CONTENTS

Chapter		Page
	Introduction	13
I	The Anabaptists	16
II	Menno Simons and the Mennonites of Europe	53
III	Cornelisz Pieter Plockhoy and the Mennonite Colony on the Delaware	81
IV	Germantown	94
V	The Pequea Colony	134
VI	Franconia	183
VII	Expansion of the Pequea Colony before 1800	192
VIII	The Amish	208
IX	During the Revolution	253
X	The Mennonites of Ontario	265
XI	The Mennonites During the Nineteenth Century	275
	1. Settlements in Ohio, Illinois, Indiana and the Western States	
	2. Schisms.	
	3. The Civil War.	
XII	The Immigration from Russia	324
XIII	The General Conference of Mennonites	343

XIV	The Mennonites and the State	353
XV	Principles, Customs and Culture	386
XVI	Literature and Hymnology	409
XVII	The Present	446
XVIII	Bibliography	456

LIST OF ILLUSTRATIONS

Germantown Church
Dirck Keyser House
Thones Kunders House
Old Bench and Table
Rohrerstown Church
Doylestown Church
Plot of Ground
Christ Herr House
Brick Graveyard
Pequea Creek
Conestoga Wagon
Skippack Meeting House
Franconia Graveyard
Bank Church
Weaver Church
Kinzer Church
Partridge Church
Bethel College
Schrock Barn
Old Amish Homestead
Landisville Log Church
Boehm Chapel
How They Went to Church
Goshen College
Bluffton College
John F. Funk
J. S. Coffman
J. H. Oberholtzer
Joseph Stuckey

THE OLD GERMANTOWN CHURCH. Built 1770. Still standing. This old building occupied the middle of the battlefield in the battle of Germantown.

INTRODUCTION

To write a history of the Mennonites of America is not an easy task. Material from which to construct the complete life story of the Mennonite people is meager, and hence in the selection of the subject matter of this book and in the method of treatment the dearth of material has made it impossible for the author to exercise much choice. If more attention is paid to the early settlements made by small colonies of the denomination throughout the land and to the various church schisms than to the history of the development of their church life, it is both because more has been recorded of the former than of the latter, and also because when this is told almost the whole of their story has been recited.

The Mennonites have almost invariably been a rural people. They formed congregations which were generally self-governing and independent of one another, and hence had little of a common organized church life. They were a sober, quiet and unassuming people, took little interest in government and the affairs of the outside world. They were seldom molested in the even tenor of their way and consequently their history is largely the story of the life of a number of individual farming communities with little of special interest to lend color to their history.

Although the story of the religious life of the Mennonites may be told in few words, yet they have been the founders of the first German colony in America and have been among the pioneers in many of the frontier settlements in the westward expansion of the American people. And for this reason their history is of interest also to the student of general American history. I have attempted therefore to trace in this volume not only the history of the Mennonite church but also the complete life story of the Mennonite people, and have treated such phases of the subject as I could find material for.

I have attempted further to cover the entire field of American Mennonite history and have tried to place every event of importance in its proper perspective. So far as possible I have tried to be impartial toward the various branches of the church and have given each the amount of space which according to my judgment its importance deserved.

It is hoped that this volume may be of interest and profit to the thousands who are no longer within the Mennonite church, but who trace their lineage to a Mennonite ancestry, as well as to those who are still to be found within the various branches of the denomination.

I am indebted to many friends for criticisms, suggestions and the use of manuscript sources. These are mentioned throughout the book in their proper places. In addition to these I wish to thank especially John F. Funk of Elkhart, Indiana, for the use of his private

INTRODUCTION 15

library; H. P. Krehbiel and Christian Krehbiel of Newton, Kansas, for kindly reading the manuscript for chapters XII and XIII; N. B. Grubb of Philadelphia for the use of a number of cuts relating to the Germantown church; D. H. Bender, for editing the manuscript; the Mennonite Publishing House, for the use of a number of cuts; and Professor D. S. Gerig, of Goshen College, for critical suggestions.

C. Henry Smith.

Goshen, Indiana, November 14, 1908.

CHAPTER I

THE ANABAPTISTS

Regarding the origin of the Mennonites there is some difference of opinion among those interested in
Origin of   Mennonite history. Some trace them
Mennonites   to the Anabaptists; others credit the Waldenses with being their ancestors;
still others try to follow, through numerous medieval sects which had certain religious beliefs in common, a continuous line of succession from the very days of the apostles themselves. While it is possible to trace several religious doctrines and practices, common to the later Mennonites, through various medieval sects and a number of individual religious reformers, yet it is merely a waste of time to try to carry the continuity of the Mennonite church, either as an organization or as to its faith in its totality, beyond the Anabaptists.

The Anabaptists were a so-called radical religious sect which developed in middle Europe during the
early sixteenth century, out of the Luth-
Beginnings of   eran and Zwinglian revolutions. In the
Anabaptists   early stages of the Reformation both Luther and Zwingli were in favor of a departure from the old system far more radical and

more literally in accord with the teaching of the New Testament than that which they adopted a few years later. When it became apparent that both favored the retention of some of the fundamental principles of the old system, those who favored a more radical and thorough change began to withdraw from the movement. Among the demands made by the radicals was the withdrawal of the magistrates from all interference in matters of religion—in other words, a separation of church and state. To the common man especially, it seemed that all his ills, religious and social, were due to an established state church. And so, many were as much opposed to a Lutheran or Zwinglian established church as they had been to the Catholic system. True churches according to their views must be voluntary and independent organizations composed of members each of whom must be individually responsible to God for his religious beliefs.

This opposition first appeared as a radical tail to the Zwinglian movement in Zurich. Dissatisfaction with Zwingli's reforms had begun as early as 1521 among some of his followers, but the first rupture took place in a disputation held in the fall of 1523 between the Catholics and Zwingli's party. In the controversy as to what should constitute the final authority on all religious beliefs, Zwingli demanded obedience to God and the Bible. He would reject what was unscriptural. Dr. Faber of the Catholic party insisted that the Universities should be called upon to judge. Hereupon Simon Stumpf, pastor at Höngg, who was in Zurich at the time and who was one of the radicals, declared that the Spirit of God must decide all matters of difference, and that furthermore each one must interpret the Bible for himself. Here we find the germ of the teaching of the people whom we later call Anabaptists—namely, that no outside authority, either lay or ecclesiastical has the right to force any religious system upon the people.

Another fundamental question, which was lightly touched upon here but which later became the chief cause of contention between the Zwinglians and the radicals, was infant baptism. Even at this time the radical element had been forced by the logic of their position to question both the necessity and scriptural basis of infant baptism. If the church was to be a voluntary, independent organization, then infant baptism, the sign of initiation into a universal church, had to be discarded.

It is impossible to designate any single individual as the author of these radical doctrines. Zurich had for some time been the rallying point for all those who were dissatisfied with the Zwinglian reform. The movement soon crystallized itself, however, and associated itself with the names of several men who, if not the founders of the sect we know as Anabaptists, at any rate became its leaders. These men were Conrad Grebel, Felix Manz, William Reublin, George Blaurock, and several others.

Conrad Grebel Conrad Grebel in the early period of the Reformation was Zwingli's admired friend. As late as 1522 Zwingli spoke of him as "a most learned and candid youth." His father was a member of the Zurich Council. Conrad was not a church man, but was educated at the Universities of Vienna and Paris. By 1523 he differed from Zwingli on infant baptism, and also opposed the union of church and state. The church ought to be composed only of true believers, he said, those who were truly converted. He agreed with Zwingli on the discarding of pictures and the mass, but differed again on the question as to what was to take the place of the mass in religious worship. The real cause of difference however, lay deeper than any of these things. In his estimation Zwingli did not go far enough in his effort at reform. The Bible must be the final authority on all these questions, and the new church must be organized after the example of the early apostolic church. Some authorities say that Grebel hoped to be elected professor of Greek in a school at Zurich but that Zwingli used his influence against both him and Manz who hoped to become professor of Hebrew, and that consequently both these men arose in opposition to him from personal, rather than religious grounds. But from what we know of the later life, religious zeal and martyrdom of these two men, it does not seem that this accusation is just.

Felix Manz Felix Manz, a native of Zurich, and also a thorough scholar and a firm friend of Zwingli's from the first, as early as 1522 began to question the scriptural grounds for infant baptism and a state church. After failing to convert Zwingli to his views he began to preach in the fields and in his mother's house. He was arrested at Chur and sent out of the city, but soon returned, and remained for some time and became one of the founders of the new independent church in 1525.

George Blaurock had been a monk at Chur, but

some time before 1523 he renounced the Roman church and came to Zurich to seek light from Zwingli. Failing to find satisfaction here he joined the radical party and was the first to be baptized into the new organization which came into existence by virtue of that act in 1525.

George Blaurock

William Reublin in 1521 became a priest in Basel. He was a deep student of the Bible and a preacher of evangelical truths. Later he became preacher at Wittikon near Zurich where he met Grebel, Manz and Blaurock. He was one of the first of the priests to marry. He soon joined the Swiss cause and became a zealous worker for the movement.

William Reublin

These are the principal characters concerned in the origin of the Anabaptists in Zurich. Many others, preachers as well as laymen, including such men as Ludwig Hetzer and Hans Brödli, soon joined them. After the disputation of 1523, it is likely that the followers of Grebel and Manz met separately for worship. Many of them said that the church must be made up of true believers, and thus they could not worship with those of the state church. They met at first in the home of the mother of Felix Manz for Bible study, and studied especially the history of the early apostolic church and made it a model for the new body. They found that the apostles and their followers said nothing about tithes, taxes and church benefices. Consequently they thought the present practices wrong and attempted to get back to the independent church and community of goods prevalent in the days of the apostles. They could not find that any of the members of the early

First Meetings

church held office, so they considered it wrong for a Christian to be a magistrate. They saw that the early church did not fight, so they could not use the sword. In fact the whole movement soon became an attempt to reproduce the letter as well as the spirit of the primitive apostolic church, with the Sermon on the Mount as the basis of their faith.

Just how general these doctrines were and how thoroughly these people believed in them at this time (1524) is not easy to say. But judging **Early** from their earliest confession of faith on **Doctrines** record (Schleitheim, 1527) and from the accusations made against them by the authorities in their trials during persecution, these practices were embodied in well defined articles of faith by 1527, and must have been believed in quite generally even at this time. In the meantime the gap between the Zwinglians and the "Brethren," as they now called themselves, was growing wider. Zwingli tried to win over his opponents by disputations, both private and public—a common practice at that time. As was to be expected, however, these debates served only to confirm each side of the truth of its own position. Zwingli, having the temporal authorities in sympathy with him, was inevitably proclaimed victorious. The most decisive of the great public disputations was held January 17, 1525. On the side of the Brethren appeared Grebel, Manz, Reublin, Castelberger, Brödli, |Hetzer and Blaurock. The principal issue was infant baptism, the Brethren maintaining that only true believers should be baptized and the Zwinglians declaring in favor of baptizing infants. Neither side was convinced, but the Brethren were declared vanquished in the debate. Zwingli, however, seeing that nothing could be hoped for from this method of coercion, determined to use his influence with the civil authorities in rooting out the dangerous doctrine. January 18, 1525, the Council issued a decree ordering the leaders to leave Zurich, and furthermore ordered that all unbaptized children were to be baptized within eight days. This last order was not observed, and on February 1, of the same year another decree ordered the disobedient to be arrested and all infants to be baptized as soon as born.

About this time, 1525, whether before or after the great disputation is uncertain, the Brethren took the final and decisive step which com-
Introduction of pletely cut them off from the state
Adult Baptism church and branded them with the name that later became odious to them —the name Anabaptists. This step was the introduction of rebaptism, or adult baptism, on confession of faith only. The scene is best described by one of the earlier authorities.[1]

Blaurock was the first man to be baptized by Conrad Grebel and afterwards to baptize others. From this time on they were called Anabaptists. How this baptism was administered and how the Lord's supper was afterwards held is discussed in the account of Rudolph Thoman who was later put into prison. The account reads as follows: Rudolf Thoman answered that he desired to eat the Lord's supper with Brödlin of Wittikon, and with this in view he had invited him to his (Thoman's) house. He had not invited any others but by and by many others came and soon the room was full. Among other things, it happened, as they read and admon-

---

1. Fuesslin, J. C., Beiträge zur Kirchen Geschichte des Schweitzerlandes. I. p. 225.

ished one another, that Hans Brubbach of Zumikon arose, wept and cried out that he was a great sinner and asked that they would pray for him. Whereupon Blaurock asked him whether he desired the grace of God. He replied, "Yes." Then Manz arose and said, "Who shall hinder me from baptizing him?" Blaurock answered, "No one." Thereupon he took a pitcher of water and baptized him in the name of the Son, Father and Holy Ghost. After this Jacob Hottinger arose and demanded to be baptized. Manz also baptized him.

This was the decisive step in the development of the new movement. It was the act which finally cut off the radicals from the state church. Its significance lay in the fact that now the new church began definite organization, and in the complete severing of church and state. Baptism became the outward sign of membership in the new organization.

This is by no means the first case in history of adult baptism, or even of rebaptism, but the rite seems now to have a new meaning. Blaurock himself confesses that so far as he knows he was the first to be baptized. Some good authorities say, however, that Storch administered rebaptism. It is not likely that Münzer rebaptized any one, although Bullinger says he did, and that Manz and Grebel learned the practice from him. Reublin probably baptized at Waldshut in 1524, the year preceding Blaurock's baptism. The Waldenses and other older sects also sometimes performed the rite. But whatever may have been the case heretofore, baptism from henceforth had a new significance. It was an indication that the baptized person had become a member of a new organization, one with a clear cut and well defined separation from the older church.

In the meantime a movement had arisen in Saxony

which in some respects was similar to the one in Switzerland. While the latter, however, was purely religious, the former was largely political and social.

The Zwickau Prophets

In Germany, as in Switzerland, there were those who were disappointed in the Reformation. The radical party here first arose in Saxony. Heinrich Bullinger, a contemporary of the leaders of that day, in speaking of these events, says:

> About the year 1521 or 1522 there arose in Saxony a number of restless spirits among whom Nicholas Storch was one of the most influential, who went about saying that God revealed himself to them through dreams and visions, that there must be a new world in which only righteousness shall prevail. Therefore all godless people must be destroyed from the earth and all godless princes and lords. They called all people godless who did not take part with them. At first they kept these matters secret. From this same school came Thomas Münzer who also had his followers, Pfeiffer, Rink and many others. This Münzer boasted that God had revealed Himself to him. All his conversation and writing was bitter against the preachers and also against the magistrates.

The leaders of this movement, Storch and Münzer, because of these claims which they first made public in Zwickau, were called the Zwickau prophets.

Storch was a weaver, and although a layman, was well read in the Bible. Münzer in speaking of him said that he knew the Scriptures better than any priest. Of his doctrinal system we have no exact knowledge. But it is thought that he imbibed his ideas from the Bohemian Picards, since he advocated many of the beliefs of that religious sect. He rejected infant baptism, although there is no evidence that he practiced rebaptism. He is also charged with teaching the rejection of oaths, of the magistracy, and of warfare, and the community of goods among Christians. He believed also strongly in visions and the inner light. An angel appeared before him one night, he said, and informed him that he would be placed on the throne of the archangel Gabriel, and that a new kingdom of the elect would be established on the earth, while all unbelievers would be destroyed. He exerted considerable influence over his fellow weavers and others of the masses in Saxony. By 1521 a separate religious organization had been established by him. After the fashion of the primitive church, twelve apostles and seventy evangelists were sent out to spread broadcast his teaching. Among those who were won over to his views and who took a prominent part in the movement was Marcus Stübner, a Wittenberg student.

Thomas Münzer was born about 1490 and was well educated. He was a restless spirit and had taken up the work of reform even before Luther had, and in 1513 he had formed a conspiracy against the bishop of Magdeburg. After leading a wandering life for several years he finally became pastor of the Lutheran church at Zwickau with the full approval of Luther. Here he became closely associated with Storch and began a fierce attack upon the avarice and corruption of the monks and priests, and denounced many of the practices of the new as well as of the old church. As a result of these attacks he was forced to leave Zwickau in 1521.

From here he traveled through Bohemia and the small towns of Saxony, preaching radical ideas. He finally came to Alstädt where he soon gathered a large following and became pastor of a congregation in 1523. Here he began his denunciation of the Lutheran and the Catholic church, and the temporal government, and soon formed an organization whose members were bound by oath to stand by each other, the purpose of which was to overthrow the old government and set up in its place a new one. A crusade against the pictures, statuary, altars and church buildings near Alstädt was inaugurated by him, all of which he said savored of idolatry and were not necessary in the worship of God. He laid more stress upon direct revelation than upon the teaching of the Bible. "One might read ten thousand Bibles," he said, "and yet it would not help him." He considered himself a prophet sent from God to set right the times. Like many of the enthusiasts of that day, he pretended to make the primitive church, together with certain teachings of the Old Testament and Revelation, the basis of his new system.

Infant baptism he rejected as useless, although in theory rather than in practice. He never baptized adults and it is not likely that he himself was ever rebaptized. In spite of his apparent rejection of the doctrine, however, he continued to baptize infants as late as 1522 and when he translated the Latin liturgy into German he retained the formula for infant baptism.

Closely associated with Münzer's religious views were many radical political ideas. He attacked the foundations of the state as well as those of the established church, and when the temporal authorities forbade him to preach he asked his followers to pay no attention to their demands. God, he said, gave the temporal princes in his anger to the world, and He will put them out of the way.

Münzer's Political Ideas

Those princes who would not repent and would not

accept the Gospel must even as the Catholic ecclesiasts be destroyed with fire and sword. They stand not only against the true faith but also against the natural rights of man. Consequently they must be strangled like dogs.

Rulers must govern for the good of the people and are accountable to them. He also seemed to favor community of goods, equality in social life and a leveling of all class distinctions.

As a result of these fanatical teachings, George of Saxony finally ordered Münzer to leave Alstädt and never return to his kingdom under penalty of severe punishment. Münzer seems to have gone to Mühlhausen and other places in South Germany. Early in 1524 he made an eight weeks tour through Switzerland and Lower Germany; at Waldshut he met Hubmeier and other leaders of the Swiss Anabaptist movement.

He entered into warm sympathy with the peasants of Southern Germany in their struggle to free themselves from the economic and social burdens to which the church and the land tenure system of that day subjected them. When the peasants' revolt broke out in 1525, Münzer became one of the leaders of the peasants and was among the number who were captured in the battle of Frankenhausen; he was shortly afterward executed.

Are Münzer and his fellow laborers at Zwickau to be regarded as Anabaptists? On this question authorities differ. The difference, how-

Were the Zwickau Prophets Anabaptists? ever, seems to be largely one of interpretation of the term Anabaptist. If the term is to include all those radical sects which followed in the wake of the Reformation, and which rejected many of the doctrines and practices of the Lutheran and Zwinglian movements, including infant baptism, then the Zwickau prophets may be regarded as Anabaptists. But if the term is to be confined to the Swiss type who not only rejected infant baptism but also instituted adult baptism, and who refused to take an oath or to hold office and regarded all warfare as contrary to the teaching of Jesus, then Münzer and his school can not be classed as Anabaptists, at least not of the peaceful, non-resistant type.

Although Münzer had traveled through Switzerland early in 1524 and had received a friendly welcome from the leaders of the Swiss Brethren, it is not likely that he exerted much influence over them, especially after they learned of his attitude toward the civil authorities

Attitude of the Swiss toward Münzer The attitude of the Swiss toward Münzer can be learned from a letter written to him by them, under date of September 5, 1524. It reads in part as follows:

> At this time we read your writings against the false faith and baptism. We were comforted and strengthened and wonderfully rejoiced to find one who had the same view of Christianity as we, and who dared to show the evangelical preachers their shortcomings, how they in all the principal articles conduct themselves falsely and set up their own good judgment instead of following the judgment of God. Therefore we beg of you as a brother to preach the true word of God earnestly and fearlessly; to set up and defend only godly practices, and value and defend the pure Gospel.

They differ with Münzer on certain minor points of practice, such as the substitution of singing for the mass, etc. In reference to baptism the letter goes on:

> We are very much pleased with your writing and desire to be taught more on the subject.

In conclusion they say:

> Regard us as your brethren and understand this writing to have been done through great joy and hope of you through God, and teach and comfort as you well can. Pray to God for us that He may help us in our faith. We desire you to write again.

This is signed by Grebel, Manz, Castelberg and others. Grebel adds a postscript to the letter in which he says that some one has written him that Münzer taught that the peasants should lay violent hands on the temporal princes. He warns him against this and admonishes him to renounce the teaching. He says the true disciple of Christ must suffer persecution but cannot offer violence to any one. He adds that he warns him because of his love for him.

This letter shows that although the Swiss were greatly impressed with Münzer's writing and that they felt that they had found in him a kindred spirit, yet they were suspicious of his teaching regarding the Christian's relation to the temporal authority. Of Münzer's influence in Switzerland, Ludwig Keller, probably one of the best and at the same time a sympathetic modern critic of Anabaptist lore says:

> Münzer may in his visit to Switzerland have gained certain individuals, yet it is true that he did not succeed in exerting any very great influence upon the heretofore leaders of the Swiss movement. The further development of this sect was not changed by him.

Let us return to the Zurich Brethren. The introduction of rebaptism gained for them the name "Wiedertäufer" or Anabaptists. They never acknowledged the term, but spoke of themselves merely as the Brethren. We shall speak of them here as Anabaptists.

The year 1525 marks the beginning of the persecution of the Anabaptists. Zwingli now saw that the new movement was becoming a menace to his **Early** state system and consequently did all he **Persecutions** could to persuade the Zurich authorities to stamp out the new teaching. Powers of persuasion were first tried, and to this end numerous public disputations were held with the Anabaptists. But when these failed, severer measures were resorted to. After the disputation of 1525, the leaders were ordered to leave the canton, their teaching was suppressed and all children were ordered to be baptized within eight days. At first the penalty for disobedience was a money fine. But when it was found that the Anabaptists were increasing in numbers and insisted on coming back, banishment and finally the death penalty was decreed for those who dared return. Blaurock was sent out of the city. Grebel died a natural death in 1526. Felix Manz was the first of the leaders to suffer the death penalty. After converting hundreds to the new faith he was finally apprehended and suffered martyrdom by drowning in 1527.

As a result of these persecutions the leaders were scattered over Switzerland and Southern Germany in a short time. Wherever they went they **Rapid Spread** preached the new doctrines and ad- **of Anabaptists** ministered the rite of baptism upon hundreds and thousands of believers. Grebel had gone to Schaffhausen, Brödli to Hallau, and Reublin to Waldshut where he had baptized Balthasar Hubmeir and his entire congregation. From here Reublin went to Strasburg in 1526. Soon churches were established in Zollikon, Grüningen, Appenzell, St. Gallen, Schaffhausen, Berne, Basel and all along the upper Rhine country in Switzerland and across the border in Germany, and soon the movement crept down the Rhine. Hetzer went to Augsburg from Zurich. In 1526 Hubmeir went to Augsburg, and later to Moravia.

Some of these congregations grew to large dimensions. The one at St. Gallen soon numbered eight hundred members, to which fifteen hundred more were added from Appenzell. The little town of St. Gallen became so full of Anabaptists that it was called the little Jerusalem. The church at Augsburg also soon contained one thousand members. In 1526 a congregation was established at Steyr and about the same time others were organized at Worms and Nuremberg. By 1527 there were thirty-eight congregations in the canton of Zurich alone.

Reublin, from Strasburg as a center, visited Rottenburg, Reutlingen, Esslingen and Ulm. All along the course of the Rhine in the large cities, Anabaptist communities were soon found. By 1528 the movement had entered the lower Rhine country and from there spread over the Netherlands. The cause for this rapid spread of the new faith is discussed later in this chapter.

Sebastian Frank, an old chronicler of that day in speaking of the movement says:

> In the year 1526 a new party arose whose leaders and bishops were Hubmeir, Rink, Hut, Denk and Hetzer. They spread so rapidly that their teaching soon covered the whole land and they soon secured a large following and also added

to their number many good hearts who were zealous toward God.

Tendencies of the Movement
Of course it is not to be supposed that a movement which spread so rapidly and which was subject to so many modifying local influences retained throughout its course all the tendencies of its early beginnings. Anabaptism was above all intensely individualistic, and in the course of its brief history it manifested a variety of tendencies according to the spirit and opinions of its chief leaders. It is impossible here to name all these leaders, but next to the founders of the sect, among the most influential and those who were most responsible for these various tendencies of the movement were Hans Denk, Balthasar Hubmeir, Hans Hut and Melchior Hoffman. Each of these stamped his own personality upon the trend of the development of Anabaptism, and each modified the interpretation of its chief doctrines to suit his own theories.

Hans Denk
Hans Denk was a student at the University of Ingolstadt and early allied himself with the reform movement. In 1523 he was made professor in the St. Albans school at Nuremberg. Already at this place his orthodoxy was questioned by the Lutheran authorities in the city, and in 1525 he was required to write out his confession of faith. His chief cause for complaint seems to have been that the reform was not thorough enough. It did not attempt to reform the life of the individual. Nuremberg was a center of Waldensian teaching at this time and it may be that Denk imbibed some of their doctrines.

As a result of these differences he was banished

from Nuremberg never to return under penalty of capital punishment. He at once went to the Swiss Brethren at St. Gallen, and soon afterward to Augsburg where he found a large congregation of Brethren. It is supposed that he was secretly baptized in 1526 by Hubmeir who was preaching there at this time. On Easter, 1526, Denk in turn baptized Hut and many others. Near the close of 1526 Denk fled to Strasburg where a large church had been organized. While there he drew many noted merchants to the church—including two members of the lower council—to the number of eleven hundred. He soon had to leave the city, however, and wandered about for another year, visiting Worms, Zurich and other centers of Anabaptism. He died at Basel October, 1527.

Denk exerted great influence upon the history of the Anabaptists of his time both by his preaching and his writings. He spent much time in defending the Anabaptists against the charges of the Catholic and Reform parties. He also helped to translate part of the Old Testament from the Hebrew to the German. In his faith he agreed, in the main, with the earlier Anabaptists, although he differed from them in some respects. This difference was great enough to attach to his followers the name "Denkianer." He was not an enthusiast on rebaptism and said in later life he was sorry that he ever rebaptized any one. He taught that Christ alone was not sufficient for salvation. Free will must also be exercised. He further taught that no man will remain forever damned. Even the evil spirits will be regenerated. In common with Hetzer he even doubted the Trinity and divinity of Christ.[2]

---

2. Arnold, Gottfried, II. p. 864.

THE ANABAPTISTS

Balthasar Hubmeir

Balthasar Hubmeir, preacher and professor at Ingolstadt, was converted from Catholicism to Zwinglianism in 1522. He first located at Waldshut from whence he often visited Basel and spoke with Denk, Grebel and Manz. In 1523 he was present and assisted Zwingli in the great debate with the Catholics. From here he went to Schaffhausen, but becoming dissatisfied with the Zwinglian movement on the ground that it did not insist strongly enough on a thorough reform of the individual and did not take the apostolic church as a model for its organization, he left the state church and cast his lot with the Anabaptists, being baptized by Reublin at Waldshut in 1525. Soon after this Hubmeir in turn baptized out of a milk pail over three hundred believers. From this time to his death two years later he lived the life of a fugitive. He first went to Constance where he spent some time in establishing Anabaptist communities and from there in 1526 fled to Moravia which at this time was an asylum for the persecuted Anabaptists of other countries. Here he labored at Nicolsburg for about a year when upon the request of the Austrian government he and his wife were cast into prison. After nearly a year of imprisonment he was finally burned at the stake on March 10, 1528. Three days later his devoted wife was cast into the Danube. Hubmeir had once been led by the excruciating pain which he suffered on the rack to recant, but later repented his weakness and when he was tied to the stake he first thrust his right hand into the flames because as he said it had been the hand with which he had written the recantation.

Hubmeir built up large congregations wherever he went. He was a learned man, being educated at the University of Freiburg, and later he became a professor at Ingolstadt. He was also a voluminous writer and many of his writings are still extant.

In his religious views Hubmeir was one of the most moderate of the Anabaptists. Unlike the radical elements of the party, he opposed communism. In most of the religious doctrines he agreed with the Swiss Brethren except that he did not follow them in their doctrine of non-resistance as regards warfare and the magistracy. He taught that a Christian might be a magistrate and even bear arms, although not for the purpose of enforcing any particular set of religious opinions. It is this half-way position of Hubmeir's among the Anabaptists of his day that leads the modern Baptists to regard him as the greatest leader of the movement, and as the one most nearly in accord with their own faith.

In the meantime the persecution of the Anabaptists went on apace. In almost every country, and by all of the established churches those who **Continued** showed any signs of belief in the new **Persecutions** doctrines were banished, imprisoned and burned at the stake or thrown into the rivers. Kirschmeyer estimates that from 1525 to 1530 over one thousand were slain in Tyrol alone. Sebastian Frank counts up six hundred as having perished at Ensisheim, the seat of the Austrian government in its southwestern dominions. In another small city seventy-six were killed in six weeks| Duke William of Bavaria issued the blood-thirsty decree that all those who recanted should be beheaded, while those who did not should be burned. Cornelius, a reliable although Catholic historian says:

The blood of these poor people flowed like water. But hundreds of them, of all ages and both sexes, suffered the pangs of torture without a murmur, refusing to redeem their lives by recanting, and went to the place of execution with joy and singing psalms.

Partly as a result of these severe persecutions, but more as a result of the fanatical teaching of certain leaders of the movement who perhaps were influenced somewhat by the teaching of Münzer and other enthusiasts, there appeared by about 1527 in Southern Germany the first signs of those chiliastic tendencies which a few years later resulted in the disastrous Münster episode.

Chiliastic Tendencies This chiliastic spirit which was potentially present in the teaching of some of the earlier leaders was openly manifested in the life and work of Hans Hut.

Hans Hut Hut was a native of Franconia, and by trade a book-binder. In 1524 he made the acquaintance of Thomas Münzer whom he assisted in printing and circulating his pamphlets. Later he fell in with some Anabaptists and was converted to that faith. In 1526 he was rebaptized by Hans Denk. He now went about, preaching and baptizing. Although now an Anabaptist in his affiliations and in many of the essential tenets of the faith, yet he did not recognize the non-resistant doctrine which at the time was still held by the majority of the Anabaptists, and had evidently not yet gotten away entirely from the teachings of Münzer. He was one of the earliest among the sect to teach millenarianism. Christ would shortly come, he said, and would give His kingdom over into the hands of the elect, which of course meant those who had been rebaptized. He himself was the special agent appointed by God to make known these things to the elect, who in the last days were to have two-edged swords in their hands. Upon the establishing of Christ's kingdom all the temporal rulers as well as the priests and pastors would be punished for their intolerance and false doctrines. This work of vengeance was to be performed by an invasion of Turks, after which the earth was to be given over to the Saints. In 1527 Hut actually gathered together a large number of his followers in Franconia for the purpose of leading them to Switzerland, Mühlhausen or Hungary to await the coming of the Turks. The advent of Christ was set for Whitsuntide 1528.

The Christian himself may use the sword in taking possession of the new kingdom but he must wait until God ordered him to unsheath it. Here we have, if not the actual teaching of the later Münsterites, at least the germ out of which that teaching grew.

These doctrines Hut preached first at Augsburg and the surrounding region and later at Nicolsburg where he tried to gain the large community in which Hubmeir was teaching, to his party. Hut was finally arrested and imprisoned in Nicolsburg. He lost his life in an attempt to escape from prison at Augsburg.

In Melchior Hoffman we have the doctrines of Hans Hut carried one step farther. Hoff-
Melchior man came originally from Suabia, and un-
Hoffman like some of the Anabaptist leaders he was a laboring man, being a leather-dresser by trade. As early as 1523 we find him in Zurich and

soon after as a Lutheran agitator in Northern Germany. In 1524 we find him in company with Melchior Rink, a disciple of Münzer, on a preaching tour through Sweden. At Stockholm he became involved in a crusade against the images in the churches, and was forced to leave. In 1525 he finally appeared in Wittenberg where he first began his teaching regarding the kingdom of the elect. Hoffman, although not an educated man, knew his Bible from cover to cover, being especially saturated with the teachings of the Prophets and Revelation, which seemed to appeal to his imagination. In common with Hans Hut he believed in a speedy coming of Christ's kingdom on earth and taught that he himself was a prophet and would be given the task of appointing the king when the time should come.

In 1527 he appears again as an agitator of these views in Holstein. In 1529 he came to Strasburg which at that time was an asylum for Anabaptists. Soon he again left for East Friesland.

Hoffman was not the first Anabaptist in Northern Germany and the Netherlands. Waldensians and other medieval evangelical sects had been found here for some time and at this time there were many communities of non-resistant Anabaptists. It is not known just when Hoffman cast his lot with them. In 1530 he advised a Zwinglian church at Strasburg to be put in charge of the Anabaptists and not long after this he was baptized at Embden, one of their strongholds. From this time on he became an enthusiastic preacher of Anabaptist doctrines as he understood them and spent several years in Northern Germany and the Netherlands. He was finally imprisoned at Strasburg in 1533, and here he remained until his death some time later.

In doctrine Hoffman agreed in the main with the large body of Anabaptists represented earlier by Grebel, Blaurock, and partly by Denk on baptism, free will, justification, church discipline and the ban; but differed in his attitude toward civil government, and also, as we have seen, on the kingdom of the elect. When he left Strasburg in 1532 for Friesland he predicted that Strasburg was to be the New Jerusalem and that the end would come in 1533. He was the Elias who was to crown the new King at that time. When the day upon which his prophecy was to be fulfilled came and passed he extended the time to successive dates as occasion demanded. Finally the belief grew among his followers that Münster, and not Strasburg was to be the New Jerusalem. From this time on the eyes of such as believed in the speedy establishment of a kingdom of the elect were turned toward Münster. Just what part the elect were to play in bringing about the new kingdom Hoffman did not explain. He did not make an appeal for an armed uprising as did his successors. Yet he taught that the non-believers must all be destroyed by the sword. This was dangerous teaching, and as we shall see prepared the way for the fierce fanaticism of Jan Matthys.

Hoffman before his imprisonment had appointed one Jan Matthys as leader of his people in East Friesland. Matthys now became the champion of millenarianism. He proclaimed himself the Enoch who was to inaugurate the new dispensation. Unlike Hoffman, who merely prophesied that the new era would come,

Matthys now immediately set about to take a hand in bringing about the new kingdom by force. The movement now rapidly lost its religious character and assumed more and more a political nature. The story of Jan Matthys and his successor, John of Leyden, and the founding of the Münster kingdom, together with its fanatical rule furnish one of the most familiar as well as most disgraceful episodes in Anabaptist history and need not be repeated here.

In this brief sketch of the development of Anabaptism the term has been used in its widest application. All classes and tendencies of the **Peaceful** movement have been included. It is not **Anabaptists** to be supposed for a moment, however, that the teachings just mentioned were everywhere accepted. These chiliastic tendencies were confined to Northern Germany and the Netherlands. The majority of the Anabaptists of Switzerland, Moravia and Southern Germany were not tainted with millenarianism, and had not departed from their earlier non-resistant doctrines. Neither had those of the peaceful non-resistant faith altogether died out in Northern Germany. They bore their persecutions patiently and not much was heard of them. There were still many in these regions who were not influenced by the teachings of Melchior Hoffman or Jan Matthys. Bullinger, the avowed enemy of the Anabaptists, and a contemporary, in his book, "Against the Anabaptists," accuses them of fanaticism but never mentions, except in the case of the Münsterites, any revolutionary tendencies. These all had to face the charge of being Münsterites but they always stoutly denied that they had any sympathy or even any historical connection with them. Judging from Anabaptist confessions of faith which are still extant, from accusations made against them by the authorities and the records of their submissive spirit under persecution, it is safe to say that outside of the Münsterites, the large majority were at least peaceable, loyal and obedient citizens, if not indeed altogether non-resistant. Sebastian Frank, one of the early authorities characterizes them as follows:

> I am thoroughly convinced that there are many simple, righteous people among this sect, and also their leaders try to fear God. Many of them desire such a holy, simple, consecrated Christian life that they no longer desire to live according to the flesh and no longer seek the things of the earth. For this reason they say a Christian should not live for the world and not care for the world, should desire death equally with life, etc.

While it is true that often individuals and communities held a variety of opinions and doctrines, some of which resembled those of the Münsterites, yet the large assemblies or conferences always rebuked any manifestations of fanaticism and always declared for the non-resistant doctrines. As early as 1526 Hans Denk presided over a large conference of leaders at Augsburg at which a warning note was raised against chiliastic and millenarian teaching, showing perhaps that already at that time these tendencies were cropping out among some of the leaders. One of the most important of these assemblages, and the one at which the earliest known Anabaptist confession of faith was drawn up, was held in 1527 at Schleitheim near Schaffhausen. This confession, called, "A Brotherly

[margin: Schleitheim Confession]

Union of Some Children of God," contains in substance the following declarations of doctrine.[3]

1. **Baptism.**—Baptism shall be administered to all who are taught repentance and a change of life, and truly believe in the forgiveness of their sins through Jesus Christ, and are willing to walk in newness of life; all those shall be baptized when they desire it and ask it by the decision of their own minds; which excludes all infant baptism according to the Scriptures and the practice of the Apostles.

2. **The Ban or Excommunication.**—This shall be practiced with all those who have given themselves to the Lord, to follow His commandments, are baptized, and call themselves brethren and sisters, and yet stumble and fall into sin, or are unexpectedly overtaken; these after admonition according to Matthew 18, if they do not repent shall be excommunicated.

3. **Breaking of Bread.**—All who wish to break "one bread" in remembrance of the broken body of Christ, and drink of "one cup" in remembrance of His shed blood, shall be united by baptism into one body which is the congregation of God and of which Christ is the Head.

4. **Separation from the World.**—The Christian must be separated from all the evil and wickedness that Satan has planted into the world. According to II Cor. 6:17,18. "We shall come out from among them and be separate:" separate from all Papistic works and services, meetings and churchgoings, drinking houses and other things which the world highly esteems.

5. **Ministers.**—The ministers shall, according to the teaching of Paul, be of good report of them that are without. He shall teach, exhort, and help all the members to advance in their spiritual life. When he has needs he shall be aided by the congregation which chose him to his work. If he should be driven away, or imprisoned, or killed, another minister shall at once be put into his place.

---

3. This confession can be found in many books on Anabaptist history. This brief summary is taken from John Horsch's pamphlet, "The Mennonites."

6. Taking the Sword.—The worldly governments of the land are to use the sword, but in the perfect congregation of Christ, excommunication is used, by which no one suffers violence to his body. Peter says: "Christ has suffered (not reigned) and has given us an example that we should follow his footsteps." Neither is it the Christian's work to have a part in civil government; because the rulings of government are according to the flesh, but the government of Christ is according to the Spirit. The weapons of the world are carnal, but the weapons of the Christian are spiritual to the overcoming of the world and Satan.

7. Oaths.—Christ, who taught the law in perfection, forbade His disciples all oaths, whether true or false. By this we understand that all swearing is forbidden.

This declaration, it will be observed, is soundly Biblical and thoroughly in accord with the doctrine of non-resistance. Later confessions embodied practically the same views.

From what has been said in this chapter the reader will readily observe that when speaking of Anabaptists one must keep in mind that there were a **Classes of** variety of sects some of which had no **Anabaptists** connection whatever with the others. The non-resistant, peaceful type, with which we are here most concerned and which maintained its identity all through this time, must not be confused with the fanatical, chiliastical element of the movement.

Bullinger in his work on the Anabaptists mentions no less than forty sects in his time under that name. Among the most prominent were: 1. **The Apostolic,** who read their Bibles very literally, traveled about without staff and shoes, carried no money. Some of them preached from the housetops, acted like children because the Bible said they must become like children to enter the kingdom of heaven, and had all their property in common. 2. **Those Excluded from the World.** They had nothing in common with the rest of the world. Their clothing was simply made and they had rules for eating, drinking, and sleeping. They had neither weddings nor banquets. In fact they discarded everything that was common to the outside world. 3. **The Holy, Sinless Baptists..** They could not sin; did not believe in original sin. They omitted the phrase, "Forgive our sins," from the Lord's Prayer; they did not need the prayers of the faithful. 4. **The Silent Brethren.** They thought that preaching was of no avail. It was not necessary for the world to hear the Word. When asked concerning their faith they kept silent. 5. **The Enthusiasts.** They were filled with the spirit of prophecy, saw visions and had dreams, and believed in an early second coming of Christ. In Amsterdam, 1535, five women and seven men filled with the spirit ran naked through the streets, preached, prayed, fell into a trance and warned the city against the wrath to come. 6. **The Free Brethren.** They were shunned by most of the others. They made the spiritual freedom a freedom of the flesh. They paid no tithes, nor taxes, and opposed slavery. Entered all sorts of disgraces. Had property and women in common. They taught that a Christian must hate all that belonged to him, even wife and child. 7. **Münsterites.** All other branches despised everything high and exalted, but these aimed at power.

It is not necessary to prolong the list. The remainder show the same basis of classification as the first seven. These different branches are classified according to the emphasis they place upon some particular interpretation of certain portions of the Bible. In the essentials of Anabaptist doctrine, such as baptism, independence of church and state, exclusion from the world, the ban, etc., they generally agree. It is the minor differences that constitute the classes. And yet they agree even in their differences— in this that they show an attempt to follow closely the teaching of the Bible as they saw it, sometimes the Old Testament, but much more frequently the New and generally the early primitive church. Generally speaking, too, all of them had to a slight extent what each one had to excess. Each one of them embodied some Biblical truth and could find passages of Scripture which seemed to substantiate the particular peculiarity for which they stood.

These classes must be taken as tendencies to excess in the entire body rather than well defined and distinct divisions, separate from all others. These were enthusiastic and fanatical tendencies that were likely to crop out occasionally but not characteristic of the body as a whole. It is difficult and impossible to say just how many belonged to one sect and how many to another, but it is fair to presume that the large body, as has already been suggested, were peaceable and law-abiding as well as deeply religious.

It is not at all strange that these differences occurred. The times offered an excellent opportunity for ambitious leaders to impress their personality upon the development of the movement. We have seen how various leaders as Denk, Hut, Hoffman, Hubmeir and others differed and how each secured a large personal following. The masses were adrift,

Reasons for These Classes

trusting neither Catholics nor Lutherans nor Zwinglians, anxiously awaiting leaders.

Persecution, which soon set in, made secrecy necessary and a common organization impossible. Each congregation was left to follow the bent of its own Biblical interpretation or fanatical impulse. Neither was system and organization consistent with the spirit of the movement. The people had just freed themselves from authority and tyranny and had just succeeded in separating church and state. The very thing they were fighting for was individual freedom in matters of religion.

Amid all of this diversity the people whom we call Anabaptists, including even the most fanatical, had many things in common; the most fundamental of which were probably:

1. The attempt to return in matters of faith as well as church discipline to the example of the early primitive church as it existed in the apostolic times. The Bible was made the final authority on all matters of faith and discipline. The New Testament was given preference over the Old, which was generally not considered binding on the true believers; yet some received from the Old Testament many suggestions for the establishing of the new Jerusalem. In addition to the Bible as authority there was the inner light or direct revelation from God. This belief was common to all to a certain extent but received different emphasis from different sects. Münzer placed direct revelation far above the Bible as the guide for life. The same tendency prevailed among the followers of Hans Hut, and Melchior Hoffman.

2. Complete separation of church and state. No

temporal or ecclesiastical authority has a right to force an unsatisfactory Biblical interpretation upon an unwilling subject. Justification must come through an individual faith. But faith alone is not sufficient (and here they differed from the Lutherans) it must be accompanied by works, the exercise of man's own free will. Baptism was the outward expression of this belief. No importance was attached to the mere act of baptism. All were agreed that infant baptism was unnecessary, but not all insisted on the necessity of the outward rebaptism. With some, the inward baptism that comes from the regeneration, of the heart was sufficient.

3. In many points of doctrine also there was a common dissatisfaction with both the Catholic and Reformed and Lutheran views. The Lord's supper was viewed only as a token of remembrance and not as containing the actual body of Christ. All agreed on the abolition of the mass. On the subject of the Trinity, incarnation and other doctrinal points there was a difference of opinion, giving rise to several distinct sects.

4. The Anabaptists always excluded themselves from the rest of the world. They were the elect and all who would not believe as they did were lost. We have already seen that politically and religiously they had nothing in common with other people. Many of them carried this spirit of exclusion into their social and business relations. In many cases members of the congregations could carry on business only with members of the same faith. Marriage with outsiders was strictly forbidden.

5. Of government there was no need by the

Christian. It was a necessity, but only for the unrighteous. This is the view found in most of the confessions of faith issued by the large assemblages of the leaders as at Schleitheim, 1527. This was the non-resistant attitude, held by the majority of the Swiss. Government was a necessity, was divinely ordained to punish the wicked and reward the righteous. A Christian, however, could not become a magistrate although he must render obedience and pay his just taxes. He could not take up the sword to kill even at the call of his country. He could not take the oath. Christ taught him to say, "Yea, yea; nay, nay."

Bullinger includes the attitude of non-resistance in his long list of tenets held in common by the large majority of Anabaptists. There were, however, two other well-defined views regarding civil government; the one represented by Hubmeir and the other by John of Leyden. The former believed in government, paid all taxes and obeyed all its ordinances that did not interfere with the free exercise of religion. It was proper to use the sword outside of persecution. The latter believed in the establishment of Christ's kingdom by the sword at the cost of sedition and revolution.

6. The disobedient were to be punished with the church ban. To be excluded from the rights and privileges of the membership at large. Later there was considerable difference of opinion on this question, which resulted in several distinct divisions.

In addition to these principles which the large body of Anabaptists held more or less in common, there were certain other well-defined tendencies which in spirit at least were also common to all, but upon which there was a greater divergence of opinion and practice than upon the six articles above mentioned. On the question of community of goods there was much difference of teaching as well as practice. Traces of a well-marked tendency in that direction, however, can be found in all. It was a characteristic of the early apostolic church. The oppression that the poor, unpropertied classes had to bear, naturally strengthened whatever natural tendency there may have been in a movement of this kind. Some actually had everything in common, others, including Hubmeir and Grebel, said it was not compulsory but that the brethren ought to be willing freely to help one another in case of need.

The belief in the early coming of Christ was also characteristic of them to a greater or less degree, in their hopes and expectations. Among the earlier Anabaptists the day may have been at some distance in the future and its coming may have been only a hope and a longing, but in the case of Hoffman and Hut, a definite time was set, while in the case of John of Leyden the day had actually come and John was to be the king of the new dispensation.

The refusal to pay tithes and taxes on the part of the more radical, had its germ in the teaching of the more conservative, many of whom taught that they really owed nothing to the government, but paid taxes simply to escape persecution. Stumpf, one of the early founders, and Grebel told Zwingli that they desired to found a church which should be made up of truly converted Christians who would live righteously, cling to the Gospel, and who would not be burdened with taxes or other forms of usury.

As we have already seen, the principles which characterized the faith of the Anabaptists can not be traced to any single individual as a source. The movement seems to have sprung up almost simultaneously over Switzerland and Southern Germany, especially along the upper Rhine country. The soil was well prepared for the reception of Anabaptist doctrine by earlier evangelical sects.

Causes for Rapid Spread   Among other deep seated causes that made possible this rapid spread, not the least potent was the increased and almost universal interest taken in the reading of the Bible among the common people. The Bible for a long time had been a sealed book to the laity, but by the beginning of the sixteenth century a new interest was taken in the study of the book. Many translations appeared about this time making it possible for the common people to get some knowledge of its contents. Between 1466-1518 there were no less than fourteen complete translations of the whole Bible in the High German language and four in the Low German dialect. In addition, up to 1518 the Gospels had appeared in about twenty-five editions, the Psalms in thirteen and other portions of the Bible in many more.

The leaders of the Anabaptists were invariably well versed in the Bible, the uneducated as well as those who had studied at the Universities. It is fair to say that in knowledge of the text of the Bible the Anabaptists were much in advance of both the Lutheran and Catholic clergy. It is not at all strange that these simple-minded people as many of them were, coming fresh upon the contents of this hitherto sealed book should attempt to interpret it literally and reinstate the conditions which prevailed in apostolic times. The times were favorable for the movement. The peasants were oppressed and had to pay heavy taxes to support a government and a church in which they had no faith. They were denied many of the privileges and rights which they believed were theirs by nature but which had not been granted to them because the old feudal regime had not yet completely died out in central Europe. In the example of the early apostolic church they found a remedy for the burdens, industrial, social and political which they were bearing. It is not at all strange that in some places the movement became political and social as well as religious. In fact it was almost impossible for a movement of this kind, under the conditions of the time, to remain entirely free from political and social questions. At any rate the hard lot of the peasant made it easier for the new faith to make its appeal to him than might otherwise have been possible.

Bibliography. Sebastian Franck, Chronica: C. A. Cornelius, Des Münsterischen Aufruhrs; Johann C. Füsslin, Beiträge zur Kirchen Geschichte; Heinrich Bullinger, Der Wiedertouferen Ursprung, Fürgang, Sekten, etc.; and the works of Keller, Egli, Erbkam, Beck, Nitsche, Brons, Müller, A. H. Newman, Belfort Bax, Heath, Burrage, etc.

CHAPTER II

MENNO SIMONS AND THE MENNONITES OF EUROPE

As we have seen, Anabaptists of several types appeared early in the Netherlands and Northwestern Germany. These were not all followers of Melchior Hoffman and John of Leyden, but many retained their peaceful and nonresistant principles. Among the leaders of the latter in this region were Dirck and Obbe Philip, Leonard Bouwens and later Menno Simons.

Early Life

Menno Simons was born 1492, in the village of Witmarsum in West Friesland. He was educated for the priesthood and entered upon the duties of his office at the age of twenty-eight in the neighboring village of Pingjum. According to his own account he had at this time very little knowledge of the Bible and no religious convictions. For several years he lived a life of ease and self-indulgence and seemed entirely oblivious of the great religious reformation that was at this time sweeping over middle Europe. This very apathy perhaps finally caused him to question the correctness of some of the traditional ceremonies of the church, for on one occasion during the early years of his priesthood while he was perfunctorily administering the mass, the thought suddenly struck him that the bread and wine he was handling could not be the body and blood of Christ. He attributed this suggestion to the devil and prayed and confessed, but the conviction did not leave him.

Once led to doubt the truth of the prevailing system, it was but inevitable that he should be impelled to study the new teachings which already at this time had found their way into Lower Germany and the Netherlands. The martyrdom in 1533 of Sicke Snyder in a neighboring town, on the charge of Anabaptism made a deep impresssion upon Menno's mind, and led him to study the question of infant baptism. He read the New Testament and found that there was no scriptural basis for the practice. He then consulted the writings of Luther, who taught that infants should be baptized on their own faith. Not satisfied with Luther's argument he next consulted Bucer, who said that infants should be baptized in order that they might more easily be brought up in the way of the Lord. He next went to Bullinger who taught that infant baptism was a sign of the new covenant as circumcision was of the old. Menno was convinced by none of these contradictory views and decided that all were contrary to the teaching of the New Testament.

During this time, 1534-5, occurred also the unfortunate Münster episode which brought shame upon the Anabaptist name and led thousands of well meaning, though fanatical enthusiasts to destruction. In February, 1535, over three hundred of these people had

MENNO SIMONS AND THE MENNONITES

taken refuge in a monastery near Menno's home and most of them, including his own brother, fell in battle.

This event made a profound impression upon Menno's mind, and aroused him more than ever to take a firm stand against the errors of the time.

He says:

> Thus reflecting upon these things, my soul was so grieved that I could no longer endure it. I thought to myself—I, miserable man, what shall I do? If I continue in this way and live not agreeably to the Word of the Lord, according to the knowledge which I have obtained; if I do not rebuke to the best of my limited ability the hypocrisy, the impenitent, carnal life, the perverted baptism, the Lord's supper and the false worship of God which the learned teach; if I, through bodily fear, do not show them the true foundation of the truth, neither use all of my powers to direct the wandering flock, who would gladly do their duty if they knew it, to the true pastures of Christ—Oh, how shall their blood, though shed in error, rise against me at the judgment of the Almighty, and pronounce sentence against my poor, miserable soul.
>
> My heart trembled in my body. I prayed to God in sighs and tears that He would give me, a troubled sinner, the gift of His grace, and create a clean heart within me, that through the merits of the crimson blood of Christ, He would graciously forgive my unclean walk and unprofitable life, and bestow upon me wisdom, Spirit, candor, and fortitude, that I might preach His exalted and adorable name and holy Word unperverted and make manifest His truth to His praise.

This may be considered a turning point in Menno Simons' life; after this he followed with unswerving loyalty, and single-minded devotion the path of duty as his conscience and the Word of God pointed it out to him.

In 1536 he openly renounced the Roman Catholic

Church and a year later at the urgent request of a small deputation of peaceful and non-resistant Anabaptists, whose leaders had all been driven out of the land or put to death, he cast his lot with that despised people and was ordained to the ministry by Obbe Philip. Henceforth he readily became their most influential leader. Thus he became not the founder of a new religious denomination, but rather the organizer of a body of people who were already more or less numerous in the land, but who were awaiting a leader to gather together their scattered forces and organize them into an efficient working body.

Renounces Catholicism

Menno immediately entered upon an active campaign in behalf of the new faith. The rest of his life was spent in preaching the Gospel, organizing new churches and writing in defence of his position. His writings are still extant and have been frequently translated from the Dutch into the German and several times into the English language.

Controversial Writings

On baptism, the supper, faith, magistracy and other church doctrines and practices he held the views of the majority of the peaceful Anabaptists of his day.

Infant baptism he renounces and says "it is a self-begotten rite and human righteousness; for in all the New Testament there is not a word or command about baptizing infants, by Christ nor by the apostles."

The true significance of baptism is set forth as follows:

The believing receive remission of sins, not through baptism, but in baptism in this manner: As they now sincerely believe the lowly Gospel of Jesus Christ which has been preached and taught to them, which is the glad tidings of grace, namely the remission of sin, of grace, of peace, of favor, of mercy and of eternal life through Jesus Christ, our Lord, so they become of a new mind, deny themselves, bitterly lament their old, corrupted life, and look diligently to the Word of the Lord who has shown them such great love; to fulfill all that which He has taught and commanded them in His holy Gospel, trusting firmly in the word of grace, in the remission of their sins through the precious blood and through the merits of our beloved Lord Jesus Christ.

They therefore receive the holy baptism as a token of obedience which proceeds from faith, as proof, before God and His church, that they firmly believe in the remission of their sins through Jesus Christ.

The Supper according to Menno is not the eating of the actual flesh of Jesus, as both the Catholics and Lutherans maintained, but merely a symbol of His suffering.

The bread is no flesh and the wine no blood; for were they flesh and blood as the idolaters pretend and teach the poor people, one of two consequences must follow; either the perishable bread and wine are changed into the imperishable and heavenly Son of God, or the Son of God must be changed into bread and wine. This is incontrovertible. Christ Jesus is not like the fabulous Proteus, now like the everlasting Son of the eternal Omnipotent God, and then a perishable creature, bread and wine. Oh, no! He is unchangeable through all eternity. Neither can He be confined in any house, church or chamber, in silver or golden vessels; for according to His eternal, divine Being, earth is His footstool, and after His holy humanity He ascended into heaven and sits at the right hand of His Father.

On the subject of the incarnation he differed not only from the leading theologians of the Lutheran and Zwinglian denominations but also from many of the leaders in his own. His views practically involved a denial of the true humanity of Christ and were the source of frequent disputes between himself and his brethren.

The fundamental tenets of Menno's belief are quite well expressed by the following extract from a treatise of his on the new birth:

> Behold, worthy reader, all those who are born of God with Christ, who thus conform their weak life to the Gospel, are thus converted, and follow the example of Christ, hear and believe His holy Word, follow His commands, which He, in plain words commanded us in the holy Scriptures, form the holy Christian church which has the promise; the true children of God, brothers and sisters of Christ; for they are born with Him of one Father, and of the new Eve, the pure, chaste bride. They are flesh of Christ's flesh, and bone of His bone, the spiritual house of Israel, the spiritual city, Jerusalem, temple and Mount Zion, the spiritual ark of the Lord, in which are hidden the true bread of heaven, Christ Jesus and His blessed Word, the green, blossoming rod of faith, and the spiritual tables of stone, with the commands of the Lord written thereon; they are the spiritual seed of Abraham, children of the promise, confederates of the covenant of God, and partakers of the heavenly blessings.
>
> These regenerated have a spiritual King over them, who rules them by the unbroken scepter of His mouth, namely, with His Holy Spirit and Word. He clothes them with the garment of righteousness, of pure white silk; He refreshes them with the living water of His Holy Spirit, and feeds them with the bread of life. His name is Christ Jesus. They are the children of peace, who have beaten their swords into plough-shares, and their spears into pruning-hooks, and know of no war; and give to Caesar the things that are Caesar's, and to God the things that are God's (Isa. 2:4; Matt. 22:21). Their sword is the sword of the Spirit, which they hold in a good conscience through the Holy Ghost. Their marriage is that of one man and one woman, according to the ordinance of God. Their kingdom is the kingdom of grace, here in hope, and after this in eternal life (Eph. 6:17; Matt. 19:5; 25:1).

Their citizenship is in heaven; and they use the creatures below, such as eating, drinking, clothing and dwelling with thanksgiving, and that to the necessary wants of their own lives, and to the free service of their neighbor, according to the Word of the Lord (Isa. 58:7). Their doctrine is the unadulterated Word of God, testified through Moses and the prophets, through Christ and the apostles, upon which they build their faith, and save their souls; and everything that is contrary thereto, they consider accursed. They use and administer their baptism on the confession of their faith, according to the command of the Lord, and the doctrines and usages of the apostles (Mark 16:16).

The Lord's supper they celebrate in remembrance of the favors and death of their Lord, and in reminding one another of true and brotherly love.

The ban extends to all the proud scorners, great and small, rich and poor, without any respect to person, who heard and obeyed the Word for a season, but have fallen off again, and in the house of the Lord, teach or live offensively, till they again sincerely repent.

They sigh and lament daily over their poor, displeasing, evil flesh, over the manifold errors and faults of their weak lives. They war inwardly and outwardly without ceasing. They seek and call the Most High; fight and struggle against the devil, world and flesh during their lives, press on towards the prize of the high calling that they may obtain it. And they prove by their actions that they believe the Word of the Lord; that they know and have Christ in power; that they are born of God and have Him as their Father.

Behold, worthy reader, as I said before, so I say again. These are the Christians who have the promise, and are assured by the Spirit of God, to whom are given and bestowed Christ Jesus, with all His merits, righteousness, intercessions, word, cross, suffering, flesh, blood, death, resurrection, kingdom, and all His possessions, and this all without merit; given out of pure grace from God. But what kind of doctrine, faith, life, regeneration, baptism, supper, ban and divine service, sectarian churches have, of whatever name; and what kind of reward is promised them in the Scriptures, I will let the reasonable meditate upon, with the aid of the Spirit and the word of the Lord.

The peaceful Anabaptists of the lower Rhine countries although in no way connected with the followers of John of Leyden yet were associated in the popular mind with the sect of Münsterites. Menno found it necessary to deny the charge. In a tract denouncing John of Leyden he says:

> I can fearlessly challenge anybody, that under the broad canopy of heaven can show and prove that I ever agreed with the Münsterites in regard to the before mentioned articles; for from the beginning until the present moment I have opposed them with diligence and earnestness both privately and publicly, verbally and in writing for over seventeen years and ever since I confessed the Word of the Lord and knew and sought His holy name according to my weakness.[1]

In their attitude toward the civil government Menno and his followers were also misunderstood. They practiced non-participation in civil government, but were by no means opposed to properly constituted authority. He says,

> We now publicly confess that the office of a magistrate is ordained of God, as we ever have confessed since we serve, according to our small talent, the Word of the Lord, and in the meantime, we have ever obeyed them when not contrary to the Word of God and we intend to do so all our lives, for we are not so stupid as not to know what the Lord's Word commands in this respect. We render unto Caesar the things which are Caesar's as Christ teaches (Matt. 22:21); we pray for the imperial majesty, kings, lords, princes and all in authority, honor and obey them.

On these and a number of other doctrines and practices Menno was generally in accord with the

---

1. Complete Works of Menno Simons, part I, p. 300.

views of the peaceful Anabaptists. Where differences of opinion existed he usually by the force of his personality succeeded in establishing his own interpretations. The Mennonites of today in America have deviated very little from the teaching of their first great leader.

On many of these questions Menno had public debates or disputations as they were called, with the leading theologians of the Lutheran and Zwinglian denominations. One of the earliest of these disputations was held in 1543 with John a Lasco on the incarnation, the two natures of Christ, sanctification, hereditary sin, etc. The debate lasted for three or four days, but, as was usually the case in such events, it ended without results, both sides claiming the victory. He later also entered into public debates and literary controversies with Martin Micronius and Gellius Faber, two well-known theologians of that day.

Public Disputations

These teachings of course brought Menno into bitter opposition to the Catholics, as well as the Lutheran and Reformed churches. Those who like him held or taught these opinions were never safe in their lives and possessions. Menno was compelled to remain in hiding during the greater portion of his life.

He spent the first few years after his renunciation of the Roman church in West Friesland where, under the tolerant Duke Charles of Gelders, the persecuted sects enjoyed a short period of rest. In 1542, however, the Emperor, Charles V, offered a reward of one hundred guilders, the equivalent of forty dollars

Price Set on Menno's Head

for his arrest. A description of his person was nailed on the church doors to make his capture the easier. He fled to East Friesland and was finally driven to the city of Cologne where he remained for two years, but he was finally driven from that place also. For the next seven years he found an asylum in the East Sea region with headquarters at Wismar where he organized a small congregation of his followers. During this time he visited Embden, the stronghold of the Mennonites of Northern Europe. In this region Menno and his followers were tolerated by the state authorities, but were compelled by the established church to lead a quiet and secluded life. Their worship was carried on in private houses, in fields and out of the way places. Their dead were buried without the sound of the church bell. Finally in 1555 the Lutheran cities of the Hanseatic league succeeded in banishing all Anabaptists. Menno again fled for his life. This time he found an asylum on the estates of Count of Fresenburg in Holstein where he remained until his death four years later.

Not only was a price set upon Menno's head but even those who gave him aid in any form were summarily punished. In 1539 a man was burned at the stake at Leuwarden for having taken him into his home. Two others met the same fate for printing his writings. In 1546 four houses were confiscated because the owner had rented one for a short time to Menno's sick wife and children.

The later years of Menno's life were saddened by dissensions and differences of opinion among his own followers and co-laborers. Among the most troublesome questions was that of the ban, and its application to the religious and social relations. In 1547 Menno met Dirck and Obbe Philip, Leonard Bouwens and other leaders at Embden to discuss this question. Some of these men insisted on a rigorous application of the practice while others favored greater moderation. The specific point on which they disagreed was with reference to the marital avoidance. Menno contended that in case either husband or wife were excommunicated from the church it was the duty of the believing member to refuse to co-habit with the one excluded. This extreme view he pushed with greater zeal than wisdom, for it resulted in driving Obbe Philip from the Anabaptist ranks and was the source of considerable trouble among his followers later on.

Differences among His Followers

In 1555 another conference was held at Strasburg of the German brethren at which the questions of the incarnation and church discipline were discussed. Menno was not present but received a report of the meeting and was dissatisfied with the results of its proceedings. He and Dirck Philip, in turn, drew up several rules of discipline which they wished the churches to follow. These rules declared in favor of a rigid application of the practice of shunning in all social and marital relations. Military service was prohibited and no one was to set himself up as a teacher or preacher until he had been chosen by the church and ordained by the elders.

The first of these rules Menno and his friends found extremely difficult to enforce. He later let up a little in his exactions and spent his last years in visiting the various churches throughout Friesland in the interests of harmony, but he was not entirely successful. He died January 13, 1559, and was buried **Death** in his own garden.

Thus lived and died one of the great heroes of the Reformation. Although he played a less conspicuous role in that great crisis than did his contemporaries—Luther and Zwingli—yet his real greatness cannot be measured by the humble part he seemed to play upon the religious arena of that time. His task in many respects was more difficult than that of the founders of the state churches. While they depended upon a union of state and church and the support of the strong arm of the temporal government, Menno considered the force of love and the simple truth of the Gospel to be vital enough to secure the permanency of his system without being propped up by the temporal authority. As an embodiment of the simple, humble and Christ-like spirit and as an exponent of the religion of the common man, based upon the example of the early primitive Christian church, Menno Simons must ever be given a pre-eminent place among the heroes of the Reformation.

Menno's influence extended throughout the Anabaptist communities of the Netherlands and Germany. Wherever he went he established new **Influence** churches and strengthened old congregations. The conference already spoken of which was held at Strasburg in 1555 referred to him for advice on several questions of doctrine. Delegates were present here from Wurtemberg, Suabia, Alsace, Moravia, the Palatinate and Switzerland. It is evident that by this time he was already considered a leader among the Anabaptists of these countries, although he had never visited any of them. His influence over these churches was such that soon they began to be known by his name. The term "Menist" was first used in 1544 by Countess Anne in West Friesland. From this time on the Anabaptists of the Netherlands as well as those of Germany and Switzerland were frequently called Menists, which term has since become in the English language, Mennonites.

The Mennonites in the Netherlands

The Netherlands remained for some time the principle stronghold of the Mennonites. Here they were severely persecuted by both the Catholic and Reformed churches. They were forced to hold their meetings for worship behind dikes and on small islands. Frequently their property was confiscated. In Friesland from 1531 to 1574 eighteen suffered a martyr's death. Duke Alva's rule was especially hard on them, for many of them held property which Alva desired for himself. In Holland and Zealand alone one hundred and eleven Mennonites lost their lives by burning and drowning.

When in 1573 William of Orange openly renounced the Catholic faith and assumed the leadership of the Dutch patriots in their **William of Orange** struggle against Spanish tyranny, **Protects Mennonites** the Mennonites were given their first taste of religious toleration. Although they refused to bear arms during these critical years, yet the Stadtholder's good will was gained by large contributions which they made to his treasury; for all through the war with Spain the Mennonites occupied the somewhat inconsistent position of refusing to bear arms, yet aiding the patriotic cause indirectly by large contributions of money.

During this period of limited toleration, the Mennonites became as a body a prosperous people.

Thrifty and Industrious They were among the most thrifty and industrious people in the land, and were noted for their honesty and uprightness.

They were also among the largest contributors to all benevolent causes. During the latter sixteenth century and all through the seventeenth they sent large sums of money and provisions to their persecuted brethren in the Palatinate and Switzerland. But their gifts were not confined to the needy of their own faith. Every appeal to help in a just cause met a hearty response from them. Although they insisted upon the greatest simplicity in every detail of daily living yet everything they used was of the very best material. The term "Menist fine" finally came to be used among the tradesmen of the Netherlands as a synonym for the best that could be secured.

As soon as the Catholic church lost its hold upon the temporal powers in the Netherlands, the Calvinistic

Persecutions by the Reformed Church Reformed church assumed the role of persecutor of the Mennonites. The Anabaptist doctrines of the separation of church and state and of the voluntary congregational form of church organization was as distasteful to the Reformed as to the Catholics, since these principles, if they could be put into practice, would put an end to the rule of all established churches. The efforts of the Calvinists proved of little consequence, however, since the

Mennonites were protected at first by William and later by his successor, Maurice of Nassau. By the time of the death of the latter the spirit of religious toleration had attained sufficient strength in the land to prevent any religious organization from severely persecuting another.

As early as 1574 the Synod of Dort resolved to ask the States General to compel the Mennonites to have their infants baptized, and if they refused, to give the Reformed ministers the right to deal with them as they thought best. They also desired the privilege of entering Mennonite assemblies to convince them of the error of their way. These privileges of course were not granted, although the latter was exercised for a short time in East Friesland. In 1577 a deputation of ministers appeared before the States General again and demanded that the freedom of the Mennonites be limited.

In 1596 a public disputation lasting for two months was held at Leuwarden between the Reformed and Mennonites. As usual in such debates both sides claimed the victory. The Reformed party published a complete report of the event which they closed with a fervent appeal to the temporal authorities to withdraw all toleration from the Mennonites, since as it was said, their principles were destructive of all religious and civil order.

In 1603 the synod asked that Mennonite bishops be forbidden to evangelize and baptize; in 1604 an attempt was made to prevent young ministers from being ordained; and in 1605 a petition was sent to the government asking that Mennonites be prevented from building any more houses of worship. In fact all through the seventeenth century the Reformed synods tried to annihilate the Mennonite faith, and if they were not successful, it was due, not to any lack of zeal on their part but only to the more tolerant spirit of the Dutch government.

Discussions on the Ban

The dissensions which darkened the last days of Menno's life were by no means forgotten after his death. Honest differences of opinion were intensified by differences of race and nationality. The chief contention was with regard to church discipline, especially the ban. On this question the denomination was split up into several party divisions. The Flemings occupied the extreme conservative position, maintained a rigid application of the ban, and severe simplicity of dress and observed marital avoidance in the case of an excommunicated member. Like the later Amish in Switzerland, they wore beards and used hooks and eyes instead of buttons on their clothes. At the other extreme were the Waterlander churches, which were very liberal in their interpretation of the ban and other forms of discipline. They were contemptuously called "Dreckwagen" by the stricter party while they in turn spoke of the latter as the "Bekümmerte." Midway between these two parties stood the High Germans and the Frieslanders who believed in a moderate discipline. These parties later became united, although the names by which they were known continued for some time. By 1649 thirty Flemish and German churches were represented in a conference held at that time. At later conferences delegates were found from all three of the divisions, although isolated congregations refused for a long while to join the main body.

In their theological thinking the Mennonites were Arminians, which partly explains why they were hated so by the hyper-Calvinistic Dutch Reformed church. The wave of Socinianism which swept over Northern Netherlands during the early seventeenth century was not without some effect upon the Mennonites. Many of their leaders were in sympathy with the movement.

In 1619 there arose another movement in Rhynsburg, Holland, which exerted some influence upon the Mennonites. The followers of this movement, the Collegiants, did not constitute a separate organization, but were to be found in all denominations. They met merely for religious worship; repudiated all creeds, and their meetings were open to all believers. They evaded all controversies and tolerated all opinions not directly condemned by the Bible, and like the Mennonites they opposed oaths and war, but administered baptism by immersion. One of their distinguishing characteristics was the abolition of the office of teacher. Teaching and prophesying was not restricted to special teachers but was open to all. In this respect they resembled the later Quakers. They admitted all spiritual-minded Christians to the communion table. Many Mennonites worshiped with these Collegiants, and many of their younger ministers exercised their gifts in these meetings. These liberal ideas and practices were not without their influence upon the church in some parts of Holland.

In their religious practices the main body of the

Religious Practices

Dutch Mennonites during the sixteenth and seventeenth centuries were extremely simple and unpretentious. Their dress was plain, all unnecessary ornaments were discarded, even buckles and buttons in some instances being taken off. Their preachers supported themselves and received no special education. During the latter half of the seventeenth century, however, it was recognized that the church was suffering from the lack of a trained ministry, and preachers were chosen from men who had been to the Universities, chiefly physicians and literary men. Later a theological seminary was established. Their children for a long while were not sent to the Universities. They refused to take the oath and to enter military service. Merchants were not allowed to arm their ships. Controversies were adjusted within the church and no recourse was permitted to the courts of law. In this respect also the Dutch Mennonites have deviated from the old customs. Their principles of non-resistance have practically all been discarded. Those who married unregenerate persons or members of other churches were excommunicated. Baptism was generally administered by affusion. In fact it is doubtful whether any church in that day or since has followed so nearly the spirit and practice of the primitive Christian church as did the Dutch Mennonites of the late sixteenth and early seventeenth centuries.

One other phase of the subject demands a brief mention here—the relation of the Dutch Mennonites to the English Baptists and Quakers.

During the reign of Elizabeth and the early

Stuarts many Dutch found their way into Southeastern
England. Some of these had come
as a result of the close commercial
connection between the two countries; others were driven out of Holland by the cruel persecutions of the
Catholics. It is said that one hundred thousand left
their homes during the bloody rule of Alva. Among
these were large numbers of Anabaptists, many of
whom were Mennonites. These were all termed
Anabaptists, however, since the latter name had not
yet been generally accepted in the Netherlands. That
the two were identical can be seen by a comparison of
their religious beliefs and practices. The records
which were kept by the authorities, of those who were
tried for heresy show that they were accused of rejecting infant baptism, and of being opposed to the
oath, warfare and the holding of office. They held the
prevailing Anabaptist view regarding the incarnation,
and stood for the entire independence of the church
from the temporal authority, and for congregational
church government.

Relation to English Baptists and Separatists

That these views must have been quite general in
this part of England during this time is evidenced by
the fact that all the leading churches found it necessary
to distinctly repudiate them in their confessions of
faith.

What influence Anabaptist doctrines had upon
English, and incidentally upon American history is
also a matter of dispute. But when we remember that
Separatism, Congregationalism, Anti-pedobaptism and
Quakerism, all of which embodied ideas that were new
in England but old in Holland, all had their inception

in Southeastern England in the very regions where the Dutch tradesmen and religious refugees were most numerous, we can not escape the conviction that these great religious movements owed their rise at least in part to the influence of the Dutch Anabaptists.

The hot-bed of Separatism was Norwich, half of whose population it is said was composed of Dutch refugees, and the surrounding region. Among the earliest of the English Separatists was Robert Brown, the "father of English Congregationalism," who in 1580 established an independent, though not an Anabaptist congregation in Norwich. Driven from England he sought refuge in Middleburg, Zealand. Here was located a Mennonite congregation. It is said that a part of Brown's church united with that body although he himself returned to England and re-entered the established church.

Another Separatist congregation was organized about 1602 at Gainsborough by one John Smyth. This church embraced a number of men who later became famous in English and American history. It contained Helwys and Murton, who with Smyth became the founders of the General Baptist church; John Robinson, the Father of the Pilgrims, the pastor of the small flock which left Leyden in 1620 to become the founders of the Plymouth plantation; William Brewster and William Bradford, two of the leading spirits of the first New England colony.

Smyth, together with Helwys and Murton, and a part of the congregation were driven out of England. They finally established themselves at Amsterdam. Heretofore Smyth had been a Separatist but not an Anabaptist, but now he went a step farther. Desiring

MENNO SIMONS AND THE MENNONITES

to receive believers' baptism, but not considering any of the churches then existing as true churches, he first baptized himself, and then the rest of his congregation. Later he became involved in a difficulty with Helwys and Murton, who withdrew from him. Smyth then, together with thirty-one others applied for membership in the Mennonite church at Amsterdam. His explanation for not joining the Mennonites earlier was that he then thought there was no church with whom he could join with a good conscience, but since then he had discovered that the Mennonite churches were "true churches" and had "true ministers." Smyth died before he could be received by the Mennonites but his followers became a part of the Mennonite congregation. Some of these together with the folfollowers of Helwys and Murton later returned to England, and there established the first General Baptist church in England. Thus the Mennonite church may be considered the mother of the modern Baptist denomination. The English church soon introduced immersion and discarded the doctrine of non-resistance.

Relation to Quakers

The Quakers, too, owe something to the Anabaptists. George Fox traveled extensively throughout Southeastern England and preached in Baptist churches. The close resemblance in almost every detail of religious belief between the Quakers and Mennonites makes it impossible to believe that it was not the result of a close connection between the two denominations. Robert Barclay, himself a Quaker, and the best authority on this subject says in speaking of the doctrines of the Mennonites:

So closely do these views correspond with those of George Fox, that we are compelled to view him as the unconscious exponent of the doctrine, practice, and discipline of the ancient and strict party of the Dutch Mennonites, at a period when, under the pressure of the times, some deviation took place among the General Baptists from their original principles.

The visit of Fox, Penn, and Caton, to the Mennonites in Holland and Germany is told in another chapter.

The Mennonites in Switzerland

The term Mennonite also came to be applied to the Swiss Anabaptists, although it was not so generally used as in the Netherlands where Menno's influence was more direct and potent. Here they were usually called Täufer or Wiedertäufer, or sometimes Taufgesinnte, which terms were also common in the German states where Anabaptists were found. All these people, however, formed one body of believers with the Anabaptists or Doopsgezinde of the Netherlands, and delegates from these various countries often met in Conferences where questions of common church polity and usage were discussed.

The story of the Swiss, like that of their Dutch brethren, is largely a recital of cruel persecution on the one hand, and patient suffering on the other. In the cantons of Berne and Zurich, which were the principal Anabaptist strongholds, persecution was even more severe and lasted longer than in the Netherlands. While in the latter country the chief oppressors were at first the Spanish Catholics, in the former they were the Zwinglians and Lutherans. Even the peace of

Westphalia in 1648, which is spoken of as the end of the religious quarrels of Europe, failed to bring rest to the Mennonites. The cause of this hostility on the part of the established church was largely the attitude of the Mennonites toward a state church and their non-participation in civil government. They taught that state and church must be independent of each other, and refused to bear arms, take the oath and hold office. Misunderstood on these questions they were considered dangerous to both the state and church and were hounded to death by both. At first they were hunted like wild beasts, burned at the stake, drowned in the rivers, or left to rot in filthy prisons. As the spirit of the times became more humane during the seventeenth century they were exiled from the country, sent to the galleys and their property was confiscated. In the eighteenth century they were punished with a money fine and denied many of the rights of citizenship.

The masses of the people were often in sympathy with the persecuted and often the same decree which pronounced death or banishment upon the Anabaptists provided also for a money fine against those who gave them aid. A decree of 1580 declared that any aid given them would result in a fine or exile for one year. In 1643, a year of severe oppression, many were exiled and an amount equal to eigthy thousand dollars was collected in fines. All through the seventeenth century they emigrated to other lands, principally to Holland, the Palatinate and Alsace. In 1671 seven hundred Bernese came to the Palatinate whither they had been invited by the Count Palatine to settle upon his waste lands. In 1709 many were sent to the galleys. In 1711 one hundred families came to Holland and established their own congregations there. The experiences of the Swiss in the early eighteenth century and the help they received from the Dutch is told more fully elsewhere in this volume and need not be repeated here. Through these measures the Mennonites of Switzerland were nearly all banished, sold as slaves and forced back into the state church, or had voluntarily emigrated to other more tolerant lands. By the nineteenth century the congregations were small and few.

The Palatinate

The Mennonites in the Palatinate experienced the same fate as did their brethren in other parts of Europe during the latter half of the sixteenth and the first half of the seventeenth centuries. The established church tried to turn them from their faith and when unsuccessful it persuaded the government to lock them up in prisons or put them to death. In 1571 the Count Palatine himself presided over a public disputation with the Mennonites at Frankenthal which lasted for nineteen days. Of the thirteen questions which were discussed the following are the most significant:

I. Did the flesh of Christ receive its substance from the flesh of the Virgin Mary?

II. Are children born in sin?

III. Does faith in Jesus Christ suffice for salvation, or are the cross and good works essential?

IV. Will the body be resurrected at the Judgment Day?

V. Can the individual Christian own property?

VI. Is the Christian permitted to be magistrate and may he use the sword?

VII. Is the Christian allowed to take the oath?
VIII. Must children be baptized?
IX. Is the communion only a symbol and a token of remembrance?

These questions it is observed strike at the root of the beliefs which differentiated the Anabaptists from the Lutherans and Zwinglians. Many such disputations were held but always without result. The Mennonites were only confirmed more strongly than ever in their faith, and the established church continued its persecutions until far into the seventeenth century. By the close of the Thirty Years' War the Count Palatine, Karl Ludwig, wishing to build up the lands laid waste by the war granted the Mennonites religious toleration and invited their persecuted brethren in Switzerland to join them. As we have already seen, a number of the Swiss accepted this invitation in 1660 and again in 1671. But here again they enjoyed a mere breathing spell of liberty. During the many wars fought between the French and Germans in the time of Louis XIV, the Palatinate was made the battle field of the struggle. Several hundred Mennonite families were driven out of the country by the French and German armies. Many of these fled to the lowlands of the Rhine where they would hardly have been able to eke out an existence had not their brethren in the Netherlands again come to their rescue with money, food and clothing. Others of the Palatines, as we have seen elsewhere, found their way to America. The churches in Amsterdam and other cities in the Netherlands supported an organization, the purpose of which was to help them find new homes across the Atlantic. By 1732 over three thousand had arrived at Rotterdam from the Palatinate.

During the first half of the eighteenth century they were oppressed by special head tax, inheritance tax, banishment, confiscation of property and were denied the freedom of worship. As a result the stream of emigration into Pennsylvania continued throughout this period.

The Church in Prussia and Northern Germany

Before the time of Menno Simons many Anabaptists were found in what is now Prussia and other parts of Lower Germany, and after his time Mennonite churches were found in most of the leading cities. Menno himself traveled for several years through this region and visited the Anabaptist congregations. His friend, Dirck Philip, became the first elder of the large Mennonite church at Danzig. Among the earliest and most influential congregations in this region were those in Danzig, Thorn, Marienburg, Elbing, Friedrich stadt, Hamburg, Altona, Königsberg and Crefeld. The Mennonites here were in close touch with those of the Netherlands and enjoyed greater freedom than their brethren farther south. As early as 1585 they were granted the rights of citizenship. Instead of the oath they were permitted the use of the "yea and nay." Both Prussia and Poland invited the persecuted from other countries to settle on the marshes and waste lands of the Low Countries. During the 17th century they were granted additional privileges. In 1660 the Danzig church was allowed to erect a building for worship. Of course, complete religious freedom was not yet offered them. In times of war they were often obliged to serve in the armies or find substitutes. Their attitude toward the state church and their non-resistant principles were always regarded with suspicion by the Lutherans. By 1710 Frederick, influenced partly by the States General of the Netherlands, invited the Swiss Mennonites to settle upon some of his unoccupied lands. Numbers of the Swiss as we have already seen accepted the invitation. These were granted religious toleration and freedom from military service.

Under Frederick William they were ordered to leave Prussian soil. This was due to Frederick's dislike of them because they dared to oppose him in his attempt to secure six of their promising young men for his famous Potsdam body guard. Few of them, however, left the country because of the order. Under Frederick the Great they were again granted freedom of worship. As a result of these liberal policies they grew steadily in numbers until by 1772 there were about thirteen thousand in Prussia.

The next year they gained from the king the following privileges:

I. Full freedom of worship in accordance with the Mennonite confession of faith.

II. The privilege of building suitable structures for worship.

III. The right to teach their children in their own schools.

IV. Freedom from military service.

V. The privilege of discarding the oath and using the "yea and nay" instead.

VI. The privilege of engaging in any industry

open to their countrymen and the right of buying and selling, and holding property.

These privileges were confirmed by Frederick in 1780 on the condition that they pay yearly into the king's treasury the sum of five thousand dollars. This sum was to go to the support of a military academy, but the Mennonites were free from military service.

Such freedom, however, could not last. Under other kings and in times of war it was not an easy matter to maintain the non-resistant faith. A few years later, these privileges were somewhat restricted and several thousand families emigrated to Russia where in turn they had been promised freedom from military service.

The story of the later Prussian, as well as of other European Mennonites, is omitted here since it is the province of this chapter merely to furnish a background for the history of the church in America.

Bibliography.—Complete Works of Menno Simons, (Elkhart, Indiana, Edition, 1871); A. H. Newman, History of Anti-pedobaptism; T. J. van Bracht, Martyrs' Mirror; Dirck Philip, Enchiridion; A. M. Cramer, Het Leven en de Verrigtingen van Menno Simons; B. K. Roosen, Menno Simons; Anna Brons, Ursprung, Entwickelung, und Schicksale der Taufgesinnten oder Mennoniten; Ernest Müller, Geschichte der Bernischen Taufer.

CHAPTER III

PLOCKHOY AND THE MENNONITE COLONY ON THE DELAWARE

Just when the first Mennonites came to the New World is not definitely known, but it is likely that a
few individuals settled in what is now
Mennonites in New York and Delaware soon after
Manhattan the first permanent English settlements were made along the Atlantic
coast. Frequent references are made in the colonial records of New York to Dutch Anabaptists in New Netherlands soon after the Dutch gained a foothold on American soil. Some of these Anabaptists no doubt were Mennonites. The first printed mention of the latter by name is found in a report on the religious conditions in New Netherlands, made by a French Jesuit, Father Jogues, who had visited this region in 1643. In a letter written the following year he says regarding the religious affairs in "Manhate"[1] island,

No religion is publically exercised but the Calvinist, and orders are to admit none but Calvinists, but this is not observed. For there are besides Calvinists in the colony,

---

1. Manhattan Island.

Catholics, English Puritans, Lutherans and Anabaptists, here called Menists.²

Long Island   The next reference so far as I have been able to discover in the same documents is in a report made in 1657 to Amsterdam regarding the early settlements on Long Island. The report says,

> Those at Gravesend are reported Menonists; yea they for the most part reject infant baptism, the sabbath, the office of preacher and teacher of God's Word, saying that through these come all sorts of contention into the world, whenever they meet together the one or the other reads something for them.³

This description does not fit the orthodox Mennonite of either that day or this day. Two explanations may be suggested to harmonize the seeming contradictory account. It is barely possible that the writer, who was a Dutchman and thus was acquainted with the Dutch Mennonites but perhaps knew nothing about the English Quakers confused the two and thus considered these people Mennonites when in reality they may have been Quakers. Their practices seem to have been nearer those of the Quakers than of the main body of Mennonites, and we know that soon after this Gravesend became a Quaker settlement.⁴ On the other hand we must remember that at this time there were several sects of Mennonites, some of which differed very little in their religious practices from the early settlers at Gravesend. If these people were Mennonites

---

2. O'Callahan, E. B., Documentary History of New York, IV. p. 15.
3. Ibid, III. p. 69.
4. In 1657. See A. P. Stockwell, Histroy of Gravesend.

MENNONITE COLONY ON THE DELAWARE 83

as the report says they were, then perhaps they belonged to the sect of Collegiants, who had their origin in Rhynsburg in 1619 and who like the Quakers did not believe in a regular preacher.[5]

The first settlement in America of which we have anything like definite knowledge is that made by Plockhoy and his small colony on the **Horekill** Horekill in what is now Southwestern Delaware. Cornelisz Pieter Plockhoy of Zeirik Zee was a liberal-minded Dutch communist and social reformer of his day. He was of Mennonite descent and was perhaps himself a member of one of the several sects of that faith. Of his early life we know little, but by 1658 we find him in London **Plockhoy in** addressing a letter to Cromwell in **England** which he laid before the Lord Protector a scheme for the social and political reorganization of English society.[6] England it will be remembered was at this time under the Commonwealth government, and at no period of her history has there been a greater diversity of opinion among Englishmen on social, religious, and political questions than just at this time. Plockhoy therefore was only one of many who felt that they had a remedy for the ills of society.

In the mean time, however, Cromwell had died

---

5. For a good description of the Collegiants see Robert Barclay; "The Inner Life of the Religious Societies of the Commonwealth." p. 90.

6. For the facts regarding this part of Plockhoy's life I am indebted to a chapter headed "Plockhoys Social Planen" in a book Called "Beelden en Groepen Studien" written by H. P. G. Quack, and published in Amsterdam, 1892 by P. N. van Kampen and Zoon.

before Plockhoy's letter had reached him, whereupon
the latter prepared a memorial to
His Communistic Parliament, which together with his
Schemes earlier letter and a pamphlet, in
which he outlined his plans for reform, he sent to that body in 1659. In his first letter
his chief ambition seemed to be to harmonize the
religious dissensions then prevalent in the Christian
church. After calling attention to the numerous sects
he outlines his plan for bringing all these sects together. He suggests that Cromwell establish as an
experiment a common church in which all are to
worship. Religious worship, however, is to be voluntary. Church and State are to be entirely separated
and there is to be no tithing for the support of a
regular ministry. During the year, however, Plockhoy's ideas seem to have enlarged, for in the above
mentioned pamphlet he includes in his communistic
plans a scheme for the alleviation of the poor. The
title page contains an epitome of his program and
reads as follows:

> A way propounded to make the poor in these and other Nations happy by bringing together a fit, suitable and well qualified people into one Household-government or little Commonwealth, wherein every one may keep his property and be employed in some work or other as he shall be fit, without being oppressed. Being the way not only to rid these and other Nations from idle, evil and disorderly persons, but also from all such as have sought and found out many inventions to live upon others. Whereunto is also annexed an invitation to this society or little Commonwealth. Psalm 42:1. Blessed is he that considereth the poor etc.—By Cornelison van Zierik Zee, London. Printed for the author

and sold at Black Spread Eagle near the West end of Pauls. 1659.[7]

This scheme it is seen, although co-operative, was not entirely communistic, for those who entered the society were not bound to hold their property in common. The little trial commonwealth which Plockhoy hoped to establish was to be composed of four classes of men—husbandmen, handicraftsmen, mariners and masters of arts and sciences. Until the society became firmly established unmarried men were to be preferred. All were to live together in houses large enough to accommodate twenty or thirty families.

Simplicity and economy were to be practiced in every detail of daily living. The women were to make their own apparel without unnecessary trimming.

Apparel should be fitted for the body and convenient for the work, without being dyed to the fashions, colors or stuffs, only the unnecessary trimmings to be forborn that God's creatures which He hath made be not misused.

Education was to be provided for all.

In religion the same spirit of equality and harmony was to be encouraged as in other interests of life. There was to be one large hall for religious purposes. All sects were to be given freedom of worship but were encouraged to worship together. During religious service the Holy Scriptures were to be read and then each member of the congregation was to be free to express his own opinions on the passages read.

In spiritual things we acknowledge none but Christ for head and master, who of old hath appointed in his church, apostles, prophets, evangelists, pastors and teachers, these

---

[7]. This pamphlet is now very rare. There is a copy in the New York city public library, perhaps the only copy in America. The British Museum also contains a copy.

having through the spirit of God brought forth and left behind them the writings in the New Testament, we own for ambassadors and their words (without any interpretation from men) for our rule and plummet, keeping in remembrance when we meet together that we must allow that liberty of speaking to others which we desire ourselves, without tying anyone to our opinion, maintaining a firm friendship with such who have renounced all unreasonable things contrary to Scripture, without stumbling at any differences, which do not hinder love and piety. . . . . . We intend that we may bring the good people of all sects to unity, setting our meeting place open to all rational men.

This in brief was to be the plan of government for a community which Plockhoy hoped with the aid of Parliament to establish somewhere in England.

At the end of the pamphlet was inserted an invitation to all the poor and needy and others interested in forming such an association to co-operate with Plockhoy. His plan was to found the association in London. But later Bristol, and finally Ireland was chosen as the place where the experiment was to be tried. We do not find, however, that the scheme ever materialized. Parliament, whose aid he sought, had far more important work in hand at this time, and Plockhoy soon left London again for Amsterdam, where he continued his efforts to secure help for putting his theories into practice. Here he was finally successful. The city of Amsterdam, being anxious at this time to secure colonists for her newly acquired territory along the Delaware river, promised Plockhoy financial aid and the privilege of establishing a colony of Mennonites on the Horekill.

The Horekill is the name of a small stream flowing into the Delaware Bay near its southern extremity in what was then New Netherlands, but now the state of Delaware.[8] The term which originated from the name Hoorn, a town in Holland, was applied not only to the stream but the entire surrounding region which was also sometimes called Swaanendael. The settlement at this place was one of the earliest made by the Dutch, south of Manhattan Island.

The first settlement in this region was made in 1631 by DeVries, a Dutch explorer, who built a fort called Oplandt near the stream.[9] The colony was soon destroyed, however, by Indians. Later unsuccessful attempts at colonization were also made by the West India Company and the city of Amsterdam to which city the region had finally been sold. Amsterdam made repeated efforts to populate her new colony. In 1656 three hundred Waldenses had been sent over. Invitations were also sent to other persecuted sects of Europe to settle in the New World. It was no doubt this eagerness for colonists that made it possible for Plockhoy to get financial aid and permission from the burgomasters of Amsterdam to establish here a colony of Mennonites, based on his plan of social, political and economic equality.

---

8. This region is described in a report sent to Amsterdam in 1657 by Alrichs to the Commissioners of the colony on the Delaware.

"I have already stated that there is a very fine country called the Whorekill abounding very much in wild animals, birds, fish, etc. And the land is so good and fertile that the like is nowhere to be found. It lies at the entrance of the Bay about two leagues up from Cape Hinlopen. I shall send a draft of it by the next opportunity. Please to keep it recommended. The place can be visited by a yacht of eight or ten lasts but some people must be there for security. This can be regularly done after numbers are sent and have arrived here and more of the place is taken up."—O'Callahan, Documentary History of New York, II. p. 19.

9. See Benjamin Ferris, Original Settlements on the Delaware, p. 22, and Francis Vincent, History of Delaware, p. 130.

On June 9, 1662, the burgomasters of Amsterdam made a contract with Plockhoy and twenty-four others, called Mennonites, regarding the conveyance of the proposed colony to the Delaware.[10] According to this contract the city was to advance two hundred guilders to each of the twenty-five families making up the association. For the repayment of these loans the whole body was to be responsible. A tract of land was granted the colony on the Horekill which was to be free from taxes for twenty years. The society was authorized to make such laws and rules as were necessary for the government of the settlement, allowing to each member the right of appeal to the city authorities in case he felt himself unjustly treated. Such laws and rules, however, were not to be in contradiction to the fundamental conditions which the city had published in 1656.

Contract with Amsterdam

In the meantime Plockhoy, in 1662, had again published a pamphlet called, "Kort en Klaer Ontwerp"[11] in which he outlined in detail the communistic scheme by which the proposed colony was to be governed, and in which he invited associates to join the new enterprise. The following September was the date set for the departure of the company.

Many of these regulations for the proposed com-

---

10. O'Callahan, Documentary History of New York, II. p. 176.
11. This is also a very rare book. S. W. Pennypacker has a copy in his private library. There is also a copy in the library of the New York Historical Society. See Collections of New York Historical Society, Second Series, Vol. III, part I, footnote page 291. A brief analysis of the book with something of its history can be found in H. C. Murphy's Anthology of New Netherland and also in G. M. Asher's Historical Essay on Dutch Books and Pamphlets relating to New

munity were similar to those suggested in London in 1658. The colony was to comprise four classes of people—agriculturists, seafaring persons, all necessary trades people, and masters of useful arts and sciences. The associates were to be either married males, or single men twenty-four years old who were free from debt. Each was to obey the ordinances of the society and not seek his own advancement over any other member. The colony evidently was not to be exclusively a Mennonite one, since as in the earlier scheme all Christian sects who composed the community were to be united. This was to be accomplished partly by the exclusion of all clergymen from the settlement, since it would be impossible to gain the desired harmony, either by electing a clergyman for each sect or by selecting him from any one sect. Preachers, furthermore, according to Plockhoy, were not necessary for religious instruction and worship. The colonists were themselves provided with the Holy Scriptures which all ministers agreed in pronouncing the best, and which they looked upon as "the most peaceable and economical of all preachers." Religious exercises were to be as simple as possible. Every Sunday and holiday the people were to assemble in the common meeting house. Here the services were to be opened by the singing of a psalm and the reading of a chapter from the Bible by one of the members. Any one present was to be at liberty to express his opinions on the passage of Scripture read. Another

Regulations for Proposed Colony

Netherland. For a further discussion of Plockhoy's scheme for establishing a colony on the Delaware see O'Callahan, History of New Netherland; and John Romeyn Brodhead, History of New York. Vol. I. p. 697.

psalm closed the services, and immediately after, the court was to convene in the same building for the transaction of the public business of the community. There was to be no deviation from these simple exercises, for even the Lord's supper and baptism were to be considered as "signs or ceremonies becoming rather weak children than men in Christ."

Public schools were to be provided, but no creeds nor religious formulas except the Holy Scriptures were to be taught.

Plockhoy evidently was not entirely non-resistant, for those having conscientious scruples against bearing arms were to pay an extra tax for the support of those who entered military service. Only defensive warfare, however, was to be waged.

Slavery was to be prohibited.

In order to secure perfect harmony within the settlement certain classes of religious sects were to be excluded from the Society,

All untractable people, such as those in communion with the Roman see, usurious Jews; English stiffnecked Quakers; Puritans; foolhardy believers in the Millennium; and obstinate modern pretenders to revelation.

Undesirable persons were to be subject to expulsion by a two-thirds vote of the entire community.

All laws and regulations for the governing of the colony were to be passed by a two-thirds vote of the members, but were to be subject to the approval of the authorities of Amsterdam. Each year ten persons were to be proposed for officers, from which the burgomasters of Amsterdam were to choose five. No magistrate was to be eligible for re-election until one year after the expiration of his term of office, nor was he to receive any compensation for his services. For the first year the oldest member was to preside over the court, but after that, the one longest in office.

For five years after their arrival in their new home the colonists were to labor for the common good and live from a common store-house, but after that time the property might be divided proportionally among the heads of families.

Such in outline were the articles of association which were drawn up by Plockhoy for the government of his proposed American colony of Mennonites—a scheme which Brodhead in his history of New Netherlands calls "one among the most extraordinary of the memorials of American colonization."[12]

Of the actual history of the colony we have little knowledge. As we have seen, the company was to leave for the Horekill by September, 1662. But we do not know whether they actually set sail at that time. It seems probable, however, that they did not start on their voyage until the following spring, for from a letter written May 5, 1663, we learn that Plockhoy sailed in the ship St. Jacob for the Horekill,[13] and in another letter dated August 4, 1663,[14] it is recorded that the ship St. Jacob arrived at the Horekill on July 28, 1663, and left there forty-one souls with

Colony on the Delaware

---

12. At first glance these regulations may seem entirely inconsistent with the doctrines and practices of the main body of the Mennonites of today. But as suggested in an earlier portion of this chapter, there were several sects of the denomination in the Netherlands during the seventeenth century which held views in many respects similar to these set forth by Plockhoy.
13. Fernow, Documents Relating to the History of New York, XII. p. 429.
14. Ibid, p. 437, 450.

their baggage and farm utensils. From these scraps of information it would seem that these forty-one souls comprised the twenty-five families who contracted with the burgomasters of Amsterdam to settle in New Netherlands. How they fared during the autumn and the following winter we do not know, but they had hardly begun their new settlement when they were unceremoniously driven out of the region by the English who were now at war with the Dutch for the possession of New Netherlands. In 1664, all the Dutch settlements along the Delaware, including the Mennonite colony, were plundered and some of the inhabitants, perhaps principally soldiers, were taken to Virginia where according to Governor Stuyvesant they were sold as indentured servants.[15] A report of the affair sent to Amsterdam in 1684 says that during this war all the possessions of the city of Amsterdam were plundered and occupied "as also what belonged to the Quaking Society of Plockhoy to a very naile."[16]

Of the ultimate fate of these Mennonites we are equally ignorant. Whether they later built up their settlement again on the Horekill, and perhaps lost their Mennonite faith; whether they became disheartened

---

15. "The Dutch soldiers were taken prisoners and given to the merchantman that was there in payment of his services, and they were transported into Virginia to be sold.—All sorts of tools for handicraft, tradesmen, and all plow-gear and other things to cultivate the ground which were in store in great quantity were likewise seized, together with a saw mill ready to set up and nine sea buoys with their iron chains. Even the inoffensive Mennonites, though thoroughly noncombatant in principle, did not escape the sack and plunder to which the whole river was subjected by Carr and his co-marauders. A boat was dispatched to their settlement which was stripped of everything 'to a naile.'"—O'Callahan, History of New Netherlands, II. 538. See also Documentary History of New York, II. 346.
16. Documentary History of New York, III. 356.

and returned to their native country; or whether like some of the Dutch soldiers they were sold as servants in Virginia we may never know. Save for a brief mention made of Plockhoy sometime later in the records of the Germantown court[17] these few facts are all that have thus far come to light regarding this, one of the earliest attempts of the Mennonites to secure a home in the New World. One day in 1694 Plockhoy now grown old and blind, accompanied by his wife, evidently friendless and penniless, having heard somehow of the later and more fortunate settlement made in the meantime at Germantown, and coming, we know not whence, wandered into the village, where he met a hearty welcome. The court appointed William Rittenhouse and John Doeden to select a suitable home in the village and provide for the needs of the aged couple. And here with his wife, Pieter Cornelisz Plockhoy, the dreamer and social reformer, and so far as known, the only survivor in America of the ill-fated colony he tried to establish, after a long life of disappointments and vicissitudes, finally ended his days in peace among his brethren and countrymen.

---

17. The Germantown Rathbuch. The original written in German is to be found in the library of the Pennsylvania State Historical Society.

CHAPTER IV

GERMANTOWN 1683-1708

The first permanent Mennonite settlement in America was made at Germantown, Pennsylvania.

Relation of Mennonites to Quakers The first settlers came from Holland and Germany, especially from the Lower Rhine region along the borders of the two countries—principally from the towns, Crefeld and Kriegsheim. The story of the early Mennonites in America is so closely intertwined with that of the Quakers that it may not be out of place here to speak briefly of the early relation of these two denominations in Europe. Even the most casual student of their history must observe that they had much in common in doctrine, practice and spirit. As already indicated it is even suggested by some historians that Quakerism may owe its origin to Mennonite influence from Holland.[1] The opinion of Robert Barclay on this subject has already been referred to.

---

1. Barclay, The Inner Life of the Religious Societies of the Commonwealth, p. 77.

Whatever their origin may have been, the English Quakers very early in their history crossed over into Holland and Northwestern Germany for the purpose of extending their faith. They were wise enough to begin their work where the soil had already been well prepared for the reception of the Quaker doctrines of non-resistance, non-swearing of oaths, and rejection of infant baptism. And so we find their first evangelists almost invariably beginning their efforts among the Mennonites; and in Mennonite communities they found their first proselytes.

One of the first of the Quakers to come to the continent was William Ames who visited Holland and the Palatinate as early as 1655. Here he found his way to many of the Mennonite strongholds. In company with George Rolfe he visited Kriegsheim in 1657 where he gained a number of Mennonite converts.[2] And it is a noteworthy fact that at a later time the entire Quaker body at this place emigrated to Pennsylvania.[3] During the same year Ames won for his faith also Judith Zinspenning, of Amsterdam, who had been a member of the Flemish Mennonite church. She was the wife of Jacob Sewell, also a Mennonite, and the mother of William Sewell, the well known Quaker historian.[4] Caton who labored in Holland at the same time, says he was well received everywhere by the Mennonites.[5] Stephen Crisp, another zealous Quaker, made a number of trips to Holland and Germany between 1663 and

---

2. Pa. Ger. Soc., IX. 170.
3. Sewell, History of the Quakers, I. 260.
4. Ibid, II. 120.
5. Barclay, 250.

1684, gained a few proselytes, visited Hamburg, Embden, Friedrichstadt and Danzig, and set up a meeting at Crefeld.[6] In all of these towns the Mennonites had large congregations.

By far the most significant missionary tour, however, was that made in 1677 by a number of the Quaker leaders, including Robert Barclay, George Keith, Benjamin Furley, George Fox and William Penn. On July 26, this party landed in Briel, a seaport town of Holland. From here they went to Leyden accompanied by Jan Roelof, a Quaker, whose father, Berend Roelof, had been a Mennonite preacher at Hamburg, and thence to Haarlem, where they attended a meeting consisting of Friends and Mennonites.[7] The travelers visited all the places where meetings had been established and many new towns where they hoped to gain new proselytes. The tour included Amsterdam, Frankfort on the Main, where Penn met a number of Pietists who had established a society in that city, Kriegsheim, Cologne, Embden and many other cities.[8] At Amsterdam Penn and Fox had a debate with the celebrated Mennonite preacher Galenus Abraham. The story of this debate is told very briefly but entertainingly by Sewell.

Penn and Fox in Germany

Galenus asserted that nobody now-a-days could be accepted as a messenger of God unless he confirmed his doctrine by miracles. Penn denied this and said miracles at present are not necessary. Fox then also spoke something

---

6. Oswald Seidensticker, William Penn's Travels in Holland and Germany in 1677, in Pennsylvania Magazine of History, II., 240.
7. Pa. Mag. of History, II. 250.
8. Sewell, II. 268.

to the matter; but he being somewhat short breathed, went several times away which some were ready to impute to a passionate temper but I well know that therein they wronged him. This dispute was a troublesome business, for the parties on both sides were fain to speak by an interpreter which generally was performed so imperfectly that at last the conference was broke off without coming to a decision although many weighty arguments were objected against the position.9

This tour of Penn's was full of significance for the future settlement of Pennsylvania. To be sure, at this time he was traveling merely in the interests of the Quaker religion. But when a few years later he was granted a large tract of land in the new world, and when he sent his agents to the continent to secure colonists, many of these persecuted Quakers, Mennonites, Pietists, and other sects more or less limited in their freedom of worship, felt a personal interest in the enterprise.

Later Quakers Among the Mennonites

Penn was by no means the last of Quaker apostles to visit the Mennonites. At Hamburg, Amsterdam, Crefeld, Kriegsheim, Altona, in fact wherever there was a Mennonite congregation the Quakers got more or less of a footing. The Mennonites evidently often heard the Quaker preachers gladly. The yearly meeting of London in 1694 reported from Holland that at Twist and Hoorne

there is found great openness and tenderness among the people who desire to be visited and salute Friends and that in some places is found good openness among the Mennists (or Baptists) to hear the Friends tell the truth.10

---
9. Ibid, 277.
10. Bealing, Epistles of London Yearly Meeting. Baltimore, 1806.

In 1709 Chalkley after a visit to Rotterdam, Haarlem, Hamburg, Embden and other places said,

I know not that I ever met with more tenderness and openness in people than in those parts of the world. There is a great people there whom they call Menonists who are very near the truth and the fields are white unto harvest among divers of them spiritually speaking.[11]

In 1714 Story reported from Holland that he "met with great kindness especially from a sect called Minists who in many respects resemble the Friends." These people whenever he met with them tendered him "the use of their meeting houses," and assisted him in his labors "as far as they were able."[12] Thus we see that the Mennonites and Quakers[13] were by no means strangers to one another when Penn opened up Pennsylvania as an asylum for the persecuted of all lands and where there was to be absolute freedom of worship. It was but natural that through his agents he should first invite those with whom he had come into such close personal contact, and who, he had reason to believe, might easily be induced to cast their lot in the new country.

Persecutions

The Mennonites at the close of the seventeenth century still felt the heavy hand of persecution and oppression upon them. The day of the stake and the rack to be sure was past, but in Switzerland the followers of Menno Simons were still sold as galley slaves or left

---

11. Chalkley, Journal, 99.
12. Story, Journal, 176.
13. Quaker preachers were not always received with open arms by the Mennonite churches, however. Occasionally individual Mennonites would join the Society but often a congregation as such would bar the doors against Quaker preachers. See Pa. Mag. of Hist., II. 242.

to starve in prisons. In the Palatinate and other parts of Germany they were allowed freedom of worship, but their refusal to enter military service and to take the oath often brought upon them great hardships, as they often had to pay large sums of money for the privilege of exemption. In Holland and Northwestern Germany, and especially in Crefeld, they enjoyed practically most of the religious and civil rights granted to other citizens.[14] Even in the most tolerant countries, however, the position of the Mennonites on the question of war, the oath and the magistracy, was a source of continual friction between them and the civil authorities, while their opposition to infant baptism, and to the domination of the state churches brought upon them the suspicions of the ecclesiastical hierarchies.

The lot of the Quakers on the continent as well as in England was even harder than that of the Mennonites. Their aggressive zeal for the propagation of their faith, their peculiar practices, in addition to their refusal to enter military service and to take the oath—two doctrines which they held in common with the Mennonites—often brought them into trouble with the authorities. On several occasions Penn wrote to the authorities in behalf of his persecuted brethren. In 1677 he petitioned the Elector of the Palatinate for milder treatment of the Quakers at Kriegsheim, for "tithes were exacted from them not only by the parson of the village but also by the popish priests of Worms. And the mayor of the town endeavored to restrain their due liberty of religious meeting."[15]

---

14. Barclay, 78.
15. Sewell, I. 268.

It was the desire, then, for fuller religious freedom, and for exemption from heavy burdens of taxation and civil obligations which they could not conscientiously accept that led the first Mennonites and Quakers to emigrate from Germany and Holland to Pennsylvania.

Crefeld, the home of the first colony, is a city on the Rhine in Northwestern Germany, near the borders of the Netherlands. This city had for many years been an asylum for various persecuted sects in Germany. It was from here also that the Dunkards came to America some years later. The Mennonite congregation had been in existence since the early part of the century.

Jacob Telner The individual who perhaps was most directly concerned with the first emigration was Jacob Telner, a Mennonite merchant of Crefeld, but resident at the time in Amsterdam.[16] Telner, who had been in America sometime between 1678 and 1681 in the interests of his business, had business relations with the Quakers of London and was on friendly terms with the leading merchants of New York. He may thus be regarded as a connecting link between Penn and the Crefeld congregation.[17] It was no doubt largely due to his influence that the enterprise was launched, partly perhaps as a business venture but principally in order that his brethren might enjoy greater civil and religious liberty.

Our knowledge of the history of the Crefeld colony

---

16. Pennypacker in Pa. Ger. Soc., IX. 177.
17. Hazard, Register, VI. 183.

begins with May 10, 1682, when William Penn conveyed to Jacob Telner of Crefeld, Jan Streypers, also a merchant, of Kaldkirchen, and
Dirk Sipman of Crefeld each five thousand
acres in Pennsylvania. On June 11, 1683, Penn conveyed to Govert Remke, Leonart Arets and Jacob Isaacs Van Bebber, all of Crefeld, one thousand acres each. These six, all Mennonites, constitute the original Crefeld purchasers. All of these men with the exception of Sipman and Remke finally found their way to Pennsylvania. Colonization was the purpose these purchasers had in view, and Penn stipulated that a certain number of families should settle in Pennsylvania within a specified time.

Crefeld Purchasers

In the meantime a group of thirteen men with their families, making thirty-three in all, nearly all related to one another were gathered together for the first colony. With the possible exception of one or two families they were all from Crefeld, although most of them were of Dutch ancestry. The names of these men are Lenart Arets, Abraham Opden Graff, Dirk Opden Graff, Herman Opden Graff, William Streypers, Thones Kunders, Reynier Tyson, Jan Siemens, Jan Lensen, Peter Keurlis, Johannes Bleikers, Jan Lucken and Abraham Tunes.

On June 18, 1683, this little company had arrived at Rotterdam whither they had been accompanied by Telner, Sipman and Jan Streypers, three of the largest purchasers. Passage had been secured for them (on the Concord) through James Claypool, a Quaker merchant in London. They were to sail July 6, but owing to delay in Rotterdam they did not begin their voyage from London until July 24.[18] The Concord had other passengers besides the Crefeld emigrants, for it was provisioned with "14 oxen, 30 (fasz) beer, bread and water enough for 120 passengers."[19] After a voyage of ten weeks they reached Philadelphia on October 6. One young woman had died on board the ship, but this loss was more than balanced by the birth of two children. Here we must leave this little band of pioneers and turn briefly to the consideration of another subject,—Pastorius and the Frankfort Land Company.

The Frankfort Land Company was composed of a number of Pietists in and around Frankfort on the Main, who at different times had bought about 25,000 acres from Penn for humanitarian purposes. The Pietists were not a distinct religious sect. Pietism began among orthodox Lutherans and was a protest against the formalism and dogmatism of the church at large. Its chief exponent was Philip Jacob Spener, who was born in 1635 in Alsace. He later studied at Strasburg and in 1666 became pastor of a church in Frankfort on the Main. It was here that he first began to discredit a mere intellectual belief as a means to salvation and to teach that a complete transformation of life was necessary. He encouraged Bible study and the cultivation of the spiritual life. In 1670 he organized the "Collegia Pietatis" which was merely a gathering of pious souls for purposes of devotion. This was the group of men with whom Penn had come in contact in 1677.

Pietists

---

18. Claypool Letter Book. Extracts in Pa. Mag. of History, X. 275.
19. Seidensticker, Bilder aus der Deutsch-Pennsylvanischen Geschichte, p. 26.

GERMANTOWN 103

    The result of this meeting was the formation of the Frankfort Land Company, whose purpose was to establish in the wilds of Pennsylvania for themselves and others, an ideal retreat where they might devote themselves, free and unhindered, more exclusively to the cultivation of the religious life. The original plan, however, was never carried out. Land was actually purchased from Penn, as we have just seen, but the company far from maintaining its original ideals soon degenerated into a mere speculating enterprise. The agent for these Pietists was Francis Daniel Pastorius, an accomplished scholar and successful lawyer, who had traveled much as a student, and practiced law in Frankfort, Worms, Mannheim and Speier, and it was at Frankfort in the spring of 1682 that he met Spener. Hearing much of Pennsylvania and of the proposed scheme of the Pietists to buy large tracts of land for colonization purposes, he was seized with the idea of going to Pennsylvania himself to enjoy the quiet, simple Christian life for which the new world seemed to afford such ample opportunities.[20] As agent for the company Pastorius later purchased land for them from Penn, and for seventeen years acted as their attorney in Pennsylvania.

    Soon after his appointment Pastorius left for America. On his way to Rotterdam from which place he was to embark for Philadelphia he visited Kriegsheim and Crefeld where he met many of the future colonists. In Rotterdam he met Jacob Telner and Benjamin Furley, Penn's agents in Holland. Telner

---

20. Seidensticker, p. 55.

and such Crefeld purchasers as did not immediately emigrate also engaged Pastorius to represent their interests in the new world. Much of the land bought by the Frankfort Company was located around what was soon to be Germantown and many of the early settlers bought their lands from this company. This explains why Pastorius played such an important role in the early affairs of the first Mennonite colony.[21]

Pastorius accompanied by several of the Crefeld purchasers had left London early in the summer of 1683 and had arrived in Philadelphia, August 20, about six weeks before the Crefeld colonists came.

These colonists did not remain long in Philadelphia, which was at that time a mere village, having been founded only the year before. They immediately set out in search of their new homes. Following, it is said, an Indian trail, which is now perhaps Germantown Avenue, they selected as their first dwelling place an elevated spot between the Delaware and Schuylkill rivers about five or six miles north of where the village of Philadelphia then stood. This Indian path was lined with laurel bushes. The surrounding region was a

Germantown Founded

---

21. In religion Pastorius has been claimed by both Mennonites and Quakers but as a matter of fact he belonged to neither denomination. He was himself baptized a Lutheran in Germany, and had his two sons, born in Pennsylvania, baptized into the same church. Being a Pietist (See J. F. Sachse, The German Sectaries of Pennsylvania). however, he no doubt felt himself very much at home with both Mennonites and Quakers. During the early years of the Germantown settlement there was no Lutheran organization in the community and so we find Pastorius taking an active interest in the religious affairs of the Quakers. His name often appears on the records as a delegate to the Quarterly Meetings (See Abington Records). There is nothing to show, however, that he took a similar interest in the religious affairs of the Mennonites.

"very fine and fertile district with plenty of springs of fresh water, being well supplied with oak, walnut and chestnut trees and having besides excellent and abundant pasturage for the cattle." [22] On October 24, Thomas Fairman, Penn's surveyor, laid out the land for the colonists in a township afterwards called Germantown or Germanopolis in honor of the nationality of the colonists. On the next day they all gathered together in the cave of Pastorius and cast lots for their portions of land.[23]

These early settlers were mostly mechanics and linen weavers "and not given much to agriculture." Consequently, instead of locating on large farms as did the Mennonites on the Pequea some years later, they established a village and divided their time between the cultivation of the soil, which soon, however, became a secondary occupation with them, and the industry of weaving. The Opden Graffs, Arets, Tunes and Lensen were all linen weavers, while Dennis Konders was a dyer.[24] In 1686 Abraham Opden Graff petitioned the Governor's Council to grant him the Governor's premium for "the first and finest pece of linen cloth."[25] Penn encouraged the linen industry and gave Telner 100 acres of Liberty land for his services in helping to establish the colony.[26]

Occupation

---

22. Letter of Pastorius, quoted in Pa. Mag. of Hist., IV. 90.
23. Watson, Annals, II. 18.
24. Pa. Arch., Second Ser., XIX., p. 270.
25. Col. Rec., I. 194.
26. Pa. Arch. Second Ser., XIX. 256.

As early as 1692 Richard Fraeme wrote:

The Germantown of which I spoke before
Which is at least in length a mile or more,
Where live High German people and Low Dutch—
Whose trade in weaving cloth is much—
Here grows the flax as also you may know
That from the same they do divide the tow.[27]

The village was laid out along one street 60 feet wide with cross streets 40 feet wide.[28] This street, Fraeme says, was one mile long in 1692, and by 1748 when the famous Swedish Botanist Kalm visited Germantown it had grown to two miles. An old chronicler, writing in 1700, relates that at that time it was lined on both borders with blooming peach trees.[29] On both sides were erected the first temporary dwelling places by the settlers. Pastorius in March 1684, writes that the community already has forty-two persons in twelve families and each family has an estate of three acres. Later, however, the village was resurveyed into fifty-five lots of fifty acres each, running along both sides of the main street.[30]

During the first few years the colonists were kept busy clearing the land, opening roads, and raising such grain as they needed for their sustenance. On October 22, 1684, William Streypers wrote to Holland:

I have been busy and made a brave dwelling and under it a cellar, fit to live in, and have so much grain such as Indian

---

27. Old South Leaflets, Number 95.
28. See Pastorius letter in Pa. Ger. Soc., IX. 145.
29. Watson, II. 46.
30. Pa. Ger. Soc., IX. 201.

corn and buckwheat that this winter I shall be better off than I was last year.[31]

First Houses The temporary houses and caves were soon replaced by other and more substantial buildings. The region abounded in sandstone and many of the settlers, before 1700, erected large and comfortable stone houses, some of which are still standing.[32] These buildings cost considerable time and labor in their erection, but were put up without very much other expense. Several of the original purchasers may have been men of means, but the actual settlers for some time were poor men. Pastorius in 1684 says,—

These honest people spent all their means on their journey

---

31. Streyper's in a letter to his brother. Quoted by Pennypacker in Pa. Ger. Soc. Preceedings, IX. 72.

32. "Most of the old houses in Germantown are plastered on the inside with clay and straw mixed, and over it is laid a finishing coat of thin lime plaster; some old houses seem to be made with log frames and the interstices filled with wattles, river rushes and clay intermixed. In a house ninety years of age taken down, the grass in the clay appeared as green as when cut. Probably twenty houses now remain of the primitive population. They are of but one story, so low that a man six feet high can readily touch the eves of the roof. Their gable ends are to the street. The ground story is of stone or of logs—or sometimes the front room is of stone and the back room is of logs, and thus they have one room behind the other. The roof is high and mostly hipped, forms a low bed chamber; the ends of the houses above the first story are of boards or sometimes of shingles with a small chamber window at each end."

"In modern times those houses made of logs have been lathed and plastered over, so as to look like stone houses; the doors all divide in the middle, so as to have an upper and a lower door; and in some houses the upper door folds. The windows are two doors opening outwards and were at first set in leaden frames with outside frames of wood."—Watson II. 18.

Since the above was written many of the old houses have disappeared. Some of those still standing have since been remodelled.

so that when provision was not made for them by William Penn they were obliged to serve others.[33]

From Indian ravages and deadly disease, the two most fatal enemies of so many of the early American colonists, the Germantown settlement was fortunately free. During the first winter there was only one death and that was of the aged mother of the Opden Graff brothers. While Abraham, who sent the news to Germany, was sitting in his room with pen in his hand an Indian squaw came into the room. Curious to know what the writer was doing she took the pen in her hand, whereupon Opden Graff took her hand in his and traced the news of his mother's death across the page. Thus was the news of the first death among the colonists sent to their friends in Europe.[34]

The colony once established, was soon increased by fresh arrivals from Germany and Holland, influenced to emigrate either by their friends here **Later** or by Penn's agents in Europe who during **Arrivals** all this time were busily engaged in securing colonists for Penn's new province. For the first ten or fifteen years the immigration was very largely confined to those of the Mennonite or Quaker

---

Among this number wholly or partially original are the Dirk Keyser house built 1738; the Thones Kunder's home now No. 5109 Germantown Avenue; the Engle house built 1758; and the Rittenhouse mansion on the Wissahickon built 1709. The Hiefert Papen home, built in 1698 was torn down several years ago. For a discussion on the old houses of Germantown see Jenkins, Guide book to Historic Germantown; and Keyser, Old Historic Germantown, in Pa. Ger. Sec., Sec., XV. (C. H. S.)

33. Pa. Ger. Soc., IX. Pastorius letter p. 141.
34. Letter of Abr. Opden Graff written to friends in Holland 1684. Translated and published by J. F. Sachse, in Letters Relating to the Settlement of Germantown.

faith but soon after that the Reformed and Lutherans
predominated, with a sprinkling of Dunkards, and
many other denominations and sects. Germantown
is not only the first home of the Mennonites in
America, but the first home of the German race in
America. Especially was it the religious cradle of
German America. Here was organized not only the
first Mennonite church in this country but also the
first Dunkard,[35] German Reformed,[36] German
Lutheran,[37] Moravian, and one of the earliest
Methodist congregations.

Among several other persons concerning whose
religious affiliations we have no positive information
came, in 1684, these Mennonites,—Hans Peter Umstat, Isaac Jacob Van Bebber from Crefeld, and
Jacob Telner. The next year added to the list
Hiefert Papen, who is said to have built the
first stone house in Philadelphia, and Klas Jansen,
and two families, Peter Shoemaker and Gerhard
Hendricks from the Mennonite-Quaker congregation at Kriegsheim. Johannes Kassel, also
a Quaker convert, came from the same place during
the following year. In 1687 came Matthias Van
Bebber, son of Jacob Isaacs Van Bebber, the founder,
a few years later, of the Skippack settlement. In 1688
Dirck Keyser, who was a well known silk merchant
of Amsterdam, arrived by way of New York. In this
year came also William Rittinghuysen, the first
Mennonite preacher in America.

---

35. Brumbaugh, History of the Brethren.
36. J. H. Dubl.s. German Reformed Church. (Am. Ch. Hist. Series) 245.
37. H. E. Jacobs. The German Lutherans (Am. Ch. Hist. Series) 710.

During the next fifteen years were added a number of names many of which have occupied a conspicuous place ever since that day, not only in the annals of the Mennonite church but in the political history of the commonwealth of Pennsylvania as

The Dick Keyser House, built 1738

well. All came from Lower Germany and Holland. They were, Hendrick Sellen, Hendrick Pennebecker, the first German surveyor for the province,[38] George Gottschalk, Hans Neus, a silversmith, four families

---

38. For much of the detailed information on the early settlement of Germantown I am indebted to the writings of S. W. Pennypacker in the Proceedings of the Pa. Ger. Society, Vol. IX. Where other references are not given I have drawn upon Pennypacker for my facts.

from the Hamburg congregation, Harmen Karsdorp, Claes Berends, Isaac Van Sinteren, and Paul Roosen, Paulus Kuster, Paul Engel, Christopher Schlegel, Evert In de Hoffen, Christian Meyer,[39] Hans Graff,[40] Cornelius Bom and Hendrick Casselberg, with perhaps several others.

In the meantime those of other religious faiths were continually finding their way into the new colony.

Other Denominations In 1694 Kelpius, a disciple of Jacob Boehm, came over with a number of followers. After remaining in Germantown for a short time they withdrew to the lonely banks of the beautiful Wissahickon a few miles to the west and there Kelpius became known as the Hermit of the Ridge.[41] With Kelpius came a party of Lutherans who held their first services in America in the house of the Mennonite, Van Bebber.[42] There were also a number of the Reformed denomination, as well as several Quakers who for the most part had been proselytes from the Mennonites in Crefeld, Kriegsheim or other places. The Reformed, however, did not organize a congregation until 1710.[43]

Relation of Various Sects There seems to be considerable confusion in the minds of writers on this subject as to the relation of these various sects. This confusion arises undoubtedly very largely from the fact that during the first few years while the community was still small and most of the denominations without preachers, the settlers

---
39. Fretz, Moyer Family.
40. Rupp, Hist. of Lanc. Co., 133.
41. For discussion of this subject see J. F. Sachse, the German Sectaries of Pennsylvania.
42. Pa. Ger. Soc., XI. 79.
43. Dubbs, History of the Reformed Church.

irrespective of their religious affiliations often worshipped in common. In 1686 a public meeting house was built which served as a place of common worship. It was only as the different denominations grew, that separate organizations developed. The Quakers built their first meeting house in 1705, and the Mennonites in 1708. There is much dispute especially concerning the religious complexion of the original thirteen families. What were they, Mennonites or Quakers?[44] We have already noticed the close and intimate associations between the two denominations on the continent. Whatever may have been the church relations of the first settlers after they came to Germantown there can be very little doubt that, with the exception of Pastorius, they were originally of Mennonite descent. According to Pennypacker[45] who has made a very exhaustive study of the family connections of these people, the Opden Graffs were grandsons of the Herman Opden Graff who as a delegate from Crefeld signed the Dortrecht Confession of Faith in 1632. Lensen was a member of the Mennonite church in 1708 and is the only one of the thirteen whose name appears on the church roll at that time. Jan Lucken has the same name as the engraver who illustrated the Martyrs' Mirror of 1685 in Holland. A certain Leonart Arets was a follower of David Joris who belonged to one of the Anabaptist sects in Holland and who died at Basel in 1556. Tunes was a common name among the Mennonite preachers of that time.

---

44. The fact that the Mennonites never kept any church records makes a thorough study of their early history extremely difficult, especially on such a question as this.
45. Pennypacker, in Pa. Ger. Soc., IX.

William Streypers was a brother of Jan Streypers[46] who was an uncle to Hermanus Kuster known as a Mennonite in 1708. The Streypers furthermore, were cousins to the Opden Graffs. The wife of Thones Kunders was a sister to Arets and a sister of the Streypers. The wife of Jan Streyper was a sister of Reynier Tyson. Keurles also was related to several of the group. This leaves no doubt as to the faith of these people before the coming of Stephen Crisp, the Quaker, into Crefeld some time before 1683.

And yet some of them may have accepted the Quaker faith before the emigration[47], but concerning this question it is difficult to reach a definite conclusion. We are certain, however, that a number of them showed decided Quaker qualities soon after they reached Germantown.

The fact that at first family ties, lack of preachers, their common hardships and common interests made it necessary for all to worship as one body **Common** irrespective of their individual religious be-**Worship** liefs, makes it difficult to tell whether or not the company represented more than one religious faith. The first meeting seems to have been in the house of Thones Kunders, whom the Quakers claim as one of their members, and it is likely that this and succeeding gatherings partook more of Quaker than Mennonite characteristics. A number of the

---

46. See Streyper Mms. in Pa. Historical Soc. Lib., Philadelphia.
47. "Before their departure from Germany there had been a Friend's Monthly Meeting held at Crefeld which was discontinued immediately after their departure, indicating that all or nearly all the full body of members had gone."—Jenkins, Guide Book to Historic Germantown, p. 18.

colonists took an active interest from the very beginning in Quaker religious affairs.

Among these was Abraham Opden Graff who later became one of the leading participants in the Keith controversy. He left Germantown some time after 1704 for the Skippack, and consequently the records of the Abingdon meetings make no mention of his name. It is likely that at Skippack he was again active in the Mennonite congregation, and he is buried in the Mennonite graveyard at that place. The name of his brother also, Derrick Up de Grave, is often found on the Quaker records as a delegate to the Quarterly meetings, as are also the names of Dennis (Thones) Kunders, Leonard Arets, Reynier Tyson (1709) and John Lukens (1705). During the first half of the 18th century the names of Conrad, Tyson, Lukens, Streyper and Updegrave, all descendants of the original thirteen, often appeared on the records of the Monthly Meetings. Many of these records it will be observed refer to a time long after the Mennonites had organized their congregation, and thus there can be no doubt that the men named had deserted the Mennonite for the Quaker faith. These men with the arrival a few years later of the Mennonite-Quakers from Kriegsheim constituted the first and for some time, the strongest religious body in Germantown.

Thones Kunders House. Built before 1688. A part of the original wall is still standing.

This view is substantiated by a letter from Jacob Gottchalk, one of the early Mennonite preachers.[48] He says:

The beginning of the community of Jesus Christ here at Germantown who are called Mennonites took its rise in this way, that some friends out of Holland and other places in Germany came here together and although they did not all agree, since at this time the most were still Quakers, nevertheless they found it good to have exercises together but in doing it they were to be regarded as sheep who had no shepherd and since as yet they had no preachers, they endeavored to instruct one another.

Whatever the religious faith, however, of the larger part of the colony may have been during the early years of the settlement, it must not be forgotten that originally they had all been Mennonites and that the leaders, Jacob Telner, Matthias Van Bebber and others remained true to that faith and that soon many other Mennonites came over. The Germantown settlement in its inception after all, must be considered a Mennonite enterprise.

As the colony and the various parties grew in numbers and wealth, the different sects began to differentiate and crystallize into separate organizations. We can get a glimpse of the religious conditions several years after the settlement was made from a letter written on June 7, 1690, by Domine Rudolfus Varick, a Reformed pastor visiting at that time in Pennsylvania. In writing to Amsterdam he says,—

Mennonites Worship Separate

I came to a German village near Philadelphia where among others I heard Jacob Telner, a German Quaker,

---
48. Pa. Ger. Soc., IX. 220.

preaching. Later I lodged at his house in Philadelphia. The village consists of 44 families, 28 of whom are Quakers, the other 16 of the Reformed church. Among whom I spoke to those who had been received as members of the Lutheran, the Mennonites, and the Papists, who are very much opposed to Quakerism and therefore lovingly meet every Sunday when a Menist, Dirck Keyser[49] from Amsterdam reads a sermon from a book by Jobst Harmensen.[50]

Although Varick's observations may not be altogether reliable, yet this much can safely be accepted, namely, that in 1690 the Mennonites had withdrawn from the Quakers in worship; that they must still have been few in number; that they were still without a regularly ordained minister; and that other denominations, which likewise were without regular organization often met with them rather than with the Quakers for worship. According to Jacob Gotschalk, to whose letter reference has already been made, these meetings were held in the house of Isaac Jacob Van Bebber. In this year the Mennonite community was increased by more of their brethren from Crefeld, who from "the first found it good or judged it better for the building up of the community to choose by a unanimity of votes a preacher and some deacons."[51] Accordingly William Rittenhouse was chosen preacher and Jan Neus, deacon. These were the first two officials of the Mennonite church in America. On October 8, 1702, two other ministers were elected—Jacob Gotschalk and Hans Neus.[52]

---
49. Keyser had not yet been ordained to the ministry.
50. Pa. Ger. Soc., XV. A translation.
51. Gotschalk letter. Pa. Ger. Soc., IX. 220.
52. This information is given in a letter written to Holland in 1773 by Andreas Ziegler, Isaac Kolb and Christian Funk. These three men get their information from the earlier Gotschalk letter. Pennypacker found the letter in Holland and published it in his "Hendrick Pennebecker."

Thus far the church was without a bishop and hence it was impossible to administer the sacrament of communion or the rite of baptism. Soon after 1700 a letter was written to the church at Hamburg-Altona, from which several of the brethren had come in 1700, asking that a bishop be sent to them for the purpose of ordaining a bishop for the American church. But no one in Altona seemed to be willing to make the long journey, and the authorities therefore advised the Americans that if their selection could be made harmoniously, one of their own ministers might install a bishop. One of the four ministers from the Hamburg-Altona church whose signature appears to this letter of advice was Gerrit Roosen, a well-known preacher of that day[53]. This advice seems to have been followed, for before 1708 William Rittenhouse had become the first bishop of the congregation.

First Bishop

In 1708 the congregation erected a building for worship. As early as February 10, 1703, Arnold Van Vossen had delivered to Jan Neus in behalf of the church a deed for three perches of land for a meeting house. The house was not put up, however, until 1708.[54] It was a log structure and stood until 1770, when it was replaced by a stone building, which is still standing. The spring of 1708 must have been a season of renewed life to the small brotherhood. On March 22, three new deacons were elected—Isaac Van Sinteren, Hendrick Kassel and Conrad Janz. On April 20, two

Log House of 1708

---

53. Brons, Ursprung, Entwickelung, und Schicksale der Mennoniten, p. 224.
54. Pennypacker, in Pa. Ger. Sec. IX.

new preachers—Herman Kasdorp and Martin Kolb, were chosen. On May 9, Bishop Jacob Gotschalk, successor to Bishop Rittenhouse, who had died in February, administered the first baptismal services to eleven applicants for church membership. On May 23, just two weeks later, all partook of the Lord's supper[55]. All this evidently took place in the little log meeting house which had just been completed. Morgan Edwards says that the membership at this time numbered fifty-two[56]. He must be mistaken, however, for he includes William Rittenhouse, who died several months before, and Gotschalk in his letter says that the congregation numbered forty-four members. Edwards no doubt included some who had either died or moved away from Germantown before May 23. The community continued to grow. In 1709 others came from the Palatinate so that by April 6, 1712, the entire membership including the settlement on the Skippack, counted up ninety-nine individuals.[57]

An old bench and table in the Germantown meeting house. Tradition says they were used by the schoolmaster Christopher Dock.

Many of the later arrivals at Germantown were

---

55. Gotschalk letter, Pa. Ger. Soc., IX. 220.
56. See Morgan Edwards, Material for a History of the Baptists, for a complete list of members at that time. The list is also copied by Cassel in Geschichte der Mennoniten.
57. Gotschalk letter, Pa. Ger. Soc. IX. 220.

GERMANTOWN 119

an agricultural people and as the land about the village was taken up it was inevitable that new lo-
Skippack cations should be sought for. Among the
Settlement fertile valleys that very early began to attract attention as suitable for new settlements was that of the Perkiomen, watered by the beautiful Perkiomen creek which empties into the Schuylkill about thirty miles above Germantown. The Skippack is a branch of the Perkiomen flowing directly through the middle of what is now Montgomery county. It was on the banks of this stream that the second Mennonite church in America was established. On February 22, 1702, Matthias Van Bebber received a patent for 6166[58] acres of land in what is now the lower part of Perkiomen township, but which was for many years known as Van Bebber's township. Most of the early settlers were Mennonites from Germantown, or recently from Europe. Among the Mennonites who bought land and located on this tract between 1702 and 1709 were Hendrick Pennebecker and his brother-in-law, Johannes Umstat, Johannes Kuster, Klas Jansen, Jan Krey, John Jacobs, Herman In de Hoffen, Hermanus Kuster, Christopher Zimmerman and Jacob, Johannes and Martin Kolb. In 1717 Van Bebber gave one hundred acres to the congregation for a place "to bury their dead as also for all and every the inhabitants of said Township to build a schoolhouse and fence in a sufficient burying place."[59]

---

58. Pa. Arch., Second Ser., XIX. 338.
59. In the early days burying grounds were frequently owned in common by several denominations. The same was frequently true of the schools held in the Mennonite churches.

The house,[60] however, was not built until about 1725.[61]

In the early development of Germantown there are two events which deserve more than a passing notice and which are of more than local significance. These events are the protest against holding of slaves in 1688, and the incorporation of the little village in the form of a borough in 1691.

It is but fitting that the Mennonites who in the old world were among the first of modern advocates for entire liberty of soul, should in the **Protest against** new be the first to raise their voice **Slavery** in public protest against the bondage of the body. On February 18, 1688, Gerrit Hendricks, Derick Op den Graff, Francis Daniel Pastorius and Abraham Op den Graff met in the house of Thones Kunders, it is supposed, and drew up, so far as is known the first public protest against the holding of slaves on record in America. This remonstrance begins immediately with the reasons for their opposition to "the traffick in menbody."

Those who hold slaves are no better than the Turks. Rather it is worse for them, which say they are Christians; for we hear that ye most part of such Negers are brought hither against their will and consent, and that many of them are stolen. Now though they are black, we cannot conceive there is more liberty to have them slaves as it is to have other white ones. There is a saying that we shall doe to all men licke as we will be done ourselves: macking no difference of what generation, descent or colour they are. And those who buy or purchase

---

60. Christopher Dock, the pioneer Pennsylvania schoolmaster, taught school here for a number of years.
61. Bean, History of Montgomery County. 101.

them, are they not all alicke? Here is liberty of Conscience which is right and reasonable, here ought to be likewise liberty of ye body, except of evil doers, which is an other case. But to bring men hither, or to robb and sell them against their will, we stand against. In Europe there are many oppressed for conscience sacke: and here there are those oppressed which are of black Colour.[62]

The Mennonites of Europe evidently had inquired regarding the Quaker practice of holding slaves, for the protest adds—

This makes an ill report in all those countries of Europe (Holland and Germany) where they hear off, that ye Quackers do here handel men, Licke they handel there ye cattle and for that reason some have no mind or inclination to come hither. But if they help to stop this robbing and stealing if possible and such men ought to be delivered out of ye hands of ye Robbers and set free as well as Europe. Then is Pennsilvania to have a good report, instead it hath now a bad one for this sacke in other Countries. Especially whereas ye Europeans are desirous to know in what manner ye Quackers doe rule in their Province and most of them doe loock upon this with an envious eye, But if this is done well, what shall we say, is don evil?

This document, which appears in the handwriting of Pastorius, was carried by Derick Op den Graff to the Quaker Monthly Meeting held at Dublin, (Pa.) on "ye 30—2 mo of 1688." The Dublin meeting, however, considered the matter of too great importance "to meddle with it here" and referred it to the Quarterly Meeting. When the Quarterly Meeting came together at Philadelphia the protest met the same fate. It was recommended to the Yearly Meeting, and that is the last action taken upon it. The Quakers, in spite of the

---

62. Pa. Mag. of Hist., IV. 28.

good service they later rendered in the cause of human freedom, were not yet quite ready to declare in favor of total abolition.

Both Mennonites and Quakers claim the credit of the authorship of this document. The Quakers maintain that it was sent to their Monthly and Quarterly meetings and that the original signers were all Quakers. This latter portion of their claim can certainly not be substantiated.

It is true that Derick Op den Graff was a Quaker in 1688, and that his brother Abraham was also inclined to accept that faith at the time, although he later again identified himself with the Mennonites. But on the other hand Pastorius, as we have already seen, cannot be counted a Quaker, while Hendricks, whose name heads the list of signers, remained true to the Mennonite faith throughout his life.

But had all of them been Quakers at this time, the protest would still have to be considered more of a Mennonite than a Quaker document. In the first place three of the signers had been brought up in the Mennonite faith and owed their abhorrence of human slavery to their German blood and to their Mennonite, and not Quaker training. In the second place it must be remembered that the Mennonites never held slaves, but the English Quakers did. So late as 1696 the Yearly Meeting of Philadelphia advised Friends to be careful to bring their slaves to meeting and to have meeting with them in their families.[63] It must also not be forgotten that the Yearly Meeting in 1688 re-

---

63. Davis, History of Bucks Co., p. 795.

fused to act on the protest. It is perfectly clear that
this appeal was made to the Quakers against a practice
which was common among them, and that it was made
as a result of Mennonite influence. To the Mennonites then, it would seem, should belong the credit for
uttering this first public protest against "the traffick
in menbody."

The incorporation of the village of Germantown
is of interest to the student of political science[64] as
well as to the student of Mennonite
Incorporation history: to the former because German-
of Germantown town was the first example in Pennsylvania of the borough type of govern-
ment, the common form of local administration in the
later history of the province; to the latter, because it
is one of the few times that the Mennonites in America
had the opportunity to test the feasibility of non-
resistant principles when applied to the establishing
of a civil government. Here we have a group of men,
all of whom inherit the Mennonite prejudice against
the holding of civil office and the use of physical force
in any form whatever when applied to government;
they ask for separate incorporation which implies the
establishing of a complete list of civil officers, the ma-
chinery for the making of laws, and courts for execut-
ing them. Theory and practice were completely inconsistent with one another, and it was inevitable that
an attempt to harmonize the two should end in failure.

The charter for the borough was obtained from
Penn in 1689 but did not go into effect until 1691. It
was granted to a corporation composed of a small

---

64. See Johns Hopkins Studies, V.

body of men to whom was given a limited power of government and opens with these words—

> I, William Penn, Proprietor of the province of Pensilvania in America under the Imperial Crown of Great Britian, by virtue of Letters Patent under the great Seale of England DO grant unto ffrancis Daniel Pastorius, Civilian and Jacob Telner, Merchant, Dirck Isaacs Optegraff Linenmaker, Herman Isaacs Optegraff, Towne President, Tennis (?) (Dennis or Thones Konders) Abraham Isaacs Optegraff Linen Maker, Jacob Isaacs, Johannes Cassell, Heywait Hapon (Hiefert Papen) Coender Herman Bon (Cornelius Herman Bom) Dirk Van Kolk, all of Germantowne, yeomen that they shall be one Body politique and corporate aforesaid in name etc.[65]

To these men was given the exclusive right of managing the affairs of the village, of electing all necessary officers and of admitting

> such and so many persons into their corporation and society and to increase, contract, or divide theire Joynt stock or any part thereof . . . . . as they shall think fitt.

The officers provided for by the charter were a bailiff, four burgesses and six committee men. To these were added later, a recorder, clerk, sheriff and coroner. ("Leichenbeschauer.") A General Court was to "govern and direct all the affairs and business of the said corporation." In the words of the charter they

> shall have power to make, ordain, constitute and establish so many good and reasonable Laws, Ordinances and Constitucons as they shall deeme necessary and convenient for the good Government of the said Corporacon and theire affairs, and at theire pleasure to revoke, alter and make anew as occasion shall require—And also to impose and set such mulets

---

[65] See Pa. Arch., p. 111 for charter in full.

and amerciaments upon the breakers of such Laws and Ordinances as in their Discrecon shall bee thought necessary.

The form of government here provided for, it will be seen, was that of a close corporation. The corporate members were granted the exclusive right of the franchise, of legislation and of admitting new members into the corporation.

The charter named the first officers. Francis Daniel Pastorius was the first bailiff; Jacob Telner, Dirck Isaac Op te Graaf, Herman Op te Graaf, and Isaac Op te Graaf, Jacob Isaacs (Van Bebber), "Tennis Coender" the first burgesses; and Abraham Johannes Kassel, Heywart Haypon, Herman Bom and Dirck Van Kolk the first committeemen. These officials were to constitute the General Court. The judicial functions were placed in the hands of a Court of Record which was composed of the bailiff and the two oldest burgesses, who as individuals were also to serve as Justices of the Peace. This court was to be held every six weeks and was to determine

all civill causes, matters, and things whatsoever arising or happening betwixt the Inhabitants of the said Corporacon, according to the Laws of the said Province and of the Kingdom of England, reserving the appeal according to the same.

Our chief interest for the purposes of our story is centered in the proceedings of the Court of Record. This court was by no means a useless institution, though for several years it was concerned chiefly with litigation relating to stray pigs, fences, and such other trivial matters as are likely to become causes for dispute between neighbors in a primitive settlement. The promptings of the non-resistant spirit were evidently not always followed to their logical result, for in 1693 we find Pastorius, the Pietist, and Shumaker, the Quaker, asking in the General Court that "stocks for evil doers" might be erected. Aret Klincken, a brother Quaker, delivered the stocks. In 1697 Klincken's house was converted into a temporary prison house, and at the same session it was decreed that all punishment imposed in the past should be annulled but for the future all decrees were to be strictly enforced.

The first Court of Record[66] was held August 6, 1691, in the common meeting house which, as was the custom in many places in early colonial times, served the double purpose of a church building and a city hall. Pastorius was bailiff, and Jacob Telner, Derick Opden Graff and Herman Opden Graff as the three oldest burgesses constituted the court. In addition to these there were present, Isaac Jacobs Van Bebber, recorder; Paul Wulf, clerk; Andrew Souple, sheriff, and John Luken, constable. All of these with the exception of the ever-present Pastorius, and the Sheriff were either Mennonites or Mennonite-Quakers.[67]

The rulings of the Court are not without interest and throw some light on the every day life of the settlement. The following extracts are characteristic of much of the work of the Court and show that

---

66. For a brief discussion of the proceedings of the Court of Record see Seidensticker, Bilder aus der Deutsch Pennsylvanischen Geschichte, p. 55, and following. For a few extracts from the laws of the General Court see Pa. Ger. Soc. Proceedings X. The complete records of the Court of Record in the original German are now deposited in the Pennsylvania State Historical Society Library in Philadelphia.

67. By Mennonite-Quakers I mean those Mennonites who had turned Quaker either in Europe or America.

occasionally even the Mennonites were inclined to forget the letter of the law.

The first meeting was called to order by the sheriff, who read the proclamation and saw that the officers were properly installed.[68] The Court fined one Carsten for menacing Constable Luken, who attempted to serve a warrant on him. The fine was two pounds and ten shillings. The Court then adjourned.

December 21, 1692.—

Court adjourned by reason of the absence of some for religious meeting over the Schuylkill.

October 25, 1694.—[69]

Jacob Isaacs[70] and Albertus Brand were called into court and told that because their fences were presented insufficient each of them was finable six shillings.

March 7, 1695.—

Peter Keurlis was attested why he did not come when the justice sent for him: he answered he had much work to do whereupon he was further attested why he refused to lodge travellers (?) Answer, he only intended to sell drink but not keep an ordinary. Then he was attested why he did not sell barley malt beer at 4d. a quart against the law of this province? Answer, he did not know such a law. Lastly he was asked why he would not obey the law of Germantown corporation which forbids to sell more than a gill of rum or a quart of beer every half a day to each individual? Answer, they being able to bear more, he could or would not obey.

September 10, 1696.—

Overseers of fences reported as insufficient the fences of Herman Opden Graff, Abraham Opden Graff, Isaac Jacobs and others. But Herman Van Bom and Johannes Umstat

---

68. Both Quakers and Mennonites.
69. Of course elections were frequently held and the officers first named were soon succeeded by others.
70. Van Bebber.

pretending they did not know the several fences in their quarter refused to perform their duty.
July 9, 1700.—

Abraham Opden Graff and Peter Keurlis were sent for to answer complaints made against their children by Daniel Fallkner,[71] but the said Abraham Opden Graff being not well and Peter Keurlis gone to Philadelphia this matter was left to next session.

John Lensen appeared in this court excusing himself from serving as committeeman because his conscience would not allow it, hereof the next General court shall consider and make an order concerning like excuses.[72]

December 9, 1701.—

All the inhabitants of Germantown shall make their fences good and lawful within three weeks and set posts in the ground with their names upon both their side fences and those which are behind the lots.

November 11, 1701.—

John Lensen gave over with the assent of the court keeping an ordinary and Peter Keurlis promised in open court to keep a good and regular ordinary in this town whereof the town does allow.

December 28, 1703.—

Abraham Opden Graff[73] did mightily abuse the bailiff[74] in open court wherefore he was brought out of it to answer for the same at the next Court of Record.

December 8, 1704.

Hermanus Kuster fined ten shillings for not appearing as a juryman.

April 18, 1704.—

Jacob Gaetschalck and John Lensen say they will not

---

71. Lutheran preacher.
72. "The General Court decreed that those having conscientious scruples would be excused. Those not having but refusing were fined three pounds."—Seidensticker.
73. Opden Graff seemed to be unusually quarrelsome. He was an active participant in the Keith controversy and was much in public life having twice been elected to the General Assembly.
74. Aret Klincken.

betray their neighbors, especially John Lensen, therefore the court appointed in his room Leonart Arets.[75]

October 3, 1704.—

Abraham Opden Graff sued David Sherkes for saying that no honest man would be in his company.

Dirk Keyser Sr. and Jr. and Van Vossen were among the jurymen. The Jury returned a verdict in favor of the defendant.[76]

The last Court of Record was held December 11, 1706-7, and the last General Court on December 2, of the same year. Soon after the borough lost its charter for want of an election to fill the offices. The village was governed after this by the ordinary laws of the township until finally absorbed by the city of Philadelphia.

The loss of the charter was due largely to the fact that the Mennonites had very little taste for civil government. At first so long as the matter of local government was hardly more than the regulating of the family affairs of the brotherhood there seemed to be little objection to the holding of office. Out of eleven of the first officers named in the charter six and probably seven were Mennonites while four of the remaining five were Mennonite-Quakers. But the village grew in numbers. Many came in who were not in sympathy with Mennonite ideals. The making of laws and the administering of justice became more

---

75. In a jury in a law suit.
76. It must be remembered that only such proceedings of the court are here selected as concern the Mennonites and their relatives. They were by no means the only source of trouble and cause for legal proceedings in the little village.

complicated. With the coming in of stocks and prison-houses the Mennonites lost their desire for politics. The offices were filled more and more by either Mennonite-Quakers or by the Quakers, who seem never to have shared the prejudice of the Mennonites against the holding of civil office. These two denominations in theory held similar views in their attitude toward the temporal power; both objected to the oath and to war. The Mennonites, however, carried out the principle of non-resistance farther than the Quakers and maintained that it was wrong to use force against the individual, and hence to be consistent no Mennonite could hold an office which involved the use of physical force in the execution of the laws. For this reason we have here the unparalleled instance of a corporation losing its charter because no one could be found to fill the offices.

As early as 1701 Pastorius in writing to Penn said that he could not get men to serve in the General Court for "conscience sake" and he trusted for a remedy in an expected arrival of immigrants.[77] Hiefert Papen had declined to be a burgess in 1701. In 1702 Cornelius Siverts had refused to serve, and Paul Engle in 1703. John Lensen and Arnold Kuster declined to be committeemen in 1702. Others declined to serve in similar capacities. But why were not the offices filled by non-Mennonites? The Mennonites in 1707 were certainly outnumbered by those who were not in sympathy with their civil and religious principles. The charter it will be remembered put the government into the hands of a close corporation. This corporation

---

77. Hazard, Register, I. 280.

began predominantly Mennonite, and although later the Mennonites declined to serve as officials, they did not hesitate to exercise the franchise. They and the Mennonite-Quakers, who had never quite forgotten their early training in Europe, held the controlling vote and were very careful not to admit those into the corporation who were opposed to their principles. The offices were handed about to a group of men who from year to year held the various positions of influence in rotation. Although the Quakers held most of these positions during the later years, yet the Mennonite leaven was strong enough to control the political sentiment in the corporation. The loss of the charter was due to Mennonite, not Quaker, influence.

The remaining history of the Germantown church can be dismissed with few words. Immigrants continued to come to America, but most of them being agriculturists, they passed the first settlement by for more promising locations on the Skippack or the Conestoga. The congregation was never large and seems never to have been in a prosperous condition. It continued, however, for a good many years; but we get only occasional glimpses of its life and activities. The old log building was replaced by the present stone structure in 1770, and at that time the congregation numbered twenty-five.[78] In a letter of October 27, 1796, from Jacob Oberholtzer of Franconia to Abraham Kolb of Germantown Township, he states that lots had been drawn for ministers to serve the congregation for the coming year. This indicates that there was no resident minister here at that time and that only one

---

78. N. B. Grubb, the Mennonite Church of Germantown.

preaching service per month was held.[79] The congregation finally became extinct but was revived again in 1863 under the pastorate of F. R. S. Hunsicker. It is at present under the control of the General Conference Mennonites and has nineteen members.

Insignificant, however, as the later history of the Germantown church may seem in itself, it has nevertheless indirectly exerted no mean influence both upon the Mennonite church at large and indirectly upon the civil and religious history of Pennsylvania. In the house of Van Bebber was held in 1690 the first service of the German Lutherans in America, and at least ten of the prominent churches of Philadelphia including one Evangelical, one Presbyterian, two Episcopal and two Lutheran were first organized in the early days in the little Mennonite meeting house.[80] Many of these congregations drew heavily upon the Mennonites for their membership.

Influence of the Germantown Congregation

In the civil and political history of Pennsylvania also we find many names with which we have been made familiar in the course of our story. In 1690 William Rittenhouse, the first bishop, erected on the Wissahickon the first paper mill in America.[81] Here in 1709 his son built a stone house, still standing, where

---

79. The original letter is in the possession of S. W. Pennypacker. The facts here have been taken from a photograph of the original taken by N. B. Grubb of Philadelphia. The letter contains the names of twelve of the ministers of the Franconia District who were to preach at Germantown during the year.
80. Per N. B. Grubb, pastor of First Mennonite Church of Philadelphia.
81. See "The Rittenhouse Paper Mill" by H. G. Jones in Pennsylvania State Historical Library. The old mill site and the old Rittenhouse "mansion" on the banks of the picturesque Wissahickon is now one of the places of interest to the sight-seer in Fairmount Park.

in 1732 was born his great-grandson David,[82] who became a celebrated philosopher and astronomer of his day, the respected friend of Benjamin Franklin and Thomas Jefferson. He was a prominent member of the Assembly during the Revolutionary war and was appointed first director of the United States mint by President Washington.[83]

Another prominent Mennonite was Heinrich Pennebecker, many of whose descendants have become well known in Pennsylvania history. He was the first German surveyer employed by Penn in the province. Among a long list of distinguished men bearing the name Pennypacker is the recent governor of Pennsylvania, and Isaac S. Pennypacker some time United States Senator from Virginia.[84] Space will not permit to speak of the Keysers, Updegraves, Cassels, and Van Bebbers but all of them could boast of a long line of men who have occupied positions of trust and influence in church and state.

---

82. D. K. Cassel, Family Record of David Rittenhouse.
83. William Barton, Memoirs of David Rittenhouse.
84. "Of the descendants of old Hendrick Pennebecker, 27 have been lawyers, including three District Attorneys, one president of a law academy and assistant editor of a legal journal, and five judges: Isaac S., long a judge of the U. S. District Court, became Senator from Virginia."—S. W. Pennypacker, in The Pennypacker Reunion, 1877. p. 31.

CHAPTER V

THE PEQUEA COLONY

The German immigration into Pennsylvania, and especially Mennonite immigration, for the first twenty years was not very large. The first settlers, as we have seen, came largely from the Lower Rhine country. But in 1710 began a second and much greater wave, which during the next seventy five years was to bring in round numbers nearly 100,000 Germans into the province, and which was to form the basis of that picturesque element of the population of Pennsylvania which we today know as the Pennsylvania Dutch. These people came from the Upper Rhine country, the region called the Palatinate, including, roughly speaking, the southwestern part of present Germany. Among the first to arrive was a small colony of Mennonites who located on the banks of the Pequea, a branch of the Susquehanna in what is now Lancaster county.

In order to understand the causes of this steady inflow of the Palatines it is necessary that we know something about the conditions prevailing at that time

THE PEQUEA COLONY 135

Unrest in the Palatinate

in the land from which they came. During the greater part of the seventeenth century there had been much distress and unrest among the people of the Palatinate, due very largely to the wars and religious disturbances of the period. This region, situated as it was, on the borders between France and the German states, in the very heart of Europe, was made the battlefield for many of the great wars of the century. Throughout the entire Thirty Years' War the armies of the opposing parties played havoc with the lives and possessions of the wretched Palatines. The year 1638 marked the climax of their misery. Rapine, plunder and fire were followed by famine and pestilence. The people

tried to satisfy hunger with roots, grass and leaves; even cannibalism became more or less frequent. The gallows and the graveyards had to be guarded; the bodies of children were not safe from their mothers. So great was the desolation that where once flourished farms and vineyards, now whole bands of wolves roamed unmolested.[1]

The Thirty Years' War was followed not many years afterward by the famous campaigns of Louis XIV, who in 1688, in order to starve out his enemies, ordered his generals to devastate the Palatinate, a command which was carried out to the letter.[2] This war was

---

1. Kuhns, German and Swiss Settlements of Pa., p. 9.
2. The following extracts from Macauley refers to an incident in one of these campaigns.
   "The commander announced to near half a million human beings that he granted them three days of grace, and that within that time they must shift for themselves. Soon the roads and fields, which then lay deep in snow, were blackened by innumerable multitudes of men, women and children fleeing from their homes. .. .. Meanwhile the work of destruction went on. The flames went up

closed by the treaty of Ryswick in 1698, but it was many years before the Palatinate recovered from these devastations.

It was during this same time that the religious question became a serious menace to the peace of the province. The Treaty of Westphalia had provided that each Prince was to determine the religion of his people. Up to 1685 the Electors were either Lutherans or Calvinists, but in that year a Catholic once more came into possession of the Electorate. Then there began a systematic policy of Protestant extermination. Lutherans and Reformed, who were by far the most numerous in the province, were deprived of their lands and churches. Mennonites, Walloons, and Huguenots, who had found a refuge in the Palatinate for many years were now driven out of the land. It was conditions such as these together with the impoverishment of the country resulting from the many wars, that paved the way for the great Palatine emigration to America and other places during the first half of the eighteenth century.

No attempt on a large scale was made, however, by the people who were oppressed to leave their native land until 1709. But during this year a perfect flood of Palatines poured into London expecting help from the English government to cross the Atlantic. Two causes may be mentioned among others for this sudden

---

from every market place, every parish church, every country seat within the devoted province. The fields where the corn had been sown were plowed up. The orchards were hewn down. No promise of a harvest was left on the fertile plains near what had been Frankenthal. Not a vine, not an almond tree was to be seen on the slopes of the sunny hills round what had once been Heidelberg." Macauley, III. 112.

desire at this particular time to seek homes in a new country. In the first place the winter of 1708-9 was unusually cold and severe throughout Europe, increasing the distress and hardships of the poor people.[3] In the second place Queen Anne had for several years been actively trying to get colonists for her unoccupied possessions in America and had sent her agents to the Palatinate for this purpose. This together with the conditions previously described, may explain the sudden German inundation of the city of London in the summer of 1709.[4] The English government was at a loss at first to know what to do with such a large number of foreigners but made the best of the situation. Several thousand were sent to Ireland. Some were sent to North Carolina; others to New York. A few remained in England. Some died; others were sent back to Germany. Many in after years found their way to Pennsylvania.[4]

Thus far we have been speaking of general conditions which affected all, and especially all non-Catholics, alike. So much of a background is necessary for an understanding of our story.[5] But we are concerned here only with the Mennonites and it is to them that we now turn with special reference to

---

3. "It was so cold that the birds froze in the air and the wild beasts in the forest." Löher, Geschichte der Deutschen in Amerika, p. 42.
4. The story of the German emigration of 1709 is told in detail by F. R. Diffenderfer in the "German Exodus to England in 1709," in Pa. Ger. Soc. Proceedings, VII.
5. There are several good histories of the Palatinate, any one of which will describe the condition of the country during this period. A very good brief account of the general European background of the Palatine emigration is found in chapter 1 of Kuhns, German and Swiss Settlements of Pennsylvania. See also a letter written by Benedict Brechbühl in 1714 quoted by Müller, in Geschichte der Bernischen Täufer, Chapter 12.

their experiences in the Palatinate and in Switzerland, immediately before and after the emigration of 1709.

The Mennonites had still other reasons in addition to those just named for leaving their homes in these regions at this time. As we have **Swiss Mennonites** already seen up to 1685 they had **under Persecution** been at least tolerated in the Palatinate. But in Switzerland throughout the latter half of the seventeenth century they had been severely oppressed. Because of their refusal to bear arms and to take the oath, they were exiled, sent to the galleys, robbed of their property, imprisoned, and occasionally put to death. As a result of these conditions many had found their way into the Palatinate before 1709. The Swiss Mennonites were found principally in the cantons of Berne, Zurich and Schaffhausen. All of these cantons tried to exterminate them, but Berne was especially oppressive. And since we know more about the Mennonites of Berne, thanks to the labors of Ernst Müller, than we do about those of the other parts of Switzerland, and since Berne furnished a large number of the later Swiss immigrants, it may not be out of order to relate briefly the experience in that canton of many who later became citizens of Pennsylvania.

As just stated, the Bernese as well as other Swiss Mennonites had been imprisoned and exiled all through the latter half of the seventeenth and the first part of the eighteenth centuries. Of special severity, however, and of special importance for our story were the persecutions of the years 1708-9-10-11. The Government had frequently imprisoned or banished those

DOYLESTOWN CHURCH

THE PEQUEA COLONY

whom they could lay hands on.[6] But since they kept back the wives and children of the banished ones, the exiles naturally returned, in spite of the threats of the authorities. Finally in 1709 it was decided to end the matter by deporting all the prisoners then in custody, about fifty-four in number, to America.

The prisoners were finally placed on board a ship in charge of a certain Ritter, and on March 18, 1710, the voyage began down the Rhine. Passports had been secured from France and other states that bordered the river. In the meantime the representative of the Bernese government at the Hague was told to secure the necessary permission from the government of the Netherlands to pass through that country and to embark at Rotterdam.[7] To gain permission for transportation proved a difficult task. There were many influential Mennonites in the Netherlands who now, as they often had done before, interested themselves in their Swiss brethren. St. Saphorin, the Bernese representative, instead of gaining the desired permission was told by the States General

> that the Mennonites (in Holland) had always proved themselves good subjects and that they (States General) therefore could by no means lend a hand to the transportation of these people to America; neither could they do anything that

---

6. In the meantime the Council had written to Zurich to learn how they rid themselves of the Mennonites, whereupon they replied that they had put a number to death; others they imprisoned; some were forced into the armies in the war against the French while still others were exiled from the land." Letter of Runkel, the envoy of the Netherlands to Bern written in 1710, and quoted by Müller, 257.

7. For information regarding the Mennonites of Switzerland during this period I have relied almost entirely on Ernest Müller's Geschichte der Bernischen Täufer. For the negotiations between Berne and the Netherlands see Müller, p. 261.

might in any way be interpreted as sanctioning the Bernese policy toward the Mennonites.

St. Saphorin hereupon turned to the English ambassador, Lord Townsend, in the hope that he might use his influence in his, St. Saphorin's, behalf with the States General. He described the desirable qualities in the Mennonites as colonists. They were "very good agriculturists, industrious, for the most part possessed of some means," and since the transportation would cost the English government nothing the advantage must all be theirs. Townsend, however, influenced by the Dutch Mennonites, decided against the request of St. Saphorin. Since neither passports nor permission for transportation were to be had, the proposed scheme of Berne to get rid of the Mennonites had to be abandoned.

But one shipload had already started down the Rhine. Thirty-two of the exiles, the old and sick had been left at Mannheim. The remaining reached Nimwegen on April 6. Here they asked permission to visit some of their brethren in the city, which permission was granted. They were now on free soil and since the Lower Rhine was closed to Ritter and his cargo he left his prisoners here and returned to Berne. Among those who arrived at Nimwegen were Benedicht Brechbühl, a bishop from Trachselwald, and Hans Burchi from Langnau. These two men appeared to be the leading men among the Swiss Palatines at this time. Brechbühl later came to Pennsylvania and was one of the ministers from Conestoga to sign the confession of Faith printed in 1727. The

Voyage down the Rhine

THE PEQUEA COLONY 141

arrival of the Swiss at Nimwegen is described by a contemporary as follows:

> Now they were free, for which we rejoiced with them greatly and we showed them every manner of friendship and love. After we had enjoyed ourselves together for a day and they had gained much strength they departed. But they could hardly walk, for their joints had grown stiff through long imprisonment. Some of them had been in prison for two years with great suffering, especially last winter during the great cold, since their feet were fettered with iron bands. I went with them several miles out of the town. We embraced one another weeping and parted with a farewell kiss of peace. Thus they turned their steps toward the Palatinate to search for their wives and children who were scatterd there , as well as in Switzerland and Alsace, and they did not know whither they had been sent. They were in good spirits even in their sorrow, although all their possessions had been taken from them. There were among them one preacher and two teachers. They were a very sturdy people by nature who could endure hardships, with long untrimmed beards, with plain clothes, and heavy shoes shod with heavy iron and large nails. They were very zealous in serving God with prayer, reading and in other ways. They were very simple in their bearing, like lambs and doves and asked me how the church here was conducted. I told them and they seemed very much pleased. But we could speak with them only with difficulty. For they had lived in the mountains of Switzerland far from villages and towns and had little communication with other people. Thus their speech is very blunt and simple and they could with difficulty speak with others who did not use precisely their speech. Two of them went to Deventer to see whether they could support themselves in this land.[8]

Such were many of the men who later settled Lancaster county.

---

8. Translated from Müller.

This letter no doubt partly answers a question which the reader may already have asked himself,— Why did not these persecuted Mennonites eagerly seize this opportunity of transportation to America where already a goodly number of their fellow believers had built homes for themselves? This question perhaps may not be difficult to answer if we remember that the wives and children of these men had been kept back in Berne. Furthermore, as St. Saphorin said, they were extremely anxious, since Switzerland was the cradle of Anabaptism, that their faith should not be rooted out in that country. In addition to all this we must not forget that this was their home land which in spite of their sufferings remained dear to them.

Many, including Brechbühl and Burchi went back to Berne and were again imprisoned. The Bernese government only redoubled its energies to destroy them entirely. They were accused of refusing to bear arms and to take the oath of allegiance. The civil authorities, however, were still largely under the influence of the predominating church. The Mennonites owe their bitter experience in Switzerland quite as much to the intolerant spirit of the Reformed church as to the suspicions of the civil magistrates. Melchior Zahler in a letter written in 1710 relates that when he was captured he was taken before the ecclesiastical authorities of the parish and interrogated regarding his belief on the following questions: Infant baptism, the oath, the ordinance of the ban, bearing the sword and concerning the office of the magistrate. Most of the fines and confiscations were usually appropriated by the Reformed church. At Hütwohl they used 500

Gulden of Mennonite fine money for building a new church. In Roggwyl the money was used for church bells. Zofingen built a hospital and poor house.

The persecutions continued. So relentless were the Swiss in their cruel treatment of the Mennonites that Townsend finally interceded in their behalf with Queen Anne and suggested to both the Anabaptists and Quakers of England that they assist the persecuted to get to America. The king of Prussia invited them to settle in his own territory. The States General interceded with the Bernese government for a more liberal policy. Finally in 1711 those in prison were allowed their freedom on condition that they pay a fine and with their families and friends leave their native country.

<small>Continued Persecution at Berne</small>

On July 13, 1711, four ships, loaded with several hundred Mennonites and Amish[9] began once more their voyage down the Rhine. Müller gives us a vivid description of these Emmenthaler and Oberländer[10] exiles as they drifted down the river and their homes disappeared behind the cathedral spires of Basle and the wooded hills of the Jura. Seated upon the chests and bundles which were piled up in the middle of the vessels were the grey-headed men and women, old and weak. On the sides were the young people watching with delight and wonder the shifting scenery of the banks as they glided by. Now hopeful, now troubled, they cast questioning glances to the North and then with longing eyes they again turned their faces to the South in the direction of their be-

<small>Exiled from Berne</small>

---

9. In 1693 Jacob Amman headed a church division, since called the Amish branch of the church.
10. The valleys in Switzerland from which they came.

loved homes which they were leaving forever, the homes which had so basely exiled them and yet the homes whose green hills and silver tipped mountains they could not forget. And when overcome with sorrow some one began a song which comforted them.

"O Herr, wir thun dich bitten, richt unser Herz und Gemüth, nach deinem heiligen Wort, durch deine grosze Güt. Zünd du in unserm Herzen eine reine Liebe an, thu für uns wachen und streiten sonst mögen wir nit bestahn."[11]

Once beyond the Swiss borders they began to leave the vessels at many of the cities along the Rhine wherever there were congregations of their brethren. And thus the Mennonites had all left before the ships reached Holland. The Amish alone arrived at Amsterdam. From these places they were finally scattered throughout the various cities of Holland and Northwestern Germany. Few of them started for America immediately but judging from the similarity of family names sometime during the next fifty years a large number of these Bernese exiles and their children must have found their way into Pennsylvania. Among this group can be found representatives of nearly all the names that have since become familiar in the history of the Pennsylvania Mennonites. Among the most characteristic of which are those of Burki, Gerber, Flückiger, Baumgartner, Gäuman, Neukomm, Wisler, Haldeman, Shallenberger, Hauri, Schlabach, Blank, Neuhauser, Meier, Reuszer, Steiner, Wenger, Streit, Stähli, Stucki, Bauer, Hoffman, Brechbühl, Krähenbühl, Bieri, Rupp, Schenk, Fahrni, Äshleman, Ebersold.

But to return more directly to the emigration to

---

11. Müller, 304. Translated from the German.

THE PEQUEA COLONY

Pennsylvania and the Pequea settlement. The Bernese exiles of 1709 and 1711, as we have seen, were not the first of the Swiss Palatines to seek new homes across the Atlantic. The first to emigrate were among those who had come into the Palatinate from Berne and Zurich many years before. Godshalk[12] says that in 1707 several Palatines came to Germantown, among them Johannes, Jacob and Martin Kolb. From a few scattered references and letters, our only source of information, we learn that others followed in the years immediately succeeding. On April 8, 1709, a letter from the "Committee on Foreign Needs" at Amsterdam states that nine or ten poor families from near Worms had come to Rotterdam asking for help to be transported to Pennsylvania. The committee advised them not to go.[13] They evidently reached England, however, for under date of August 6, Jacob Telner wrote from London that eight families had gone to Pennsylvania and that there were six more Mennonite families in London too poor to pay their passage across. He asks the brethren at Rotterdam to come to their rescue.[14] It was during this year that the Yearly Meeting of the Quakers at London voted fifty pounds to help the Mennonites to get to America.[15] It is of these same people also no doubt that Penn wrote to Logan who was then in Pennsylvania.

First Palatinate Immigrants

---

12. See the Godschalk letter quoted by Pennypacker in Hendrick Pennebecker.
13. Scheffer, Mennonite Emigration to Pennsylvania, translated in Pa. Mag. of History, II.
14. Ibid, II. 122.
15. Barclay, The Inner Life of the Religious Societies of the Commonwealth, p. 257.

The latter is dated, "26th, 4th mo. 1709." Penn says,—Herewith come the Palatines, whom use with tenderness and love and fix them so that they may send over an agreeable character; for they are a sober people, divers Menonists and will neither swear nor fight. See that Guy uses them well.[16]

All of these, whoever they were, no doubt reached America safely and located somewhere near Germantown or on the Skippack.

The first notice that we have of the founders of the Pequea colony is in a letter written from London on June 27, 1710, by Martin Kendig, **Pequea Colony** Jacob Miller, Martin Oberholtzer, **of 1710** Martin Maili, Christian Herr and Hans Herr to friends in Amsterdam. They were on their way to America and sent a letter of thanks to the brethren in Holland for assistance that the Dutch had rendered them.[17] These were likely of the earlier exiles into the Palatinate from Zurich and Berne.[18] The next appearance of the names of these men is on a warrant dated October 10, 1710, for a tract of ten thousand acres north of Pequea Creek in what is now Lancaster county.[19] The warrant is drawn up in favor of John Rudolf Bundely, Martin Kendig, Jacob Müller, Hans Graff, Hans Herr, Christian Herr, Martin Oberholts, Hans Funk, Michael Oberholts and Weyndel Bowman "Switzers, lately arrived in the province." The tract is to be located on

---

16. Penn-Logan Correspondence, II. 354.
17. Entire letter in Müller, 366.
18. In 1731 in the church near Ebingen there was a Heinrich Kündig and a Jacob Oberholzer. In the church at Thirnheim near Sintzheim there was a Hans Herr, a Christian Herr and a Jacob Meili. All of these no doubt were of the same families as the emigrants to Pennsylvania. See Müller, 209, 210.
19. In the office of the Secretary of the Interior at Harrisburg.

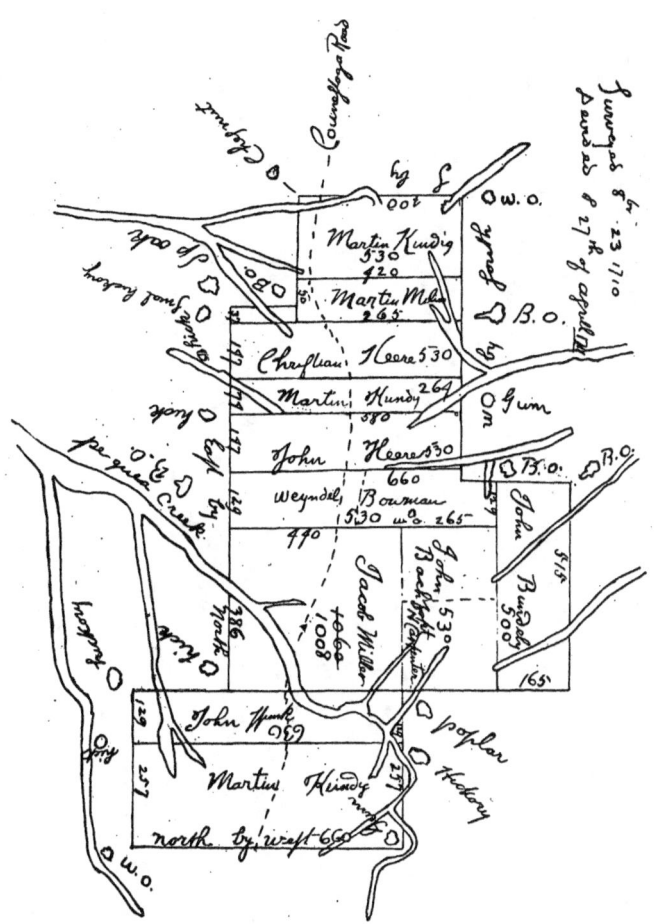

"This diagram shows the location and size of the plots of land secured by the first Pequea settlers. The largest holder it will be seen was Jacob Miller and not John Heer as is usually supposed. The Pequea here sketched is south of Willow Street. This sketch has been made from the original plot in the office of the Secretary of the Interior at Harrisburg."

THE PEQUEA COLONY

"the northwesterly side of a hill about twenty miles easterly from Conestoga near the head of the Perquin Creek." For these ten thousand acres the purchasers were to pay five hundred pounds sterling money, and in addition one shilling sterling quit rent for every hundred acres. On April 27, 1711, six thousand four hundred and seventeen acres were distributed among the purchasers.[20] The remainder was divided among later comers. It will be observed that in the first division several new names appear, while those of Hans Graff and Martin Oberholts are not to be found. Of all these it is likely that Carpenter, (Zimmermann)[21] Funk and Bowman joined the Kendig-Meilin colony at Germantown.

Of the early incidents leading up to this settlement and of the early life of the settlers we know nothing above what we are able to glean from these land records. It is to be supposed, however, that while in England they met either Penn or his agents and there contracted for their land. Since Germantown and the surrounding country was already taken up by immigrants, they consequently turned their faces westward, and traveling about sixty miles out of Philadelphia they reached a rich limestone region along the banks of the Pequea, in what was then Chester, but now Lancaster county. Here they decided to put up their first log cabins, in spite of the fact that they were in the very heart of Indian territory and that with the exception of a few scattered Scotch-Irish hunters and

---

20. For plot of original tract see Old Rights, Lancaster Co., in office of Secretary of Interior.
21. Many of those names were early Anglisized. Henry Zimmerman came to Germantown 1701, returned to Germany, and brought back his family 1706.

fisherman they were the only white men for many miles around. Conyngham, a local historian, speaks of this region one hundred and twenty years later as a rich limestone country, beautifully adorned with sugar maple, hickory and black and white walnut, on the border of a delightful stream, abounding in the finest trout. . . . The water of the Pequai was clear, cold and transparent, and the grape vines and clematis intertwining among the lofty branches of the majestic button wood, formed a pleasant retreat from the noon beams of the summer sun.[22]

As already said, we know very little about these early days.[23] The colonists evidently were well pleased with their new home, for they immediately decided to send for their friends and relatives in the old country.[24] A voyage across the ocean in those days was no small undertaking, and consequently they agreed to cast the lot to decide who was to carry the news to Europe. The lot fell on Hans Herr, but either because he was their preacher whose services could not well be dispensed with or for some other reason, Martin Kendig offered to take his place. Kendig succeeded in his mission and some time during that year brought back with him Peter Yordea, Jacob Miller, Hans Tschantz, Henry Funk, John Houser, John Bachman, Jacob Weber, Christopher Schlegel[25]

Kendig's Mission to Germany

---

22. Hazard, Register, VII. 151.
23. For some of the traditions of the early settlement see Mombert, History of Lancaster County, p. 421; also an article by G. N. Le Fevre in the "Home," Aug. 5, 1905, published at Strasburg, Pa.
24. The details of this story are a matter of tradition. See Rupp; History of Lancaster County and G. N. Le Fevre in the "Home" Aug. 5, 1905.
25. Schlegel had come to Germantown 1701. Pa. Ger. Soc., IX. 191. See also Pa. Arch. 2nd. Ser., Vol. XIX. 56.

THE PEQUEA COLONY 149

and others,[26] most of them with their families. During the next fifteen years many others took up land near the Palatines. From the minute books of the Board of Property and from other sources we learn that in addition[27] to those already named there were added to the settlement before 1715 the following, most of them heads of families,—Christian Brenneman, Hans Haigy, Christian Hershi, 'Hans Pupather (Brubaker), Heinrich Bär, Peter Lehman,[28] Benedictus Witmer, Melchior Brenneman,[29] Heinrich Funk, Michael Schenk, Johannes Landes, Hans Huber, Isaac Kaufman, Melchior Erisman, with others, sons of the first settlers who had in the meantime reached the age of twenty-one, and a very few more who were non-Mennonites.[30] During the next two years there were added either from Europe or the Germantown settlement, Jacob Hostetter, Jacob Kreider, Hans Graff,[31] Benedictus Venerich[31], Jacob Böhm,[32] Hans Faber, Theodorus Eby[33], Heinrich Zimmerman and others.

The settlers from 1711 to 1717 came as individuals and in small groups. But in the latter year there was another wave of immigration including many of those

---

26. Rupp, History of Lancaster County, p. 81.
27. Pa. Arch. 2nd. Ser., XIX. See Index for well known Mennonite names.
28. A minister in Oberpfalz in 1699. See J. Moser, Eine Verantwortung gegen Musser.
29. See Müller, 201.
30. Mombert, History of Lancaster County, p. 422; Rupp, Thirty Thousand Names, 436. Graff came to Lancaster county 1716. See Rupp, History of Lancaster County, p. 15.
31. Name appears on the 1710 warrant.
32. Father of Martin Boehm, one of the founders of the United Brethren church.

150   MENNONITES OF AMERICA

who had been exiled from Berne in 1710 and 1711.
Wave of 1717 These refugees, as we saw, were scattered throughout the Palatinate and other parts of Germany. They were never in prosperous circumstances. The country was wasted by wars. The churches were poor. They had to gain a livelihood as best they could, often by the help of their brethren in the Netherlands. Their numbers, furthermore, were continually increasing by fresh exiles from Switzerland.[33] At this same time came a special invitation from King George I to settle the lands west of the Alleghanies.[34] The glowing description of the new country given by the king's agent together with the promising reports of friends who had already come across, as well as their own distressed condition finally prevailed over the love for their native land which had made these Swiss exiles so averse to deportation several years previously. They had now been absent long enough to be partly weaned from their love for the hills and valleys of their beloved even though cruel native land. Consequently, in February of 1717 a number of elders, including Benedict Brechtbühl and Hans Burghalter, met at Mannheim and decided to emigrate to Pennsylvania.[35] The "Committee on Foreign Needs" which had been organized some time before at Amsterdam for the purpose of helping their needy brethren in the Palatinate, and to whom these exiles now applied for assistance, dis-

---

33. See de Hoop Scheffer, in Pa. Mag. of History, II. 126; also de Hoop Scheffer's catalogue of documents for list of Swiss letters in the archives of the Mennonite church at Amsterdam.
34. For glowing descriptions of the country as given by these agents and the terms of settlement see de Hoop Scheffer in Pa. Mag. of Hist., II. 127.
35. Ibid, p. 132.

THE PEQUEA COLONY 151

couraged the movement. They feared that if a precedent were once established there might be more calls for money than they could supply. In spite of all the endeavors, however, of the committee to check the emigration it was reported to them on March 20 that more than one hundred persons had started. This number was soon increased to three hundred. In spite of their own refusal to render assistance, the committee nevertheless helped the needy ones across the ocean. This was the history of the proceedings of this committee for many years to come. They publicly discouraged all attempts to emigrate but secretly rendered assistance when called upon for help.

This year, 1717, must have been especially conducive to emigration for we find that many others besides Mennonites came into Pennsylvania at this time. In fact their great numbers began to excite some alarm among the English, in the province. Governor Keith fearing lest the English speaking population might be outnumbered by the foreigners, recommended that some steps be taken towards restricting future immigration. The minute books of the Board of Property contain many entries of land sold during the year near the Mennonite settlement in the Pequea. These newcomers were all "Relations, Friends or acquaintances who are honest conscientious people."[36] Martin Kendig and Hans Herr were the richest and the most influential members of the colony, and much of the land for the new settlers was first taken up in the names of these two men.[37]

---

36. Pa. Arch. 2nd. Ser., XIX. 679.
37. "Feb. 8, 1717."
  "Agreed with Martin Kendigg and Hans Herr for 5000 acres of land to be taken up in several parcels about Conestoga and

The Mennonite settlement occupied at this time the southern half of what was then (in 1718) Conestoga township. The northern part of the township was composed largely of Scotch-Irish and English. It must not be forgotten that although what is now Lancaster county has from that day to this been predominantly a Mennonite settlement yet by 1718 many others besides Mennonites had found their way to the community. The first assessment of the township was taken in 1718,[38] and the list of tax payers for that year gives us a fair idea of the size of the Mennonite settlement. These names, however, do not include all the immigrants who had up to this time come into the province, for several of their number had moved away by this time, while others had not settled originally within the domain of what was then Conestoga township. The list shows that in this immediate neighborhood there were added by 1718 among per-

---

Pequea Creeks at 10 pounds ct. to be paid at the returns of the surveys and usual quit rents, it being for settlements for several of their countrymen that are lately arrived here." The warrant for this land is signed on September 22, to the following:

Hans Moyer	350 acres
Chr. Hearsay and Hans Pupather	1000 "
Hans Kaiggy	100 "
Mich. Shenk and Henry Pare	400 "
Hans Pupather	700 "
Peter Lehman	300 "
Molker Penerman	500 "
Henry and John Funk	550 "
Chr. Fransicus	150 "
Michael Shank	200 "
Jacob Lundus and Ulrick Harvey	150 "
Emanuel Herr	500 "
Abr. Herr	600 "
Hans Tuber, Isaac Coffman and Melkerman	675 "
Mich. Miller	500 "

Minute Book of Board of Property, Pa. Arch. 2nd. Ser., XIX. 622.

38. Ellis and Evans.—History of Lancaster County, p. -9.

haps others the following names: Joseph Stemen, Isaac LeFevre,[39] Hans Houre, Martin Bear, Henry Kendig, Andrew Kauffman, Isaac Kauffman,[40] Jacob Brubaker, Melchior Erisman, Hance Burghalter,[41] Hance Neucommer, Jacob Landes,[42] Hance Henry Neff, Franz Neff, Felix Landes, Jacob Landes Jr., Martin Boyer, Hance Boyer, Benedictus Brackbill [Brechtbühl] and Christian Schans.

Later Arrivals

The wave of immigration in 1717 evidently relieved the immediate pressure in the Palatinate and for a few years there seem to have been few, if any new arrivals in Lancaster county. But soon they began once more to come. In 1722 Nicholas Erb[43] and others arrived from Europe and some time later settled on Hammer Creek

---

39. See Rupp, Hist. of Lancaster County, for good sketch of the life of Isaac Le Fevre. Le Fevre was a Huguenot. In 1709 he was one of the company that located in New York at New Paltz where the name Lefevre is still very common. In 1712 he and his wife, Catherine, daughter of Madam Ferree came to Lancaster County. Here he became one of the largest landholders in the settlement. Either he or some of his immediate descendants joined the Mennonites. There are many Lefevers and Le Fevres in the Mennonite church in the county to-day. See also History of New Paltz, by Ralph Le Fevre.

40. See J. Moser; Eine Verantwortung, etc. This pamphlet contains the names of many of the ministers in Switzerland who took part in the trouble between Amman and Reist in the years 1693-1710. Among them was Isaac Kauffman.

41. Müller, Geschichte der Bernischen Täufer, p. 200.

42. In 1717 three brothers, Rev. Benjamin, Felix, and John Landis, Swiss Mennonites came to America from Mannheim on the Rhine whither they had been driven from Zurich. Benjamin's descendants are found mostly in Lancaster county. In 1718 the first assessment in Conestoga township contained the names of Jacob Landis and Jacob Jr. The name Jacob is probably a mistake. It should have been Benjamin. D. B. Landis, The Landis Family, p. 12. Benjamin located in East Lampeter township. Felix in 1719 received a patent from London Company for 400 acres in Conestoga township. John located in Bucks county but in 1720 took up 300 acres at the junction of Middle and Hammer Creeks.

43. Alex. Harris, Biographical History of Lancaster County, p. 194.

in what is now Warwick township. Christian Bamberger[44] and Peter Reist[45] also located in the same region. Each year brought a few more. Before 1727 we meet the following additional names of Mennonites who had come into the county,—Christian Mosser, Samuel Hess, Abraham Burkhalter, Johannes Hess, Joseph Buchwalter, Peter Baumgartner, Jacob Nüssli who settled in Mt. Joy township,[46] Hans Schnebele, Jacob Guth, Jacob Beyer, Hans Jacob Schnebele,[47] Heinrich Musselman, Jacob Kurtz,[48] John Ulrich Huber, Johannes Lichty,[49] Johannes Stauffer,[50] Johann Heinrich Bär, Jacob Weber, Heinrich Weber, Johannes Weber, George Weber, David Longenecker,[51] Peter Eby,[52] Matthias Stouffer,[53] Johannes Guth, Christian Steiner,[54] Adam Brandt,[55] Simon König,[56] Johannes Rupp,[57] Philipp Dock,[58] Rudolph Nägeli,[59] and Michael Eckerlin.[60] There may perhaps have been

---

44. Ibid, 62.
45. Ibid, 480.
46. Ibid, 425.
47. Müller, Geschichte der Bernischen Täufer, 225, 290.
48. Possibly Amish.
49. The name Lichti frequently occurs in Müller's book.
50. Müller, 202.
51. Pennypacker, Hendrick Pennebecker, p. 16.
52. A relative to Theodore.
53. Pa. Arch. Second Ser., XIX. 134.
54. Müller, 277.
55. Possibly Amish.
56. Possibly Amish.
57. Müller, 277.
58. Father of Christopher, the pedagogue who came to Germantown in 1714. This list of names is taken largely from Mombert..
59. See Brumbaugh, History of the Brethren, p. 161; also Moser, in Eine Verantwortung.
60. Came to Germantown in 1725, to Conestoga, 1727. There he joined the Mennonites but soon cast his lot with Beissel and became one of the founders of the Ephrata movement.

others of whom no record has been preserved.[61]

In the meantime the original settlement on the Pequea was spreading itself over the central portion of what is now Lancaster county. The Herrs, Meylins and Kendigs as we have seen were located on both sides of the Pequea southeast of the present village of Willow Street. The settlement soon spread across what are now Conestoga, Pequea, West Lampeter, Strasburg and Providence (northern part) townships. This region was soon taken up, however, and it became necessary for those who desired large and cheap tracts of land to locate on the outskirts of the original settlement. Hans Graff was one of the first to begin a new community. The story goes that sometime in the year 1717 while in pursuit of his stray horses he wandered into what is now known as Graff's Thal in West Earl township. He was so well pleased with the beauty

Graff's Thal

---

61. I have taken great pains throughout this treatise to insert the names of the early immigrants who I was reasonably certain were Mennonites. This I have done for several reasons. In the first place since the Mennonites kept no church records, one of the difficult problems of the Mennonite historian is to ascertain who were and who were not Mennonites. These names all appear in all histories of the early settlers in these various localities and I have thought it worth while here to place them within their proper religious affiliations. In the second place these names are still representative of many Mennonite families throughout the country and may be of interest to many Mennonites of today. The task was by no means an easy one. In a few instances I may have been mistaken but very few if any of those mentioned were other than Mennonite. I have relied very largely for my information on family histories, letters, lists of European Mennonites, local histories, naturalization lists, controversial pamphlets, records on tombstones, family traditions and my own personal knowledge of the Mennonite names of today. By a careful process of elimination and comparison in the study of these various sorts of evidence I have been able to make a fairly complete and I think quite accurate list of at least the most prominent of the early Mennonite immigrants.—C. H. S.

and fertility of the surrounding country that he decided to remove his family and belongings from the Pequea to the new location.⁶² During the same year he received a warrant for 1150 acres on what is now Graff's Run, a branch of the Conestoga. Hans Graff was soon followed by others,—Mennonites and non-Mennonites. The preponderance of the names Groff, Graff, and Grove in the cemetery of the Groffdale Mennonite church, near the little station called Groffdale indicates that many of the descendants of old Hans remained faithful to the church of his choice. That he must have been a man of considerable influence in the community is shown by the fact that three townships—the three Earls—now bear his name although in an Angelicized form.

A little later, in 1724, another Mennonite settlement was made about six miles east of Graff's Thal.

Weber's Thal Here in what soon became known as Weber's Thal, three brothers, John, Jacob and Henry Weber bought from the Penns about three thousand acres of land between the Welsh Mountain near which some Welsh had settled, and the Conestoga. With them was associated Hans Guth a brother-in-law of one of the Webers. These were joined soon after by the Martins, Schneiders, Zimmermans and Ruths. These names are found today almost exclusively on the oldest tomb-stones in the graveyard of the Weaverland Mennonite church. Fully two thirds of the inscriptions bear the names of Weber or Weaver and Martin. This locality is undoubtedly the original home of nearly all the Mennon-

---

62. For this story see Diffenderfer, The Three Earls; and Rupp, History of Lancaster County, p. 132.

THE OLD CHRIST HERR HOUSE. Built in 1719. This is the oldest building standing in Lancaster county. Here the early pioneers met for worship before a meeting house was built.

ite Weavers found in America today.⁶³ At the same time settlements were being made in the west and northwest. In 1717, John Brubaker and Christian Hershey took out a patent for one thousand acres about two miles west of Lancaster city in East Hempfield.⁶⁴ Here Brubaker erected the first grist mill in Lancaster county near the present Abbeyville.⁶⁵ Later the tract of land was divided, Hershey taking the northern half and Brubaker the southern.⁶⁶ In the north we have already seen that as early as 1720 John Landes took up land at the junction of Middle and Hammer Creeks, which form a tributary of the Cocalico.⁶⁷ A little farther to the west Peter Reist, Christian Bomberger and Nicholas Erb soon after became early settlers in this region. Land was also purchased very early west of the Conestoga in what was then Conestoga Manor but now Manor township. A draft made of the manor in 1718 shows that land had been purchased before that time by John and Abraham Herr, John Shenk, Michael Shenk, Martin Funk, Michael Baughman and many others. It is perhaps not necessary to proceed further with these details. Enough has already been said to show that the Mennonites were taking possession of the land. It was not long until the richest portions of the country were in their hands.

The year 1727 marks another epoch in the history

---

63. See Rupp, 124, and Diffenderfer, 26.
64. Pa. Arch. Second Series, XIX. 628.
65. Harris, 88. Brubaker had nine sons. John and Daniel later settled in Elizabeth township, while Abraham went to Virignia.
66. Per. J. N. Brubaker, Mt. Joy, Pa.
67. See Landis Family, by D. B. Landes.

158   MENNONITES OF AMERICA

of the immigration of Mennonites as well as that of
other Palatines.[68] So many foreign-
Passenger Lists ers came over this year that the
Required 1727 English Quakers again became
alarmed. The Provincial Council on
September 14, adopted a resolution which was embodied into law to the effect that all masters of vessels
importing Germans and other foreigners should prepare a list of such persons together with the place
from whence they came, and further that all such
immigrants should sign a declaration of allegiance to
the king of Great Britain and of fidelity to the Proprietary of Pennsylvania.[69] These lists begin with
September 21, 1727, and continue to the Revolutionary
war. They have since been printed by Rupp in his
"Thirty Thousand Names" and can also be found in
the Pennsylvania Archives publications.[70] These lists
are of great value to any Pennsylvania German who is
interested in the study of his ancestry. They show us
that Mennonites continued to come to Pennsylvania
more or less irregularly up to the time of the Revolutionary war. Not all of these immigrants, to be
sure, came to Lancaster county. Many settled in
Chester, Bucks, Berks and Montgomery counties.

Many of these early ship passengers bear names
that sound familiar to the ears of the student of
Mennonite genealogy. The second ship to arrive
under the new law, the James Goodwill, which regis-

---

68. For the reasons for this emigration and for the efforts of the Committee on Foreign Needs to stem the tide of emigration see Scheffer in Pa. Mag. of History II. 130.
69. Colonial Records. III. 282.
70. Pa. Arch Second Series, XIX. See Index for genealogical purposes. Index, however, is not reliable.

tered on September 27, 1727, had on board Abraham Ebersohl, Peter Zug,[71] Ulric Zug,[72] and Ulric Stauffer. On September 30, the ship Molley brought over seventy Palatines including Peter Gut, Felix Gut, Hans Gut, Sr., Hans Funk, Martin Kendigh, Samuel Gut, Samuel Oberholtz and Christian Wenger.[73] On board the Adventurer which arrived at Philadelphia on October 2, were Ulrich Pitscha,[74] John Jacob Stutzman, Johannes Kurtz, Ulrich Riesser, John Beydeler and Hans Halteman.

These ships arrived usually in the fall during the months of August, September and October. The first vessel to arrive in 1729, the Mortonhouse, had among other passengers Dielman Kolb, Uldric Root, Jacob Crebil, Jacob Eschelman, Christian Longacre and Hendrick Snevele. On August 11, 1732, among the passengers on board the Samuel from London we again meet many familiar Mennonite names, among others those of Jacob Oberholtzer, Oswald Hostetter, Hans Musselman, George Bender, Ulrich Burkhalter, Jacob Gut, Jacob Albrecht, Michael Kreider, Jacob Staufer, Jacob Gut, Andreas Shetler, Johannes Brechbil, Wendel Brechbiehl, Heinrich Ramsauer and Peter Shellenberger. During the remainder of that autumn there were added to the list,—Conrad Frick, Michael

---

71. Located in Milford township, Bucks county. See Battle, History of Bucks county. He later joined the Ephrata Monks. See Chronicon Ephratense.
72. Hartzler Genealogy, p. 329.
73. The founder of the Mennonite Wenger family. See Wenger, Wenger Family History.
74. Possibly an Amishman.

Witmer, Lenhart Mumma, Christian Martin, Johann Landis and Jacob Steli.[75]

The Mennonites, it will be seen, came in small groups during all these years. On September 21, 1742, on the ship, Francis and Elizabeth, there were brought over a large company of Amish and Mennonites, among whom were the three Zug brothers, the ancestors of most of the Amish Zooks in this country. The names of these men are,—Michael Kolb, Christian Newcomer, Ulrich Neuschwanger, Jacob Yoder,[76] Moritz Zug, and two brothers,[76] Christian Jotter,[76] Andreas Bachman, Johann Heinrich Schertz,[77] Jacob Kurtz, Jacob Guth,[78] Johannes Gerber.[79] On September 30, 1754, the ship, Brothers, arrived at Philadelphia with two hundred and fifty Palatines on board, twenty-seven of whom are designated in the records as Mennonites and seven as Catholics. Judging entirely from the names themselves we may conclude that the following were perhaps the twenty-seven Mennonites,—Jacob Brubaker, Franz Burghart, Abraham Mellinger, Johannes Hershberger, Johannes Eicher, John Jacob Brubaker, Michael Burckhart,

---

75. A large proportion of these names are of Bernese origin and their duplicates can all be found in Müller's Geschichte der Bernischen Täufer.
76. Amish.
77. The name Schertz is not very common but where it is found in Illinois and Ohio its bearers all belong to original Amish or Mennonite families.
78. Rupp in his History of Religious Denominations says that by 1735 there were about five hundred families in Lancaster county, mostly Mennonites.
79. It is not necessary to continue these names. Enough has been said to illustrate the value of these lists to the student of Mennonite immigration. Any one personally interested in the subject is referred to the sources mentioned.

I am not absolutely sure that all the names mentioned here were those of Mennonites. But the exceptions, if any, are very few.

THE PEQUEA COLONY 161

Christian Eicher, Johann Christian Witmer, Jacob Detweiler, Johannes Frey, Peter Frey, Johann Jacob Witmer, Abraham Strickler, Wilhelm Eschelman, Heinrich Heistand, Jacob Kauffman, Jacob Huber, Heinrich Graff, Valentine Noldt, Abraham Hackman, Joseph Lemann. On October 1, of the same year the ship, Phoenix, had on board twenty-five Mennonites, including such names as Neuenschwander, Burckhalter, Aeschliman, Newcomer, Brechtbühl, Burckhart, Hunsicker and Geyman. Later lists do not mention the Mennonites specifically, but it is likely that a few came each year as late as the Revolutionary war. By about 1755, however, the steady inflow of immigrants from the Palatinate had practically ceased.

We have thus far confined our attention to the formation of early settlements. Let us turn now briefly to a subject of more interest—the
Secular secular and religious life of the people.
Life But to tell this story is not an easy task, for these people left no record of themselves, except in the land offices and on their tombstones. Of church records there is not a scrap. Our story of these early days must be pieced together from what we can glean from their land entries, family Bibles, petitions for naturalization or military exemption and an occasional letter to Europe preserved in European archives.

The first thing to notice is that these men, unlike their brethren at Germantown, were agriculturists. In their Swiss homes most of them had been small farmers and dairymen.[80] Consequently while the Germantown settlement took the form of a village

---
80. Müller, 290.

that on the Pequea was spread over large farms, varying in the first few years from two hundred to several thousand acres in extent. Thus the problem of government was with them a simple matter. Although the Mennonites were the first white settlers to come to Lancaster county, and although they have ever since far outnumbered all others in the rural districts, yet they have always been ruled politically by others. They never took to politics. The local government was usually managed by their Scotch-Irish neighbors who orgainzed and named the townships and filled the various local offices. The Mennonites were a peaceful, quiet and industrious people, well satisfied with their quiet life on the farm. They were willing to leave the matter of government to the Scotch-Irish whom they gradually dispossessed of such rich farms as were not already in their hands. Today the descendants of these Scotch-Irish are found almost altogether in the southern township, a region in which the soil is so poor that no industrious Mennonite has ever located there. A glance at the county map will indicate that with the exception of the three Earls most of the townships bear Irish and English names. Two of them only, Strasburg and Manheim, are named for the places from which the German settlers came. In the small villages and less conspicuous localities, however, where places are more likely to be named after some original settler, more German names appear. Bareville, Beyertown, Eby's Post Office, Groffdale, Herrville, Hess Station, Landis Valley, Landisville, Martinsdale, Weaverland, Mast's Post Office, Rohrerstown, Weavertown, Witmer Station, Hertzler, Lapps, Brubaker, Neffsville and Good-

"The water of the Pequea was clear, cold and transparent, and the grape vines and clematis intertwining among the lofty branches of the majestic buttonwood, formed a pleasant retreat from the noonday beams of the summer sun."—Conyngham.

ville,—all these names indicate that the Mennonites have everywhere been pioneers in building up the county.

Their industry very early attracted the attention of travelers through this region. In 1744 one of the delegates to the Indian conference at Lancaster describes their beautiful farms:

"They sow all kinds of grain," he says, "and have very plentiful harvests. Their houses are chiefly built of stone and generally near some brook or stream of water. They have very large meadows which produce a great deal of hay and feed therewith a variety of cattle."[81]

Before the days of the railroad all this produce had to be carried from the Conestoga region in large heavy wagons. These were the famous Conestoga wagons which were used not only to transport farm produce from Conestoga to Philadelphia but in later years when the fever of western emigration began, they also became the means of carrying the emigrant and his family across the mountains and down the valleys to his new home.[82] In more recent years on the western plains the same vehicle but under a new name, "The Prairie Schooner" has been used for the

---

81. Witham Marshes Journal, Mass. Historical Society, First Series; VII. 175.
82. Albert Cook Myers, of Moylan, Pa., a careful student of Pennsylvania history, tells me that the earliest reference found to the Conestoga wagon is in 1716.
 "In this wagon, drawn by four or five horses of a peculiar breed, they convey to market, over the roughest roads, 2000 or 3000 pounds' weight of produce of their farms. In the months of September and October it is no uncommon thing on the Lancaster and Reading roads to meet in one day fifty or one hundred of these wagons on their way to Philadelphia, most of which belong to German farmers." Benj. Rush, in 1789 quoted by Kuhns Swiss and German Settlements in Pennsylvania, p. 98.

same purpose. But the railroad has put an end to the old Conestoga wagon. Nothing but an occasional remnant of a few broken bows, an old wagon bed, or a few ponderous wheels found in obscure corners in Indiana, Ohio or Pennsylvania is left now to remind us of the famous old wagon that was once so essential to the well-being of these early pioneers.

The Mennonites, as we saw, were a country people. They never took a liking to city life. And thus it is that while the central portion of the county was settled almost exclusively by Mennonites, Lancaster city, in the very center of the county, was composed largely of German Lutherans or Reformed, Scotch-Irish, English, and children of Mennonite parents but who had left the church of their fathers. It is only within very recent years that members of the Mennonite church have begun to find their way into the city. A large percentage of the present inhabitants of the city, however, trace their ancestry back to the early Mennonite immigrants.

With the Indians the Mennonites were usually on good terms. We saw that at the time of the first settlement the Indians were still found in the immediate neighborhood of the colony. Both Conestoga and Pequea Creeks were named after the tribes of Indians found along the banks of these respective streams. The Conestoga Indians were early transferred across the Conestoga to a reservation in the Manor where they had a village bordering on the land purchased by some of the early settlers. As early as June 8, 1711, Governor Gookin visited these Indians and in a speech to them said that Penn intended to present them with

Relation to Indians

a belt of wampum and that he required their friendship to the Palatines settled near Pequea.[83] The Indians replied that since they were at war with the Tuscaroras they did not think the place safe for any Christians. They were afraid furthermore that if any damage should happen to these the blame would fall upon them.

The Mennonites evidently felt no alarm and do not seem to have been molested by the Indians during the earlier years. But as the settlement grew they found themselves encroaching upon the lands of their red skinned neighbors. On November 2, 1717, the Board of Property reported that

the late settlements on and near Conestoga Creek hath made it necessary that the Indian fields about the town be enclosed by a good fence to secure the Indians corn from the horses, cattle and hogs of these new settlers that would otherwise destroy it and thereby cause an uneasiness in those Indians.[84]

It was not until the French and Indian war, from 1754 to 1763 that the Mennonites suffered seriously at the hands of the Indians. The frontier line at this time was run along the Susquehanna on the west and the Blue Mountains on the north. This whole region was occupied by the Germans, among them the Mennonites in Lancaster county and the Amish in Berks. Just how many Mennonites were killed by the Indians will never be known but from a few scattered references we can make at least an estimate. A letter written to Switzerland by Ulrich Engel, Christian Brechbühl, and Isaac Neuschwander under date of December 7, 1755, says that Hans Jacob König had left his wife and three young children with Abraham Herr at Con-

---
83. Colonial Records, II. 532-3.
84. Pa. Arch. Second Series, XIX. 626.

estoga but that he, with a son, daughter and a servant had settled on the frontier among the Indians at a place called "Shamogen". Other families followed. The Indians having warned them repeatedly that they had trespassed on Indian territory, suddenly fell upon the settlers, murdered six families and burned their houses. Thirteen persons were killed, including König. His son and daughter were carried away as captives.[85]

So great was the loss of life and property all along the frontiers of Pennsylvania and Virginia where the Mennonites had settled that in 1758 they found it necessary to send to Holland for aid. They sent over two of their number Martin Funk and Johannes Schneyder with a letter dated September 7, 1758, written by Michael Kaufman, Jacob Borner, Samuel Böhm and Daniel Stauffer,—all Lancaster names. This letter says that over two hundred families in Pennsylvania had during a recent incursion in May lost all of their property and that fifty of their number were dead. Of course this number refers to all the frontiers-men who suffered, but must no doubt include a number of Mennonites. The envoys succeeded in obtaining a contribution of fifty pounds sterling and departed again for America December 17, 1758.[86]

We have already seen that the Provincial authorities early became suspicious of the increasing number of German immigrants. The privilege **Naturalization** of naturalization without which no one could enjoy the full rights of citizenship

---

85. Müller, Geschichte der Bernischen Täufer, 365. See also Rupp, Lancaster County 353, and Pa. Arch., First Series III. 194.
86. Pa. Mag. of History, II. 136. For the list of letters written at this time to Amsterdam see de Hoop Scheffer's catalog of documents in the Amsterdam Mennonite Church.

THE PEQUEA COLONY 167

was often very grudgingly conferred. In 1683 before German immigration had begun it was provided that all foreigners[87] who had taken the oath of allegiance to the king and to Penn were to be thereby to all intents naturalized.[88] This law was repealed in 1705 by Parliament, and from this time until 1742 naturalizations were by private act. It often took years of petitioning and waiting before the Assembly would grant the rights of citizenship. The unnaturalized were under many disadvantages. At first these disadvantages were not so apparent and we find the Mennonites rather slow in becoming British subjects. As early as 1691, however, Hendrick Casselberg and Clas Jansen of Germantown were naturalized. They were followed in 1698 by Hans Neus, Paul Engle and others.[89] Petitions by others were sent to the General Assembly in 1706[90] and again in 1709.[91] But it was not until September 29, 1709, that the Mennonites as a body in and around Germantown were granted the rights of naturalization and thus were given equal civil rights with their English neighbors.[92] No Lancastrians seem to have been naturalized until 1729.

The disadvantages under which the unnaturalized were placed is very well stated by an entry which appears in the minute book of the Board of Property

---

87. Foreign here means non-English.
88. For a good discussion on Naturalization in Pennsylvania see American Historical Review, IX. 300 ff.
89. Pa. Ger. Soc. VIII. 189.
90. Colonial Records. II. 241.
91. Votes of the Assembly. II. 48.
92. Col. Rec., II. 493. The full list is given here including Pastorius, Dirk Keyser, Kunders, etc. See also Statutes at Large, II. 299.

under date of September 22, 1717. The entry is as follows:

Martin Kendig, Hans Heer and Hans Funk with several other of the Palatines, their countrymen having applied to purchase land near Conestoga and Pequea Creek to accommodate those of them who have lately arrived in this province, who are their Relations, friends and acquaintances and whom they assure the board are Honest and Conscientious people. Their request being considered and the circumstances of those people in relation to their holding of Lands in the Dominion of Great Britian were asked if they understood the Disadvantage they were under by their being born aliens, that therefore their children could not inherit, nor they themselves convey to others the Lands they purchase according to the laws of England which may in such case be extended hither. They answered they were informed thereof, before. However, inasmuch as they had removed themselves and families into this province they were, not with standing the said disadvantages willing to purchase lands for their own dwelling. It was further said by the commissioners that it was their business to sell and dispose of the proprietor's lands to such as would purchase it yet at the same time they were willing to let them know as they are aliens the danger that might ensue if not in time prevented, also that some years ago a law was enacted here and afterwards passed by the late Queen Anne for enabling divers Aliens particularly named therein to hold and enjoy lands in this province and that the like advantage might probably be obtained for those amongst themselves that were of good report if a petition were preferred to this present assembly, when they sit to do business. With this advice they seemed pleased and desired to be informed when such a sitting of the assembly would be that they might prefer a petition to them for such a law as is above mentioned.[93]

Petitions for the above privilege were sent to the Assembly, but this was just the time, it will be remem-

---

93. Pa. Arch. Second Series, XIX. 624.

THE PEQUEA COLONY 169

bered, when Governor Keith was especially alarmed at the German immigration, and it appears that no attention was paid to the demands of the petitioners. Keith was followed by Gordon, who was more liberal, and it was under Governor Gordon's administration that the Mennonites of Lancaster county were finally permitted to become British subjects and thereby acquire the right to "sell and bequeath" their lands. Before naturalization had been granted them they were obliged to swear[94] to the value of their possessions and declare their religious views. They were denounced as being peculiar in dress, religion and notions of political government and resolved to speak their own language and acknowledge but the great Creator of the Universe.[95]

The bill of 1729 was the result of a petition made November 27, 1727, by "Wendal Bowman, Martin Meiling and Benedick Hearsay in behalf of themselves and others called Menists" asking permission to bring in a bill "to enable them to hold lands and trade in the said Province" which was presented to the House, read and ordered to lie on the table.[96] The year 1727 was another year however, of heavy immigration and the petition was not immediately granted. It was discussed at various times during the following year and finally on December 14, 1728, permission was given by the Assembly to present such a bill.[97] In the meantime the Governor had made inquiry regarding the general character of the petitioners. In his message to the Assembly in 1729 he reported that these people

---

94. Or affirm.
95. Diffenderfer, Odds and Ends of Local History; in Lancaster County Historical Society report on June 1, 1906.
96. Votes of the Assembly, III. 42, 45, 70.
97. Votes, III. 71, 72.

are principally such who many years since came into this province under a particular agreement with our late honorable Proprietary at London and have regularly taken up Lands under him. It likewise appears to me by good information that they have hitherto behaved themselves well and have generally so good a character for Honesty and Industry as to deserve the esteem of this Government and a Mark of its regard for them. I am therefore inclined from these considerations to favor their request and hope you will join with me in passing a bill for their naturalization.[98]

The bill was accordingly passed[99] but efforts were made at the same time to discourage further immigration of Germans by providing for a levy of a head-tax of forty shillings on every alien who should come into the province. This was the last Mennonite petition for naturalization except the one in 1742 when the Amish of Lancaster county, as we have already seen, asked for the right of naturalization, but a little later the general law was passed which was made to cover the cases of all aliens.[100]

Most of the Palatine immigrants in Pennsylvania during the eighteenth century were poor people, and the Mennonites were no exception. With the exception of Telner and Van Bebber of Germantown and Herr, Kendig and Meilin of Pequea, all of whom became owners of from one to six thousand acres, the early settlers owned very little of this world's goods when they landed at Philadelphia. And even

---

98. Votes and Proceedings, III. 100.
99. The names of all who were naturalized by this act are found in Pennsylvania Statutes at Large, IV, 148. The list is made up almost exclusively of Mennonites and no doubt contains practically all the Mennonite male inhabitants of twenty-one years of age in the county. The list contains one hundred and thirteen names.
100. For further legislation on naturalization and the dispute between the assembly and Governor Thomas in 1741 see Votes and Proceedings III. 451-3, 460, 466, 472, 488, 505, 515, etc.

these men are likely to be considered wealthier than they really were. One thousand acres of wild land at that time was by no means a fortune.[101] The fact that by 1745 the whole Pennsylvania colony of Mennonites did not consider itself able to print the Martyrs Mirror, and that in 1758 they felt obliged to ask help from Holland to make good the losses from Indian incursions shows that by that time they could by no means be considered rich.

During the period preceding the Revolutionary war, and even later it was the practice of all emigrants, who did not have sufficient money to pay their passage across the ocean, to sell their services for a number of years to some ship captain in return for free passage. The captain then owned the labor of the emigrant and could dispose of it as he saw fit. Usually the services of such people was sold by the captain at auction to the highest bidder soon after the ship's arrival.[102] The persons who thus sold their

Redemptioners

---

101. The price of land in 1717 was ten pounds per hundred acres and one shilling quit rent.
102. "Every day Englishmen, Dutchmen and High German people came from the city of Philadelphia and other places, some from a great distance, sixty miles and one hundred and twenty miles away and go on board the newly arrived ship that has brought and offers for sale passengers from Europe and select among them the healthy persons such as they deem suitable for their business and bargain with them how long they will serve for their passage money, for which most of them are still in debt. When they have come to an agreement it happens that adult persons bind themselves in writing to serve three, four, five or six years for the amount due by them, according to their age and strength. But very young people from ten to fifteen must serve until they are 21." Gottlieb Mittelberger, Journey to Pennsylvania, (1754), p. 26.

"The reason we (Lutherans) are invited to go to a distance here and there are the following: Our German Evangelical inhabitants for the most part came latest into this province. The English and

services were called redemptioners. A large portion of the immigrants into Pennsylvania were of this class of settlers.

The number of Mennonite redemptioners was perhaps comparatively small, because, although many may have been poor, their friends who were already here, if necessary, paid their passage money which was to be returned later either in money or perhaps in labor. But this was not always the case. There are many family traditions which point to the fact that Mennonites were occasionally sold as redemptioners, sometimes to their own Mennonite brethren. Jost Yoder,[103] the founder of a long line of Yoders, well known in the Amish church today, bound his children to service to help pay the passage money for the family. Frederick Alderfer in 1734 was sold in Philadelphia to a man who lived in Montgomery county.[104] The traffic in redemptioners was profitable, and frequently ship captains would steal young children or entice both children and grown people into their vessels and then sell them on this side of the water. Melchior Plank, an Amishman, an ancestor of Bishop David Plank of Logan county, Ohio, was in-

---

German Quakers, the Inspired, the Mennonites, Separatists and other such small sects came in first when the land was still cheap. These selected for themselves the richest tracts of land and are now enriched. But in later years after the poor Evangelicals also found their way and numerously came into this country also some perhaps here and there still found good land. Most of them, however, had to serve for their passage as men-servants and maid-servants and afterwards shift with the poor land and eat their bread in the copious sweat of their brows." Muhlenberg in "Hallische Nachrichten" II, 51.

103. An Amishman. Landed at Philadelphia, 1744. Settled later in Berks County.
104. See Heckler, History of Lower Salford Township, p. 220.

vited together with his wife by a ship captain on board
a vessel just ready to sail. They were both brought to
Pennsylvania and sold to a Mr. Morgan either in
Berks or Lancaster county. Philip Lantz, when a boy
of five was kidnapped in Europe and brought to
Baltimore. From here he was taken to Lancaster
county, where he was bound to Peter Yordy of
Lampeter township until he was twenty-one years old.
Lantz served Yordy until his time had expired and
then married one of his master's daughters.[105] These
are only a few instances of this practice. No doubt
many of the early Mennonite settlers of Lancaster
county had similar experiences.

  Concerning the church life of the Pequea colonists
we know even less than of their secular life. But since
they had at least one minister among them
Church in the person of Hans Herr, it is likely that
Buildings a church was organized immediately after
the settlement began. The meetings of
course were held for a number of years in private
houses. These houses at first were made of logs, but
as the settlement became older these were replaced
frequently by large stone buildings made from the
lime and sandstone with which the county abounded,
many of which stood for over one hundred years. In
1719 Christian Herr erected a large stone dwelling
house north of the Pequea which is still standing,
today the oldest building in Lancaster county.[106]
Within the heavy walls of this old building was often
heard the message of the Gospel as it fell from the lips

---

105. See Egle, Notes and Queries, vol. III.
106. For a good description of this house see article in the "Home"
  August 5, 1905, by George N. Le Fevre.

of old Hans Herr, Benedict Brechtbühl, or some other devoted preacher of the time.

The earliest settlement, as we saw, occupied the tier of townships immediately south of Lancaster city. The nucleus of the colony evidently was near where the present Brick church stands near Willow Street. From here to the east, west and gradually to the northwest and northeast centers of worship with church houses were gradually established. The settlement, as we have seen, never extended very far to the south because of the poor soil in that region. Wherever centers of settlements were established, congregations were organized. The congregation usually, of course, preceded the meeting house by a number of years. South of Lancaster city a log house was erected in the region now called Byerland as early as 1747; another at Millersville in 1756. These were both replaced later by more substantial buildings. The so-called Stone meeting house was put up in 1755 and was repaired later. In the Strasburg region meetings were held for many years in private houses. There is still standing near Strasburg a house built in 1740 by John Herr, the upper story of which was especially constructed for holding church services.[108] The present stone church in Strasburg village was erected in 1804. Further south, in what is now Providence township, a meeting house was put up as early as 1766. One mile west of Lancaster city a log house was erected about 1730 on the tract of land purchased by Brubaker and Hershey in 1717. In the northwestern townships of the county one of the earliest houses to be erected was the Hernley meeting house built in 1766, the land being

---

108. Still standing one-half mile south-west of Strasburg.

OLD LOG CHURCH AT LANDISVILLE, PENNSYLVANIA. Built in 1790 and still in good condition. It is now used as a home for the sexton.

bought in 1745. The Landisville church, made of logs in 1790, is still standing. The Chestnut Hill, Risser and Erisman houses were all built before 1800. About three miles east of Lancaster stands the Mellinger or what was formerly the Lampeter meeting house which replaced in 1884 a stone building put up in 1767. In the northeastern part of the county the first log building for worship was put up at Groffdale about 1755. The Weaverland house was erected in 1766 and a part of the walls are still standing. Farther east the Bowmansville church was erected in 1794.[109] These are a few of the oldest buildings. Many others were erected during the nineteenth century throughout the county. There are at present fifty-one places of worship in the county.

Few of these old meeting houses are left. The present buildings in the older centers are of the third or fourth generation of meeting houses, the first being of logs, the second usually of stone, and the third of stone or brick. In the walls of most of them are inserted stone blocks with the date of the first stone structure and a short inscription. The inscription on the Strasburg church reads as follows:

> Built by the
> Mennonite Society
> in the year of Christ
> whom they worship
> 1804

Many of the later inscriptions have the word " old " pre-

---

109. Most of the information regarding these meeting houses has been gained from personal observation and from Ellis and Evans' History of Lancaster County, corrected from other sources.

fixed to Mennonite to distinguish the main body from the New Mennonites or Herrites who took their rise in 1811.

Near each of these buildings were laid out the earliest graveyards. The oldest cemetery in the county is undoubtedly the one near the Brick church, between the church and the old Christian Herr house. Here lies buried old Hans Herr and perhaps others of the early settlers. The earliest graves either were unmarked or have long since lost all signs of identification. The Mennonites were so much opposed to publicity and outward display that for a time it appears they were even religiously scrupulous against the use of tombstones. The very earliest immigrants furthermore, may have been buried in some out-of-the-way corner of their farms. The stones that were used to mark their last resting places, if any were used at all, were small and made of slate or sand stone and may long ago have succumbed to the wear of rains and frosts. Whatever the reason, it remains true that with the exception of Hans Groff whose grave lies distinctly marked in the Groffdale cemetery, we are unable to locate with certainty the final resting place of a single one of these early pioneers of Lancaster county. The earliest grave with any record in the Brick church cemetery bears the inscription.

L. G.
1741

So far as I have been able to discover, this is the oldest marked Mennonite grave in the county.

The Mennonites on the Pequea did not suffer for

THE BRICK CHURCH CEMETERY. Old Hans Herr is buried here. His grave is not marked but it is supposed to be somewhere in the middle of the cemetery among the old stones which have decayed.

THE PEQUEA COLONY

Early Preachers

want of preachers. Many of the early immigrants were ministers. Old Hans Herr, the first bishop, was followed by his son Christian, Benedict Brechtbühl, Jacob Hostetter,[110] Benjamin Hershey[111] and others. In 1725 a conference was held, but where is not known, of the entire Pennsylvania church, including the congregations of Skippack, Germantown, Great Swamp, Manatant and Conestoga, as the Pequea settlement was then called.[112] The purpose of the conference is not definitely known but one of the duties of those present was to subscribe their names to an appendix which had been added to the Confession of Faith which had been translated into English in Amsterdam in 1712. The Conestoga ministers present at this conference were Hans Burghaltzer,[113] Christian Herr, Benedict Hirschi,[114] Martin Baer and Johannes Bowman.[115] Among other ministers and bishops who lived during the eighteenth century there have come down to us the names of Benjamin Landis,[116] Ben Schantz,[117] Martin Boehm,[118] Tobias Kryter,[119] Friederich Kaufman,[119] Hans Schantz,[119] Christian Bomberger,[120]

---

110. Per. Abr. R. Burkholder of Willow Street, in New Era (Lancaster), Feb. 1, 1905.
111. Ellis and Evans, History of Lancaster County. See Index.
112. Lancaster county was not organized until 1729.
113. Came in 1717 with Brechtbühl. See Gotschalk letter quoted by Pennypacker in Hendrick Pennebecker.
114. Still living in 1770. See Morgan Edward's "Material for a History of American Baptists" under Mennonists. Three brothers, Andrew, Benjamin and Christian were all ministers.
115. See Confession of Faith of 1727, printed by Bradford, Philadelphia.
116. Harris, History of Lancaster County, 360. Located four miles east of Lancaster.
117. See Gotschalk letter in Hendrick Pennebecker by Pennypacker.
118. Ordained by lot, 1756.
119. See Gotschalk letter.
120. In Hammer Creek District. Ellis and Evans. See Index.

Christian Burkholder,[121] Henry Martin,[121] Peter Risser,[122] Jacob Brubaker,[123] and no doubt a host of others who were faithful preachers of the Gospel in their day, but whose names now if not entirely forgotten are preserved only in family traditions.

Lancaster county like Germantown soon became a center for the peace sects. The Mennonites were followed by the Dunkards in 1724, and **Relation to** by the Moravians some time later, who **Dunkards** settled in the region of Lititz. The Dunkards in their early history usually followed up the Mennonites in their wanderings. They first associated with them in Crefeld, then followed them to Germantown, and thence to Conestoga, Oley, Great Swamp, and to many other of the early centers on Mennonitism. This was due, no doubt, to several reasons. The Dunkards, like the Mennonites had an instinct for finding the best lands. They were so much like the Mennonites in faith and practice that they felt very much at home among them, and moreover the Mennonites furnished good proselyting material, and were a fruitful field for Dunkard missionary zeal.

So great is the similarity between these two denominations that we can but conclude that the Dunkards must have borrowed many of their religious practices and doctrines from the Mennonites. Both reject infant baptism, oppose the bearing of arms and the taking of oaths. Some of their religious practices are similar; the kiss of peace, the use of the prayer

---

121. In Weaverland District.
122. In Root District.
123. Ordained bishop in 1783 in East Hempfield. Ellis and Evans.

THE PEQUEA COLONY 179

head-covering and bonnet for the women, and feet-washing at the communion service.

There is much in the early history of the Dunkards to bear out this proposition. Alexander Mack was their founder. At first a member of the Reformed church he became dissatisfied with the formalism and ritualism of the Reformed religion, and with seven others he left the church in 1708. During the year he traveled among the Mennonites of Germany in the hope of finding among them the people nearest to his ideals of the Christian life. But learning that they would not admit that immersion was the only true mode of baptism he turned from them and was himself immersed by one of the group which with him had left the Reformed church.[124] He then baptized by trine immersion the rest of the group and thus became the founder of a new church. They were soon driven to Crefeld and there gained several adherents among the Mennonites. In 1719 they came to Germantown and there again won over some of the Mennonites, among them Peter Keyser, son of Dirk Keyser and for many years a leading minister in the Dunkard church. In 1724, as we have seen, a party of them came into the Conestoga region. This was purely a proselyting tour, for having heard that "in the Conestoga country were a number of awakened souls"[125] they decided to go to that locality. Starting one November day from Coventry on the Schuylkill where a congregation had been established, they divided at the close of day into two parties for the night. They had by this time arrived in the Groffthal and Weberthal region, and on that

---
124. Brumbaugh, History of the Brethren, p. 38.
125. Brumbaugh, 161.

night those afoot remained with Hans Groff and those who rode spent the night at Jacob Weber's. The next day the party again reunited at the house of Rudolf Nägele, also a Mennonite. From here they visited Conrad Beissel, who was soon to cause the Dunkards much trouble.[126] Beissel was a Pietist, who came over from Germany in 1720, and at this time was leading a hermit's life on the Conestoga. This little band of enthusiasts left its mark wherever it went. A few days later a congregation was formed on Mill Creek with Beissel himself as the first preacher. There do not seem to have been any Mennonites in this first group; but it is likely that Rudolf Nägele joined them a little later, for soon the meeting was held in his house in Earl township where this first Dunkard congregation in the Conestoga region worshiped for seven years.[127] During the following years a number of familiar Mennonite names are found among the Dunkards— John Landes, Samuel Good, Henry Sneider, Peter Zug, Henry Neff, Hans Graff[128] and many others concerning whose previous religious faith we know

---

126. "Once we visited Conrad Matthew at Germantown who advised us to leave those regions because the people there lived in vanity and to go to the Conestoga where the people lived in great simplicity and which was like a new Switzerland to look upon. In August, 1727, we moved there. For a while we adhered to the Mennonites bcause their simplicity pleased us, but their mode of worship we could never adopt ourselves. .. ..It is yet to be remembered that these same good people (the first congregation of solitary brethren, I think) had after the manner of that people a certain simplicity and lowliness of life and the superintendent (Beissel) in spite of the fact that he had had experiences in the world of vanity and show could so thoroughly adapt himself to their ways that his clothing, dwelling and household were fashioned on the poorest scale." Chronicon Ephratense, p. 35.

127. Brumbaugh, 299.

128. Not the pioneer of Groff's Thal. Perhaps a son.

nothing but whose names bear almost certain evidence that they were of Mennonite descent.[129] In 1728 Beissel withdrew from the Dunkards and established on the Cocalico Creek at Ephrata the well known Seventh Day Baptist monastic community. Several Mennonites also became involved in this movement, among them Michael Eckerlin[130] who was soon to become one of the leading spirits and John Meylin, son of Hans Meylin, the pioneer.[131]

The attempts in 1741 of Count Zinzendorf, the Moravian, to unite the religious efforts in Pennsylvania did not affect the Lancaster county Mennonites as it did their brethren in Berks county. The Wesleyan revival struck the county a little later and resulted in the apostacy of Martin Boehm, a leading Mennonite minister south of Willow Street. Boehm became one of the founders of the United Brethren church and later one of the pioneer Methodists in the region.

The Mennonites, as has already been said, were not a proselyting people and gained very few adherents from other churches. The Lutherans and Reformed were, during the early years, without much church organization and in that condition no doubt would have fallen an easy prey to missionary zeal among the other churches. Many of them found their way into the Dunkard church, but few into the Mennonite. On the contrary many Mennonites in later years joined the Reformed and Lutheran churches. A few of the Huguenots, however, who drifted into

Mennonites not Proselyters

---

129. See Brumbaugh, p. 307 for complete list of members up to 1770.
130. Pa. Ger. Soc. Proceedings, XV. 205.
131. Rupp, History of Lancaster County, p. 74.

Pennsylvania from New York, such men as the Le Fevers in Lancaster county and some of the De Turks in Berks county, the Bertolets and Fahrnis, cast their lot with the Mennonites. The entire number, however, that the Mennonite church received from other

Conestoga Wagon. See p. 163.

churches was much smaller than the number it lost. Had it been able to keep its young men and women in the church it might today possess the solid wealth and influence of one of the very best counties in the state.

CHAPTER VI

FRANCONIA

We have already seen that the region around Germantown was soon all occupied by the immigrants, and thus the later arrivals had to seek **The Skippack** homes in other localities. By 1702 a **Region** new settlement had already been begun on the Skippack near the present little village of Skippack. From this center a large community gradually grew by natural increase and by constant immigration from Southern Germany and has since expanded to the north on both sides of the Skippack over an area about ten miles in width through the north central part of Montgomery county, and the western part of Bucks county, with a few scattered settlements in Eastern Berks, and Lehigh and Southern Northampton county. This region in this chapter is spoken of as the Franconia district because among the Old Mennonites who still control most of the congregations here it constitutes what is known as the Franconia conference district.

It will be impossible here to name the first settlers in the various communities in this region and to tell

Expansion of the Pioneer Settlement

the exact dates of the organization of each congregation. They are all the result of the gradual expansion to the north of the original settlement, and a few dates and names must suffice to indicate the growth of the church in this part of the state during the eighteenth century.

The first congregation to be detached from the Skippack community was the one at Salford, just a few miles to the north. As early as 1718 Henry Ruth and Hans Reif had located here. These were soon followed by Christian Allebach, Christian Meyers, Hans Ulrich Bergey, Nicholas Holderman. Frederick Alderfer, Christian Stauffer, Jacob Funk, Dielman, Martin, and Jacob Kolb and others. The first meeting house for this congregation was built about 1738.

At about the same time a congregation was organized at Franconia in what is now Franconia township. The pioneer in this region was bishop Henry Funk who settled on the Indian Creek in this township in 1719. The tax list for 1734 shows that by that time there were in the region, among others those bearing the names Frey, Rosenberger, Oberholtzer, Moyer, Godschalk, etc.[2]

At the same time also the Mennonites were occupying the region to the east of the Skippack. The Towamencin congregation, north of Kulpsville, was organized perhaps as early as 1750. Settlers, however, had located here long before. Herman Godshalk

---

1. For a detailed account of the early settlement of Salford township see James Y. Heckler, History of Lower Salford Township.
2. For a detailed account of Mennonite settlements in Franconia Township see History of Franconia Township, by Souder, pub. by Benj. L. Gehman, Harleysville, Pa. 1886.

THE FRANCONIA BURYING GROUND. The old burying grounds in the Franconia district are surrounded by stone fences. Some of the earliest pioneers lie in nameless graves in these cemeteries. At first no stones were used, and later the stones were of sand-stone which have long since succumbed to the frost and rain. The stones in the oldest quarter of this cemetery have decayed. The stones which appear in this picture all mark recent graves.

SKIPPACK MEETING HOUSE

bought land as early as 1720.[3] The oldest marked grave in the churchyard bears the date 1733. The Methacton congregation, north of Fairview, was organized before 1773.

On the Perkiomen the Mennonites made few settlements, being preceded by the Schwenkfelders who still occupy nearly the whole valley, but as early as 1742 Muhlenberg, the Lutheran preacher, mentions a meeting house south of the Trappe, near the Perkiomen. Before the close of the century a congregation had also been established near Schwenksville.

In what is now Bucks county,[4] the oldest congregation is the Swamp in Milford township, near the headwaters of the Perkiomen. One of the earliest settlers in the locality was Velte Clemmer, who came here in 1717. By 1725 a congregation must have been established, for the name of Clemmer appears as the minister from the Swamp church in a conference which was held that year. Among other residents by 1734 were Samuel Musselman, John Byler, John Yoder, Sr., Jacob and Christian Clemmer, Abraham Shelley, Jacob Musselman, etc. A little to the east of this church was built the East Swamp meeting house in 1771 on land donated by Ulrich Drissel and for that reason it is sometimes called the Drissel church. North of the Swamp in what is now Lehigh county on Saucon creek, a branch of the Lehigh, a congregation had been established very early. Hans Yoder bought land here in 1724[5] and was followed by

Bucks County

---
3. See article on this congregation in Family Almanac 1875.
4. The most reliable history of Bucks County is the one written by W. H. H. Davis, A. M. and published in Doylestown, Pa. 1876.
5. Pa. Arch. Sec. Ser., Vol. XIX, p. 726.

men bearing the names Moyer, Gehman, Schliefer and a number of immigrants from Holland who settled near Coopersburg. A little later, but before 1760, a congregation was also organized to the east in Springfield township, Bucks county. Another early settlement was likewise made in the center of Bucks on the Deep Run creek. By 1746 the first meeting house was built. The ministerial force at that time consisted of Abraham Swartz, Hans Friedt, Samuel Kolb and Martin Oberholtzer. The Line Lexington congregation erected its first house in 1753.[6] To the northwest of the Lexington settlement is the Hilltown or Perkasie church, within the region which originally comprised the Perkasie Manor. Among the earliest Mennonite settlers here were Henry Funk, Christian Lederich, Andrew Godshalk, Valentine Kratz and many others, all of whom purchased land before 1750.

In the eastern part of Berks county a community must have been established nearly as early as on Indian creek and the Swamp, for the conference report of 1725 already referred to mentions Daniel Longenecker and Jacob Bechtley as the two ministers representing the Manatant settlement in the region of the Manatawny creek. Among the earliest settlers in this region were Jacob Stauffer,[7] Henry Stauffer,[8] Hans Bauer, Hans Jacob Bechtley, and Daniel Longeneker. These pioneers have left after them many descendants and have given names to two of the largest towns in this locality, Boyertown and Bechtelville. A congregation now

Berks County

---
6. Cassel, D. K. Geschichte der Mennoniten, p. 242.
7. Bower, H. S. Genealogical Record of Daniel Stauffer, Harleysville, Pa. 1897. p. 27.
8. Ibid, 196.

called Hereford was organized north of the Manatant in the northeastern part of the county. The first meeting house was built in 1755. To the north of Hereford in Upper Milford township, Lehigh county, another meeting house was erected about 1740.* Among the early settlers here were those bearing the names Schiffler, Basler, Mayer, Schantz,[10] etc.

In the meantime several Mennonite communities had been located along the Schulykill in Chester county.

Chester County South of Pottstown in East Coventry township stands an old church which contains a stone with the date 1728 inscribed upon it.

In Schuylkill township near what is now Phoenixville a congregation was also early established. Hans Stauffer, who came to America in 1710, soon after his arrival located near Valley Forge, several miles to the east of Phoenixville. In 1720 Francis Buchwalter,[11] the progenitor of a large family, also settled near here. These were followed by others with such names as Showalter, Bender, Haldeman, etc. By 1750 they were worshiping in a house which was also used by other denominations, but by 1772 they had erected a building of their own. Among their well known ministers were Matthias Pennebeker,

---

9. Cassel, 264.
10. See account of this settlement in History of Lehigh County, pub. by Matthews and Hungerford. Phila., 1884.
11. "Buckwalter, a Protestant refugee from Germany, was subjected to many persecutions in the Fatherland because of his faith and it is a matter of family history that he was compelled to read his Bible by stealth concealed in a cow trough. He finally concluded to flee and after leaving his home was pursued for three days by his vindictive Catholic brothers who were determined upon his destruction. His children were Joseph, Jacob, Johannes, Mary, and Yost, and from him are descended all the Buckwalter family in this vicinity." S. W. Pennypacker in Annals of Phoenixville, p. 20.

the great-grandfather of ex-Governor S. W. Pennypacker.

These are the earliest Mennonite communities of the Franconia district. Other congregations were established in the same general locality before the Revolutionary war. But soon after the war many from here moved to Ontario and other newer regions. This together with the fact that many of the younger element deserted the Mennonite church for other denominations accounts for the slow growth in the district during the nineteenth century. Few new congregations have been organized since 1800, while several have become extinct.

Communities in America by 1773
From a letter written to the church at Amsterdam in 1773 by Andrew Ziegler, Isaac Kolb, and Christian Funk we learn that the following communities had been established in America at that time:—

Germantown, Schiebach, Indian Krik, [Franconia] (to which belong also Salford, Rokkil [Rockhill] and Schwammen), Deep Ron to which belong Berkosen on the Delaware and Aufrieds, Blen [Plain], Grooten Swamb, to which belong Sacken and Lower Milford, in two places, Hosenak, Lehay and Term, Matetschen [Methacton] Schuylkill (meeting two places).

These are the congregations embraced within the region described in this chapter. Farther away they say are

Conestogis, where are many large congregations, Quitophilia [Lebanon county], great and little Schwatara [Dauphin county], Tulpehocken [western Berks county]. On the other side of the Susquehanna by Yorktown, great and little Conewago, Mannekesie [Monocacy]. To Virginia, Meriland,

Schanatore [Shenandoah] and further to Carolina[13] where are many and large congregations.[12]

In their every day life the Franconians differed very little from their brethren in Lancaster county.
Every Day Life
Many of them came from the same region in Germany and had the same customs and practices. In Pennsylvania both were among the earliest pioneers and as such endured all the hardships of pioneer life. The settlements in Berks county forming at that time the frontier line were frequently subject to Indian depradations, especially during the French and Indian war.[14] In August 1757 during one of these incursions a band of Indians murdered a number of the settlers including an Amish family by the name of Hostetler. According to the traditions handed down by the Hostetler descendants the whole family with the exception of the father and one son, Joseph, was killed. These were taken captive, but the boy after being held by the Indians for seven years, finally made his escape.

In industry the Franconians were not behind the Lancastrians, but living upon a thinner soil they never became so wealthy and prosperous.

---

12. Quoted by S. W. Pennypacker, in Hendrick Pennebecker.
13. It is difficult to obtain facts regarding the settlement in Carolina but it is evident that a settlement was made in that colony very early. Hans Stauffer, as we saw, landed there in 1710. Many of the Palatines who left Germany in 1709 found their way to Carolina, and it is not improbable that among them may have been some Mennonites. The congregation however could not have been very large.
14. "Jan. 16, 1756. Den Tag vorn neuen Yohr haben die Menisten von Schiebach und die ferner hinauf wohnen 7 wagen mit mehl und anderm Proviant nach Bethlehem und Nazareth gesandt vor die arme Leute welche dahin geflüchtet sind wegen die Indianern." Quoted from Sauer's paper in "The Perkiomen Region," by H. S. Dotterer, Vol. 1. p. 30.

In literary activity, however, they surpassed their more prosperous brethren. The men who signed the letter which was sent to Amsterdam demanding a translation of the Martyrs' Mirror were all from Franconia. Failing in interesting the church at Amsterdam in the project, the work of translation was finally undertaken in Pennsylvania under the supervision of two Franconians. The first Mennonite writers of America, Henry Funk and Christian Funk, were both from Montgomery county. In 1790 two men by the name of Hirstein and Smutz[15] from the same county went to Europe where they had five hundred copies of Denner's Sermons printed at their own expense and brought them to America in the hope of selling them. Many were sold in Montgomery county but few in Lancaster. Finally the first religious paper for the Mennonites was published in 1852 at Milford Square in Bucks county.

Literary Activity

The influence of these early settlements upon the Mennonite church at large has not been small. The Canadian Mennonites came, as we saw, largely from Bucks county. Montgomery, Berks and Bucks counties are also claimed as the original home of many of the Mennonite communities throughout the country. Among the most common names within this district are the following: Funk, Staufer, Godshalk, Ziegler, Clemmer or Clymer, Roth, Bechtel, Boyer, Moyer, Bergey, Detweiler, Hallman, Gehman, Bauman, Kolb, Pennebecker, Frey, Showalter, Kratz, Oberholtzer,

Influence

---

15. Mennonite Year Book and Almanac, 1906, p. 8.

Longenecker, Yoder, Hunsicker, Alderfer, Wambold, Haldeman, Fretz, High, Geisinger, Schliefer, Geil, Benner, Heistand, Souder, Allebach and Beidler. Many of these have become familiar throughout various parts of the country both within and without the Mennonite church.

CHAPTER VII

THE EXPANSION OF THE PEQUEA COLONY FROM 1750 TO 1800[1]

Long before the middle of the eighteenth century the best lands of Southeastern Pennsylvania had been occupied by the German and Scotch-Irish immigrants. Consequently the rapid growth of the native population together with the continuous stream of new arrivals which kept pouring into the province as late as the French and Indian war made it necessary for the younger generation as well as the later immigrants to seek homes farther out on the frontier. The Scotch-Irish, bolder and given more to a roving life than the Germans, usually ventured out first into the wilderness. Here they frequently built their cabins along some stream and devoted their time to hunting, fishing and a little farming. Or sometimes they located in the fertile valleys, but if they did they soon made way for the

Overflow of Southeastern Pennsylvania

---

[1]. Most of the information in this chapter has been gained from various county and other local histories, from the records in the deed books at the various county seats, and from manuscripts kindly furnished by such local historians as Bishop L. J. Heatwole of Dale Enterprise, Va., and D. S. Lesher of Shippensburg, Pa.

more thrifty Germans who, coming for the purpose of establishing permanent homes, usually spied out the most fertile spots for their future dwelling places. Since the two races never were congenial neighbors, the Scotch-Irish usually moved on, thus leaving to the Germans the fat of the land.

Very early the Germans of Lancaster county crossed the Susquehanna into the Cumberland Valley, in what are now York and Cumberland counties, and then down the valley, through Maryland into the fertile Shenandoah. **The Cumberland Valley** Others, soon after the French and Indian war, ascended the Susquehanna, and crossing the Alleghenies, established homes along the banks of the Juniata. Among the earliest of these pioneers were the Mennonites, who occasionally came as individuals with their neighbors and friends, but more frequently settled in small colonies, which were large enough, however, to form church congregations.

We have already seen that such communities were established before 1773 in Dauphin county, near the mouth of the Swatara, and in Lebanon county, on the Quittaphia and on the Little Swatara.

The first settlement west of the Susquehanna in York county was made even earlier, perhaps about 1750, between the Conewago and Little Conewago in Dover township. **York County** Just when the first Mennonite settlers located in this region is not known but by 1753 the colony was large enough to effect a church organization. Another early congregation was organized east of Hanover in Heidelberg township. In 1774 John and Thomas Penn granted to Michael Danner twelve acres of land for the use of the Mennonite church. The colony must have existed some time before this, however, for Michael Danner, evidently a Mennonite, resided here in 1749 in which year he was made one of the commissioners to organize York county. Soon after the grant of land was made, a building was erected for church and school purposes. Some time after this a church was also established east of York near Stony Brook station. This was followed later by other congregations in the southwestern part of the county, between the headwaters of the Little Conewago and Codorus creeks. All of these churches were established by settlers from Lancaster county as can be seen by the appearance in the land records of such familiar names as Hershey, Reiff, Rodes, Brubaker, Bare, Kauffman, Frantz, Danner, Shenk, Welty, Roth, Garber and so forth.

Cumberland and Franklin Counties Cumberland and Franklin counties occupy a valley between two parallel ranges of the Blue Ridge which form a gateway from Southeastern Pennsylvania through Maryland into the Shenandoah country. This valley, called the Cumberland, is drained by the Conococheague which flows south into the Potomac, and the Conedogwinet which flows northeast into the Susquehanna. It was through this gateway that the Pennsylvania Germans early passed into Virginia, and it was along these streams that the first Mennonite settlements of the region were made. Mennonite communities seem to have been established in Franklin county earlier than in Cumberland, which was nearer to Lancaster and York than was Franklin, but later than in Washington county, Maryland, and in the Shenandoah Valley. It is altogether likely that of the stream of settlers that began to enter the Shenandoah Valley about 1730 individual Mennonites settled here and there through the Cumberland Valley in Franklin and Cumberland counties and in Maryland, perhaps even before the Shenandoah settlements were made. There is no record, however, of such settlements.

Several Mennonites seem to have located in Franklin as early as 1735, among whom were Jacob Schnebele and Samuel Bechtel. Others may have followed but not enough came to form a congregation until after the Revolutionary war. The largest number entered the county during the last decade of the eighteenth century when a small colony located on the Conococheague, east of Chambersburg.. One of the first to settle here was Daniel Lehman who became the first resident minister. The first meeting house for this congregation was built in 1804. Soon after this, other communities were established near Strasburg and several in the southern part of the county along the Conococheague.

No settlement seems to have been made in Cumberland county until about 1800 when near Shiremanstown there was organized what is now known as the Slate Hill congregation, the first building for which was erected before 1820. Before the middle of the nineteenth century congregations were also established in the western half of the county, near Shippensburg, Huntsdale, and Carlisle.

In the meantime a small colony had gone up the Susquehanna and the Juniata and had located on the Mahantago near what is now Richfield, in Snyder county. The pioneer Mennonite as well as one of the very first of white men in the region was John Graybill, who came from Lancaster county in 1772. He was followed soon after by Jacob Moyer, Michael Lauver, John Shellenberger, Jacob Sellers and others. John Graybill, son of the pioneer, became the first minister of the congregation, which was soon organized. From this settlement have developed several small congregations in the extreme northern part of Juniata county. Among the prominent Mennonite names still to be found here are Graybill, Winey, Leiter, Bergey, and others. Soon after this a large community of Amish located a little farther west in Mifflin county, but of these more is said elsewhere.

Up the Juniata

At about the same time small colonies were being formed across the Alleghenies, in the southwestern part of the state, along the valleys of the Monongahela, Youghiogheny, and the Conemaugh rivers within the region of the headwaters of the Ohio. The earliest and most important communities were located in Westmoreland, Fayette and Somerset counties. These were followed later by a few scattered settlements in Cambria, Blair, Center, Clearfield and Butler counties. The first Mennonite to cross the mountains into this locality was Christian Blauch, from Lancaster county, who located in the county near Berlin, in 1767, a year before this region was opened to settlements.[2]

Near the Headwaters of the Ohio

In 1790 Jacob Blauch, brother of Christian,

---

2. Per. D. D. Blough, Johnstown, Pa.

located at the junction of the Quemahoning and Stony creek, in Conemaugh township, Somerset county. These were perhaps of the Amish branch of the church, but Mennonites were found in the same locality soon after. Jacob Blauch, son of the above mentioned Jacob, became the first Mennonite preacher in the settlement and in 1814 he was ordained bishop. From these early beginnings have since developed several congregations in this part of the county. By about 1780 a colony had also been established along Casselman creek, near Myersdale in the southern part of the county.

At the close of the eighteenth century two settlements were made in Fayette and Westmoreland counties. The one in Fayette was located in the southwestern part of the county between Masontown and Uniontown; the one in Westmoreland, on both sides of Jacobs creek which forms part of the boundary between these two counties. The settlers on the Westmoreland side of the creek came principally from Bucks county while those on the Fayette side came from Lancaster.

At the same time too, a colony was planted near Martinsburg in Blair county where Frederick Rhoads became the first bishop. In the early part of the nineteenth century small settlements were also made near Rockton in Clearfield county and near Harmony in Butler, where in 1816 Abraham Ziegler, David Stauffer, John Boyer and others bought the land upon which George Rapp, the founder of the Rappites, who later moved to Indiana, had tried to establish his communist colony. The first meeting house was erected in 1816.

From these original settlements, all of which were established during the latter part of the eighteenth century and the first of the nineteenth, other congregations have since developed within the counties named. During the first three-fourths of the past century, the growth of the church was very slow, some congregations becoming almost entirely extinct. But during recent years, with the introduction of more aggressive methods of work, the church in this part of the state has shown a continued increase in its membership.

Maryland

The first Mennonite settlement in Maryland was made in Washington county. This county forms part of the same Cumberland Valley through which the Germans of Pennsylvania passed on their way to Virginia. The settlement here is older than those farther up the valley in Pennsylvania and almost as old as those in Virginia. The first church was located in what is known as the Leitersburg district between Conococheague and Antietam creeks. Christian Burkhart had come here as early as 1755 and John Reiff and Jacob Good as early as 1765. By 1776 the community had grown large enough to demand some recognition upon their refusal to bear arms during the Revolutionary war from the State convention which at the time was establishing a new constitution, as well as from the county Committee of Observation. Both the constitutional convention and the local committee exempted them from military service, but required them to furnish transportation for the county troops and contribute to the support of the families of the men in the army. Before 1800, among others, the following had found their way into this region:, Michael Miller, Andrew Reiff, John Newcomer, John Strite, John Barr, Jacob Miller and John Shank. The community at present comprises four congregations. Several congregations have also been established in the western part of the state.

Virginia

As already said, the fertile valley of the Shenandoah early attracted the attention of the thrifty Germans of Pennsylvania. As early as about 1730 settlers from Lancaster and York counties had entered this region by way of the Cumberland Valley.

Germans in the Shenandoah

Among the earliest of these German pioneers, who were the first permanent settlers of the Valley, were several Mennonites. Dr. John W. Wayland of the University of Virginia says that Abraham Strickler from Lancaster county, Pennsylvania, bought a tract of land from Jacob Stover, at Massenutin in what is now Page county as early as 1729.[3] Strickler thus became one of the very earliest of the settlers in the Shenandoah Valley, preceding by three years the well known Jost Hite who is usually spoken of as the pioneer of the valley. This man Dr. Wayland believes, was a Mennonite. He bases this belief upon the fact that the later Stricklers of this

First Mennonites in the Valley

---

3. For much of the information regarding these earliest settlers I am indebted to the excellent book by Dr. John W. Wayland, The German Element of the Shenandoah Valley.

region were of that faith. It may be added as a further evidence of the correctness of this opinion that among a list of the names of twenty-seven Mennonite passengers who landed at Philadelphia on September 30, 1754, on the ship, Brothers, appears the name of Abraham Strickler, a relative no doubt of the pioneer in the Shenandoah. Jacob Strickler, said to be a Mennonite preacher and son of the Abraham who bought land in Page county in 1729, located near Luray in 1731. In a petition sent to Governor Gooch in 1733 appear the names of Abraham Strickler and Michael Kauffman, originally from Lancaster county. Kauffman, Dr. Wayland thinks, was also a Mennonite. The name appears several times among the lists of the Bernese exiles who were deported from Berne, Switzerland, some years before this.

After this, characteristic Mennonite names are met frequently in the records of the early valley counties. From the Orange county deed books we learn that in 1735 Jacob Funk and John Prupecker (Brubaker) both from Lancaster county, bought land along the North fork of the Shenandoah. In the same documents are recorded under the year 1736 the names of Martin Coffman, John Prupecker, and Christian Niswanger. In 1739 Peter Ruffner, the ancestor of a later well known Mennonite family, bought a tract of land along the Hawksbill in what is now Page county. He found living here at the time families by the names of Strickler, Heistand, Beidler and Stovers—all familiar Mennonite names. In the same year in a petition to Governor Gooch from inhabitants of the lower valley appear the names of Henry, John and Jacob Funk, and Christian Blank. Dr. Sachse of Philadelphia thinks

BANK CHURCH. VIRGINIA

WEAVER CHURCH. VIRGINIA

Jacob Funk was a member of the society of the Ephrata Brethren. But the Funks were originally of Mennonite stock and it is likely that some of the Virginia branch were still of that faith. Christian Blank is a name that frequently appears in the records of the religious controversy between Hans Reist and Jacob Ammon in Switzerland in the last decade of the seventeenth century, and among the Pennsylvania Amish.

These early settlers all came from Lancaster county, and since in that county those of a similar name were almost invariably Mennonites, it is but reasonable to suppose that these also were either of that faith at the time or at least of Mennonite descent.

This view is supported by more definite evidence a few years later. The Moravian missionaries from Pennsylvania often visited the various German settlements in Virginia. Joseph Spangenberg and Matthew Reutz, in a visit made through the valley in 1748, wrote of themselves in the third person as follows:

On July 27, they journeyed from this place (Timberville) to Messinuty, where Germans of all kinds of denomination live—Mennonites, Lutherans, Separatists, and Inspirationists.[4]

In the same year another Moravian, speaking of the Massenutin settlement in Page county says:

Many Germans live there. Most of them are Mennisten, who are in a bad condition. Nearly all religious earnestness and zeal is extinguished among them. Besides them a few church people live there, partly Lutherans, partly Reformed.[5]

The deed books of Frederick county show that

---

4. Virginia Magazine, Vol. XI. No. 3. p. 240. Quoted above from Dr. Wayland's "German Element, etc."
5. Virginia Magazine, Vol. XI. No. 3. p. 229. See Wayland, German Element, p. 112.

soon after this familiar names are also found in what is now Shenandoah county. The records indicate that Jacob Good bought land on the North Fork between what are now Woodstock and Strasburg, in 1752, and that John Funk came in 1755. Between 1755 and 1765 there appear in this region such names as Grove, Brubaker, Plank, Mellinger, and Niswander, all from Lancaster county, and undoubtedly of Mennonite ancestry.

These early settlements in what are now Page and Shenandoah counties were perhaps never very large. Just when the first churches were organized among these early pioneers it is difficult to say. But since the settlers were few in number and scattered over large tracts of land, it is not likely that there was much church organization before about 1750. By 1758 nineteen families were compelled to leave the valley for Pennsylvania because of Indian depredations. But these returned after the French and Indian war, and with them a number of others.

During the French and Indian war the Indians made several raids upon the inhabitants of the valley.

Indian Raids An incident which occurred during the last of these raids and which was related by an old lady early in the last century to Samuel Kercheval, the historian of the valley, illustrates the dangers to which these early pioneers were exposed during this war. The story refers to the murder of John Rhodes, a Mennonite minister and his family in Page county in August, 1766.

A party of eight Indians and one white man, approached the house and shot Mr. Rhodes dead, while he was standing in his doorway. His wife and one of the sons were killed

EXPANSION OF PEQUEA COLONY

in the yard. Another son was at the distance of one hundred yards from the house in a corn field. Hearing the reports of the guns, he climbed a peach tree to see what it meant, when he was discovered and was instantly killed. A third poor lad tried to save himself by running to cross the river, but was overtaken and killed in the river. The place where he attempted to cross is still known as the bloody ford. The eldest daughter, Elizabeth, at first remained within the house, but later caught up her little sixteen or eighteen-months old sister and ran into the barn. An Indian followed her and tried to force open the door that she had secured behind her. Not succeeding, he with oaths and threats ordered her to open it, and as she of course refused, he ran back to the house to get some fire. While he was gone, Elizabeth crept out at an opening at the opposite side of the barn, and with her little sister in her arms ran through a field of tall hemp, crossed the river, reached a neighbor's house and thus saved herself and little sister. The Indians, after setting fire to all the buildings, started off on their trip across the mountains, taking with them two sons and two daughters that remained alive, as captives. The youngest of the sons, being sickly and not able to travel fast enough, they killed him. The two daughters then refused to go farther, upon which both were killed. After three years of captivity with the Indians, the remaining son made his escape and came back to his friends.[6]

This was the last raid made into the valley by the Indians. They soon disappeared across the mountains into the back country and the inhabitants were comparatively free from danger after this.

The Fairfax Controversy

The Mennonite settlement in this region, however did not prosper. The congregations which were established have long since become extinct. This was due largely to the fact that the colony was located in what was called the Northern Neck,

---

6. Samuel Kercheval: A History of the Valley of Virginia, p. 91.

a region to which Lord Fairfax for many years tried to establish a private claim. During the controversy which followed, many of the settlers in the locality, including the Mennonites, feeling that their titles to their lands were uncertain, moved farther up the valley into what are now Rockingham and Augusta counties. Before the Revolutionary war families by the name of Brannerman, Showalter and Shank were found on the north side of the North Shenandoah, near the present town of Broadway in what was then Augusta, but now Rockingham county. By about 1800[7] the Mennonites had occupied the greater portion of the Linville Valley, the most fertile portion of Rockingham county. The settlement embraced the region extending from Linville creek on the east to the North mountain on the west and the Shenandoah on the north to Linville and Singers Glen on the south, a district about ten miles long by eight miles wide. After 1780 when Harrisonburg was established as the county seat of the newly organized Rockingham county many of the settlers of the Linville district moved southwest of the new town where a large Mennonite community has since developed. This and the settlement above mentioned are still the stronghold of the church in Virginia.

The Linville Valley

The Harrisonburg Region

---

7. By about 1780 the principal families among the Virginia Mennonites were Allebaugh, Burkholder, Beery, Brunk, Branner, Brannerman, Driver, Fultz, Funk, Frank, Good, Geil, Hoover, Kiser, Kauffman, Minnich, Roadcap, Ruebush, Rhodes, Shoalter, Swank, Shank, Trissel, and Wenger. Before the close of the eighteenth century there were added to these, families by the name of Blosser, Hartman, and Weaver from Page County, and Swope and Swartz from Shenandoah, and Heatwole, Hildebrand, Harshbarger, Graybil,

No meeting houses appear to have been built by the Virginia Mennonites until nearly a whole century after the first pioneers entered the valley. During these years religious meetings were held in private houses.[8] The first church house to be erected was the Trissel meeting house near Broadway, built in 1822. Three years later the Pike church, four miles west of Harrisonburg, at the southern end of the settlement was erected. Between these two were built the Brannemans, west of Edom in 1826 and the Weaver church in 1827. Many other houses have since been built and new congregations have been established in various parts of Rockingham, Augusta, Frederick and Shenandoah counties. The Virginia Conference, including several congregations and mission stations in West Virginia now comprises thirty-

Early Meeting Houses

Grove, Fry, Landis, Layman, and Niswander directly from Pennsylvania. Later on a few of the Fauber, Grove, Hildebrand, Harshbarger, Kendig, Roadcap and Stauffer families removed to points in Augusta County, while several Kauffman, Fry and Wenger families located at a point west of the Allegheny mountains near what is now Lewisburg, Greenbrier County, West Va."—L. J. Heatwole, in Hartzler and Kauffman's Mennonite Church History, p. 200.

8. "With the increase of population, there came a time, however, when the congregations that were assembled could no longer be accommodated in private family residences. The women and older members occupied all the room, which left the children, the boys and the girls and the worldly minded people out of doors to pass the time as best they could—which was done in a way that gave to the outside gathering at least, the appearance of a Sunday social, where sports and games of various kinds were common, as a means of diversion for the crowd. Besides, if the dinner hour was prolonged, which was generally the case, it was no uncommon thing for the cellar, the spring house, and even the orchard to be drawn on to such an extent that there were not sufficient provisions left to provide dinner for those who occupied their time at worship."—L. J. Heatwole, in Hartzler and Kauffman's Mennonite Church History, p. 202.

two congregations with a total membership of about twelve hundred.

The Virginia settlement, although comparatively small in point of numbers and separated some distance from other communities, has nevertheless exerted no mean influence upon the church at large. It has become the mother church of many of the newer western settlements, including the congregations in Medina, Columbiana and Allen counties, Ohio, and Tazewell and Livingston counties, Illinois.

Being the only Mennonite settlement within the Confederacy during the late Civil war it also serves as an illustration of the experiences of a non-slaveholding and non-resistant people when their principles are put to a test. The Mennonites of Virginia, by refusing to hold slaves and to go to war when the war was waged to save the institution of slavery and when every able bodied man in the South was needed for the struggle, naturally became objects of suspicion to the state and Confederate authorities. They stood by their convictions, however. Their experiences during the war are told elsewhere in this volume, and their position on the question of holding slaves can be learned from the records of a conference of the churches which was held April, 1864.

The subject of hiring slaves was introduced by Bishop Geil.

Attitude Toward Slavery Decided that inasmuch as it is against our creed and discipline to own or traffic in slaves; so it is also forbidden a brother to hire a slave unless such slave be entitled to receive the pay for such labor by the consent of the owner. But where neighbors exchange labor, the labor of slaves may be received.

In literature and music the Virginians have con-

EXPANSION OF PEQUEA COLONY

Literature and Music tributed more than their share to the progress of the Mennonite church. We have already seen that Joseph Funk's printing press during the middle of the last century was often used to promote the literary interests of the Mennonite people. The first English song book, Burkholder's Confession of Faith, and other publications had their birth here. To the cause of music also Funk's services were great. The printing of song books, especially the Harmonica Sacra, and the teaching of singing schools for which the region around Singers Glen was well known did much to interest not only the local Virginia community but the entire church in the subject of sacred music. It was from this region that the most talented musicians of the church—the Funks, Goods, Brunks and Showalters—have come. And finally Virginia gave the church John S. Coffman, the pioneer evangelist, who did more than any other man of his day to inspire the Mennonite people everywhere with higher ideals of culture and service.

By the close of the eighteenth century, then, the Mennonites of Southeastern Pennsylvania had appeared among the pioneer settlers in the fertile valleys of Pennsylvania, Maryland and Virginia. No new communities have been established in these states since that time. But with the opening of the Northwest Territory these settlements became in turn the mother communities of many congregations organized early in the next century in Ohio, Indiana and Illinois.

CHAPTER VIII

THE AMISH[1]

Jacob Amman

The Amish branch of the church derives its name from one Jacob Amman, a Mennonite preacher in the canton of Berne in Switzerland. Not much is known of his life. But he was evidently a man of conservative tendencies and decided opinions, for in 1693 we find him visiting the Swiss churches and urging a closer observance of earlier and more conservative customs and practices. He advocated especially a more rigid application of the practice of "avoidance" or "shunning" of such as had been excommunicated by the church. The practice of the Swiss church at the time was to "shun" one who had been expelled from their body only at the communion table, but now if Amman were to have his way, the practice was to be extended

---

1. Most of our information of the origin of the Amish division of the church is obtained from a series of letters written at the time, which have been preserved by the church at the Emmenthal. These letters have been published by Joseph Stuckey in a pamphlet called "Eine Begebenheit," and by Johannes Moser in a pamphlet entitled "Eine Verantwortung gegen Daniel Musser." Ernst Müller in his history of the Bernese Mennonites devotes a chapter to the subject.

to many social and even domestic relations. Not even
the wife and children of such an ex-member, if they
were church members, were to be permitted to eat
with him at the same table. The usual conjugal relations also between husband and wife were to be suspended.

Amman soon gained a small following. His principal opponent was Hans Reist, and the two factions
were locally named after these two leaders. There
was much bitter discussion between the two parties all
through the Oberland and Emmenthaler regions, and
many conferences were held to settle the controversy,
but none were successful. Reist and his party failed
to appear at one of these appointed meetings, whereupon Amman immediately pronounced them under
the ban. Reist soon after retaliated with the same
measure.

Among other conservative customs which Amman introduced among his followers were the use of
hooks and eyes instead of buttons on the clothes of
men, and the practice of feetwashing, which had been
neglected among the Swiss by this time.

For many years there was bitter feeling between
the two factions throughout the canton. As late as
1711, at the time of the exodus from Switzerland, the
bitterness was still so strong that the two parties refused to enter the same ship in their voyage down the
Rhine. Attempts at reconciliation also proved fruitless. In 1700 Amman and several of his leading followers wrote a letter to Reist, asking for forgiveness.
The signatures to this letter are those of Isak Kauffman, Niggli Augsburger, Ulrich Amman, Jacob

Amman, Christen Blank, Jacob Kleiner, Hans Bachman, Felix Jäggi, and Hans Bieri—with a few exceptions all familiar names among the Amish of America today. Reist, however, refused to extend the olive branch and the division has remained to the present time.

The Amish church in Europe[2] has never been large. It began in the canton of Berne and from there emigrants carried the division to Alsace,Lorraine, and the Palatinate where still exist a number of congregations. From these places have come the immigrants to America.

Just when they first came to America it is not possible to say. The assertion made by some local historians that they arrived with the Mennonites at the Pequea in 1710 is based on no evidence. But since there were a number of Amish among the exiled Bernese at Amsterdam in 1711, it is barely probable that a few may have reached this country soon after that date. If there were any, however, they must have been few in number. An examination of the names of the early settlers of Lancaster county shows that by 1725 Jacob Hostater, who came in 1715,[3] Johannes Lichty, Adam Brandt, and Simon König were residents of the county. These are all characteristic Amish names, but whether their bearers were of that faith is not certain. Soon after 1727, however, Amish names appear frequently in the lists of passengers on the immigrant ships.[4] In 1727 there arrived

First Amish in America

---

2. The name "Amish" is no longer in common use in Europe.
3. Pa. Arch., Second Series, Vol. XIX. p. 632.
4. See Rupp, I. D. Thirty Thousand Names.

among others in Philadelphia Jacob Mast, Peter Zug, Ulrich Pitscha, John Jacob Stutzman and Johannes Kurtz. The fact that these men bear characteristic Amish names and that they arrived on the same vessels with others whom we know to have been Mennonites, makes it quite probable that they were Amish men. Between 1727 and 1740 appear such names as Jacob Mast, Jacob Beuler, Johannes Lapp, Jacob Lantz, Christian Blank, Oswald Hochstetler, John Jacob Kauffman and a number of others. The period of heaviest immigration appears to have been between 1742 and 1745. One vessel, the Francis Elizabeth, had on board in 1742 Moritz Zug and his two brothers, John and Christian, the ancestors of hundreds of Zooks in this country, a number of Jotters, Johann Heinrich Schertz, John Gerber and others. In 1744 among others came Peter Jutzy. During the next twenty years Amish names are found frequently on the immigration lists. In 1749 came Jacob Hartzler the ancestor of a long line of Hartzlers in this country. He was followed the next year by the Blauch brothers, Christian and Hans, and Andreas Hoelly. Nicholas Stoltzfus landed at Philadelphia in 1766 and Peter Bietch (the founder of the Peachy family) in 1767. All of these as well as others who came with them if living today could count their offspring by the hundreds both within and without the Amish church. By the time of the Revolutionary war Amish as well as Mennonite immigration had practically ceased and no foreign additions were made to the American Amish settlements until near the middle of the nineteenth century.

Just where the first immigrants located is also

uncertain, but one of the very earliest congregations
was established about 1740 in the north-
Pioneer western corner of Berks county, along
Settlements the North Kill creek, near what is now
Hamburg. Among the pioneers in this
community were the Zugs, Jotters and others whose
descendants can be found today in nearly every Amish
settlement in America. By 1742 enough had located
in this region to petition the Provincial Assembly for
exemption from the oath in becoming naturalized, a
privilege which had already been granted the Quakers
and Mennonites of Pennsylvania. This request was
granted.[5]

Another early congregation was established in
Lancaster county, near the head waters of Conestoga
river.

And within these two pioneer communities most
of the first immigrants located. The entire immigration could not have been large as can be seen by the
comparatively small number of family names which
are to be found in the Pennsylvania church today.
The following list is practically all-inclusive—Yoder,
Zook, Mast, Plank, Stoltzfus, Stutzman, Hooley,
Beiler, Koenig, Beachy, Miller, Hostettler, Kauffman,
Jutzi, Troyer and a few others.

Of the early history of these people we know very
little except that they were extremely conservative in
their religious customs, simple in their tastes and
habits and generally prosperous. They
Early Life never erected public church buildings,
but worshiped in private houses. In their
everyday life they had to meet the usual hardships of

---

5. Watson, J. F. Annals, II. 109.

the frontiersman. On several occasions and especially during the French and Indian war the outlying settlements fell prey to the Indian tomahawk and scalping-knife.

It is not possible to say which of the two above mentioned pioneer settlements is the older, but it is evident that soon the one in Berks county became the more prominent. It was the home of the Zug brothers, the Yoders and other pioneers of 1742. Not long after, other communities were established in Berks county, one on Maiden creek, one near Oley, and another in the southern part of the county near the Lancaster line. Most of the early congregations of Berks have since become extinct, the settlers having left for other more promising localities. Very early a number of the Zooks and others moved to Chester county where a church was established. Some of the Hartzlers and Beilers began a settlement in Lebanon county near the headwaters of the Tulpehocken.[6]

From all these communities many emigrated in turn to Mifflin county before the close of the eighteenth century.

The Lancaster county settlement near the headwaters of the Conestoga and the Pequea has always been prosperous and is now one of the largest communities in America. In 1900 there were eight congregations with an estimated membership of about eleven hundred.

From these various pioneer churches all the later settlements in western Pennsylvania—in Somerset,

---

6. See article by J. K. Hartzler in Herald of Truth, June 1, 1902. "Fifty Years in the Amish-Mennonite Churches of Pennsylvania."

Westmoreland, Mifflin, and Juniata counties—were made, and indirectly many more in Ohio, Indiana, Illinois, Iowa and other western states.

The Amish do not seem to have followed the Mennonites and other Germans southward into the Cumberland and Shenandoah Valleys. **Somerset County** The first movement away from Southeastern Pennsylvania was across the Alleghenies, into what is now Somerset county. Here as we have already seen came the Blauchs, Jacob and Christian, who we have reason to believe were Amishmen, into Conemaugh township, the latter as early as 1767. In 1776 two men by the names of Yoder and Hooley settled in what is called the Glades region in the same county.[7] About the same time another community was established in the southern part of the county, along Casselman creek. One of the earliest settlers here was Christian Gnaegi who in 1774 took up five hundred acres of land two miles east of Myersdale.[8] Most of these settlers came from Berks, Chester and Lebanon counties. The Glades church has since become extinct. The membership in this entire region in 1900 was three hundred and twenty-nine. The church in Somerset county has in turn become the founder of congregations in Elkhart and Lagrange counties, Indiana; Douglas and Moultrie counties, Illinois; and has furnished new settlers to many other Amish communities.

Before the close of the century another large

---

7. D. D. Miller in Herold der Wahrheit, Feb. 1, 1893.
8. Gnagey, Elias. Gnaegi Family History.

colony was begun in the beautiful and fertile valley of the Kishocoquillas, a tributary of the Juniata, in what is now Mifflin county. This valley is about three or four miles wide and about fifteen miles long, lying between Jacks mountain on the southeast and another low range on the opposite side. This picturesque retreat was discovered by the Amish of Berks and Lancaster about 1790, and they soon began to buy large tracts of land from the Scotch-Irish who had been in the region since about 1760. The deed books at Lewistown, the county seat, show that the earliest purchasers were the following —John Zook (1792),[9] John Yotter, Christian Zook, John Hooley, Jacob Yotter and Christian Yotter, all in 1793; and John Hartzler, 1794. These were followed during the next twenty years by the Beilers, Beacheys, Kauffmans, Blanks and others. The colony grew by natural increase and by new settlers until the middle of the next century. The Amish now occupy nearly the entire valley.

The Kishocoquillas Valley

Being hemmed in, however, on both sides by the mountains, it was impossible for the community to accommodate the coming generations with new homes after all the available land in the valley had been bought from the Scotch-Irish. Hence, as the settlement grew, the younger members were forced to seek homes elsewhere. From about 1840 to 1870, Mifflin county furnished many members for new congregations in Champaign, Logan and Wayne counties, Ohio; in McLean county, Illinois; and in other places in Indiana and other western states. The entire mem-

---

9. Runk, J. M. Biographical Encyclopedia of Juniata Valley, p. 745.

bership, including the various branches is still about one thousand.

During the last few years of the eighteenth century and the early part of the nineteenth, a small congregation was located in Buffalo Valley, Union county, and two in Tuscarora valley and Lost Creek valley, in Juniata county. These latter, however, have since disappeared. About the middle of the last century a settlement was also made in Lawrence county, which still has a membership of about one hundred and fifty.

The Amish of Mifflin county are still very conservative and are still principally of the several varieties of the Old Order type. Consequently church houses are scarce. The first one was erected in 1868 by the progressive wing of the church.

Few new communities were established in Pennsylvania after 1800. By that time more inviting prospects for settlement were afforded by the cheap lands of the newly organized North-west territory and soon in the state of Ohio.

Ohio

The first Amish to cross over into Ohio came from Somerset county, just a few years after Ohio became a state.[10] In the fall of 1808 preacher Jacob Miller and his two sons, Henry and Jacob, together with their wives, located on farms they had purchased on Sugar creek in the west-

Tuscarawas and Holmes Counties

---

10. See article by S. H. Miller in Mennonite Year-Book and Directory for 1908. Also History of Tuscarawas County, published by Warner, Beers Company. 1884.

An OLD AMISH HOMESTEAD. In Holmes County.

ern part of what is now Tuscarawas county. Two years later Jonas Miller, Joseph Mast, John Troyer, Christian Yoder and perhaps others, also from Somerset county, settled in this same region, but along Walnut creek in the eastern part of Holmes county. Others were ready to come from Pennsylvania, but the Indian incursions of the war of 1812, not only stopped emigration from Pennsylvania for a few years but drove back to their original homes some who had entered Ohio before 1812. After the war, however, many new settlers were added to the community bearing such names as Miller, Yoder, Gerber, Hershberger and others. Judging from the prevalence at present of the Millers, however, most of the early settlers must have belonged to that family. The first religious services were held near Shanesville in 1810 by the above mentioned Jacob Miller, familiarly known as "Yockle" Miller. The settlement soon outgrew the two small valleys where the first pioneers located and spread out over the hills of the eastern part of Holmes and the western part of Tuscarawas county until now it is the largest Amish community in America. The entire community, including the three congregations which worship in meeting houses and the seven districts of the Old Order contains about two thousand church members. These congregations have furnished a number of settlers for the churches which later were established in Logan and Geauga counties, Ohio; Howard and Elkhart counties, Indiana; Johnson county, Iowa; Seward county, Nebraska, and in other newer communities.

The second Amish colony in the state was located in Wayne county. The pioneer settler was Jacob

Wayne County

Yoder who came from Mifflin county, Pennsylvania in 1817. He was followed during the years immediately succeeding by Jonathan S. Yoder, David Stutzman, John Zook and Christian Lantz from the same county, and Peter, Jacob and Abraham Schrock from Somerset. Christian Brandt from Switzerland was the first minister and David Zook from Pennsylvania, the first bishop. Later other settlers came from Europe as well as from the older congregations in Pennsylvania. The settlement has since grown to a fine large congregation of about five hundred members. This congregation is perhaps the most progressive and cultured Amish community in the country. It has produced and kept within the church more intelligent and educated young men and women than any other single congregation in the land. Here was also the home of the late John K. Yoder, for many years one of the best known and most influential bishops in the church.

Butler County, a New Element

The next settlement was made in Butler county along the Miami river. This congregation is of special interest because it introduced new blood into the Amish church of America. The communities thus far described in Pennsylvania and Ohio were all outgrowths of the parent settlements in Berks and Lancaster counties. But now, beginning about 1820, a new stream of European immigrants of both Amish and Mennonite persuasion again sets in. The causes of this general movement to America has been discussed elsewhere and needs no repetition here. The immigrants usually first reached the older settlements in the East and from thence started out in quest of new homes in the states farther west. The Amish who located in Butler county first came to Lancaster, and from thence struck the Ohio river at Pittsburg. From here they floated down the Ohio to the Miami, then up that stream as far as what is now Butler county where they established their first settlement.

The pioneer in this immigration seems to have been Christian Augsburger, who with a family of twelve and five other families, arrived here in 1819.[11] Other families bearing the names of Imhoff, Naffziger, Kennel, etc., soon followed, and by 1830 a flourishing congregation had been established. These early settlers came mainly from near Strasburg. In 1832 several new families bearing the names Iutzi, Hooley, Kinsinger, etc., came from Hesse-Darmstadt and located near the original settlement. These Hessians, coming from a different German state, did not always agree with their Strasburg brethren in their religious practices. They held more liberal views on many questions, among others on the use of musical instruments, and in the matter of the conventional dress. These differences culminated in 1836 in a division. The Hessians were served in their religious worship by a minister who had come to them from Europe by way of Canada, Peter Naffziger, familiarly known in later years as "The Apostle"; and the conservatives by Jacob Augsburger. This breach lasted until 1897 since which time the two congregations have again acted in harmony in their religious work.

Butler county afforded a stopping place for a few

---
11. See History of Butler County, published by Western Biographical Publishing Company, Cincinnati, 1882; also Centennial History of Butler County by B. S. Bartlow. 1905.

years for many European Amish who during the next twenty years drifted down the Ohio, enroute for the Illinois settlements which had been begun in the mean time.

A number of Germans about 1820 also located in Stark county.

Still another colony, composed mostly of immigrants from near Mühlhausen was established in Fulton county. From 1834 to 1850 many families settled in what is now Germantown township. Among the earliest settler were Nicholas King, Jacob Bender, Christian Lauber, Christian Rupp, Henry and Jacob Roth and John Gunday, who came in 1834. These were followed in 1835 by Peter Rupp, Christian Beck and others, and in the following years by those bearing the names Burkholder, Rivenaugh, Stutzman, Gascho, Schmucker, Klopfenstein, Stuckey, and Wise.[12] This congregation has since grown to large dimensions, and although it has within recent years furnished a number of recruits for the Egli branch of the church, it still contains a membership of about six hundred.

Two more colonies of Pennsylvanians were planted in the state before the middle of the century, one in 1834 in Fairfield county,[13] the other in 1840 in Logan county. The Fairfield county congregation was located principally in Pleasant and Berne townships, near the earlier Mennonite settlements. It has since disappeared, however, most of the members having

---

12. See History of Henry and Fulton Counties, pub. by D. Mason and Co., Syracuse, N. Y. 1888.
13. See article by Joseph Kurtz, in History of Fairfield County, by Harvey Scott. 1877.

gone to Lagrange county, Indiana, and Champaign county, Ohio.

The church in Logan county was founded by the Yoders, Troyers, Kings, Bylers, and Kauffmans, who had come from Mifflin county between 1840 and 1850. The first settlers were Peter Yoder in 1840, followed by Daniel Yoder the next year, both of whom had come from Mifflin, by way of Wayne county, Ohio. Several of the later families came from Holmes county. The church was organized in Harrison township in 1845 with Joseph Kauffman and Jonas Troyer as first ministers. By 1850 the settlement had expanded over into Champaign county, and in that year the first services were held there. In 1863 the first Sunday school was organized in Logan county. This was the first Sunday school ever held by the Amish in America as well as by the Old Mennonites.[14]

Logan and Champaign Counties

Indiana

The first settlement in Indiana[15] was the result of an extended tour of inspection made by a group of land seekers from Somerset county, Pennsylvania, in 1840. By that time this community again found it necessary to seek new homes for its surplus membership. Accordingly a group of four men, Daniel S. Miller, Joseph Miller, Nathan Smeiley and Joseph

---

14. See article by Bishop David Plank, in Historical Review of Logan County, by Robert P. Kennedy. 1903.
15. For printed information regarding the church in Indiana see, Family Almanac, 1875; The Amish Mennonites, by S. D. Guengerich, in Gospel Witness, April 5, 1905; Eine Geschichte der ersten Ansiedlung der Amischen Mennoniten im Staat Indiana, by John E. Borntreger; and History of Lagrange and Noble Counties, published by Batley and Co., Chicago. 1882.

Speicher undertook to look up a suitable location for a colony in what was then the far "West." They took a boat at Pittsburg down the Ohio to the mouth of that river, and then ascended the Mississippi to Burlington, Iowa. From here they traversed by foot the present counties of Henry, Johnson, and Washington as far as Iowa City. They were well pleased with the fertile, rolling prairies of this region and started back to report to their brethren at home. The return was made across northern Illinois to the little village of Chicago, thence across Lake Michigan to the mouth of the St. Joseph, and thence up that river by boat. Leaving this river after they had ascended it some distance, they again started on foot across northern Indiana. They soon reached the fertile region east of Goshen in Elkhart county. They were so well pleased with this locality that they decided to make this, rather than Iowa, their future home, and returned to Pennsylvania to report their decision.

Accordingly the next summer four families, consisting of twenty-four souls, arrived from Somerset, and located first on the Elkhart prairie, but later on the wooded lands east of Goshen. The heads of these families were Daniel S. Miller, preacher Joseph Miller, Joseph Borntreger, and Christian Borntreger. Two of these soon moved ten miles east into Lagrange county. During the years immediately following many other settlers came to both of these pioneer communities from Pennsylvania and Holmes county, Ohio. The first church services were held in the spring of 1842 in the house of preacher Joseph Miller in Clinton township.

Pioneer Congregation in Elkhart County

The church which was organized contained fourteen members. From these small beginnings there have since developed in Elkhart, Lagrange and Noble counties eleven congregations, six of which are of the Old Order, with an aggregate membership of about twelve hundred.

Before the Civil war, small colonies had also been established in Marshall and Adams counties, and since that time a number of congregations, principally of the Old Order, have located in Newton, Howard, Miami, Allen, Jasper, Davies and Brown counties. These settlements are composed largely of Pennsylvanians, and the combined membership at present counts up about six hundred.

Several small congregations have also recently been organized in Michigan, principally by settlers from Indiana and neighboring states.

Iowa

West Pont Colony
The first settlement in Iowa[16] was made near West Point, in Lee county, before 1840, along the banks of the Mississippi in the extreme southeastern part of the state. The first settlers were European immigrants who had stopped for several years in Butler county, Ohio, long enough to earn a little money to purchase homes for themselves on the cheap lands of Illinois and Iowa. Among these men were John Rogie, C. Werey, C. Kinsinger, and Andrew Hauder.

---

16. See Amish Mennonites of Iowa, by B. L. Wick, printed in Publications of Iowa State Historical Society, 1894, and article by S. D. Guengerich in Gospel Witness, April 5, 1905. Some of this information has also been received from John Goldsmith of Wayland, Iowa, son of the pioneer bishop of the state.

A little later others came from Wayne county, Ohio and Canada. In 1846 Joseph Goldschmidt, the first bishop in the state came from Butler county. This colony had located on a tract of land which had been set apart as an Indian reservation, and because of some difficulty in getting clear titles to their lands most of the early settlers later left for other localities, some for Illinois; several others for Henry and Davis counties, Iowa. Before the Civil war the congregation had disappeared.

In 1845 another small prospecting party composed of Daniel P. Guengerich from Garfield county Ohio, and J. J. Swartzendruber from Alleghany county, Maryland, came to Iowa in search of cheap lands. After remaining for awhile with the colony in Lee county they traveled through the present counties of Lee, Henry, Washington and Johnson, and decided upon the last for their prospective homes. They returned east and the next spring these two men, together with one William Wertz and their families began the first Amish settlement in Johnson county. These were followed in succeeding years by many others from Germany and from Pennsylvania and Ohio, and in recent years from Illinois, who settled in all of the above mentioned counties and in Iowa county. In the early fifties a small community was established in Davis county by one or two Lee county settlers and others from Ohio.

Later Settlements

The largest congregation in the state at present is to be found in Henry county. The earliest settlers here in addition to those who had moved from Lee and Davis counties came principally from Alsace by

way of Butler county, Ohio. Among them were
Daniel Conrad, John and Peter Roth, Abraham and
John Hostetter, J. Lichty, J. Graber and others.

The combined membership of these settlements
including several large congregations of the Old Order
is about eleven hundred. Within recent years small
communities have also been established in Pocahontas,
Wright and Calhoun counties.

The "Eicher" Church
Some years ago a division occurred in Henry
county which under the late Benjamin
Eicher developed into a large congregation. This congregation, with two
places of worship, is now a member
of the General Conference Mennonites.

Immigration from 1820 to 1850

As we have already seen, there was very little
immigration of either Mennonites or Amish, from
about 1760 to 1820. But from the latter date to about
1850 large numbers again left their European homes
for this country, owing to the hardships resulting
from the Napoleonic wars, together with the great
prosperity which the people of America enjoyed during this period. The Amish came largely from Alsace,
Lorraine, Bavaria, and Hesse-Darmstadt, and settled
as we have seen in Butler and Fulton counties, Ohio;
Lewis county, New York; Wilmot township, Ontario;
Lee and Henry counties, Iowa; and in Woodford,
Tazewell and Bureau counties, Illinois. A study
of the names of these immigrants shows that
they were for the most part of different stock
from the Pennsylvania Germans who had come
to America in the early eighteenth century. The

most common of these names were Naffziger, Oesch, Virkler, Gascho, Schertz, Fahrney, Roggy, Rupp, Stucki, Gerber, Guengerich, Belsley, Auer, Zehr, Moser, Burkey, Roth, Litwiller, Schrock, Steinman, Albrecht, Bachman, Kennel, etc. They were usually poor men and women who upon coming to America found their way to the older settlements, generally to Lancaster county, but later to Butler county, where they remained long enough to earn a little money which they could invest in cheap lands in the newer countries.

Canada

Pioneer Christian Naffziger

The region which next to Butler county evidently offered the greatest attraction to these homeseekers was Ontario, for there the second settlement was made. The history of the Canadian Amish begins with the wanderings of one Christian Naffziger from Bavaria, who came to America to look up a suitable location for a proposed colony from his native congregation. Naffziger landed at New Orleans in the spring of 1822, from whence he finally found his way by foot, to Lancaster county. Here he was directed to Waterloo township, Ontario, where a thriving Mennonite community had been established some twenty years before, and near which there was still plenty of cheap land to be had. He arrived at Waterloo in the fall of the same year, and being well pleased with the country he secured at a nominal cost from the governor of Upper Canada a large tract of land, just west of Waterloo in Wilmot township, for his proposed colony. Returning to Bavaria by way of London where he had secured a confirmation of his grant from the king, he prepared to lead a colony to the new home. He was detained, however, and was not able to come back to America until 1826. But in that year he and his family, together with a number of friends, including two ministers, Peter Naffziger, a bishop, and Christian Steinman, arrived safely in Wilmot township.

In the meantime, however, Naffziger and his small colony had been preceded by several German families who had reached this region by way of Lancaster county. Among these were John Brenneman, Joseph Goldschmidt, John Guengrich, Jacob Kropf, Jacob Burky, Isaac Moser, and Joseph Becher. The first church was organized in 1824 with John Brenneman and Joseph Goldschmidt as the first ministers. This colony has since developed into four large congregations near the original settlement, and one near Lake Huron, founded in 1849.[17]

Wilmot Township

New York

A little later, between 1830 and 1835, several families bearing the names Virkler, Fahrney, Naffziger, Zehr, Moser, and Ringenberg, located near the headwaters of the Mohawk, along Beaver creek in Lewis county, New York. This congregation, which now numbers about one hundred and fifty members,

---

17, C. M. Bender. Die Amischen-Mennoniten in Canada, in Familien Kalender. 1903.

as well as those in Canada, is still very conservative in all matters of religious practice.[18]

Illinois

Wesley City Colony By far the largest and most important settlement made by the immigrants of this period was the one made in 1831 along the banks of the Illinois in what are now Woodford, Tazewell and Bureau counties. In the spring of 1831 a small company of young men and women, most of them unmarried, arrived on the banks of the Illinois near what is now Wesley City, Tazewell county, and began here the first Amish or Mennonite community west of Ohio. These pioneers had come from Alsace and Lorraine the year before and had reached the Illinois country by way of Pennsylvania, then down the Ohio, up the Mississippi and Illinois as far as Fort Clark, now Peoria, a few miles to the south of which they began the first settlement. This company included David Schertz, a miller, and his father; Christian Roggy with three daughters; Joseph Rusche and two sisters; Jacob Auer and Peter Beck.[19]

At about the same time other immigrants from Alsace began to locate about ten miles farther up the river along Partridge creek, between Spring Bay and Metamora. During the year, "Red" Joe Belsley pur-

---

18. This information was furnished by Christian Roggi of Croghan, N. Y.
19. See in appendix autobiographical sketch of Christian Ropp, manuscript in possession of John Ropp, Bloomington, Ill. The information regarding the Illinois settlements has been secured almost entirely from the oldest settlers.

THE PARTRIDGE CHURCH, ILLINOIS. Built in 1854. This is the second Amish church to be built in Illinois and perhaps the second building erected by the Amish in America. It is now deserted.

chased a farm in the bottom lands of the Illinois, near
Spring Bay, and John Engle who
Woodford and had spent several years in Penn-
Tazewell Counties sylvania on his way westward,
located near the eastern edge of
the Illinois river's wooded belt, and one mile west of
Metamora. In 1833 several additions were made to
the Partridge settlement. Christian Engle, father of
John, Peter Engle and several Engle sisters, John and
Joe Virkler settled near Metamora. "Black" Joe
Belsley, Christian Smith, and John Kennel located
near Spring Bay. To the Wesley City colony were
added this year Peter Guth, John Sweitzer, and Joseph
Summer.

Up to this time the colony had been without a
minister, but after the arrival of Christian Engle, a
bishop ordained in Europe, a
The First church was organized in 1833, in
Church Organized the home of John Engle. This
was the first church of any denomination to be organized in Woodford county.

The colony grew rapidly. Each year new immigrants came from Alsace, Lorraine, Bavaria, or occasionally from Hesse-Darmstadt, at first by way of
Pennsylvania and the Ohio river, but later by way
of New Orleans and the Mississippi. Between 1834
and 1850 in addition to those already mentioned came
the ancestors of those families now bearing the names
Schertz, Bachman, Garber, Naffziger, Litwiller, Esch,
Yordy, Burkey, Zehr, Slagel, Summer, Oyer, Ropp,
Springer, Guth, Sweitzer, Belsley, Allbrecht, Camp,
Imhoff, Rediger, and several others. By 1840 the
settlement extended along the Black Partridge creek

from Spring Bay to Metamora, along the Ten Mile creek from Peoria to Washington, along Dillon creek in Tazewell county, along the Mackinaw river in Woodford county, and along Rock creek in McLean county.

In the meantime a few families had also located in Putnam county on the banks of the Illinois. In 1835 a Burkey family from Butler county settled near Hennepin. The next year several others by the name of Burkey came from Bavaria. These were followed in 1837 by the Allbrechts from the same place, Hooleys and Brennemans from Ohio, and others from Germany came later. In 1838 the Allbrechts moved across the river into Bureau county, near Tiskilwa. Others followed and soon the entire colony had moved across. For a while the congregation was in charge of Bishop Andrew Ropp from the Dillon creek congregation, but later Joseph Burkey was ordained as the resident bishop, a position which he still holds.

Putnam County

For several years after the first pioneers arrived the various settlements in Woodford and Tazewell counties formed but one congregation, and services were held on Sundays in turn in each locality. But as the colony grew separate congregations were organized in the several centers of the settlement. Before 1840 the following congregations had been formed —Partridge, Wesley City (known as "Die Busche Gemein"), Dillon creek (now Pleasant Grove), and Rock creek, or Mackinaw. The following were the first bishops of these respective congregations—Christian Engle, Michael Moseman, Andrew Ropp, and Christian Ropp, all ordained before 1840.

THE AMISH   231

All of the early settlers thus far mentioned had come from Europe, but between 1848 and 1852 several families—Lantz, Troyer, Yoder, Kauffman—from Mifflin county, Pennsylvania, located on the wild prairies near the present town of Danvers, close to the Rock creek settlement. With them came Jonathan Yoder, a well known bishop of his day and also Joseph Stuckey from Butler county. In 1853 the Rock creek congregation built the first Amish meeting house in the state and one of the very first in the country.

Pennsylvanians in McLean County

In the early fifties a number of Hessian immigrants also settled near Danvers. One of their earliest and best known preachers was Michael Kistler, who had originally come from Butler county, but directly from Putnam county, Illinois, where a small colony of Hessians had also settled. Kistler and his congregation who had brought with them from Europe many religious practices and customs at variance with those of their brethren from Alsace and in America, soon found themselves out of harmony, especially with that part of the congregation which had come from conservative Mifflin county. Yoder and Kistler represented the two extremes of Amish practice of that day. Accordingly about 1854 the Hessians formed a separate congregation, as their countrymen had done in Butler county some time earlier, and in 1862 built what is known as the South Danvers church. The old Rock creek congregation is now the North Danvers church.

Hessians

These pioneer settlements, with the exception of

the last one mentioned were all made in the timbered sections of the country along the Illinois river and its tributaries. Beginning with the early fifties, however, many of the descendants of the original settlers moved to the more fertile prairie lands, and in course of time the original congregations were transplanted to the prairies near by. In this way churches were established, beginning in 1854 at Hopedale, Delavan, Gridley (on the Gridley prairie), Roanoke and Fisher. The original Partridge congregation has erected a church building several miles east of Metamora.

The Prairie Congregations

From these original settlements there have developed ten congregations. Exclusive of several congregations which have joined the "Egli'" and "Stuckey" branches of the church, and of many who have moved to other western states the combined membership, made up almost exclusively of the descendants of the early immigrants, is still about eleven hundred.

In addition to the settlements made by the immigrants from Europe, a colony of the Old Order was also established soon after the Civil war in Douglas and Moultrie counties by Pennsylvanians. In 1865 Mose Yoder and Dan Miller and Dan Otto from Somerset county visited Illinois for the purpose of finding suitable homes for themselves and friends. They decided upon the fertile lands of Moultrie and Douglas counties, in the vicinity of the town of Arthur. They moved to the new location the following year and were soon followed by their friends

Old Order from Pennsylvania

from Somerset county, and others who had gone to Johnson county, Iowa, some time before, and also by a number from Holmes county, Ohio. The settlement has since developed into four large congregations or districts.

The Illinois churches have in turn furnished many settlers for colonies in Missouri, Nebraska, Kansas and other western states.

Missouri

The pioneer congregation in Missouri was located in Hickory county about the middle of last century, partly by European immigrants, and partly by Amish from the East. Joseph Naffziger was the earliest settler and was followed by those bearing the names Reber, Yoder, Klopfenstein, etc. Soon after the Civil war another settlement, now by far the largest in the state, was made in Cass county. Small congregations have since been founded also in Johnson, Vernon and Boone counties. Jacob Kenagy was the pioneer bishop of this community and was for many years a man of great influence among his people.[20]

Nebraska

The cheap lands of Nebraska attracted the Amish soon after the state was organized. The first settlement was made by a small colony of eight families in 1873 in Seward county. The colony grew rapidly from the beginning by the addition of many homeseekers from Iowa, Illinois and other states. Illinois

---

20. See Mennonite Church History, by Hartzler and Kauffman.

has furnished the larger part of the new settlers.[21] Bishop Joseph Schlegel came to the congregation in 1879 from Iowa, and has ever since exerted a commanding influence over the churches in the western states. The congregation now numbers about four hundred members. Other settlements, including some of the Old Order, have been made in Fillmore, Cummings, Holt, Hamilton, and Snell counties.

Kansas

The earliest settlements in Kansas were made by the Old Order in the early eighties in Reno county where they now have three congregations. Later colonies were established by either one or the other of the two branches of the church in Harvey, Pawnee, Reno, Lyons, Decatur and Anderson counties.

Within recent years small communities of Amish have been located in Oregon, North Dakota, Colorado, Arkansas and Oklahoma, and the work of searching for cheaper lands in the newer states is still being carried on, largely by the poorer members of the older settlements.

Doctrine and Practice In doctrine there was not much difference between the Amish and the Mennonites. Both adopted the Dort confession of 1632 as the best expression of their faith. The Amish, however, insisted on a more rigid application of the ban and the practice of "shunning." They held no conferences and each community was independent of every other in its religious government.

---

21. See History of Seward County by W. W. Cox.

Like the Mennonites they had developed a strong denominational spirit. They always settled in small colonies and thus came very little in contact with outsiders.

They were in many respects even more conservative than the Mennonites and slow to adopt new customs in their daily living and religious worship. In Europe they had had no meeting houses. Religious services were always held in private houses. When they came to America, at first necessity, but finally custom fixed the same practice here. Meeting houses before 1850 were everywhere looked upon as worldly, and few were erected. Since the members of the congregation often were scattered over a considerable territory and many had some distance to the place of meeting, the members with whom the congregation met, served dinner to all those present. Services were generally long, lasting until late in the afternoon, and were conducted in the German languge, or in the East in the "Pennsylvania Dutch." Preachers usually were plentiful. The Partridge congregation in Illinois at one time was blessed with thirteen, four of whom were bishops. Preachers and other church officials were chosen by lot and were of three classes, "völlige diener" (bishop), "diener zum buch" (preacher), and "armendiener" (deacon). The old hymn book, the Ausbund, popularly known as "Das dicke Liederbuch" was still used exclusively in religious worship. In their singing all sang the melody or "einstimmig" as it was called. To sing more than one of the four parts seemed worldly and hence was not permitted. The use of notes with the hymns was regarded as savoring of pride and for that reason also prohibited.

The conservatism of the Amish manifested itself especially in their personal appearance and manner of dress. Pride is apt to show itself most conspicuously in bodily adornment, and hence in order to be "unworldly" which to them frequently meant to be unlike other people, they were slow to adopt any changes, and frequently went to absurd lengths in their customs. Their clothes were home made, of prescribed material and cut. The men wore no suspenders, for these were considered useless and worldly innovations long after they had come into common use among their fellow men. The most conspicuous departure from the usual customs of dress was the use of hooks and eyes instead of buttons on their coats and vests. This also was a relic from an earlier day when buttons were unknown. Amman in 1693 had insisted on the maintaining of the older custom. For this peculiarity the Amish were known in some localities in Europe as "Häftler", while the Mennonites on the other hand were spoken of as "Knöpfler" Täufer. Every young man also was required as soon as he was able, to grow a beard, but was not permitted to wear a mustache. This custom in some European communities had given them the name of "Bartmänner." The hair was worn long and was cut according to a prescribed rule. The women, likewise, were extremely plain in their clothes. Their dress was of a plain color, made with a cape over the shoulders and always accompanied with an apron. On their heads they wore the old fashioned, long, "slat" bonnet.

In their homes and in their everyday life the Amish were equally plain and simple. Pictures, curtains, carpets, and everything that did not serve some immediate useful purpose was discarded as an evidence of pride. In the early half of the nineteenth century modern top-buggies and in some cases wind mills and other modern improvements and conveniences were often regarded as too worldly.

They were opposed to higher education as were also the Mennonites, but were in sympathy with such elementary training as would enable their children to read and write.

In spite of these peculiarities, however, the Amish possessed the sounder and homelier virtues to a high degree, and always won the respect of those among whom they lived. They were hardworking, industrious, frugal, honest, and usually prosperous, owning the finest farms and best houses in their communities. Above all, they were religious. Wherever a colony was located there a church was soon organized.

This characterization does not apply equally to all the Amish before 1850. The Hessians as we saw, and to a slight degree the immigrants from other parts of Europe differed somewhat in their customs and practices from their Pennsylvania brethren.

Up to 1850, with the exceptions just mentioned, the Amish of America were one body and differed little in their social customs and religious faith and practices. But by that time, owing to the new element from Europe, the lack of conferences and the disintegrating influences due to the practice of settling in small colonies in various parts of the country, slight differences both in opinions and customs began to creep into the church.

The first question to arouse a general discussion

was that of baptism. About 1850 Solomon Beiler, a bishop in Mifflin county, declared that baptism ought to be administered in a running stream, and not within a house, as had been the practice up to that time. The question was taken up by others in the Kishocoquillas Valley, and created considerable discussion. Beiler's chief opponent was Abraham Pitsche, another bishop in the valley. Under the leadership of these two men the discussion was kept up for the next ten years. The dispute was never compromised and resulted in a division of the Mifflin county church. The followers of Pitsche during this time are now called the "Pitsche" church.

Discussions on Baptism

In the meantime the question was taken up in other localities.[22] In 1850 Jacob Yoder, a minister in Wayne county, Ohio, declared in favor of Beiler's views. He succeeded in getting a small following in his own county, but was strongly opposed by the Holmes county churches which were still very conservative. Differences of opinion on other questions also had arisen between these two communities during this time. So by 1860 one of the Holmes county adherents, in speaking of Wayne says,

> Es wurde nicht für gut oder notwendig angesehen dasz die Diener in dem Abrath gehen. Und es wurde zu zeiten Rat gehalten bei offnen Thüren in der Gegenwart von auswärtigen Personen. Die alten dicken Liederbücher wurden verworfen und die neuen Springweisen eingeführt. Auch die Gebetbücher brauchten sie nicht mehr. Bann und Meidung wurden selten geübt. Hochmut, Pracht und Übermut nahm überhand. Es hiesz es kommt nicht auf das äuszerliche an, wenn nur ihr Herz gut ist. Die Häuser wurden prächtig

---

22. See Shem Zook. Eine Wahre Darstellung, etc, and David A. Troyer. Ein Unpartheiischer Bericht, etc.

ausgeziert. Alles das und noch viel mehr von solcher art entstand durch den obengemeldeten J. Yoder und seinen Anhang.[23]

It was for the purpose of harmonizing these and other differences which had arisen among the various churches of the country that a series of general conferences were held.[24] The first of these conferences, which were known as "die Diener Versammlungen," was called together in 1862 in Wayne county. At this session there were present seventy-two ministers from Pennsylvania, Maryland, Ohio, Indiana, Illinois and Iowa. Jonathan Yoder of Illinois was chosen as the first moderator. The question which had been the source of so much discussion for ten years, was taken up for consideration, but after various opinions had been expressed, the subject was dropped without any definite agreement having been arrived at. This, however, was not the only subject upon which the churches differed. Levi Miller of Holmes county, representing the conservative element, said that other subjects also needed consideration, such as lightning rods, photographs, lotteries, large meeting houses, insurance, etc.

Diener Versammlungen 1862—1878

That there was considerable dissension throughout the church at this time is shown by the fact that the conference appointed special committees to investigate the troubles existing between the congregations of Holmes and Wayne counties, Elkhart and Lagrange, and Champaign and Logan. Complaint

---

23. David A. Troyer.
24. For a detailed account of the proceedings of these conferences see the reports published annually under the title "Die Diener Versammlung," Elkhart, Ind. 1862-1878.

was also made that the congregation in Butler county permitted the use of musical instruments. The subject of "kleiderpracht" likewise received some attention.

After a two days' discussion of these various subjects, evidently without coming to any definite conclusion on any of them, the conference adjourned to meet again the following year in Mifflin county, Pennsylvania.

These meetings were held annually for some years in various states. Questions relating to the general policy of the church were discussed. Generally discussions were plentiful, but definite decisions, few. One of the sessions held during the war decreed that no member could serve as a teamster in the army, neither could any one who had been in the war and had been disabled before he had been a member lay claim to any pension that might be due him. In 1868 it was decided that since the Amish were a nonresistant people, they could not deliver up a thief to the civil authorities for punishment. During several of the following years the trouble with Joseph Stuckey claimed some attention from the conference, but the later sessions with a few exceptions are not of great interest. Among the leading spirits of these conferences were J. K. Yoder of Wayne county, Jonathan Yoder and Joseph Stuckey of Illinois, John P. King of Logan county, and Shem Zook, a layman from Mifflin county, who frequently acted as secretary of the conference. Although these meetings may have been productive of some good, yet they failed to bring about the object for which they were first called—harmony among the various factions. The last session

THE JONATHAN SCHROCK BARN of Wayne county, Ohio. Here was held in 1862 the first of the series of the Amish "Diener Versammlungen." The meeting houses were not large enough to accommodate the large crowds that used to attend these meetings and so many of the conferences were held in large barns.

BETHEL COLLEGE

was held in 1878 near Eureka, Illinois. The reasons for the discontinuance of the sessions were lack of interest on the part of the ministry, failure of the conference to bring about harmony, and to a slight degree petty jealousies among some of the leaders. Some years later the general conference was replaced by state and district conferences.

During this time the church had become divided into several permanent factions. On the one hand the congregations in Butler county, Ohio, and McLean county, Illinois, discarded some of the earlier restrictions on dress and adopted a more liberal church policy. On the other hand a goodly number of the extreme conservatives withdrew from the conference and together with others who had never favored it, maintained without any modification the good old customs of the fathers. These are now generally known as the Old Order. In between these two were left a large number of congregations which occupy a middle position. These have gradually assumed the name Amish-Mennonite, and are found principally in Ohio, Indiana Illinois and the western states.

The Old Order furnish an interesting relic of the customs which prevailed among all the Amish several generations ago. In spirit they have **Old Order** changed none at all within the last fifty **Customs** years, and in practice very little. The men still use hooks and eyes and wear beards and long hair. Their clothes are still homemade and cut after a pattern common generations ago. Many are still suspenderless. The women still wear the plain tight-fitting dress, with the cape and apron, and the old fashioned bonnet. In addition, their conservatism has kept them from adopting many of the daily conveniences as well as religious practices which have come into use during the last fifty years. Among the "new" things which are still under the ban are telephones, top-buggies, dashboards, bicycles, furnaces, carpets, window curtains, musical instruments, "note" books, "store" suspenders, etc. They have no meeting houses and are opposed to conferences, Sunday schools, revivals, and evening meetings.

Even within these limitations, however, there are slight differences among the various communities. The church in Mifflin county serves as a good illustration of the different varieties of Amish. There are five in the valley, ranging from the most conservative, locally known as the "Nebraskas" whose women still wear the old Shaker hat, the predecessor of the bonnet, tied under the chin, and whose men are not permitted to adorn themselves with suspenders; and the "Peacheyites", two steps higher, who may wear one single suspender provided it be home made; and next, those who may hold up their trousers with the double suspender but who insist on most of the other restrictions; the congregation organized a few years ago by Abe Zook, then last the Amish Mennonites who worship in church houses, maintain Sunday schools and have discarded most of the restrictions on dress with the exception of the bonnet.

The principal centers of the Old Order are Lancaster and Mifflin counties, Pennsylvania, Holmes county, Ohio, Lagrange, Elkhart, Howard and Davies counties, Indiana, Douglas and Moultrie counties, Illinois, and Washington and Johnson counties, Iowa, with smaller communities in many other places.

While these events above mentioned were taking place, the church in other parts of the country was being agitated by the appearance of a new sect from Switzerland—the so-called New Amish.

The "New Amish"

These "New Amish," as they are called in Illinois, or "Neu Täufer," as they are known in Ohio, or the Apostolic church, as they name themselves, are not a branch of the Amish as their name might suggest, but their early history both in Europe and America is so closely associated with that of the Amish that a brief sketch of this connection is not out of place here.[25]

The Apostolic church was founded by Samuel Frölich, a theological student at Zurich, who in 1832 was deposed from the ministry of the Reformed church in Argau. He immediately began to organize a church of his own. While engaged in this work he visited Emmenthal, and there was well received by Christian Gerber and Christian Baumgartner, two Amishmen who were dissatisfied with their own church. Two years later George Steiger, a disciple of Frölich's, and at that time a young man of twenty-one, appeared among the Amish of Emmenthal and organized a large church of sixty dissatisfied Amish, including Gerber and Baumgartner, and of a larger number of the national church. Steiger rebaptized all the new proselytes and taught that only those who followed his teaching could be eternally saved. All other teaching was false. The new sect grew rapidly and early manifested that seclusive and self-righteous spirit which has been characteristic of them to this

---

25. See Ernst Müller, Geschichte der Bernischen Täufer, p. 389.

day. They kept themselves from contact with the outside world as much as possible, and would not send their children to public schools, but established private schools. They followed to the letter the teaching of Luke 10: "Salute no man by the way."

In 1846 seven of these people came from Switzerland to Ohio, where they soon found their way to the Swiss Mennonites in Wayne county and secured a small following among them.[26] In 1852 several more appeared among the Amish of Lewis county, New York, and won over to their faith some of the Verklers, Fahrneys and others. From here one of the Verklers and a certain Weynet, one of the leaders from Switzerland came to Woodford county, Illinois, and began proselyting among the Amish. Their first converts were Joseph Graybil, who became their first minister in Illinois, John and Joseph Verkler, cousins of their namesake from New York, Peter Engle, one of the earliest settlers of Woodford county, and others who had been more or less dissatisfied with the church, and thus fell an easy prey to the proselyting zeal of the strangers. A small following was also gained in the Dillon creek settlement. Graybil was a zealous devotee of the new sect and labored unceasingly to win new converts. In 1862 he went to Butler county, Ohio, and established a small church among the Amish at that place.

Small congregations have since been organized in other states, but Illinois is still the stronghold of the sect. The growth at first was slow. By 1877 they numbered in all only eighty-nine members. But during recent years there has been a heavy immigration

---

26. See introduction to "Glaubens Bekenntnisz der Neuen Baptisten."

from Switzerland and now there are a number of large congregations in central Illinois, aggregating in all perhaps several thousand members.

In doctrine and practice this sect has been influenced somewhat by the fact that many of its earliest adherents came from the ranks of the Amish. They are thoroughly non-resistant, and have nothing to do with civil government. In dress they are extremely plain, but as a result of Swiss influence the women are permitted to wear plain hats instead of bonnets. In doctrine, however, they differ in several respects from the Amish. They baptize by immersion and observe the practice of feetwashing, although not in connection with the communion service. They are very exclusive and have as little business and social relation with others as possible. Religious association with other churches they have none whatever. They are forbidden by the rules of their organization to listen to the preaching or praying, or any religious exercise performed by a minister not of their faith, and for that reason they never attend the funeral services of even their nearest relatives if such relatives or friends were not members of their sect.

They make free use of the ban in their religious discipline, and insist on a rigid application of the practice of "shunning of such as are expelled. This practice shuts out an expelled member from all business, social and religious association with his former fellow-members. Frequently the ban completely disrupts the domestic relations of the family. Husband and wife are not even permitted to eat at the same table when one or the other has been excommunicated. The practice has worked havoc in a number of families in central Illinois. The most notorious case was that of Samuel Moser, who because of strained family relations was led to brutally murder his wife and three children several years ago. This case and several others similar to it have given the New Amish within recent years considerable notoriety, and called forth a great deal of unfavorable criticism throughout the state.

Hardly had the excitement which was caused by the appearance of the New Amish in New York, Ohio and Illinois subsided when another church trouble arose, this time in Adams county, Indiana. The principal in the factional strife here, which was the beginning of another church division, was Henry Egli, a minister of the Amish congregation in this county.

The "Egli" Defection

About 1864 Egli began to urge the necessity of a definite experience of regeneration in the religious life. His charges against the church were that it was too formal, that applicants for membership, especially among the younger element, were received with insufficient preliminary instruction, that the members were lacking in spiritual life and that they were not strict enough in maintaining the old customs, especially with regard to dress. Some of these charges no doubt were the result of personal contention, but that the church at this time frequently paid more attention to the letter than to the spirit there can be no doubt. Even though some of these charges were well founded, it cannot be said that Egli and his immediate followers reduced this formality to a very appreciable extent. It simply cropped out among them in another direction.

Egli in 1866 withdrew from the church and organized another which has since been called the "Egli" Amish by those of the organization which he forsook. A large part of the congregation in Adams county later became identified with the movement.

A few years later the same contention arose in Livingston county, Illinois, under the leadership of Joseph Rediger, bishop of the congregation. Rediger, with the assistance of Egli, who was a distant relative of his and with whom he had had some communication before on the subject organized a small "Egli" church out of a few of the dissatisfied members of the Gridley congregation.

In the Wesley City congregation almost the entire membership, including Michael Moseman, one of the pioneer bishops of the state, and Nicholas Roth, another minister, turned to the new faith. From these small beginnings have developed large congregations at Gridley and Groveland, Illinois, Berne, Indiana, Archbold, Ohio, and a number of smaller congregations in other states.

This church although spoken of as the Egli Amish by the members of the parent organization, calls itself officially the Defenseless Mennonite church. The name is somewhat misleading to those unacquainted with Mennonite history, since "defenselessness" is no more characteristic of this than of other branches of the Mennonite denomination. The name was officially assumed during the Civil war when in negotiating for a deed to the church property at Gridley this term was hit upon.

At first the Egli people were very strict in their

discipline and were more rigid in maintaining the old regulations with regard to dress than the Amish. They were quite exclusive and had little religious or social affiliation with the church from which they withdrew. They insisted on a definite "religious experience" and rebaptized all those that could not confess that they had been truly converted at the time of their first baptism, a confession which of course under the circumstances few could make.

During recent years, however, a marked change has taken place in the relation of the two organizations. The second generation of the Egli branch has assumed a more liberal attitude toward the old church, and the latter too has changed decidedly for the better, and so the two are again working in harmony in the interests of a broader Christianity.

Hard upon the Egli division followed the trouble between Joseph Stuckey and the general conference already mentioned. Stuckey was a bishop in the Rock creek, Illinois, congregation, and was one of the leading men in the church. He was intelligent, of strong personality, a writer of some ability, and talented with more than ordinary executive power. He was one of the leading spirits in the general conference, and was more liberal minded on religious questions than most of his fellow ministers. This brought him into friction occasionally with other leaders even before 1870, about the time when his troubles began.

Illinois Conference of Mennonites

Joseph Stuckey

About this time a certain Joseph Yoder, a member of Stuckey's congregation, a school teacher and a dab-

bler in verses, wrote a long poem which he published
under the title of "Die Frohe Botschaft."
"Die Frohe The leading thought in the poem was
Botschaft" that all men will be saved eternally and
none punished for their sins. This sentiment was rank heresy among the Amish and naturally aroused a good deal of resentment. The conference which met in Fulton county, Ohio, in 1870 discussed the question, What is to be done with those members who do not believe in future punishment? and finally resolved after a long discussion to expel such from the church if they persisted in their errors. Stuckey who evidently was of the same opinion as Yoder on this question refused to excommunicate the latter and thus ran counter to the decision of the conference. The next session, held in Livingston county, Illinois, took up in secret meeting the contention between Stuckey and his fellow ministers. A committee of seven was appointed to investigate the matter. Another committee of three—Abner Yoder of Iowa, Samuel Yoder and Moses B. Miller of Pennsylvania—was appointed to visit the churches in Illinois and report their condition at the next conference. The conference of 1872 met in Lagrange county, Indiana. After reading the report of the above committee which was carefully worded so as not to make any definite charges but was full of general admonition, Stuckey was requested to make a public confession. Stuckey was present at the conference but his name does not appear on the official register, being withheld at his own request, as he said that he was absent part of the time, and did not wish to subscribe to the proceedings with which he had nothing

to do. There is no evidence from the records that he made a confession. "Die Frohe Botschaft" again came up for discussion at this session. Several verses were read before the conference and it was again declared that all members holding such opinions as were expressed in the poem were to be placed under the ban.

In the meantime another committee consisting of J. K. Yoder, J. P. King and A. Yoder, all easterners, was appointed to visit the Illinois congregations and adjudicate the difficulties between Stuckey and Christian Ropp, another bishop in the same locality. In October of 1872 this committee visited Stuckey and among other questions asked him whether he acknowledged the author of "Die Frohe Botschaft" as a brother in the church. He replied in the affirmative and added that he had permitted Yoder to participate in the communion service. Whereupon the committee declared that they could no longer consider him in harmony with the church at large, and consequently they were obliged to withdraw from him and his congregation. Most of the churches in Illinois accepted the decision of the committee as final and it was announced in the various congregations that Stuckey and his congregation were no longer considered a member of the general conference. After this he was no longer present at the conferences which continued to be held for several years. There was no further formal division however. The Illinois congregations were independent of each other and each went its own way. But when in the eighties, the Western district conference was organized Stuckey's church was not

[Margin note: Eastern Committee]

included. Since then, his followers have been considered as a separate branch of the church.

This is the story as it appears in the conference reports. Of course this does not tell everything. Back of it all there were in addition to the contentions already mentioned, many petty jealousies and lack of forbearance on the part of various conference leaders. Stuckey was without doubt more liberal minded than most of the ministers of his time, but on the other hand many of the others, especially the easterners, were still addicted to formalities which have since been discarded. Had the Illinois congregations been permitted to settle the controversy in their own way it is altogether probable that there would have been no division.

As we saw, Stuckey's congregation stood by him in this contention. He also retained supervision over a small church at Meadows, which he had served as bishop before 1870. Soon after, he also organized a church near Washington among a number of members of the Partridge congregation who had become involved in a church quarrel. His brother, Peter Stuckey, had charge of this congregation for many years. Since then many of the old church have gone over the Stuckey following, which has grown continually from the first. There are at present twelve congregations in central Illinois and nearly as many more scattered throughout Ohio, Nebraska, Iowa and Indiana. The entire membership approximates two thousand.

The Stuckey Congregations

In 1899 these congregations organized a conference now known as the "Illinois Conference of Mennonites." Although a branch of the Amish church they disown the name as well as the term "Stuckey" Amish, by which they are commonly known among the old church, and have assumed the more comprehensive name of Mennonite.[27]

Conference Organized 1899

In doctrine this branch of the church does not differ from the main body. In their practices they are a little more liberal, especially with regard to dress. Women are permitted to wear hats instead of bonnets. Under the leadership of such men at Peter Schantz, Valentine Strubhar, Joseph King, Emanuel Troyer and Lee Lantz, all of them comparatively young men and talented, the church is making steady progress both in numbers and spiritual life.

Leading Men

---

27. This tendency manifests itself in all the branches of the denomination. All, with the exception of the Old Order Amish, are now assuming the name Mennonite. The factional names are used in this book merely for the sake of convenience and greater clearness.

CHAPTER IX

DURING THE REVOLUTION

The Mennonites during the Revolution were generally opposed to the war.[1] It was not because, like the Tories, they favored the English crown, but because they were antagonistic to all war and rebellion as inconsistent with their religious principles. Their attitude toward the questions at issue was generally one of neutrality, although at heart many of them may have secretly wished well to the cause of the colonies.

Opposition to War

How they were exempted by several of the col-

---

1. See Pa. Arch., V. 767. Also Governor McKean's letter to John Adams, written Jan. 7, 1814, quoted in Mass. Hist. Coll. Fifth Ser., Vol. IV. p. 506.

"Dear Sir—In your favor of the 26 of November last you venture to say that about a third of the people of the colonies were against the Revolution. It required much reflection before I could form my opinion on this subject, but on mature deliberation I conclude you are right and that more than a third of the influential characters were against it. The opposition consisted chiefly of Friends or Quakers, the Mennonists, the Protestant Episcopalians whose clergy received salaries from the Society for the Propagation of the Gospel in Foreign parts, and from the officers of the crown and proprietors of Provinces with their connections, adding the timid and those who believed the colonies would be conquered and that of course they would be safe in their persons and property from such conduct, and also have a probability of claiming office and distinction, and also the discontented and capricious of all grades."

onies in the early years of the war from active military service has been told elsewhere. This ex-
Fines and emption was secured, however, by the
War Taxes payment of a money fine, or in other cases by other service such as hauling provisions, and similar work.

That these fines were imposed and collected can be seen by an examination of the records of the war officials of that time. From Lancaster county in 1780 among others, the following fines are reported,[2]

	£
Martin Funk	50
John Shank	50
John Hostater	90
Michael Stauffer	110
Peter Yorty	110
John Hertzler	50

From Chester county are reported among others[3]

	£	d.	d.
John Buckwalter	26	12	10
Christian Holdeman	13	0	0
Matthias Pennypacker	55	5	1
David Buckwalter	55	5	1

These fines as well as the regular war taxes were not always paid willingly nor without some attempt to evade them. The question of war taxes
Fines led, as we shall see, to dissension among
Opposed some of the congregations of the Franconia conference district. Being a nonresistant people, many of them, like the Quakers, felt that to pay a fine or a special tax for the support of war was as inconsistent with their religious principles as to enlist in

---
2. Pa. Arch., Sec. Ser., VI. p. 433.
3. S. W. Pennypacker. Annals of Phoenixville, p. 118.

the army for actual service. How general this view was among the Mennonites it is difficult to say, but Christian Funk,[4] writing of the conditions at this time says,

> The majority of the ministers in the western part of Montgomery county were opposed to the payment of a new war tax of three pounds, and ten shillings which had been levied in 1777.

The Mennonites objected not only to service in the army and the payment of fines and occasional war taxes, but also to the new oath which soon after the Declaration of Independence was required of all subjects of the newly formed sovereignties. Pennsylvania, like all the other states required a new oath of allegiance from all its citizens. To the usual objections to oaths in general, the Mennonites added to this one in particular the fear lest it might obligate them to espouse the Revolutionary cause and to take up arms in its defense.

That this opposition was quite general is shown by a letter written in 1778 by a local official in Lancaster county to a Mr. Bryan, at that time the Vice President of Pennsylvania. He says,

> You will forgive these hints which will give your weightier affairs but little interruption to be used as you think they deserve. I have been in several parts of three counties of this state and find in all great complaints made by Menonists and Quakers, of the oath of allegiance now required of its subjects as including an obligation to fight contrary to their known principles. They say, a good many at leastp that they would affirm to be faithful subjects of the state endeavoring nothing to its hurt, but discover all they

---

4. See Christian Funk's Mirror for all Mankind.

knew doing so etc., in consistence with their principles against bearing arms. To require more of them they say is persecution. And though the constitution promises the rights of subjects to all denominations, presently oaths are required which they cannot take unless otherwise qualified, without renouncing their principles and they are sincere in their profession. I find some of our sensible Whigs say that an oath of allegiance suited to these people's known sentiments might increase the Friends of the state and lessen the warm discontents of many, and then levy more from them than others under the name of a Tax for the use of the state, but not fines, as they would enjoy greater advantages by not bearing arms. And such as refuse qualifications so framed would have no excuse but appear plainly to be enemies.[5]

Many of the Mennonites refused to take the oath and in some cases such as did take it were excommunicated from the church.[6] The state authorities, however, knowing them to be peaceable citizens and not enemies, were lenient toward them.

It is not at all surprising to find that the motives of the Mennonites in their refusal to support the war and take the new oath were misunder-
Misunderstood stood and frequently misconstrued. Not to take up arms against the British and not to take the oath were construed as indications of loyalty to the king of England and of unfriendliness to the state of Pennsylvania. As we have seen, both the state and colonial governments in Pennsylvania were generally considerate of Mennonite and Quaker consciences on these questions. Usually also Mennonites were not seriously disturbed by the radical patriots in their own immediate localities. Occasionally, however, when the heat and ex-

---

5. Pa. Arch, First Ser., VI. p. 572.
6. See case of Henry Funk. Pa. Arch., Sec. Ser., III. p. 463.

citement of the struggle was at its highest, attempts were made by irresponsible mobs to deprive them, like the Tories, of their property, and in other ways to intimidate them. A broadside now to be seen in Independence Hall in Philadelphia shows that even in Lancaster where their principles ought to have been best understood by their neighbors, they were not altogether secure from mob violence. The broadside was issued by the Committee of Inspection and Observation of Lancaster county under date of May 29, 1775, and reads in part as follows,

> The committee having received information that divers persons whose religious tenets forbid their forming themselves into military associations have been maltreated by some violent and ill disposed people in the county of Lancaster not-withstanding their willingness to contribute cheerfully to the common cause otherwise than by bearing arms, etc.

The Committee then proceeds to discourage such mob spirit.

In still another sense were the Mennonites, especially those of Southeastern Pennsylvania, brought face to face with the realities of war. Many of the campaigns for the possession of Philadelphia during the year 1777 and later were carried on within the Mennonite settlements. The little stone church at Germantown which had been built just a few years before occupied the very center of the battle-field in the battle of Germantown and it was from behind the stone fence which surrounded the churchyard that one of the leading British generals was shot. The famous winter quarters of 1777-78 were located in the Skippack region and in Chester county between Phoenixville and Valley Forge. A number of the

Mennonites in this region were impressed into the teaming service during this time.

Lancaster Raided — Lancaster county was not invaded by either army during these campaigns, but the commissary department of the Continental army during the later years of the war cast longing eyes upon the fair fields and well fed cattle of the rich farmers of this region. Horses and wagons were also frequently impressed into service for hauling provisions. The following list of articles impressed from the farmers of Manheim township in 1780 shows the valuation placed upon horses and wagons at that time in terms of continental money.[7]

Benjamin Landis..Wagin, cloth feeding trough, lockchain, water Bucket and Tar Pat. £1,080.
Henry Landis..Black horse, hind geers and two bags £1,800
Christian Meyers..1 Grey horse, hind geers and 2 bags, £1,300

The well to do German farmers of the county, most of whom were Mennonites, had no intention, however, of trading their stock for worthless continental scrip, if they could escape it. A member of the Commissary department in writing to President Reed in 1780 regarding the difficulty of getting cattle, says,

Your excellency will please observe that many of the wealthy Mennonists who live in the neighborhood of Lancaster, Manheim and Conestoga drive Flocks of cattle over the mountains in the Spring season to the great distress of the poor inhabitants. These men have them undoubtedly to spare, otherwise they would keep them on their farms and therefore ought to be taken from them. But this cannot be done without the assistance of 10 or 12 men to drive them

---

7. Pa. Arch., Sec. Ser., III. p. 376.

KINZER CHURCH

together which would be attended with extra charges. Therefore wait your Excellency's particular Instructions in the Premises[8].

As we have already seen, the majority of the Mennonites during the Revolutionary war, although in real sympathy with the cause of the colonists, yet tried to maintain a strict neutrality so far as taking active part in the controversy was concerned. Some, however, were out and out in sympathy with the Crown and after independence had been won a number of them, principally from Bucks and Montgomery counties, emigrated to Canada where they might still enjoy the rule of the king. Others again, were as eager to declare their sympathy for the American cause. Among these was Christian Funk of Indian creek in Montgomery county who in bringing this question to an issue was the author of the first division in the Pennsylvania church.

Funk Schism

The trouble began in 1776 when a meeting was held in Indianfield township (now Franconia) two-thirds of the inhabitants of which were Mennonites, for the purpose of choosing three men to represent the township in a general convention which was to determine whether or not Pennsylvania should join the other colonies in the war and whether she should acknowledge her independence from England. Most of the Mennonites who were present took the position that since they were a "defenseless people and could neither institute nor destroy any government, they could not interfere in tearing themselves away from the King." In this opinion Funk seems at the time to have concurred. But when during the following year

---
8. Pa. Arch. First Series. VIII. p. 38.

his fellow ministers felt that their nonresistant principles obliged them to refuse to pay a special war tax which had just been levied he disagreed with them. The fact that the prospects of American success at this time seemed gloomy may have had something to do with determining the attitude of the majority, for "the Congress and American Government," Funk says, was rejected as rebellious and the King acknowledged by my fellow ministers under the idea that Congress would soon be overpowered. I now began to say that we ought not denounce the American government as rebellious.

Funk contended that the tax ought to be paid and said, "Were Christ here he would say give Congress that which belongs to Congress and to God what is God's." Andrew Ziegler, the spokesman for the opposite party, replied, "I would as soon go to war as pay the three pounds and ten shillings."[9]

This was the beginning of a difference of opinion which soon spread among the churches of Montgomery county. Funk in the fall of 1777 was denied the right of communion, then soon after the right to preach and finally in 1778 he was excommunicated because, as he says, he paid the "three pounds and ten shillings and would not oppose Congress." He organized a small band of his followers into a church which gradually built up small congregations at Evansburg, Line Lexington, Towamencin and several other places.

In 1805 and again in 1806 Funk tried to heal the breach which he had helped to make in 1778, but he was not successful. After his death, his son, John, assumed the leadership of the "Funkites," as the sect was called. The organization never developed much strength. Meetings were held in the scattered con-

---

9. See Christian Funk's Mirror for all Mankind.

gregations for some time, but the sect began to decline and by 1850 became extinct. One of the chief causes of this decline, according to the author of the Funk Family history, was

allowing one John Herr, a heretic from Lancaster county, to preach among them and divide them, some taking sides with John Herr in his peculiar doctrines, and others opposing which caused a division among themselves a part adhering to the Herrites and a part opposing.[10]

Martin Boehm
About the time of the Funk schism, occurred also the apostasy of Martin Boehm. This event, while in no way the result of the Revolutionary war, yet occurred during that period of our story and may as well be told here as elsewhere. Martin Boehm was a grandson of Jacob Boehm who came to Pennsylvania in 1715 where he soon joined the Pequea settlement in Lancaster county. Martin was born in 1725 and when he entered manhood inherited the family homestead, one mile south of Willow Street. In 1756 he was ordained a Mennonite minister by lot, as was the custom at that time among the Mennonites. Four years later he was chosen in the same manner to the office of bishop. We know very little about his ministry until a few years later when he visited Virginia, and there came into contact with the so-called "New Lights." These New Lights were a by-product of the great religious revival which at that time was sweeping through the colonies. As a result of this revival a few of the churches of the several denominations of that day were divided into two classes, the New Lights, as those were called who laid great stress upon inward

---

10. A. J. Fretz. Funk Family History, p. 340.

experience and outward manifestation of the Spirit in religion, and the Old Lights, or those opposed to the revival and its methods. It was this wave of revival excitement which caught up this man, who had begun to preach, as he said, not because of inward conviction, but because he was formally chosen by lot. This must have taken place in 1761, for his son Henry, a well known pioneer Methodist preacher in Pennsylvania, says in his Reminiscences that in that year he (Martin) "found redemption in the blood of the Lamb and became a flame of fire and preached with the Holy Ghost sent down from Heaven. His success was wonderful and the seals of his ministry were numerous."[11] From this time on no doubt the relations between Boehm and his fellow ministers became strained, although we do not find that any definite action was taken against him until about 1775.

From an old manuscript written during the Revolutionary war and quoted by John F. Funk in his Mennonite Church and her Accusers we learn that after repeated efforts to reconcile Boehm with his congregation, the church finally expelled him on the following charges,[12]

1. Because he had too much intercourse and fellowship with professors who admit and allow war, and the swearing of oaths.

2. In this that he says that Satan is a benefit to mankind.

3. He said the Scriptures might be burned. The word is a dead letter.

4. He said that Faith cometh from unbelief, life out of death, and light out of darkness.

---

11. See Henry Boehm. Reminiscences of Rev. Henry Boehm.
12. John F. Funk. The Mennonite Church and her Accusers, p. 41.

BOEHM CHAPEL, in Lancaster county. Built 1791 by Martin Boehm. This building which is still standing is considered by the Methodists as their first church in Lancaster county, and one of the very first in the state. Boehm, the one-time Mennonite preacher and builder of the Chapel, lies buried near the building. The stone farthest to the right of the two large stones near the middle of the building marks his final resting place.

5. He said that the old men (bishops and ministers) lay so much stress upon the ordinances, viz., baptism and communion, and the people are thereby led to the Devil and not to God.

In the meantime the Methodists had just entered Pennsylvania, and began their preaching in Lancaster county. Boehm soon became attracted to them by their fervent appeals. In 1775 a Methodist "class" was organized in his home and his wife became one of the charter members. During the years immediately following, his house was frequently used as a stopping place for pioneer Methodist preachers, and he himself frequently preached with them. In 1791 he built a small chapel on his farm in which services were held. This building, which is still standing, is considered by the Methodists as their first meeting house in Lancaster county, and one of the very earliest in the state. Although working with the Methodists, yet Boehm did not wholly identify himself with their organization. He was rather for a time an independent preacher, laboring with any church which he found congenial.

A little later he became, in connection with Otterbein, a minister of the Reformed church, the founder of the United Brethren organization. The story of the beginning of this church is told briefly by Henry Boehm as follows:

Mr Otterbein's church was built on Howard's hill. My father and he met at Isaac Long's a few miles from Lancaster. Various denominations had been invited to meet there and my father preached the first sermon which was attended with peculiar unction and when he had finished, Mr. Otterbein arose and encircled him in his arms and exclaimed, "We are brethren." Shout after shout went up and tears flowed freely from many eyes, the scene was so pentecostal. Such was the origin of the United Brethren church.

In 1800 Boehm and Otterbein were both elected as the first bishops of an organization which grew up soon after the above mentioned episode. Boehm was re-elected in 1805. But in the meantime he had his name also enrolled in the Methodist class book. It is difficult to say just what his church connections were during this time. His own son says that in his later years he was a Methodist. He died in 1812 and lies buried near the little chapel which he built in 1791. The epitaph on the stone which marks his final resting place fittingly describes his checkered religious career.

> Here lie the remains of Rev. Martin Boehm who departed this life (after a short illness) March 23, 1812, in the 87th year of his age. Fifty four years he freely preached the Gospel to thousands and labored in the Vineyard of the Lord Jesus in Pennsylvania, Maryland and Virginia among many denominations but particularly the Mennonites, United Brethren and Methodists with the last of whom he lived and died in fellowship. He not only gave himself and his services to the church but also fed the Lord's prophets and people by multitudes. He was an Israelite in whom was no guile. His end was peace.

CHAPTER X

THE MENNONITES OF ONTARIO[1]

Emigration from Pennsylvania after The Revolution

As we have already seen, the attitude of the majority of the Mennonites toward the Revolutionary war was one of neutrality. Some, however, and especially those of western Bucks and Montgomery counties, while apparently neutral, yet at heart favored the cause of the king. The period of anarchy which followed the close of the war from the signing of the treaty of peace to the formation of the constitution naturally did not lessen the distrust of these loyalists, of the new government.

At the same time some of the younger and poorer people of Lancaster, Bucks, Montgomery and other of the older counties in Pennsylvania were looking for cheaper lands in newer regions, since the land in the southeastern part of the state had already all been taken up. Even before and during the war colonies had emigrated to Maryland, Virginia and across the

---

1. For the facts of this chapter the author is indebted largely to the work of Ezra E. Eby. A Biographical History of Waterloo Township. (1895)

Alleghenies into the valleys of the Juniata and Youghiogheny. Colonization societies were being formed for the purpose of helping the poorer members of the older communities to find homes.

Why not go to Canada? Here the home seeker might find large tracts of cheap uncultivated land not far from the American line, and the loyalist, an opportunity to serve the king. Among the first to turn their eyes in this direction were a small group of men from the region of Plumstead, Bucks county. As early as 1786[2] John, Dilman, Jacob and Stoffel Kulp, Franklin Albright and Frederick Hahn left this community for the Canadian border. Following up the Susquehanna through Pennsylvania and then through New York they crossed the Niagara River and located in Lincoln county, about twenty miles from Niagara Falls. In 1799 there were added to the colony Jacob Moyer, Amos Allbright, Valentine Kratz, Dilman Moyer, John Hunsberger, Geo. Althouse, Abraham Hunsberger and Moses Fretz; and in 1800 John Fretz, Daniel High, John Wismer and a number of others. Later several small scattered settlements were made to the south in Wellington, Welland and Haldimand counties.

Lincoln County Colony 1786

This settlement thus far was without a minister. In 1801 one of the members wrote to the church in Bucks county, asking that the parent church send a bishop to help them ordain a minister. The Bucks county church advised them to select one of their own number to serve them. In accordance with this

---

2. W. H. H. Davis, History of Bucks County.

advice Valentine Kratz became the first minister of the settlement in 1801; and Jacob Moyer in 1807 was elected as the first bishop.

In the meantime another colony had been established farther out on the frontier. In 1799 Joseph Schoerg and Samuel Betzner from Franklin county crossed Pennsylvania and New York for the region beyond the lakes. After spending the winter on the Canadian side near Niagara, the next spring they started out on a tour of investigation, and finally selected the fertile and heavy timbered regions along the Grand river in what is now Waterloo county as their future home. This part of the country was as yet still unsettled, except by a few fur traders who had erected temporary quarters along the banks of the river. Returning to Niagara, these two pioneers the next year took their families to the new country and located about thirty miles beyond Dundas, Waterloo county, which then marked the line of settlements. Schoerg bought a tract of land on the east side of the Grand river directly opposite the present village of Doon, and Betzner, on the west side near the present village of Blair.

Waterloo County

Later in the spring of the same year several families from Lancaster county came with teams, wagons, and household goods, and located in the same neighborhood. This second party was composed of Samuel Betzner, Sr., John Reichert and Christian Reichert.

These early settlers, although they had to endure all the hardships incident to pioneer life, yet were well pleased with their new homes and wrote encouraging accounts of the possibilities of the new country to their relatives and friends in Pennsylvania. As a result several families from Lancaster and Montgomery counties decided to emigrate to Canada the following year.

The first party to arrive in the spring of 1801 was composed of David Gingerich and family, and his father Abraham, from Lancaster county. These were followed a little later by a small company of seven families and several unmarried men from Montgomery county, composed of George, Abraham and Jacob Bechtel, Dilman Kinsey, Benjamin Rosenberger, John Biehn, Sr., John Biehn and several others. During the same year also came Michael Bear from York county. By the fall of 1801 there were twelve families in the new colony, all of whom located in the southern end of Waterloo township near the Grand river. During the following year, in 1802, the colony was increased by new settlers from Cumberland, Montgomery and other counties in Pennsylvania.

These early settlers had to endure many hardships. The journey from the Pennsylvania settlements to Waterloo covered about five hundred miles and had to be made over mountains, **Through Swamp** through forests and almost impass- **and Forest** able swamps. Some went on horseback, but most of them loaded their household goods upon the well known Conestoga wagons to which were hitched four or five horses. The earliest pioneers frequently took their cattle with them and thus were often supplied with milk on their way. The road, usually followed, led across the Allegheny mountains, thence up the Susquehanna through

New York and struck the Niagara a little below Buffalo. From here the journey was made to Dundas by the way of what is now Hamilton, and from there through the almost impassable "Beverly Swamp" to the new settlement along the Grand. The time occupied in the entire journey was usually from four to eight weeks.

This region was all heavily wooded and the first few years were occupied largely by the settlers in making small clearings from which they might extract a scanty living, and in erecting their first log cabins.

The land thus far had all been purchased from one Richard Beasley who owned the greater portion of Waterloo township. The purchasing price ranged from one to four dollars per acre. In 1803 it was accidentally discovered that the land owned by Beasley was under a heavy mortgage, amounting to twenty thousand dollars. Those who had already bought tracts became alarmed and feared lest their titles might prove defective. Others refused to buy, and immigration to the colony ceased for the year. Beasley now suggested to the settlers that they buy the entire township and assume the mortgage. The settlers accordingly in 1804 met and sent Samuel Bricker and Joseph Shoerg to Franklin and Cumberland counties for the purpose of raising the required amount among their relatives and friends. They were not successful here and Bricker returned to Canada. But Shoerg proceeded to Lancaster county in the hope that he might enlist the sympathy of the Lancastrians in the enterprise. Here too his efforts would have come to naught had it not been for old Hans Eby, who ad-

The Beasley Fraud

vised his brethren at a meting which had been called to consider this question, not to regard the matter from the standpoint of a profitable investment, but as an opportunity of helping their brethren in distress. His advice prevailed and soon a stock company was organized for the purpose of buying the entire township. Samuel Bricker was appointed as the agent for the newly organized company, and Daniel Erb as his assistant. These men then finally were given twenty thousand dollars, all in silver, which it is said was placed in a large box and carried in a light wagon to Canada, where finally it was turned over to Beasley, while the company in return received a clear title to 60,000 acres of land in what is now Waterloo county. A draft of the township of Waterloo was then made and a copy sent to the stockholders in Lancaster. The entire tract was then divided into lots of 448 acres each, and each stockholder drew by lot his share of the entire tract according to the amount of stock which he held.

Hans Eby's Advice

In the meantime, while these events were taking place in Waterloo, the tide of immigration had been turned in another direction. In the same year in which the Beasley fraud was detected, 1803, a new settlement had been made in York county, near Markham, about twenty miles north of Toronto. Among the first settlers here as well as one of the earliest ministers was Henry Weidman. The community now consists of four small congregations. Soon after this a stock company was also formed in Pennsylvania for buying land in Woolwich township, just north of Waterloo. Forty-five thousand acres were purchased in 1807.

BERLIN CHURCH, ONTARIO

After 1804 Waterloo township again received the largest share of Pennsylvanians. Each year brought a few new colonists from Lancaster, Berks, Bucks, Montgomery, Franklin and Cumberland counties. Some years brought more than others. During the war of 1812 immigration was light, but it was heavy in the years 1825 to 1829, owing to rather hard times in Pennsylvania during those years. By 1835 Pennsylvania immigration had practically ceased, although a few individuals continued to come as late as the American Civil war. The Canadian settlements also received a part of the European wave of immigration during the second decade of the century. The colonists of Waterloo located as we have seen on both sides of the Grand river near Doon and Preston. Later, settlements were made to the north until all of Waterloo township was occupied by the Mennonites and finally the community extended over Woolwich and surrounding townships. Berlin, the principal town in this region, was once called Ebytown and in 1827 it was given its present name upon the suggestion of Bishop Benjamin Eby. Among the most common names to be found among the descendants of these early pioneers to Canada are Bauman, Bechtel, Bergey, Betzner, Brubacher, Burkholder, Cressman, Detweiler, Eby, Erb, Gehman, Gingrich, Reist, Sherk, Stauffer, Groff, Hagey, Hallman, Kolb, Horst, Honsberger, Hoffman, Martin, Moyer, Musselman, Reichert, Weber, Schneider, Shoemaker, Shantz, Witmer, and others.

During the war of 1812 communication between the Canadians and their Pennsylvania brethren of course was broken off, and there was no immigration for a few years. The Mennonites were not forced to

War of 1812 serve in the army, but a number of them were impressed with their teams into the transportation service. None lost their lives while engaged in the service, but in the battles fought around the Niagara peninsula and in the vicinity of Detroit several of them lost their teams and wagons. After the war the British government made good these losses and paid them for actual service. Christian Schneider, Jr., was paid $5.00 per day for the time he served with a two horse team, and $8.00 for service with a four horse team.

First Minister We have already seen that at "The Twenty" Valentine Kratz was ordained to the ministry in 1801. When the settlers of Waterloo first organized for religious purposes we do not know, but no doubt very soon after their arrival. In 1806 Benjamin Eby came to the settlement. Three years later he was ordained to the ministry and in 1812 to the office of bishop. From this time till his death in 1853 he exerted a strong influence over the Canadian church. In 1813 the first Mennonite church building, made of logs, was erected on his farm and was known as the Eby church. Here bishop Eby preached and also taught school during the winter months for many years. He was a man of more than ordinary talent, and wrote several books the most important of which is a short history of the Mennonites.

The first conference of the Canadian church was held about 1820. By this time there were, as we have seen, three Mennonite communities in Ontario each of which became a conference district—Waterloo, Lincoln and York county.

The Mennonites of Canada like their brethren in the States did not escape internal dissensions. About the middle of the last century there be-
Internal gan a movement in Lincoln county in
Dissensions favor of more aggressive church work. The leader of the movement was Daniel Hoch, a minister, who advocated more modern methods of church work and especially greater evangelistic activity. The result of this agitation was a division of the church. Hoch soon affiliated himself with Oberholtzer in Franconia, who, as we shall see elsewhere, led a similar movement in Pennsylvania. Hoch warmly seconded the efforts of Oberholtzer in 1860 for the establishing of a general conference of a number of liberal independent congregations in America and was one of the organizers of that movement. His followers in Canada never developed much strength and in 1875 affiliated themselves with the "New Mennonites."

The New Mennonites, under the leadership of Solomon Eby and others, founded another schism which soon united with the Reformed Mennonites of Indiana.

The Martinites or "Woolwich people", as they are spoken of locally, include a number of members of the Woolwich township church who in the early seventies sympathized with Jacob Wisler of Indiana in his stand for conservative ideas. In the eighties these formally withdrew from the church and now form an independent body, although they associate in religious work with the Wisler Mennonites of Indiana.

The general awakening of the Mennonite church

throughout the United States in recent years of which mention is made elsewhere, also manifested itself in Canada. In 1890 the first Mennonite Sunday school conference in America was held in Canada. This was soon followed by the evangelistic work of John S. Coffman. Here Coffman did some of the best work in his entire evangelistic career. Immense crowds were drawn to the meeting houses to hear him preach. Large numbers of young people were converted and brought into the church, and the churches everywhere revived. From this time on the Canadian Mennonites have made steady progress both spiritually and numerically. There are at present about thirty congregations in the three districts in Ontario, most of which are in Waterloo county, with a total membership of about fifteen hundred.

Coffman's Work in Ontario

CHAPTER XI

THE MENNONITES DURING THE NINE-

TEENTH CENTURY

1.

Settlements in Ohio, Indiana, Illinois and the Western States

In the settling of the North West Territory the Pennsylvania Germans were not far behind the New Englanders, who established the first colony in Ohio in 1788. Just ten years after Marietta was founded a small group of Germans from Lancaster county, Pennsylvania, on a prospecting tour, floated down the Ohio, past the village of New Englanders to the Hocking river, then up that stream as far as what is now Fairfield county. Here a few years later was founded a little village called Lancaster in honor of the county from which these early settlers came. In this group there was at least one Mennonite, Martin Landis, who having returned to Pennsylvania,

Pioneers in the Hocking Valley

came back again the following year, 1799, and located two miles south of the town of Lancaster.[1]

Landis built a church on his land which was to be used, however, by all denominations. No Mennonite congregation was organized until several years later when a number of Mennonites came to this region from Virginia and Fayette county, Pennsylvania. Among these were Henry Stemen,[2] who located near the present town of Bremen in 1803. He was followed by families bearing the names Good, Brenneman, Beery, Lechrone, Culp and Steiner. In 1809 Stemen became the first resident minister of the congregation which must have been organized some time before this, and in 1820 he became one of the pioneer Mennonite bishops of Ohio. For over thirty years he performed the duties of his office—visiting his scattered congregations in various parts of central Ohio, and was finally succeeded by J. M. Brenneman.

The second settlement in the state was made in 1811 in what is now Stark county,[3] on the left bank of the Tuscarawas creek, near the present city of Canton. The first settlers in the community, the Lehmans, Rohrers, McLaughlins, Oberlys, Sheffards and others came from Lancaster county, Pennsylvania, and Rockingham county, Virginia. The first log church house was built in 1823. This was replaced by a larger building in 1874, but the congregation is now almost extinct.

Stark County

---

1. See A. A. Graham. History of Fairfield and Perry Counties.
2. See C. B. Stemen. History of the Stemen Family.
3. For much of the information regarding the church in Ohio I am indebted to manuscript sketches compiled by various local authorities for M. S. Steiner, of Columbus Grove, Ohio, and kindly loaned by him to me.

MENNONITES—NINETEENTH CENTURY

Soon after this, another colony was established along the borders of Mahoning and Columbiana counties. In 1815 Jacob Oberholtzer, a preacher from Bucks county, Pennsylvania,

Mahoning and Columbiana Counties

located on a farm in Beaver township. He was followed during the years immediately succeeding by the ancestors of the present Blossers from Virginia, Metzlers from Lancaster county, Lehmans from Franklin county, Detweilers from Montgomery county, Yoders from Bucks and Lehigh counties, and others from Southeastern Pennsylvania. All of these settled in the southeastern part of Mahoning county and near Leetonia in Columbiana county. In 1817 Bishop Jacob Nold from Bucks county, Pennsylvania, located near Leetonia and became the first Mennonite bishop in the state, and later organized congregations in Georgetown, Canton, Orrville and Wadsworth. In 1825 a meeting house was erected in the northern part of the settlement and in 1828 another in the southern. The community now comprises several congregations with an aggregate membership of about three hundred and is the largest Mennonite settlement in the state.

In the meantime a number of Mennonites from Switzerland had immigrated to Ohio. As we have already seen, the martial spirit engen-

The Swiss Immigrants

dered by the Napoleonic wars in Southwestern Europe during the early part of the nineteenth century drove many Mennonites and Amish from Switzerland and Southeastern France, and Germany, to seek homes in America, which at this time appealed especially to the Europeans as the land of opportunity for the oppressed. This immigration began about 1817 and continued until the early fifties. The Amish, as we saw elsewhere, began to arrive about 1820 and located principally in Butler and Fulton counties, Ohio, Canada, Lewis county, New York, Illinois, and Southeastern Iowa. The Mennonites settled in Ohio, Indiana, St. Clair county, Illinois, and Southeastern Iowa.

The Mennonites from the canton of Berne in Switzerland led this stream of immigrants.[4] In 1817 Benedict Schrag left for America, and arriving in Ohio not long after, located on a farm near Orrville, Wayne county. He wrote to his friends in Switzerland, urging them to cast their lot with him. In 1819 he persuaded Isaac Sommer, David Kirchofer, Peter and Ulrich Lehman to join him. These men left Berne in April and took ship for New York at Havre. After a voyage of forty-seven days they landed at New York from whence they came to Wayne county on foot by way of Philadelphia, Lancaster, Pittsburg and Canton. They all purchased land in the eastern part of the county in the very center of what later was called the Sonnenberg congregation. In 1821 seven families with several single men were influenced to join the new colony. These were followed by other small parties in 1822, 1824 and 1825. Between 1825 and 1835 the immigrants came in large numbers.[5] It soon

---

4. For a more detailed sketch of the Swiss settlement in Ohio see article by D. A. Schneck in Gospel Witness, Scottdale, Pa., for Jan. 1, 1908. See also History of Allen County by R. H. Harnson, Phila.
5. Among the Swiss immigrants to this locality from 1821 to 1825 were Bishop John Lehman, Abraham Zuercher, Jacob Bixler, Peter Hofstetler, Jacob Moser, John, Christian and Abraham Lehman, David and Samuel Zuercher, Ulrich, Jacob and Michael Gerber, Christian Beer, Peter and John Welty, John and Abraham Tschantz, John

became necessary to found new settlements. In 1833 Michael Neuenschwander, who had located in Wayne county in 1823, moved to Putnam county.[6] He was soon followed by others from Wayne and Holmes counties, and new arrivals from Switzerland. Here was organized what has since become a large and prosperous congregation, near Bluffton. About the same time also others moved to Adams county, Indiana, where there has since developed a large congregation. Some of these settlements have grown into large communities. The original Sonnenberg congregation has a membership of about four hundred, the Bluffton, about seven hundred, while the congregation at Berne, Indiana, numbers about seven hundred and fifty.

The Swiss Mennonites did not affiliate themselves with the main body of the American church. They brought with them from Switzerland, and maintained after their arrival, new customs, new forms of dress, and a strange dialect, all of which tended to separate them in religious worship from the Old Mennonites. The congregations at Bluffton and Berne, together with a part of the Sonnenberg church have within recent years affiliated themselves with the General Conference Mennonites.

In 1825 a number of Mennonites from South-

---

and Christian Wahley, Christian and Abraham Gilliom, Abraham Falb, Nicholas Hofstetler, Michael Boegly, John Lugibihl, David Baumgartner, Ulrich Sommer, Peter Schneck, David Althaus, Ulrich and Peter Moser, Bishop Daniel Steiner, Ulrich and Christian Steiner.—D. A. Schneck, in Gospel Witness, Jan. 1, 1898.

6. See Mennonite Year Book and Almanac (Eastern Mennonite Conference). 1907.

eastern Pennsylvania, bearing the names Overholt, Geisinger, Weidman, Leatherman, Rohrer, Hoover and Tintsman established a community near Wadsworth, in Medina county. This community in spite of the fact that it has been the battle ground of three church controversies during the last half century has since developed into several good-sized congregations.

Pennsylvanians in Medina County

In 1834 another settlement was made by Pennsylvanians, just south of the Medina county community, near Orrville in Wayne county. The first settlers were John Rohrer and Jacob Buchwalter, followed soon after by families bearing the names Horst, Brenneman and others.

During the next thirty years numerous attempts were made to establish congregations in the northwestern part of the state—in Wood, Seneca, Williams, Ashland, Clark, Franklin, Hancock, Allen and Putnam counties. With the exception of the last three, however, the congregations in this region never made much progress. The largest and most prosperous community in this part of the state is now near Elida, in Allen county. John Thut who came here in 1849 was for many years a prominent Mennonite bishop in the state.

Later Settlements in Northwestern Ohio

During all this time of early settlement numerous Amish communities were also being established within the state, but their story is told elsewhere.

The history of the church in Ohio differs very little from that of the same body in other states. Being among the earliest settlers in the state, the Mennonites experienced all the hardships of pioneer life. Their communities were small and scattered, and perhaps for this reason they were a little less conservative and more open to outside influences than the larger and older settlements from which they came in Pennsylvania. Within recent years especially, the Ohio conference has occupied a position well to the front in all educational, missionary and other progressive movements of the church at large.

New York.

In the meantime several small settlements had been made in Northwestern New York.[7] It is said that one Johannes Roth from Lancaster county located near what is now Williamsville, in the northwestern part of Erie county, before the Revolutionary war. It does not seem, however, that he was immediately followed by others. But by 1824 families by the name of Leib, Lehman, Martin, Frick and others had settled near by. John Lapp became the first minister. Several other families came later, including Jacob Krehbiel, who arrived from Weyerhof in Rheinpfalz in 1831.

A little earlier, in 1810 and 1811, another colony had been located a little farther north. Hans and Abraham Wittmer from Lancaster county had settled in Niagara county. These communities never made much progress and are now nearly extinct.

---

7. John Krehbiel, Clarence Center, N. Y., in D. K. Cassel's **History of the Mennonites**.

Indiana

The first Mennonites to come to Indiana, as just indicated, were the Swiss who settled in Adams county in 1835. The Old Mennonites located **Swiss in Adams** in the state a few years later than **County 1835** either the Swiss or the Amish and in the same county as the latter,—Elkhart.[8] In 1843 one John Smith from Medina county, Ohio, visited the county and de- **John Smith in** cided to locate in Harrison town- **Elkhart County 1843** ship. He went back to Ohio but two years later returned with his son Joseph, Christian Henning and Bishop Martin Hoover, all from Medina county. In the Spring of 1848 Christian and Jacob Christophel and Jacob Wisler came from Columbiana county, Ohio, and on Ascension day of that year the first meeting was held in a log school house. Sixteen persons were present on this occasion. During the course of the same year twenty-four families, including those by the names of Hartman, Holdeman, Moyer, Rohrer, Weaver, Nussbaum, Freed, Weldy, Yoder, Brundage and Smeltzer from Wayne, Medina and Columbiana counties, all settled in the southwestern part of Elkhart county. The next year the first meeting house, now known as the Yellow Creek church, was erected.

In 1853 a small colony of Dutch led by R. J. Schmidt and N. J. Symensma immigrated to the same

---

8. See Family Almanac, Elkhart, Ind., 1876.

locality from Holland. For a number of years these
people held separate services in their own
The Dutch language, but finally most of them joined
Colony what is now known as the Salem congregation, and their descendants now make
up a large part of that community.

From these beginnings there have developed eleven congregations in Elkhart and surrounding counties with a membership of about eleven hundred. There are also several congregations in Michigan which are included in the Indiana Conference district.

The church in this state, being composed largely of Ohioans has differed very little in its development from the church in Ohio. Some of the leading men among the Mennonites in the state during the last half century have been Jacob Christophel, Daniel Brenneman, Jacob Wisler, John S. Coffman and John F. Funk, none of whom, however, were born in Indiana.

Two enterprises which have grown up in the state have exerted considerable influence upon the entire
body of Mennonites. One, the Men-
Influence of the nonite Publishing Company located
Indiana Church at Elkhart, has done more than any
other agency for the last forty years through its church papers and other publications to inspire Mennonites of all branches with a deeper respect for their common faith and history and with higher conceptions of religious duty. The other, Goshen College, recently established at Goshen, is beginning to exert considerable influence upon every phase of religious and intellectual activity, especially among the younger element in the church. Neither

of these institutions, however, can be claimed by the churches of Indiana. Both began as individual enterprises, and both have very largely been under the control of men who originally came from without the state.

Illinois

Mennonites settled in Illinois even before they came to Indiana. In the Spring of 1833 Benjamin Kindig, a member of the original **Kindig Settles in** Lancaster county Kindig family, to- **Tazewell County** gether with his family left his home in Augusta county, Virginia, to seek better opportunities for himself on the cheaper lands of Illinois.[9] Loading all his worldly possessions on three wagons, he began his journey overland through Kentucky, Indiana and Illinois for his new home. In October of the same year, after a journey of eight hundred miles which was made in seven weeks, he reached what was then known as Hollands Grove in Tazewell county.

Kindig was a Mennonite and was soon followed by other families from the same region in Virginia, who although not of the same faith at that time were undoubtedly of Mennonite descent. Soon after, other Mennonites came. In 1837 Peter Hartman arrived from Bavaria, Germany, by way of Lancaster county, Pennsylvania. From the same county came also Ben Kauffman, in 1842. Ben Brubaker arrived from Richland county, Ohio, in 1851. These were followed by families bearing the names Althaus, Hirstein and others. The first minister and bishop was one Yost

---

9. See Journal of David Kindig.

Bally, who had come to Illinois very early from Pennsylvania. Not much is known of his early life as a minister except that for many years he was the pioneer bishop of the early settlements in the state. He was later assisted by Henry Baer, who afterward became the first preacher in the congregation which was established in Livingston county. This first congregation in Illinois never prospered. Its membership has always remained small. Nearly all the descendants of the earliest settlers have left the church. Among these are the Kindigs, Kauffmans and Brubakers, names which today are well known in central Illinois.

Soon after, beginning about 1842 several families immigrated from Bavaria and located near Galena in Jo Davis county. The first to come was Henry Musselman. He was followed some years later by Johannes Baer, Peter Neuenschwander and others. A congregation was organized but had a feeble growth.

Jo Davis County

Another settlement of Bavarians and other Germans was made a little later, from about 1843 to 1860 in St. Clair county, near Summerfield. Among the earliest immigrants were Jacob Pletcher, 1843, Christian Baer, 1844, and Jacob Leisy, 1852. At this time, from about 1840, many of the German immigrants located in Iowa. Some of these moved to Summerfield between 1855 and 1860. Others came later from Germany and the community has since grown to large dimensions. This congregation has been one of the most progressive in America and has had among its pastors some of the ablest men in the entire church. In 1861 it formed, together with

Bavarians in St. Clair County

three congregations in Iowa, the General Conference of Mennonites of North America. It has ever since held an influential position in that organization.[10]

About the same time, also in the forties a small settlement was begun in Stephenson county, near Freeport. Among the earliest families to locate here were those of Godfrey Groff, John Brubaker, and Martin and Samuel Lapp from Clarence Center, New York. Others came later from Canada and Pennsylvania. The first resident minister was Martin Lapp, who also later became the pioneer bishop of Missouri.[11]

Stephenson County

In 1858 four families, those of Abe Harshbarger, Samuel Graybill, Samuel Harshbarger and John Heckelman came from Virginia to Livingston county, and located on what was then still a raw prairie near the present town of Cullom. These were soon followed by others from Grundy county, Illinois, where a settlement had been formed some time earlier but which has since disappeared, and from Woodford county.

The Cullom Congregation

During this time too a number of families had located in Whiteside county, near Sterling. Among the first settlers were Jacob Snavely, Leonard Hendricks, Henry Heckler, and others, principally from Bucks and Lancaster counties, Pennsylvania. This has since grown to be the largest Mennonite congregation in the state.

Settlement Near Sterling

---

10. For information regarding this settlement I am indebted to Rev. C. van der Smissen of Summerfield, Illinois.
11. John Horsch, in Herald of Truth for December 1, 1891.

In 1865 William Gsell from Franklin county, Pennsylvania, settled near Morrison. He was followed by Henry Nice and several other families and a church was organized in 1868.

In this same year also was organized near Sterling a congregation of Reformed Mennonites who had come from Pennsylvania.

No new communities were started in the state after 1865. By that time the states farther west afforded greater attractions for such Easterners as were seeking cheaper lands and broader opportunities. The Old Mennonite church in Illinois has never grown to large proportions. This was due partly to the fact that the various congregations have been scattered throughout the state and have come from different localities in the East and from Europe, and thus having little in common but their faith, they did not unite their efforts to extend their cause. There are at present six congregations with a total membership of scarcely four hundred.

Western States

Although the Amish had located in Iowa as early as 1839, few Mennonites from the older states seem to have crossed the Mississippi before the Civil war.[12] In Missouri a small colony had been established in Shelby county during the fifties. In Iowa also quite a number of immigrants from Bavaria and the Palatinate had located in the southeastern part of the state

---

12. For more detailed information regarding the recent settlements and history of the Mennonites and Amish in the western states the reader is referred to Hartzler and Kauffman's Mennonite Church History.

during the early forties and fifties.[13] The three congregations which resulted from this German settlement as we have seen were among the charter members of the General Conference of Mennonites.

These two settlements, however, with perhaps several individual members in other parts were the only Mennonites to be found west of the Mississippi before 1860.

Soon after the war there was considerable immigration of all classes into these western regions, and among some of these settlers were several

Missouri bands of Mennonites. In Missouri small colonies were planted in Shelby, Cass, Moniteau, Morgan, Chariton, Cedar, Hickory and Jasper counties. Some of these communities were hardly formed, however, before they were again broken up. The hard times of '73 together with the poor judgment which some had exercised in the choice of their lands drove some back to their eastern homes, and others to Kansas where they fared even worse than they had in Missouri. For a number of years the church decreased in membership, but finally with what may be called the general awakening of the Mennonite church all over the country during the early eighties, the church in Missouri was also given a new lease of life. With the help of eastern evangelists, foremost of whom was John S. Coffman, old communities were revived and new ones established.

---

13. In 1845 John Miller, one of the pioneer Mennonite ministers of the state, and Henry Leisa were cruelly murdered in their log cabin by a gang of robbers. The leader of the robbers was finally executed. The trial was given wide publicity at the time.

Iowa In Iowa the earliest Old Mennonites were found in Page county and later in Keokuk county, which now contains the only congregation in the state.

Kansas and Nebraska Settlements in Kansas and Nebraska were begun about 1870. Henry Yother, a Pennsylvania bishop was one of the first to locate as far west as Nebraska. During the years immediately following, others, principally from Pennsylvania and Virginia, settled in Marion and McPherson counties, Kansas. About the same time also several families of the "Holdeman" branch of the church and large numbers of Russians came to Kansas, but of these we have spoken elsewhere. Later new congregations were formed in Osborne and Harvey counties, Kansas, and in Adams county, Nebraska.

The early settlers in these states had to endure many hardships during the early days. Many were poor and had located on homesteads. They lived in sod shanties and often were able to eke out a bare existence. Hot winds and grasshoppers drove some back to their former homes in the East or other more favorable parts. But others remained and have since become fairly prosperous.

From these states and from some of the churches in the older states small communities have within recent years been established in Idaho, Oregon, North Dakota, Colorado, Oklahoma and Texas. Most of these congregations are small. The entire membership of the Old Mennonite church west of the Mississippi is hardly more than fifteen hundred.

The reader has perhaps already been struck with the fact that the Mennonites and Amish have everywhere appeared among the pioneers in the settlement of the unoccupied lands of our country. By founding Germantown in 1683 they not only became pioneer settlers in Pennsylvania, but established the first regular German settlement in America. In 1710 they were the first white settlers of the Conestoga region and followed hard on the heels of the Scotch-Irish huntsmen who had blazed the way for the first permanent settlers. Before 1750 they appeared in the Shenandoah Valley with the earliest Germans to venture into that region. In 1772 they crossed the Alleghanies and established one of the earliest communities in the valley of the Juniata. Again before the Revolutionary war they appeared among the first settlers in Southwestern Pennsylvania, near the headwaters of the Ohio.

Mennonites as Pioneers

In Ohio they ascended the Hocking river and located in Fairfield county just ten years after the founding of Marietta. In Illinois they began to clear the timber along the banks of the Illinois in 1831, just ten years after the first log cabin had been erected in that part of the state. In Iowa in 1839 they located in the southeastern part of the state before the raw prairies had ever been occupied by white men. And so all through the West and the Northwest—in Kansas, Nebraska, the Dakotas, Oregon, Oklahoma and the Canadian Northwest, wherever new lands have opened up for settlement there the Mennonites have been among the first to put up their log cabins and sod

MENNONITES—NINETEENTH CENTURY

shanties, and among the first to organize pioneer churches.

2

Schisms

No other religious body has been divided into so many factions as has the Mennonite denomination.

Causes of Schisms The cause is to be sought partly in the form of church government and partly in the spirit and the character of the people composing the church. The congregational form of government permits each congregation to develop such religious practices and customs and to a certain extent such opinions as it thinks fit. This is destructive to uniformity, for uniformity is much more easily maintained where the entire body is controlled by a central authority. 1. The Mennonite as well as the Anabaptist faith before it always fostered a strong spirit of individualism. From the beginning, Mennonites were taught that each individual must interpret the truth as expressed in the Bible for and by himself, not by a priest. This spirit of independence, while it tends toward the development of the strongest character, yet necessarily does so at the expense of uniformity and harmony. 2. As a class the Mennonites have come from the humbler walks of life and were not trained to subordinate the nonessentials to the broader and more important interests of life. 3. And finally they were thoroughly religious and took their religion seriously. Hence such convictions as they had they clung to persistently. Several divisions took place in Holland, Germany, and Switzerland during the seventeenth and the eighteenth centuries. Some of these, however, were again united.

The Reformed Mennonites[14]

The first schism of the century in America must be laid to the account of John Herr, the founder of the Reformed Mennonite church.[14] The history of this sect really begins with the excommunication of the father of John Herr, Francis Herr, of Lancaster county. Francis, who was born in 1748, was the son of a well known Mennonite minister of that day and was himself a member of the organization. During his later years, however, he became dissatisfied with the church and finally near the close of his life he became involved in a dispute with several of his fellow members which resulted in his excommunication on the alleged ground that he had taken undue advantage of a neighbor in the sale of a horse.[15]

Being evidently of a religious turn of mind, however, he, together with several others who had a grievance against the congregation of which they were members, Abraham Landis, Jacob Weaver, David Buckwalter and several others held meetings for religious purposes in their houses. Although no attempt was made to organize a separate church, these meetings were kept up until Herr's death in 1810.

John Herr, now a young man of twenty-eight, who had never been a member of the Mennonite de-

---
14. For a complete history of the Reformed Mennonites from their own point of view see Daniel Musser's The Reformed Mennonite Church (1873). John F. Funk published a reply to Musser's book in his Mennonite Church and Her Accusers (1878).
15. See letter of Susannah Herr in J. F. Funk's Mennonite Church and her Accusers, p. 110.

nomination, now after the death of his father became
"convicted of sin" and began to attend the meetings
of his father's associates. Being a man of some influence
he soon assumed the leadership of the small
group. John Herr, prejudiced against the Mennonites
by his father, would not cast his lot with them, while
his associates had already left the church. And so the
logical result of these meetings was the organization
of a new body. This took place finally in the spring
of 1812 in the house of John Herr, in Strasburg township,
Lancaster county, when Abraham Landis, who
had already been baptized as a Mennonite, now baptized
Herr, who in turn baptized Landis and Abraham
Groff. Immediately Herr was elected bishop, Landis
preacher, and Groff deacon of the new organization.
Thus was launched what soon became known as the
Reformed Mennonite church among themselves, but
among others as the "New Mennonites" or frequently
as "Herrites." Others, chiefly relatives and friends of
the charter members joined the organization. Meetings
were at first held in dwelling houses, school
houses and barns.

Herr, whose mind it is reasonable to suppose had
been poisoned against the Mennonites by his father
now in seeking an apology for the organization of a
new sect began a bitter attack upon the church, his
main contention being that it had become, since the
days of Menno Simons, a dead, spiritless and corrupt
body, and that its ministers were no longer the true
ministers of God. In one of his controversial pamphlets
appears the following rather elopuent, although
unjust paragraph in which he compares the Mennonites
of the days of Menno Simons and Dirck Philip

with those of his own generation, very much to the discredit of the latter:

Therefore I will direct thee, my dear reader, to them. Search the above mentioned writings with an unprejudiced heart, and spiritual mind, and observe how they pictured the church of Christ and how gloriously they set it forth by the testimony of Apostolic truth and Divine power, and which also their church members testified by their fruits and sealed with their blood; and when thou hast rightly apprehended this truth, then look over also on the present community with a spiritual eye, and view their spiritual life: their arrogant deportment, and their careless heart in Divine things, their insatiable world spirit, their dealing and their way, how sensual it is in every point, almost through the whole of them. And when thou hast observed this, then go a little further, where thou wilt find a great many defenseless, unarmed men. Then ask the judge and the attorney, they will tell thee that some are engaged in strife and law-suits, as much as others. And go and ask the debtors and criminals; they will tell thee that they see none more frequently on the seats of judgment passing sentence upon them and assisting to judge them, than these. Then ask the tavern keepers and they will also tell thee that many resort thither who are lovers of spirituous drinks, and from which even some of their teachers are not free; and if thou wouldst ask the race riders and their like they would tell thee that they also have some as spectators, as well as others. And if thou wilt search all of these fruits impartially according to the Gospel, then thou wilt soon find that they falsely term themselves the church of Christ; and so far as the evening is from the morning, or darkness from light, so far are they separated from our first reformer's doctrine or the community of Christ. And it is to be feared that the candlestick is removed from them, that they cannot see; and even if they do see it and do not repent, it will ultimately be taken from them because they will not receive the truth which is yet offered to them.[16]

---

16. Quoted from Herr by J. F. Funk in Mennonite Church and her Accusers, p. 14.

Daniel Musser who later became the leading defender of the sect continued Herr's policy of denunciation and in his history makes these interesting charges against the Mennonites:

From such persons as were friendly to the church, I learned in my early youth, that at the time alluded to, viz: the latter part of the last and the beginning of the present century, the members of the church were, in regard to inward or spiritual life, as ignorant, cold and dead as any carnal, unconverted person could be. It was the custom generally, that when their children would grow up to years of maturity, they were baptized and received into the church; that their preachers or teachers were altogether inexperienced, and ignorant in spiritual matters; and as a consequence, their preparatory instruction, and examination was a mere matter of form. They had neither the knowledge of sin or righteousness. Their parents belonged to the church and they were told that they also should be joined to it. There was nothing in the step which forbade the enjoyment of what the flesh could have life and glorification in, and they generally agreed to the proposition of their parents. The natural result of such a course was a carnal, cold and senseless religion. The public service was generally cold and formal, and private religious exercises was something almost unknown. They had their amusements and pastimes in rustic sports and plays, telling stories, jesting and making fun generally. They were generally what the world accounts moral, industrious, frugal and honest. But as there are always dispositions which tend to extravagance in conduct and behavior, there were not wanting many instances where the conduct rather exceeded the bounds of propriety; but there were so many precedents where these were passed over without notice, that they had to be very flagrant, if any notice was taken of them by the church authorities; and if notice was taken, it was in a mere formal manner which excited more merriment and sport in the church, than grief and sorrow. At that time spirituous liquor was more freely used in all families than at present; and inebriation was a thing not at all uncommon, and had to be very aggravated if any notice was taken of it.

Cases were related to me, where members got outrageously disorderly and no notice was taken to it.

It was a very customary thing, at the time we refer to, for the younger members to meet together on Sunday afternoon, from church service, and spend the afternoon in such sports as wrestling, jumping, running foot-races, playing ball, or whatever sports and games of the kind were in vogue at the time. The older members, with preachers would look on as spectators, and had for a proverb, "Honorable sports or diversions no one can forbid." At their marriages, feasting, drinking, and noisy mirth were carried to great extremes.

At that time the old-fashioned fairs were annually held at all the towns of any size, even down to small villages. At Lancaster, the gatherings were usually very large. Numbers of the members of the church attended also. There was, as may well be supposed, all kinds of wickedness and ungodly deeds practiced there. I have no information how far the members of the church took part in these acts of wickedness, but by their presence they showed them such countenance as tended to uphold and support them. The old portion of the community usually attended the second day, when many of the elderly members also attended. It was the custom of these old men to have their bottle of wine, round which they would sit, and often become partially intoxicated, and sometimes considerably more than partially. At this time nearly all attended elections, and many of them participated very actively in electioneering, to further the chances of their favorite candidate. This I have myself seen, and heard one say openly that he had on one occasion voted twice at the same election. These things were not of accidental or private occurence. They were common, open and known to the world; and well known to the church also, and even some of their preachers were not free from the charge.

They still as a general thing, were plain in their dress and manner of life. They also still professed to be nonresistant, and refused to swear; but they very grossly violated their nonresistance, by acts tending to countenance and abet warfare, and more especially, by seeking redress of grievance at law, and defending themselves at law against claims which they considered just. This was violating a very decided principle of Menno Simons' profession. The washing of feet if not rejected, was at least practically omitted for many years. The kiss of peace was very little, if at all practiced. The refusal to hear the service, or join the worship with those who reject and refuse to obey the plain commands of the Gospel, together with avoiding excommunicated members, both of which Menno so strenuously upheld, they rejected altogether and do so still, to the present day, in our part of the country. A church that does not walk in the love of God, must be destitute of the Spirit, and consequently a dead body. If the members of this church lived and walked as we have related that tradition reports they did, they certainly were not obedient to Christ.[17]

Of course it is to be expected that such partisans as Herr and Musser should fail to find any good in the Old Mennonites, but see only their faults which they have unduly magnified. It is true that in some respects the church in 1800 was more addicted to the forms of religion than now, and some of the charges made by these men may not be altogether unfounded, but that the whole body was hopelessly corrupt is an accusation that could come only from such a bitter and ultrapuritanical spirit as that of John Herr's. That the new sect which he founded was even more formal than the church which he denounced, but of which he never was a member can be seen by an examination of the discipline and religious practices of the new body.

In doctrine and practice the Reformed Mennonites have borrowed much from the main body. As is true of most of the other factions which have separated from the church, so here the differences between Herr and his friends, and the church were more of a personal than of a doctrinal character. And so the new organization has deviated very little from the funda-

---

17. Quoted in Mennonite Church and her Accusers, p. 10.

mental doctrines of the Old Mennonite body. In some of their practices, however, they have carried several of these principles to extreme length. They are still severely plain in their dress, and in the furnishings of their houses. They believe in a rigid application of the ban and the avoidance, and are very exclusive. They consider it a sin to worship with those who are not members of their own organization, or even to listen to the preaching of ministers of other denominations. In this respect they resemble the so-called "New-Amish" of Illinois.

In numbers they have not grown strong. Lancaster county is still the stronghold of the sect, the largest congregations being in Lancaster city and near Landisville. They also have a small number of congregations scattered throughout other counties and states. Their influence has not been great, but in Lancaster county there was often much bitter feeling for many years between the "New" and the "Old" Mennonites.

The Oberholtzer Schism

The next church division commonly spoken of as the Oberholtzer schism,[18] appeared first in Montgomery county, Pennsylvania, in 1847. To appreciate the

---

18. The principal printed sources of information regarding this controversy are to be found in several pamphlets written by Oberholtzer, and in a brief of an appeal to the Supreme Court of Pennsylvania, in 1877 which was printed in 1883. This appeal was the result of a lawsuit between the two factions for the possession of the Mennonite meeting house at Boyertown, and contains the statement of Oberholtzer himself and others regarding the events of 1847. A copy of this printed appeal can be found in the library of J. F. Funk, Elkhart, Ind.

reasons for Oberholtzer's withdrawal from the church one needs to remember that the Mennonites in this part of Pennsylvania, the Franconia conference district, were at this time still very conservative in regard to all religious as well as secular customs and practices. Out of this ultra-conservatism and partly because of it there developed a small element of ultraliberalism. The two sides came into conflict and the natural result was another division. The following extract from an article which was written recently from the ultra-liberal point of view by one no longer a member of either branch of the denomination, perhaps states fairly well a few of the conflicting interests of the time. This writer, speaking of the customs of that day says,

My father was an ardent Whig, and he supported the measures that looked for the lightening of the burdens the country was under.

He attended the township primaries, the county conventions that framed the ticket, and attended political meetings, believing as a good citizen it was his duty to do so. He was waited upon by minister Eli Landis and elder John Gotwals, warning him of having offended the rules of the meeting, assuming that such was the duty of the people of the world. This may be said to be the beginning of church troubles.

It was about this time when linen covers on dearborns were giving way to black oilcloth covers. When my father availed himself of a black oilcloth cover for his dearborn he was charged with violating a long established custom of the Mennonites in making such a change; and when a year or so later he had elleptic springs put on the running gears of his carriage he sinned even more grievously. Then too came the charge that his children did not conform to the style and dress of the Meeting. Though my father always wore the Mennonite garb, he laid no stress on it and allowed his boys and girls to dress like others around them. I remember it was under discussion that my sisters must wear caps at meeting, and be otherwise plain in dress. Other matters came up, such as forbidding marrying outside of the denomination, attendance on civil duties, such as voting at election, resorting to process of law to recover property, favoring liberal education, etc. I remember a deep impression was made on me by these outside restraining influences to my ambition in striving to obtain an education, as father was charged with being worldly minded and allowing too much latitude to his children, and thus also influencing others growing up around him.

My father was regularly ordained to the ministry on New Year 1847, some months before the split took place. My uncle, John Hunsicker, who was then bishop in the district comprising Skippack, Methacthen, Providence and Zieglers (now Gotwals) died in the autumn of 1847, and my father became bishop of the above named district.

This continued and intensified opposition by the Mennonites as referred to above, and perhaps some I have omitted, culminated in a schism or split at the conference at Franconia in May, 1847, when John Hunsicker, my uncle, John H. Oberholtzer, William Landis, Israel Beidler and my father Abraham Hunsicker, ministers ordained as Mennonites, were literally put out of the meeting for holding liberal views in advance of the church.[19]

Among the liberal minded men of the church at the time was a young school teacher and minister by the name of John H. Oberholtzer. Oberholtzer was born in Montgomery county in 1808. At the age of sixteen he began to teach school, and at thirty-four he was ordained to the ministry in the Swamp church. Being a young man with perhaps a little better education than his fellow ministers and of a more progressive spirit, he did not always work in harmony with them.

---
19. Henry A. Hunsicker, in Mennonite Year Book and Almanac, for 1907.

His troubles began soon after he entered the ministry. Among the prescribed customs for the ministers of those days was the wearing of the so-called "regulation" coat, which was collarless and of a prescribed cut. This, Oberholtzer together with a few others refused to do, but continued to wear his usual dress. In speaking of this matter some time later he himself says,

Soon after I began to preach some of the members were displeased with the way I was operating, and for different reasons. One because I did not change my coat from what it was before; some thought it unbecoming for me to wear a collar on my coat, or to have buttons on both sides. Most objections were made against the form, some contending that it ought to be round. But as the Mennonite creed did not say what form of coat the minister had to wear, in view of the Gospel I exercised my own privilege as to what would be appropriate and continued to wear my usual dress.

The question was finally taken up by the Franconia conference which in 1844 decided in favor of the conventional coat, and further declared that all who disregarded this ruling would be denied the right to vote in the conference. Oberholtzer refused to comply, but the next year declared that he would wear the coat provided the resolution of 1844 were withdrawn, which of course the conference refused to do. Thus the quarrel on this and perhaps other questions continued until the spring of 1847 when matters were brought to a crisis at the spring meeting of the conference. To the old subject of dispute there was now added another. Heretofore no records had been kept of the conference sessions. Neither had there been any constitution nor by-laws for the regulation of its proceedings. Oberholtzer, feeling that both would serve the best interests of the conference drew up a constitution which he first read to several of his friends and then submitted it to the conference in the spring session. The majority of his fellow ministers, however, either because they objected to any departure from the old methods of work, or because they had lost patience with Oberholtzer, who for some time had not been in good standing among them (although at this meeting he appeared with the conventional coat) refused to consider his draft by a vote of 60 to 16. Oberholtzer and his friends, however, insisting upon thrusting their constitution upon the conference again submitted it at the fall session of the same year. Being again refused a hearing, Oberholtzer with fifteen other ministers and deacons from the western end of the district withdrew from the Franconia conference and Oberholtzer was at the same time expelled from the conference, and on October 28, 1847, the party met in the old Skippack church and there organized a new conference.

This is the story of the division as it is told by Oberholtzer and others who lived at the time, and as it lives in tradition. But the real cause of the trouble lay deeper than in a difference of opinion over the cut of a coat or the adoption of written by-laws for the conducting of conference sessions. These disputes were mere superficial evidences of more fundamental differences between Oberholtzer and his friends on the one hand, and the majority of the Franconia Mennonites on the other. Judging from the statement of principles which the new body drew up soon after their formal withdrawal, the two parties were irreconcilably at variance in their doctrinal views. The new organization declared in favor of open communion, and a loose interpretation of the ban. They expressed themselves in favor of using the law whenever necessary to protect their interests. They permitted intermarriage with members of other denominations, and also soon instituted a salaried ministry and other liberal policies.[20] On most of these questions they differed radically from the main body of the church. A division under these conditions was inevitable.

The withdrawal of these sixteen from the conference soon had its influence upon various congregations within the district. That there was quite a considerable liberal element in the church in this region is shown by the fact, that immediately several entire congregations went over to the new organization. In the churches at Schwenkville, Skippack and Swamp, the few who were left of the old church had to build new meeting houses. At Bally und Deep Run the new wing erected new houses of worship, while at Boyertown the two parties occupied the same building on alternate Sundays for many years, but finally became involved in a lawsuit for the possession of the building. Other congregations were later established at Saucon, Springfield, Phoenixville, Philadelphia and several other places.

These "Oberholtzer" congregations finally united with many of the Russian churches in the western states and with a number of independent congregations in various parts of the country in the formation of a general conference. All of these are now members of the General Conference of Mennonites.

---

20. See J. H. Oberholtzer. Verantwortung und Erläuterung der Wahre Character.

Jacob Stauffer

At about the time of Oberholtzer's withdrawal there appeared another man in the Pennsylvania church who became the leader of a small following. This was Jacob Stauffer, who, becoming involved in a church dispute, was excommunicated, whereupon he soon tried to build up a new organization. Unlike Oberholtzer, who found the old church too conservative, Stauffer accused it of being too liberal. Like John Herr whom he resembled in many respects he now suddenly discovered after his expulsion that the church had drifted from its original foundation and had recently fallen into decay, and that he was called upon by Providence to restore the old principles in a new organization. His specific charges against the denomination were "worldliness" and "pride".

There are many whose whole heart is turned to earthly things. They speak and think only of worldly things, of buying and selling, of planting and building. One advises the other how he can make and win much money, and that even on Sunday on the way to and from the meeting house. One asks the other what is the market worth, have you sold your grain, etc? One very seldom hears of salvation and the eternal heavenly treasures. Many instruct one another on worldly elections, and even electioneer for their favorite candidates. They become jurymen to judge the lawsuits, thievery, and murders of worldly people. Some have joined insurance companies. Others, even bishops and preachers put lightning rods (through lack of faith) upon their houses. Much pride has also entered into the hearts of many. They pride themselves in their finely ornamented clothes, in the combing and braiding of hair and in the wearing of gold. Their houses are adorned with all sorts of colored and gaudy tinsels, and upon the walls hang many idolatrous pictures.

Among other "worldly" practices to which Jacob

Stauffer objected were camp meetings and singing schools.

Thus appeared to the eyes of this puritan, the Mennonites of his day, who in all matters of dress and outward display at least, must still have been severely plain and modest. His attempts to build up a new church, however, never succeeded, and his following has been small.

The Church of God

The next attempt at a reformation was made in Wayne county, Ohio, by John Holdeman, a member of the congregation in charge of Bishop John Shaum and minister Peter Troxel. Holdeman was a man of unusual learning among his brethren, of strong conviction, and of bold egotism. He was a believer in dreams and visions and was largely guided in his religious life by "the voice of the Holy Spirit" which called to him sometimes in his dreams and sometimes in his work during the day. These visions, he says, began soon after his baptism at the age of twenty, in 1853. At this time and even before, he said he had a strong conviction that he would some day be a minister of the Gospel. This conviction he confided to Bishop Abraham Rohrer on the day of his baptism. In the meantime he also had a vision through which he understood that some one would be converted through his ministry. In a dream he saw before him stems, and upon them were pieces of glass triangular in shape, some of which were turned into ice, and one melted in his hands.

No sooner had he joined the church than he began to find fault with many of his fellow members. Many he said had come into the church unconverted. He was also troubled because of the "worldly and light minded conversation amongst the brethren, the great lack in the raising of children and the neglect of the avoidance of the excommunicated". This faultfinding spirit brought him into trouble with those in authority.

Finally after four years of fruitless effort to impress his views upon the church, and of disappointment for not being called into the ministry, he decided upon a new course of action. One Sunday in the winter of 1858, he again heard the "voice of the Spirit" which told him that the melted ice which had appeared to him in his earlier vision meant his father, who that day would be converted. Whereupon he invited his father and others to his house on that day and preached to a little company of eleven for two hours. He says,

I was much moved, and spake in fervency of spirit. I placed before them the decay of the church. I taught the raising of children, and reproved the corruption therein; and reproved their going to election; and taught the avoidance of the excommunicated; and I also reproved the manner of giving testimony under what I believed (and yet believe) to be an oath. I also affirmed my calling; and taught that the lot was no command whereby to ordain ministers into their office. I also was moved to say that God would divide the church into two parts, and if it would not take place, then I would be a liar and not sent of God; and if it would not come in one year, then it would come in two; if not in two, then in three.[21]

These meetings were continued irregularly for some time and naturally brought Holdeman more than ever into disfavor with his fellow members. Not satisfied with the church, and yet not quite willing to withdraw from the denomination entirely, he and his

---

21. John Holdeman. History of the Church of God, p. 189.

father visited the so-called "Stauffer" people and the "Herrites" in Pennsylvania, in the hope of finding congenial association among them, but not satisfied with either, they organized a new sect commonly known as the "Holdeman" branch of the church, but officially as the Church of God in Christ. Holdeman now took up his pen in defence of his action and, like Herr and Stauffer before him, maintained that the old church had departed from the ways of truth, and that his organization was the true church of God which had maintained the lineage of saints from the apostolic days.

The sect grew very slowly. Outside of his own family Holdeman for a while received scant recognition. By 1865 the congregation consisted of twenty members. It has since grown, however, into a number of small congregations in Kansas, Michigan, Missouri, Manitoba, and several other western states.

In faith and practice this branch differs little from the Old Mennonites, except that, in addition to the differences noted above they also oppose the "taking of usury" and practice the "laying on of hands" after baptism.

The "Wisler" Mennonites

The next church division took place in Elkhart county, Indiana, in what is called the Yellow Creek congregation.[22] Among the pioneer settlers in this community was Jacob Wisler from Ohio, who soon became the first bishop of the church in the state. He

---

22. For information on the Wisler and the Brenneman divisions I am indebted among other sources to a manuscript prepared especially for my use by Daniel Brenneman of Goshen, Indiana.

was a man devoted to the principles of his faith, but exceedingly conservative by nature, and opposed to the introduction of all "new things" in forms of worship and religious practice. The church under his charge was slow to adopt some of the newer methods of work common to other communities. The services were all conducted in the German language. Four part singing was still considered worldly. Sunday schools, evening meetings, protracted meetings and in fact every slightest departure from the customs of the fathers was looked upon with disfavor by Wisler and a considerable portion of his congregation. Some of them, however, demanded a more progressive policy, desiring especially some English preaching and good singing.

About this time, 1864, there came from Fairfield county, Ohio, another minister in the person of Daniel Brenneman, who was much younger than Wisler, more progressive in his ideas, a better speaker and more attractive in personality.

Around these two men were grouped respectively the conservative and progressive elements of the church. Wisler was the bishop and as such dictated the practices and forms of worship. He favored neither four-part singing nor English preaching. Brenneman met the demand for both by holding meetings in school houses, and other places where he often spoke to crowded audiences. This practice Wisler disapproved of on the ground that it savored too much of protracted meetings.

Thus the rivalry continued and grew more bitter until finally Wisler, who was possessed of a stubborn will, determined to forbid on pain of excommunication the introduction of everything "new" into church worship. His arbitrary method of enforcing this policy, together with other quarrels with some of his brethren finally resulted in a church trial which was held at Yellow Creek in 1870, by a committee of bishops from neighboring states and Canada. Wisler's conduct at this trial was such that he was deprived of his ministerial office by the committee. After vainly trying to settle his difficulties with the church, Wisler, during the next year formally withdrew and together with his followers organized what is commonly spoken of as the "Wisler" branch of the denomination.

Wisler had a number of followers in his own and other congregations. These sympathizers were principally from those who preferred the good old customs of the fathers to the innovations which always follow in the path of progress. In 1872 a number of members of the Mennonite congregation in Medina county, Ohio, joined his organization. In more recent years several new divisions in the old church in Canada and in Pennsylvania have slightly swelled the ranks of the Wislerites.

In 1886 a number of conservatives from Woolwich townships, Waterloo county, Ontario, withdrew from the main body on the ground that it tolerated English preaching, Sunday schools, evening meetings, "falling" top buggies, all of which were considered too worldly for pious Christians. These people known sometimes locally as "Woolwichers," finding in the Wislerites kindred spirits now work in harmony with that body. They have about a dozen small congregations scattered throughout Waterloo, York, and Lincoln counties.

In 1893 Bishop Jonas Martin of the Weaverland

congregation in Lancaster county, Pennsylvania, becoming involved in a dispute with some of his members regarding a new pulpit which he considered too fine for his church, withdrew from the congregation and by posing as a conservative on other church questions retained about one third of his congregation.

In 1901 there was also a "Martinite" church of about one hundred members established in Rockingham county, Virginia, which was made up of the extreme conservatives of that region.

These four small bands of conservative Mennonites, which hardly deserve the name of a separate branch of the church, now count up all told hardly more than two thousand members scattered through about thirty congregations in Pennsylvania, Indiana, Ohio, Canada, Michigan and Virginia.

In doctrine the Wislerites, including the other above mentioned communities, do not differ from the main body. In religious customs and practices, however, they are extremely conservative. In dress, in language, in forms of worship and in social customs they are slow in accepting new ideas. They occupy among the Mennonites a position similar to that of the Old Order Amish among the Amish people. They might well be called the "Old Order" Mennonites.

Mennonite Brethren in Christ

Hardly had the trouble with Wisler been settled before a new difficulty arose in the Yellow Creek church. The larger part of the congregation was still conservative in all methods of religious work, even after a few of the ultra-conservatives had withdrawn.

Protracted meetings and other practices now recognized as helpful were then still under the ban. Brenneman both because of his early training, and more liberal spirit and superior talents favored more aggressive church work. The strained relations between himself and a majority of the congregation, which resulted from these differences, were brought to a head when he and J. Krupp, a fellow minister, went to Canada to investigate a revival which had broken out among the Mennonites at that place, under the influence of one Solomon Eby, a Mennonite preacher at Berlin, who as he said had preached for thirteen years before he had been converted. Both Krupp and Brenneman seemed favorably impressed with the revival. Returning to Indiana, they were closely questioned by their fellow members regarding what they had seen. Krupp, upon whom the revival had made a deep impression, spoke unreservedly of it in glowing terms. Brenneman, however, knowing that protracted meetings or revivals were not regarded favorably by either the Canadian or Indiana Mennonites, said little, But he determined to go to Canada a second time for a more thorough investigation. During his absence, Krupp in the meantime by his unwise conduct and too zealous speech, had brought the displeasure and suspicion of the conservative elements of the church upon his head, and had been expelled. Brenneman upon his return seemed more than ever impressed with the Canadian revival. Finding that Krupp had been expelled on what he considered insufficient ground, he openly espoused his cause, and finding that the differences between himself and the church could not be adjusted, practically withdrew from the organization. Soon after this the congregation formally expelled him on the following charges:

    1. For leaving the church and supporting an excommunicated minister.
    2. For teaching and preaching unscriptural customs.
    3. For causing dissensions and working disorderly at home and abroad.

Brenneman and his friends having now been cast out looked about for another church with which they might worship. They were still at heart Mennonites, however, and after considering respectively the Dunkards, Quakers, Evangelicals, and Free Methodists all of whom either had many doctrines in common with the Mennonites or had shown Brenneman some kindness during this time by offering him the use of their meeting houses for the services which he continued to hold, they finally decided to establish a separate organization. This decision was carried out in 1874 when at Eby's meeting house in Berlin, Ontario, they, together with their Canadian sympathizers, formed the "Reformed Mennonite" church. Of course by the congregation from which they withdrew they were always known as "Brennemanites." In doctrine and religious practices the new organization differed little from the old, except that they manifested a greater zeal for the propagation of their views, and laid greater stress upon "inner experience" and the necessity of a definite "change of heart" in conversion.

The new church at first was small in number, being confined to Brenneman's friends of the Yellow Creek congregation and Canada. But as a result of their zealous missionary spirit, and by uniting with several other small offshoots of the main body, it has grown to a church of no mean strength. These small bodies had arisen under similar circumstances, and having much in common in spirit and religious opinion they finally, one after another united their forces.

The New Mennonites was the name adopted by a small group of Canadian advocates of revivals, who had withdrawn from the church for the same reasons as had the Reformed Mennonites.

In 1875 in the Bloomingdale meeting house in Waterloo county, Ontario, these two branches united into one society under the name of the United Mennonites.

Some time before this, as early as 1853, a small division under the leadership of William Gehman had been made in Bucks county, Pennsylvania. In 1879 in Ontario this branch known as the Evangelical Mennonites, formed with the United Mennonites a new body called the Evangelical United Mennonites.

In Ohio near Jamton, in 1883, these Evangelical United Mennonites united with the Brethren in Christ, a small branch of the River Brethren, to form the church now called the Mennonite Brethren in Christ.

Thus by a series of amalgamations with a number of these small bodies, all of which sprang either directly or indirectly from the Old Mennonite church, the original socalled "Brenneman" organization has developed from a local faction to an institution of considerable size and influence. With these unions there have come slight changes in both the doctrine and practices of the original body. The Reformed Mennonites differed from the main body very little. The Mennonite Brethren, while still insisting in general upon modest attire, have let up a little on their restrictions on dress. In doctrine they maintain the fundamental principles of the Mennonite faith—non-resistance, non-swearing of oaths, opposition to secret societies, life insurance, etc. But in several respects they have developed certain differences. They baptize by immersion and believe strongly in "entire sanctification," and the millennium. They are quite demonstrative in their worship, and their camp meetings have lost nothing of the noise and excitement of those of the old time shouting Methodists.

3

During the Civil War

In the North during the Civil war, as we have already seen, the Mennonites were not forced to serve in the army. The Conscription Act of 1864 provided for the exemption of such as were conscientiously scrupulous against bearing arms if they were drafted, by a payment of three hundred dollars. A number of the Mennonites and Amish throughout the country were struck by the draft in 1864. Such were compelled to appear before the local recruiting officer and satisfy him that they were members in good standing of a non-resistant religious organization and that they were conscientiously opposed to the bearing of arms and that their conduct had been consistent with their profession. Usually they were then dismissed upon the payment of the three hundred dollar exemption.

Experiences in the North

Sometimes this exemption was the source of ill-feeling and jealousy among those who lived in the same communities with the Mennonites, and who felt that the latter enjoyed greater privileges than they. In Fulton county, Ohio, on one occasion while a company of Amish had assembled for the purpose of securing exemption, they were attacked by a mob of men some of whom had been less fortunate than they in escaping the draft, and barely escaped serious bodily injury. Such occasions however, were rare.

In the South the Mennonites did not escape so easily. Neither Virginia nor the Confederate government were as liberal toward them as was the North. And besides, the Virginia settlement was located in the very heart of the Shenandoah Valley, the scene of Sheridan's raid. The experience of the Virginians during this time is best told by Bishop L. J. Heatwole who was a young man at the time, and was an eyewitness of the events he describes. The following sketch was prepared by him for Hartzler and Kauffman's Mennonite Church History:

The Mennonites of the South

With the beginning of this period (1861), there were in the Virginia church three bishops: John Geil, Sr., (Lower district); Samuel Coffman, (Middle district), and Jacob Hildebrand, (Upper district); twelve ministers and six deacons, with a membership all told of about three hundred fifty. In the three districts were seven meeting houses, in each of which worship was held once every four weeks.

For a number of years prior to the outbreak of the Civil war, the state of Virginia maintained a strict military organization known as the State Militia, which required every able-bodied man in the state, if not otherwise exempted, to attend in time of peace, no less than four days' drill each year, in the tactics of war. The exemption laws, as they were then framed, afforded no opportunity for our brethren to escape this service, except in the payment of the minimum fine—50 cents for absence from each muster drill. With but a few exceptions, this was always done and hence our brethren avoided doing violence to the principle of non-resistance and deliberately ignored each call as it was made to serve in the muster drills.

But with the outbreak of the war, the military laws became a far greater menace to the brotherhood, and in time proved a severe test of their loyalty to the church. First, there came the call for all the Militia to take the field. Such of our brethren whose names were on the muster rolls found themselves no longer excusable from military duty by paying their muster fines, but had to go into the ranks or be dealt with as deserters.

It was a time of sore distress to the church. What were they to do in the face of such circumstances? To remain at home meant sooner or later to be taken away by force before a court martial to be tried and shot. To go voluntarily into the ranks and line up for the field of battle would be treason to the church. When the final test came, a few of the younger brethren went into the army with the first volunteers; others hid themselves away in the mountains and timbered sections of the country and made frequent visits to their families under cover of night; while others— along with such as were drafted into service later in the fall of 1861—were taken into the army under protest with the understanding among themselves and their families at home, that neither of them would strike a blow or fire a gun. Though these brethren were with the regular army and were in action near Winchester, and before Harper's Ferry, they proved true to their pledges, and in consequence, a number of them were soon reported to the officers, as such who refused to shoot when the order was given to open fire on the enemy. In their refusal to obey orders on this point, some were threatened to the point of being court-martialed and shot; this threat not having the effect to change their minds in the least, a number of the men found themselves detailed, by and by, as cooks, teamsters and on the relief corps, to attend to the sick and wounded. When the army lay in camp it was a custom with them to meet when off duty, to join together in singing some of the old familiar church hymns to which they were so well accustomed when at home. It was not an uncommon thing for the soldiers to have their attention drawn to some particular tent or corner of the camp where a number of earnest voices were joined in singing:—"O, For a Closer walk with God," or "Am I a Soldier of the Cross," etc.

During the winter of 1861-62, while the army lay in winter quarters at Winchester, nearly all these brethren found their way back to their homes, but with the opening of the campaign of 1862, there came the general call from the Confederate government for every man between the ages of eighteen and forty-five years and capable of bearing arms, to go to the front. This call being made universal, there was no avenue of escape left, and to respond to this universal call was looked upon by the church as equivalent to volunteering for military service. Owing to the force of circumstances and the highly exciting nature of the times, some of the younger brethren responded and went into the ranks. Bishop Coffman, however, took the bold stand and preached his convictions from the pulpit that Mennonites could not go into the army and at the same time be loyal to their church, and that our people must, notwithstanding their opposition to slavery, occupy neutral ground in the present crisis.

From this time on was the real crisis for the Mennonites. A considerable number of the brethren went into their former custom of hiding away in secluded places; others continued about their homes as usual. Threats were made against Bishop Coffman by some of the military authorities, for his public declarations, one certain Colonel having sent word that he was coming with his regiment to take Bishop Coffman and all his members, capable of bearing arms, into the army; there was, of course, some consternation among the brotherhood. Brother Coffman, thinking it prudent to leave the state for a time, passed through the lines safely and reached the communities of our people in Maryland and Pennsylvania, where he remained until the feeling against him at home had sufficiently subsided for him to return to his family.

In the meantime, quite a number of the brethren, together with a number of their sons and others, who were not at the time members of the church, to the number of about seventy persons, all met at a certain rendezvous ground not far from the mountains where they decided to travel together in a body across the mountains to West Virginia to Ohio and other states, expecting to remain there as refugees until the close of the war. The ministers who remained were not molested, but some of the brethren who yet remained in hiding about their homes, were either apprehended on surprise or hunted down by scouting parties of the provost-marshal and were taken forcibly into the army or confined in the county jail at Harrisonburg. Strange as it may seem, some of the brethren who were yet of military age, remained at their homes unmolested through all this trying period, while others, who were known to be in hiding, were hunted and chased from place to place like wild beasts of the forest—it was those who had been taken into the army and afterwards deserted, that were made thus to suffer—those who had managed to keep out of the ranks from the beginning of the war, had not nearly so much trouble. Those who managed to elude the scouts spent their time at camping places far up in the mountains, and returned occasionally to their homes for supplies. Others had hiding places under their dwelling houses that were reached by means of trap-doors covered with carpets or bedding to throw the searching party off the trail, and several instances are recalled when the fugitive brother lay with only the thickness of a board and carpet between himself and his would-be captors.

The company of seventy, who started on their journey across the mountains early in the spring of 1862, were surprised and captured by a squad of Confederate cavalry, near Petersburg, West Virginia, on the second day after leaving home. They were immediately marched from that point some sixty miles to the southeast of Staunton, from which place they were sent by train to Richmond, which had already become the seat of the Confederate government. Here, with two exceptions, they were all lodged as common prisoners in the famous Libby Prison, at that place. These exceptions were two brethren who effected their escape, and came home immediately and reported the fate of the rest of the party. Had it not been for this, it might not have been known for a time indefinite, that matters had taken the turn

MENNONITES—NINETEENTH CENTURY   319

they had, and besides the brethren might have been languishing in prison much longer than they did, without their condition being known at home.

It was a "serious and a solemn time," when genuine and earnest supplication was made to God for help. By the time the excitement and intense anxiety caused by the news of the capture at Petersburg, had sufficiently subsided at home, the members came together for calm consultation.

Officers connected with the Confederate government at Richmond, who were known to have some acquaintance with the Mennonites and their doctrine, were notified of the condition of things. With a copy of the Mennonite Confession of Faith placed in their hands, these officials were enabled to impress upon the Confederate Congress the fact that the fathers and sons of our people, whom they were then holding as prisoners, were far from being enemies to the government, but were a peace-loving people and that the only motive they had for leaving their homes was because of the encroachment upon their religious liberties.

With this convincing explanation, the Confederate Congress was moved to adopt a bill that led to the release of, not only the Mennonites who were in prison, but also liberated such who were in the army and such as were in hiding near their homes. This bill provided that all people professing the peace doctrine as part of their religion, such as the Mennonites, Dunkards, Quakers, and Nazarites, residing within the Confederate States, would be exempt from military duty on condition that each male member of such religious bodies who was subject to bear arms, should pay into the treasury, the sum of five hundred dollars. After this bill was adopted the required amount was made up as soon as possible, a brother delegated by the church to go to Richmond to see that it was paid, and the brethren liberated from a confinement that had already been prolonged to six weeks in a prison that was reeking with filth and vermin, and a ration that barely kept them alive.

The unfeigned joy that was experienced by the church over the home-coming of the captive brethren, as well as the happy reunions brought about in the restoration of the others, who had been in the army or in hiding, was profoundly deep and sincere. Their unexpected release from prison and military bondage was attributed to the same "Mighty Hand" that had brought Israel of old, from under the bondage of Egypt. . . . . . One unpleasant feature still remained, and that feature lay in the fact that not all of the seventy who were captured were members of the Mennonite or Dunkard Church and hence could not be released from prison on the payment of five hundred dollars fine. They were, however, liberated from confinement on condition that they went immediately into the army as conscript soldiers. The fact that they were about all either sons or relatives of the brethren who were exempted did not count for anything in their case. There was no other course for them to take but to go into the army, and it is sad to relate that some of these poor boys never again reached their homes alive. After serving as soldiers for a time, the most of them, however, left the army, came home, and spent the rest of the war period either in hiding or refugeeing in the Northern or Western states.

During the next eighteen months of the war, the Mennonites, as a rule, were left undisturbed on their farms, except that the government levied heavily upon their crops for army supplies. The commissary wagons came with unpleasant frequency to haul away wheat, corn and other supplies, all of which they usually took without leave or license or a cent of pay.

In the summer of 1864 the war cloud again settled thick and dark over the Mennonite homes in the Shenandoah Valley. With the suddenness of a thunderclap there came from the seat of government at Richmond, the announcement that the substitute Exemption Law was abolished and that all able-bodied men from seventeen to sixty years of age were now required to go into the army. This of course started off many of the seventeen-year-old boys and most of the older brethren to hiding again, numbers of them going in squads of three and four across the mountains into West Virginia and Ohio until by September and October, the exodus of brethren from the state was so general that it is remembered as the time when the Sunday congregations were composed of a few old men, the younger boys and the women. The meetings at this time are remembered as being made all the more solemn because of the many sad and weeping faces that were seen in the audience. It sometimes happened that these meetings were seriously disturbed and even stampeded by the real or imaginary approach of soldiers, and at times for a period indefinite no meetings were held by reason of soldiers being quartered on the grounds and occupying the meeting house where our people were accustomed to meet for worship.

Then, to cap the climax, there came the never-to-be-forgotten Sheridan's raid through the Shenandoah Valley. From the evening of Oct. 6th, 1864, to the morning of the 8th following, nearly all the barns and mills, and in some cases the dwelling houses also, were set on fire in that part of Rockingham county where the Mennonites were located. These buildings being burned, together with their stores and provisions, and the live stock driven from the farms—the whole country being overrun by troops of both sides, keeping up a desultory warfare between them—with the fences obliterated in a way that left their farms a desolate waste. It is not to be wondered at that quite a number of our Mennonite families and nearly all the sixteen and seventeen-year-old boys bade farewell to the hallowed surroundings of the dear places they used to call home, and rather than to longer bear the hardships of a war-ridden country, took the opportunity to remove to Pennsylvania and Ohio under the protection of Sheridan's army as it marched northward in October, 1864.

Before the hard, cold winter of 1864-65 had fully set in, those of our people who remained at their homes managed to provide some shelter and to divide with one another the scanty supplies that remained for them. There was perhaps, never a time before this that Mennonites in America had things more "in common" than during the war period of 1864-65. Every possible article of wearing apparel had to be manufactured at home—no leather to make shoes except that which was tanned at home; no hats were worn except the home-made article; no sugar or salt or pepper or spices to season food with; no coffee, except such as was made from parched wheat or rye. Upon the whole, it was like going back to the purely primitive life of the grandfathers of a hundred years before.

The citing of a few instances, with reference to the trying experiences of such of the brethren who were in hiding, may not come amiss before closing this chapter.

A certain brother who had spent much of his time hiding away from the observation of the military officials, was accused, not only as a fugitive from the ranks of the army, but also for rendering aid to others and acting as guide to some of the numerous squads of refugees that were finding their way across the mountains to the Federal lines. By some means it became known to the military authorities that he was at home on a certain night when some soldiers were sent out with the order that he be shot on sight. The soldiers approached and surrounded the house in the dead hour of the night. Calling him to the door, he was told that they were there with orders to kill him. He coolly replied that before doing that, they would certainly give him time to bid farewell to his family and also to write his will. This being granted, he waked his wife and a number of children, and after telling what the soldiers were there for, sat down in perfect composure to write his will. As he proceeded with the writing, he suggested to one of the soldiers that his neighbor would be needed to sign the paper as witness. While the messenger was gone to bring in the neighbor, the brother's personal coolness, together with the pathetic attitude of the family, so operated upon the minds of the soldiers that they left their intended victim unharmed and made a hasty departure.

Another brother had repeatedly been searched for by detachments of the provost-marshal's guards, but in each case he managed to elude them. Finding that he was no longer safe at or near his home, he went back into the mountains where he spent many days in a solitary cabin all alone. By some unknown means his hiding place was located by the provost-marshal and several soldiers were sent to capture him. The soldiers were already more than half way on the road to his camp, when they were seen by a near family relative, who, surmising what their errand was, himself started off at full speed and like Ahimaaz, who outran

Kushi, he outstripped the marshal's guard and reached our brother's place of concealment just in time for him to save himself by flight. But as there was snow on the ground at the time, he was easily followed by his pursuers. After going some distance up a mountain ravine, he performed the feat of climbing to the top of a high mountain, walking backward in the snow and by this means succeeded in throwing his would-be captors off his trail. The first night of his flight he spent at a cold and cheerless place under a spruce tree, fifteen miles or more away from the haunts of civilization. Fearing to come back to his home, or even to his cabin in the lonely mountain glen, he traveled on westward for several days, until he reached the eastern slope of the Allegheny mountains. Finding himself among a people who treated him with great kindness, he made his home among them. From him these people soon learned something of the doctrine taught by the Mennonites, and by means of a copy of the Confession of Faith, which he had with him, they became greatly interested in the peace doctrine taught by the church. It only remains for us to add that the very means that served to drive this brother across the mountains as a fugitive from military service, has resulted ultimately in the establishing of a church and the building of the first meeting house in the state of West Virginia.

CHAPTER XII

THE IMMIGRATION FROM RUSSIA

Catherine's Invitation

The Mennonites of Europe during the eighteenth century were everywhere recognized as an industrious and thrifty people. Peter the Great first came into contact with them at Zaandam while serving his ship-building apprenticeship in Holland, and while there selected one of their number as his private physician. In 1786 Catharine the Great, desiring to build up the waste lands of Southern Russia, invited the Mennonites of Prussia to locate on her crown lands near the mouth of the Dnieper, in the province of Jekaterinoslav. As an inducement to immigration she promised them free transportation, free lands, religious toleration and freedom from military service. Although denied passports by the Prussian government, many of them accepted these terms and established a colony among the wooded hills along the lower Dnieper, not far from the town of Jekaterinoslav. By 1788 about two hundred families had settled in this region.

In 1796 Catherine died and the new colonists, fearing lest her successor, Paul I, might forget the promises of his mother to them, sent **Charter of Paul I** two men to St. Petersburg to ask that Catherine's concessions might be continued. These men secured from the Czar in 1800 a charter of privileges which is still preserved in a fire proof building at Chortitz. Paul, not only renewed his mother's promises, but in order to encourage further immigration he offered them even added privileges. The most important provisions of the charter were:

1. Religious toleration.
2. Exemption from military service.
3. The substitution of the affirmation for the oath.
4. Sixty-five dessatin of free, arable land for each family.
5. Freedom from taxation for ten years.
6. The right to fish, and to establish distilleries, of which they were to have a monopoly within their settlement.
7. Freedom from the quartering of soldiers among them.

As a result of these privileges the emigration fever again seized the Prussians. The first colony had been made up largely of the poorer people, but now even many of the well-to-do decided to emigrate to Russia. The lands offered them were on the treeless plains of Taurien, some distance east of the old colony. The first settlers came in 1803 and located on the river Molotchna, not far from where the stream enters the Azov. During the first two years three hundred and four families found their way to the new settlement. Others came during the succeeding years and by 1836 the entire population of the Molotchna colony was estimated at ten thousand, grouped into forty-six villages.

In addition to these two colonies another was established in 1860 in Crimea, largely by settlers from the Molotchna community.

In the meantime many other Germans besides the Mennonites had also settled in these regions. It is estimated that by 1870 there were several millions of Germans in Southern Russia. The Mennonites of course constituted only a small portion of this entire number, perhaps between thirty and forty thousand. These Germans had settled in villages as the first occupants of the soil and thus they still kept up their German customs and habits, and spoke the language of the Fatherland, and maintained their various forms of religious worship. They were thrifty, and many had grown rich. None were more prosperous than the Mennonites. An American traveler, passing through these Mennonite villages in 1874 speaks as follows:—

The Germans in Russia

> The dwelling houses were large brick structures with tile roofs, a flower garden between the street and the house and well kept vegetable garden and orchard in the rear. The stables with splendid work horses of every build, and the sheds with vehicles of every description, among them family coaches and all kinds of farming machinery. They were certainly the best appointed farming communities I had seen anywhere. Scattered over the country were large, isolated estates, with buildings reminding one of the feudal baronial castles of Western Europe. Their owners were millionaire Mennonites, who had acquired large tracts of land by private purchase. I was entertained by one of them, who had the reputation of being the largest sheep owner in Europe. When I asked how many sheep he owned he could not tell,

but said he had three thousand shepherd dogs taking care of his flock. A little figuring developed that he owned over a million sheep, scattered in flocks all along the coast of the Black Sea.[1]

This prosperity, together with the exclusiveness of the German colonists, engendered on the part of the native Russians a strong feeling of jealousy and suspicion against them. This feeling was intensified by the special religious and political privileges which had been granted them at the time of their immigration into the Empire. For in addition to the military exemption enjoyed by the Mennonites, all Germans were still more or less under the political guardianship of Prussia from which state most of them had come, and thus enjoyed certain privileges denied the native Russians.

And so the Russian government was importuned to withdraw these privileges. As a result of this pressure it soon became evident that the Czar intended to Russianize his German subjects as soon as possible.

Withdrawal of Privileges

As early as 1869 it was rumored that a new treaty was to be made with Prussia regarding the rights of the Germans. During the Franco-Prussian war it was agreed between the Czar and Bismarck that the newly created German government should withdraw its political guardianship over the Germans in Russia on the condition that all Germans who did not wish to become full-fledged Russian subjects might be given ten years in which to dispose of their property and

---

1. C. B. Schmidt: Reminiscences of Foreign Immigration Work. An address at the fourth annual convention of the Colorado State Realty Association. Held at Colorado Springs, June 20-23, 1901.

emigrate to some other country. This international agreement was received by all the Germans with disfavor, and by the Mennonites with consternation. To the latter it meant not only that their children must now be educated in Russian schools, but their young men must now also enter the Russian army, for at the same time it was also rumored that universal military service was to be established. Several delegations were sent to St. Petersburg for the purpose of securing military exemption in the proposed law, but nothing was accomplished.

Nothing seemed to be left for the Mennonites now but either to violate their non-resistant principles, or leave for some other land where they might still enjoy the freedom of their religious convictions. Many decided upon the latter alternative. But where were they to go? Some suggested Africa; others Australia. A delegation was sent to Siberia to hunt for a suitable place for a colony and a small colony actually set out for that country. Of all the places suggested, however, America seemed the most promising. Here were many of their own faith who, centuries before, had come for the same purpose. Here also was still much raw land where large communities might be established on the plan of their native Russian villages. Here also they could enjoy freedom of religious opinion. But with all of these advantages there were misgivings in the minds of many to whom America still meant little more than an asylum for European convicts, and the haunt of untutored savages. In the language of one who later became a leader in the emigration to the West, America was a

Looking for a New Home

country "interesting for the adventurer, an asylum for
convicts. How could one think of finding a home in
peace under his vine and figtree among such and other
like people in addition to the wild natives."[2]

In the meantime several families already began
to leave for America. In 1870 and 1871 several individual travelers made inspection tours
through the country. In 1872 a small
delegation, among whom was Bernhard
Warkentin, who later took an active part
in the emigration movement, reached the Mennonite
congregation at Summerfield, Illinois. From here
they were directed to the western states as best suited
for colonization. The Russians were becoming more
and more restless, and in 1873 another delegation
reached America for the purpose of looking up a good
location for a large colony. This committee was
composed of twelve men from Russia and West
Prussia. Their names were Jacob Buller, Leonard
Suderman, William Ewert, Andreas Schrag, Jacob
Buller, Tobias Unruh, Jacob Peters, Heinrich Wiebe,
Cornelius Buhr, Cornelius Toews, David Classen,
Paul Tschetter and Lawrence Tschetter.

Delegation to America

Accompanied by John F. Funk of Elkhart, Indiana, and J. Y. Schantz of Berlin, Ontario, this delegation proceeded on an inspection tour down the Red
River valley through Dakota and Manitoba. Here
were still large tracts of raw prairie land to be had
almost for the asking. They were best pleased with
the region south of Winnipeg and here is where a few
years later the largest settlement was made. From
here the committee also visited Minnesota, Nebraska

---

2. Leonard Suderman.

and Kansas, and several members also went to Texas.

In the meantime the western fever had also taken hold of a number of members of the Summerfield, Illinois, congregation. As early as 1871 a small group of men under the direction of Christian Krehbiel, had visited Kansas with a view to planting a colony of their own in that or some other western state. And so such Russian home-seekers as came under the influence of the Summerfield congregation were directed to that region. Many of them later settled in this state and in Nebraska.

When it became known that there was a probability of a large immigration of industrious Europeans to these western regions, various inducements to settlement were offered them by such agencies as were interested in having these lands occupied. The Canadian government through its agent at Winnipeg offered large tracts of cheap lands and freedom of conscience. In Kansas, the Atchison, Topeka and Santa Fe Railroad, which was built about this time, offered railroad land at two and one half dollars per acre. So determined was this railroad company to get these immigrants for Kansas that in 1875 it sent a special agent to Russia for the purpose of influencing the Mennonites who expected to emigrate, to locate upon its lands. Other roads in Nebraska and Minnesota seemed equally bent on selling their lands, but none of these sent special representatives to Russia.

Americans Interested

In the meantime the delegation which had visited these regions during the summer of 1873 had returned home and made such a favorable report of what they had seen that many of the Russians prepared to leave for America immediately. Many sold their property, always at a loss, and applied to the government for free passes for emigration.

But the Czar, now upon hearing the rumor of the intended emigration, regretted the prospect of losing so many of his most thrifty people, and sent a member of his ministry, von Todtleben, as a special agent among the Mennonite colonies to persuade them not to leave the country. Von Todtleben dwelt upon the hardships of the long voyage to America and promised the Mennonites certain exemptions from military service in the proposed new military law. This exception in favor of the Mennonites as it finally appeared is as follows:

> Von Todtleben

The Mennonites who shall be called out for military service shall be assigned to duty only at other places than at the front, as in hospitals, in military works and similar establishments, and are exempt from bearing arms. This provision, however, shall not include such Mennonites, who shall unite with the church after the new military law shall have come into force or such as shall come into the Russian Empire from any foreign country.[3]

The majority of the Mennonites accepted these conditions and remained in their native land, and these selected the forestry service in lieu of the military service, which was soon demanded of all the young men of Russia.

To a large minority, however, the promises made by von Todtleben were not convincing. To this class belonged many of the more scrupulous and some of the poorer families. To these, forestry service seemed

---

3. Isaac Peters, in Herald of Truth.

little better than military service. Their point of view is best expressed in the words of one of their number:

> Although the forestry service in and of itself embodied nothing that can be called contrary to the Scriptures, it nevertheless always means or stands for military service on the statute books and is not consistent with our non-resistant confession, since this always implies alliance or connection with military life and affairs, where the soldier is taken and trained and is subject to the army officials yoked together with them and the profession they represent. Besides this, the forestry service is for the present limited to twenty years, and thus the government keeps the back door open for the introduction of new things at any time, and perhaps assign the soldiers at any time to service in any of the branches named in the provisory clauses of the new military law, all of which are designed to foster war.[4]

And so the preparations for departure continued in many of the villages. Although a few individuals had already crossed to this country during 1872 and 1873, the general breaking up of the Russian settlements did not begin until the summer of 1874. In both colonies, the Molotchna and the old colony, many sold all their possessions and secured their passports. In some cases whole villages emigrated bodily to the new country. In others only a few members left their native homes. But everywhere the emigration fever had seized the people.

Exodus of 1874 Although the great exodus from the two largest colonies did not begin until early in the summer of 1874, several families had arrived here in the fall of 1873 and began settlements in Kansas, Dakota and Minnesota. From the files of the Herald of Truth we

---

4. Isaac Peters, in Herald of Truth.

learn that by January, 1874, there were ten or twelve families near Mountain Lake, Minnesota, and several families in Marion and McPherson counties, Kansas. In the same issue it is announced that one thousand families are to start for America in April. By May the stream had begun. The issue of the Herald for May 5, announces the arrival of fifty-eight Mennonites from Poland. By May 20, fifty more Poles under the leadership of Andreas Schrag have arrived and located near Yankton, Dakota. By June forty more from the same place were brought by William Ewert to Summerfield, from which place they soon after went to their new homes in Kansas. On July 8, seven more families stopped at Summerfield enroute to Kansas. And so they continued to come in an increasing stream throughout the summer.

In the meantime this expected exodus of Russian Mennonites to America was not awaited by their brethren here without interest **American Mennonites** and some anxiety as to how **Aid Immigrants** they were to provide for them. As soon as it was known that they would come in large numbers, steps were taken to furnish them with such money and care as might be necessary to settle them in their western homes. For many of the new arrivals were not rich. Some were poor to begin with. The expenses of transporting entire families were heavy. Such as had property in Russia had to dispose of it at a loss and so, very few of them were left rich when they arrived at their new homes.

In 1873 the western conference of the General Conference Mennonites, under the influence of Christian Krehbiel had appointed a committee to collect money for such of the immigrants as might need help, and to direct them to their new homes. About the same time a similar organization was effected under the influence of John F. Funk among the Old Mennonites of the middle west. These two movements were soon consolidated into the Mennonite Board of Guardians, with Christian Krehbiel as president; David Goerz (an immigrant), as secretary; John F. Funk, treasurer; and B. Warkentin (an immigrant), agent. The Mennonites of Eastern Pennsylvania organized the Mennonite Executive Aid Committee, and the Canadian church under the leadership of J. Y. Schantz, of Berlin, Ontario, also appointed a committee. All of these organizations did valuable service in providing for the needs and the conveniences of the Russians while they were becoming settled. It is estimated that a total of about $100,000 was collected and expended in this work. In addition to this sum, there were many individual loans, and in Manitoba the Canadian government loaned the settlers of that region a sum of $96,000 at six per cent interest upon securities furnished by the Mennonites of Ontario. Within twenty years almost all the money loaned to the Russians both in Manitoba and in the United States was paid back by them.

Aided and directed by these organizations, the immigrants continued to find their way to the western settlements by the hundreds throughout the summer and autumn of 1874. The Herald reports that on July 18, eighty families had reached Burlington, Iowa, enroute to Nebraska. July 19, thirty arrived at Elkhart, Indiana, where they remained for the night in the

Mennonite meeting house at that place, and the next day left—some for Kansas, others for Yankton, Dakota. The total number of arrivals at the harbor of New York by July 18, was six hundred. In the meantime many had arrived at Toronto, Canada. On July 20, three hundred and seventy are reported, and on July 30, two hundred and ninety more. The next day five hundred and four left for Manitoba. And thus they continued to come in a steady stream throughout all the summer and fall. A report made in November, 1874, shows that the Mennonite Board of Guardians reported from the Inman line the arrival of two hundred families. The Pennsylvania Aid Committee reported thirty-five families from the Red Star line and three hundred and eighty-six families on the Hamburg line. The Canadian committee reported the arrival of two hundred and thirty by way of the Allan line for the year. The total estimate for the year was about twelve hundred families with the prospect that at least a thousand more families were preparing to come during the following year. And the year 1875 saw no less come across than the previous year. Whole vessels were chartered by the immigrants. In December, 1874, seven hundred had arrived in the "Fatherland," and four hundred in the "Abbotsford." On July 25, 1875, the "Netherlands" steamed up to the dock at New York with five hundred and fifty Mennonites on board. And soon after the "Nevada" unloaded five hundred and seventy. By the fall of 1875 the greatest rush was over, but they continued to come in small bands up to 1880. In August, 1879, it was estimated that in Manitoba alone, which was however the largest settlement, there were seven thousand three hundred and eighty-three Mennonites.[5] Perhaps nearly an equal number came to all the other settlements combined—Kansas, Nebraska, Dakota and Minnesota. No reliable statistics are at hand at present regarding the present number in these various settlements, but it would be safe to place the estimate at more than double that of the above number.

In the meantime a number of Mennonites from West Prussia also emigrated at this time to America. These located in Harvey and Butler counties, Kansas.

As we have seen, the first settlers in 1873 located near Mountain Lake, Minnesota, and in Dakota and Kansas. Soon after in Manitoba two colonies were established, one twenty-five miles south of Winnepeg and the other about eighty miles south. To the former the Canadian government granted a reserve of eight townships; to the latter, a reserve of seventeen townships. Here, on the raw prairie, secluded from the outside world, they were at liberty to establish such forms of religion and, within certain limits, such civil government as they wished. The Manitoba settlers were principally from the old colony in Russia, which was more conservative than the other settlement. These immigrants from the latter colony settled principally in Kansas. Naturally the colonists built up such civil and religious institutions as they were accustomed to in their native land. They grouped themselves over their vast reserves in small villages, containing from five to thirty families each. These villages were scattered

---

5. See Herald of Truth, January, 1877, and August, 1879.

irregularly over the reserve, and sometimes two or three were built quite close together, and then again sometimes there were long distances between them. Their houses the first year were dug half in the earth, for the nearest timber was ten to twenty miles away, but later were made of oak logs, covered with prairie grass. A traveler passing through the colony in 1877 describes one of these villages in the "Pembina" settlement which at that time contained twenty-five villages, occupied by four hundred and eighty-five families.

The houses are built on both sides of the street, about one hundred feet back from the street, giving ample space for trees, flowers, etc., between the houses and the streets. The houses are built on a line with the street about two hundred feet apart, and all with the gable end toward the street, giving them a regular and handsome appearance. In this colony they have erected a building for a steam mill, and expect to have it all completed yet this fall with two run of stones. This mill is situated within two miles of the timber.[6]

According to another writer there was frequently a mill and nearly always a blacksmith shop in every village. In addition there was also the village school house which sometimes

is used as a place of worship and this sometimes has extra rooms in which a teacher resides. In the larger villages they have separate buildings for religious service. These meeting houses are usually very plain buildings and the roofs, like some of their dwellings, are thatched with straw.[7]

These settlements also furnish an interesting

---

6. J. Y. Schantz, in Herald of Truth, December, 1877.
7. Family Almanac, 1896.

study in the religious and civil government of their native Russian Mennonite village, for on the raw prairies of Manitoba they were left almost entirely free to institute such local form of government as they might choose. Naturally they reproduced as nearly as their new environment would permit such institutions as they were familiar with. As is always the case with a religious people when they are given an opportunity to form their own civil government, this government was that of a theocracy, and here with the highest source of authority vested in a bishop chosen by the whole settlement. The following description of the local government of one of these settlements, the Reinland, which consisted of twenty-five villages, was written in 1877 by Peter Wiens, himself an immigrant from Russia.

Government of Colony

> In matters concerning the church there is one bishop for the whole settlement, and seven ministers, which are elected for life, and preach the Word of God in their public meetings. In the management of affairs of the church the bishop occupies the highest position and is looked to first in deciding and settling any difficulties that may arise in the church. The bishop and preachers are chosen by lot by the church during life.
>
> For the management of their temporal affairs, to see after roads, bridges, etc., the colony has a district office in Reinland. To fill this office the whole colony elects a general superintendent, each village a director and two assistants. A secretary for the district office is hired for a year. The general superintendent or director and the village directors or village superintendents, as they are sometimes called, and their assistants are elected for two years. The general superintendent and the village superintendents are each paid a small salary.
>
> The general superintendent gives all general orders, or

when anything is to be done, the order is made through the secretary of the district to the superintendents of the villages who in turn make it known to the village. When matters of importance are to be attended to, the general superintendent through the secretary calls the village superintendents to a general conference in which all the village superintendents in the district must appear in Reinland and sometimes also the bishop of the church takes part in the councils. The general superintendents, when considered necessary, makes known the proceedings of the council through the secretary to the superintendent of the villages, who make it known to the villages. Ofttimes also when the proceedings are short and they can remember them without difficulty, the proceedings are delivered verbally to the village superintendents.

As long as everything goes on in peace and all are obedient, the general superintendent and the village superintendents have only to give the needful instructions, but if any become disobedient and refuse to obey the instructions of the general and village superintendents, they are, after they have been exhorted several times, given over to the bishop of the church. He again exhorts them to obedience. If they hear him, all is again well. If, however, they refuse to hear him, the bishop and general superintendent together visit them several times in order if possible to adjust the difficulties, sometimes also some of the ministers go with them to assist in settling the difficulty. If they hear these, all is well again, but if they refuse to hear them they are called into the church before the whole congregation where the bishop is the director of the meeting. The bishop presents the matter to the congregation and makes the necessary inquiries of them, and if the whole congregation agrees, when these disobedient persons are not willing to hear after the matter has been again seriously and solemnly presented to them, then these disobedient persons are excommunicated from the church until they become obedient, acknowledge that they have done wrong, and ask for forgiveness. When an excommunicated member comes again in this manner penitent and sorry, he is presented before the congregation, and when he there makes his confession, he is again, according to the Word of God, received into the church.

The entire colony has an office for the care of the orphans to fill which two persons are elected for three years. These have in charge all money of the orphans, widows and other weakly persons, which they loan out at five per cent on good security and are required to keep a correct account of all their transactions.

The colony has a fire office to which a fire overseer is chosen. In this office every family is secured and a record is kept of the amount of property that each family has secured. When a fire occurs the fire overseer makes an estimate of the percentage of the loss. He then reports to the village superintendents who collect the money and hand it over to the fire overseer who pays it to the person who sustained the loss. Each village has also a school teacher who is employed by the village for a year for such salary as they can agree upon. The bishop and ministers receive no pay.

The above is briefly an account of the manner in which our colony is conducted.[8]

Although there has been some dissatisfaction with this form of government on the part of the younger and more aggressive members of the colony, yet the local government here described with slight modifications is still in vogue in the Manitoba settlement.

Kansas Colony

The Kansas colony, which was next to those in Manitoba in size, was composed largely of immigrants from the Molotchna settlement. Here too, although they came from a less conservative community, they at first tried to reproduce the village life of their native land. In the fall of 1873 the first arrivals purchased twelve sections of railroad land in Marion county, and laid out two villages, "Gnadenau" and "Hoffnungsthal." Each of these villages "occupied

---

8. Peter Wiens, in Herald of Truth, November, 1877.

one section of land, the main street running through the center, with the dwelling houses and flower gardens facing the street, the barns, the stables, orchards and vegetable gardens in the rear of the lots. The remaining ten sections of land were devoted to the farms proper."[9] This manner of settlement, however, was abandoned by the later immigrants to the colony, who adopted the American plan of having their houses on the land they farmed.

The Kansas settlers at first met with many hardships. They came into the state in the year of the financial panic of 1873, which was followed the next year by the grasshopper plague. As a result many of them had to call upon their brethren in the eastern states for the necessaries of life. They have since, however, become among the most prosperous people in the western states. They have also become among the most useful and faithful of American citizens. One of their number, Peter Jansen, a wealthy landowner and sheep raiser, was at one time a member of the Nebraska legislature and was appointed by President McKinley as one of the commissioners from this country to the Paris Exposition in 1900.

In their conference relations the Russian churches are not a unit. A small division had taken place in Crimea a short time before the immigra-
Conference Relations tion. This branch, known as the "Brüder Gemeinde," practices baptism by immersion and is more conservative in its religious life than the main body. It is represented in this country by several congregations in the western states.

---

9. C. B. Schmidt, in Reminiscences of Foreign Immigration Work.

The Manitoba settlements have remained isolated from the American churches. But in the United States there has been a closer connection between the native and Russian congregations. The majority have affiliated themselves with the General Conference Mennonites. About thirty congregations, principally from Kansas, including the large Alexanderwohl church of about eight hundred members in Harvey county, are now included in that body.

A number of small congregations in Nebraska and Minnesota have united in the Minnesota-Nebraska conference. The leading spirit in the movement had been Isaac Peters, from Henderson, Nebraska, and hence these churches are sometimes spoken of among other Mennonites as the "Peters" churches.

Several of the congregations of Kansas have furnished a number of members for the so-called "Holdeman" people, while a number of churches in Minnesota have remained independent of all conference relations.

CHAPTER XIII

GENERAL CONFERENCE MENNONITES[1]

As already seen in another chapter, J. H. Oberholtzer and his followers after their expulsion from the Franconia conference in 1847 immediately organized themselves into a new religious body. Oberholtzer began an aggressive campaign for the spread of the new movement. For the advancement of the religious interests of his congregations he founded in 1852 the first Mennonite religious paper in America, called Religiöser Botschafter. This paper soon changed its name to Christliches Volksblatt and is still published at Berne, Indiana, under the name of Christlicher Bundesbote.

Although Oberholtzer was active in promoting the interests of the new movement, he had not entirely abandoned the hope of effecting a reconciliation with the mother church. He was earnest in his desire for union and as late as 1860, he suggested in a

---

1. For the infomation in this chapter I am indebted almost entirely to the excellent history of the General Conference movement written by H. P. Krehbiel.

pamphlet called Verantwortung und Erläuterung, terms upon which the two churches might unite. These terms, however, were rejected and no reconciliation was brought about.

In the meantime a liberal movement similar in many respects to the one in Franconia had made headway among a few of the scattered churches near Niagara Falls, in Lincoln county, Ontario. The movement was one in behalf of more aggressive church work, especially of greater evangelistic efforts, and the leading spirit was a minister by the name of Daniel Hoch. In 1853 Hoch was appointed by these congregations as evangelist to visit some of the scattered churches in the region. He also evidently came in touch with a small congregation near Wadsworth, Ohio, for in 1855 these churches organized themselves into the Conference Council of the Mennonite Community of Canada West and Ohio. The purpose of the organization seems to have been to promote a greater evangelistic and missionary zeal among the churches.

Liberal Movement in Ontario

Oberholtzer had taken a great interest in the Canada movement from the very beginning, for here might perhaps be an opportunity of enlarging the circle of churches that favored a more liberal policy, and of beginning the realization of a dream which he already began to cherish, namely, the unification of all the Mennonite churches of America. Consequently in the Volksblatt in 1856 he advocated the union of the Canada-Ohio conference already referred to with his own Pennsylvania conference in the interests of the mission cause, and suggested a general council of the two conferences. The plan was favorably received by the Canadian churches but no action was taken upon it.

While this subject was being discussed in the East, a question of a similar nature had arisen in the West. In Lee county, Iowa, there **Iowa Movement** were two congregations which were composed largely of Bavarian immigrants who had come to the state a few years before. They were located near the Amish settlement which had been made here some time earlier. But being more recently from Europe than the Amish and differing from them in some of their customs, they never worked in harmony with them. Consequently these two congregations found themselves isolated from the other Iowa churches. Feeling the need of united effort, especially in evangelistic work among such members of the church as had settled some distance from the main body of the two congregations, in 1859 they held a joint meeting of which J. C. Krehbiel was the chairman, near West Point in Lee county, for the purpose of "devising ways on the one hand for the centralization of the Mennonite churches, but chiefly on the other for supplying isolated families with the Gospel blessings." The ideal of a union of all Mennonite churches in the interest of the mission cause, or at any rate of such Mennonite churches as were in sympathy with a more aggressive church policy seems also to have taken hold of the imagination of the leaders in the Lee county congregations. Near the close of the meeting it was decided to invite other churches to meet with them in another conference to be held the next year near West Point. The report of the meeting together with this invitation was published in the Volksblatt.

Oberholtzer naturally was interested in the Iowa movement. During the year he repeatedly urged through the columns of his paper that his own and the Canadian congregations send representatives to the coming meeting in Lee county. Neither, however, seemed enthusiastic in responding to the invitation, and that for several reasons. In the first place Iowa was at that time on the frontier line of American civilization, and why should the eastern churches go so far west to attend a meeting the purpose of which was to form a union of congregations almost all of which were located in the East. Secondly, the Iowans were recent European immigrants in whom the easterners, whose ancestors had been in this country for two centuries, felt little interest. Neither of the local conferences appointed delegates to the western meeting. Hoch and Oberholtzer appeared to be the only individuals who manifested any interest in the enterprise, and it seemed doubtful whether even they could go. But finally at the very last moment Oberholtzer with one companion contrived to attend and they were the only representatives at the meeting outside of the Iowa congregations.

The conference, if such it may be called, was held May 28-9, 1860, near West Point, and was composed of the two congregations already mentioned, another minister from a nearby settlement and the two representatives from Pennsylvania. J. H. Oberholtzer was chosen chairman, and Christian Showalter of the home congregation, secretary. Although

The Conference of 1860

unpretentious and local in character, this meeting was not deterred by that fact from discussing an ambitious and lofty ideal, namely, the unification of all the Mennonites of America under one working organization. Deploring the fact that there was so much strife among the congregations and that the "denomination has never since its existence in America constituted an ecclesiastical organization," the assembly drew up a set of resolutions which might serve as a common platform upon which all might unite for the extension of the mission and other church interests. These resolutions are as follows,—

1. That all branches of the Mennonite denomination in North America regardless of minor differences, should extend to each other the hand of fellowship.

2. That fraternal relations shall be severed only when a person or church abandons the fundamental doctrines of the denomination; namely, those concerning baptism, the oath, etc., as indeed all those principal doctrines of the faith which we with Menno base solely upon the Gospel as received from our Lord Jesus Christ and His apostles.

3. That no brother shall be found guilty of heresy unless his error can be established on unequivocal Scripture evidence.

4. That the General Conference shall consider no excommunication as scripturally valid, unless a real transgression or neglect conflicting with the demands of scripture, exists.

5. That every church or district shall be entitled to continue without molestation or hindrance and amenable only to their own conscience, any rules or regulations they may have adopted for their own government; provided they do not conflict with the tenets of our general confession.

6. That if a member of a church, because of existing customs or ordinances in his church, shall desire to sever his connec-

tion and unite with some other church of the General Conference, such action shall not be interfered with.[2]

Its Purpose As indicated, the motive for this united action was for more effective evangelistic efforts, but two other subjects were discussed during the meeting,—the establishing of a publishing house, and of an institution for theological training. Both of these measures had been advocated by Oberholtzer and Hoch before, and the former no doubt introduced them in the discussions at this time. After a two days session the assembly adjourned, but not before it was decided to meet again the following year at Wadsworth, Ohio.

Thus was launched the General Conference of the Mennonites, or what became popularly known as the General Conference Mennonites. The aim of the movement was an ambitious, but a worthy one. Just how seriously the leaders of the cause at this time entertained the thought of a union of all Mennonites it is not easy to say. It may be safely inferred, however, that none expected to see the work accomplished in their own generation, for the task was almost an impossible one. The gap between the opposite extremes of Mennonite custom and practice of that time was too wide to be bridged over easily. But a union of some of the more liberal of the native American churches and a number of the recent immigrant congregations was entirely feasible, and the leaders of the movement perhaps hardly hoped to accomplish more than that.

The General Conference, however, was hardly a

---

2. Krehbiel. p. 57.

fact as yet. Neither the Canada-Ohio Council nor the several other independent congregations which it was hoped might be brought into line had accepted the first invitation. It remained to be seen what action these would take at the next meeting at Wadsworth.

This session, the second of the General Conference, was held at Wadsworth, Medina county, Ohio, May 20, 1861. It was soon found that the unification movement was growing, for now eight congregations were represented, including in addition to those represented the previous year, those at Waterloo, Ontario, Wadsworth, Ohio, Summerfield, Illinois, and several from Pennsylvania. Two new subjects were discussed at this session. A new article discouraging secret societies was added to the platform adopted the previous year, and the first steps were taken toward the establishing of a theological school. This was founded several years later at Wadsworth. The conference was now a fact. After this, sessions were held regularly, at first biennially, but later triennially. Under the leadership of such able men as J. H. Oberholtzer, Daniel Krehbiel, Christian Showalter, A. B. Shelly, Christian Krehbiel, Ephraim Hunsberger, S. F. Sprunger and many other younger men within recent years, the movement grew steadily from the beginning along the lines laid down at the first meeting in Iowa. Each session since then has shown an addition of new congregations.

Second Session at Wadsworth

The largest additions have come from the more recent immigrant churches,—the Swiss of Ohio and Indiana, and the Russians of Kansas and other western states.[3] Among the largest congregations are now the magnificent church at Berne, Indiana, with a membership of over seven hundred, and the Alexanderwohl congregation of Russians, in Harvey county, Kansas, which has a membership of about eight hundred. In 1908 the Conference embraced a total membership of about twelve thousand.

It will be seen that the General Conference of Mennonites is not a separate division of the church. It is rather a conference whose ultimate aim is the union of all branches of the denomination. This it hopes to do along the lines laid down in 1860. No restrictions or limitations are placed upon the congregations composing it. Each governs itself and determines its own church policy. But all unite upon certain lines of Christian activity—such as missions, education, publication interests and evangelistic efforts. The purpose of the General Conference is best set forth by H. P. Krehbiel, the historian of the movement. He says,—

Character of the General Conference

The churches constituting the General Conference have by their union not become something else from what they were before. Each church remains just what it was and retains all peculiarities she had if she chooses. Each church retains her individuality as well as her independence. It is not a separate class or division of Mennonites which may be distinguished from others by special doctrines or customs. It is impossible to class the Conference as such a division because her membership list contains churches which differ very

---

3. This was because both the General Conference and the recent immigrants were in favor of heathen mission work while the old Mennonites still opposed such work, and because both were more liberal in their views regarding religious customs and practices than the main body of the native American church.

much in customs and special views, and which to this day retain these differences precisely as they did previous to uniting with the Conference. The General Conference is therefore in no sense a branch or division of the denomination.

After all, however, the members of the organization necessarily have certain common interests and religious opinions and practices which differentiate them from all other Mennonites, and which give them many of the characteristics of a separate branch of the church. In fundamental doctrines they differ little from other divisions of the denomination. In the main they accept the same confession of faith as all others—the Dordrecht Confession of 1632, and they accept all the fundamental doctrines of the Mennonite faith with the exception that some of them insist on rather a modified form of the doctrine of non-resistance as applied to war and especially as applied to the practice of availing one's self of the law in personal controversies.

In practice and customs, however, they differ in some respects from the main body of Old Mennonites. They do not practice feetwashing, and no restrictions are laid on the form of dress. They maintain a salaried ministry and favor in general a liberal church policy.

And consequently they have made little headway in interesting the more conservative bodies of the church in the movement for union. For among both the Amish and the main body of native American Mennonites, these earlier practices are still firmly rooted. Whether the various branches will ever again reunite and if so, whether the union will be along the lines suggested by the General Conference Mennonites, is a question the solution of which no one can foretell.

It is but natural that this, the most liberal wing of the denomination, should be the first to venture out into new lines of Christian activity. It is **Christian** here that the first church paper, the first **Activity** church school, and the first missionary enterprise among the American Mennonites were established. Although at times there has been considerable friction between the eastern and western churches, due to the fact that the former were native Americans while the latter were recent European immigrants, yet the growth of interest in educational and missionary enterprises has been constant from the beginning, and the General Conference movement has done much to enhance both the interests and the good name of the whole denomination.

CHAPTER XIV

THE MENNONITES AND THE STATE

The purpose of this chapter is to show how in America the non-resistant principles of the Mennonites often came into conflict with the civil authorities, but how, also, absolute religious liberty was finally secured. The subject will be treated from the standpoint of the civil powers, and I shall not discuss here the experience of the Mennonites in the application of these laws. In this respect the Quakers and Mennonites have in many instances had a common history, and the two must necessarily be treated more or less together.

No part of their creed has subjected the Mennonites to more misrepresentation and misunderstanding than their attitude toward the civil authorities. They adopted bodily the faith of the peaceful type of Anabaptists, and that was a rejection of all civil and a great deal of the prevailing ecclesiastical government as unnecessary for the Christian. The Non-resistant Anabaptists of whom the Mennonites were the direct successors, went no further, however, in their opposition to the temporal authority than to declare that the true church

Attitude toward Civil Government Misunderstood

and the temporal powers had nothing in common and must be entirely separate; not only must the state not interfere with the church, but the true Christian must be entirely free from participating in civil matters. The temporal authority must needs exist since it was instituted of God to punish the wicked, but in that work the Christian had no hand. This position they reached from a literal interpretation of the Sermon on the mount where Christ taught his disciples among other things to "love their enemies", and to "swear not at all." Hence their position involved opposition to the oath, holding of office and bearing of arms. This often brought them into trouble with the civil authorities, and in Europe they seldom got exemption from these civic obligations. This was one of the causes of their emigration. Nor were they granted entire exemption in America without many years of struggle.

The earliest Anabaptist confession of faith drawn up at Schleitheim in 1527, teaches very distinctly that the use of the sword is ordained by God to punish the wicked but no Christian can wield it. As to the right of the Christian to be a magistrate, this declaration states, "it was intended to make Christ King and He fled and did not regard the ordinance of the Father. Thus should we do, and follow him and we shall not walk in darkness." Neither can the Christian take an oath, for "Christ who teaches the perfection of the law forbids to his people all swearing whether true or false." This was the position taken by Menno Simons[1] and by all those Anabaptists

Anabaptist View of the Sword

---

1. See Menno Simons' Complete Works, Elkhart, Ind., Edition. Part II. p. 301.

who later were known as Mennonites. The Anabaptist movement was not confined to Germany and Holland but soon appeared also in England. That this view of the Christian's attitude toward the civil authorities had made some headway in the latter country is evidenced by the fact that the earliest confessions of faith of the Presbyterian, Anglican and Baptist churches found it necessary to explicitly state that it is not unlawful nor inconsistent for the Christian to swear, bear arms, or be a magistrate.[2] On the con-

---

2. The following extracts taken from various Confessions of Faith and other sources illustrate the prevalence of these ideas:

(a) "It is lawful for a Christian to be a magistrate or civil officer and also it is lawful to take an oath so it be in truth and judgment and in righteousness for confirmation of truth and ending all strife and that by rash and vain oaths the Lord is provoked and this land mourns." Article 49. Confession of Faith of so-called Anabaptists in London, 1646,—See Schaff, Confessions of Faith of Baptists in the Seventeenth Century, p. 46.

(b) "We ought to pay tribute, custom, and all other duties. Magistrates may be members of the church of Christ, retaining their magistracy; for no ordinance of God debarreth any from being a member of Christ's church. They bear the Sword of God; which Sword in all lawful administrations is to be defended and supported by the servants of God that are under their government, with their lives and all that they have, according as in the first institution of that holy ordinance."—Declaration of Faith of English people remaining at Amsterdam, printed 1611. See Schaff, p. 10.

(c) "A lawful oath is a part of religious worship wherein upon just occasion the person swearing solemnly calleth God to witness what he asserteth or promiseth."
It is lawful for Christians to accept and execute the office of a magistrate when called thereunto."—Westminister Confession 1647.

(d) "It is lawful for Christian men at the commandment of the magistrate to weare weapons and serve in the wars."
"We judge that Christian religion doth not prohibite, but that a man may sweare when the magistrate requireth in a cause of faith and charitie, so it be done accordyng to the prophet's teaching in justice, judgment and truth."—The Book of Common Prayer of Church of England. 1571 Edition.

(e) "The Sword—An ordinance of God, to punish the wicked. The Christian can not use it." "Magistrate—It was intended to make Christ king and he fled, and did not regard the ordinance of

tinent several peace sects borrowed a part or all of these doctrines from the earlier Anabaptists or later Mennonites. The most prominent of these, most of whom followed the Mennonites to America early in the eighteenth century, were the Moravians, Schwenkfelders and the Dunkards.

His Father. Thus should we do and follow Him and we shall not walk in darkness." "Oath—Christ who teacheth the perfection of the law forbids to his people all swearing whether true or false." Substance of the Schleitheim Confession of Faith 1527 as quoted by Armitage in his history of the Baptists. This is the first Anabaptist confession and was adopted by the Mennonites.

(f) In as much as we thus confess and cordially believe and besides confess that no emperor or king may rule or command contrary to his word since he is the head of all princes and is the king of kings and that unto Him every knee shall bow which is in heaven in earth or under the earth, and as he has plainly forbidden us to swear and points us to yea and nay alone, therefore it is that we swear not by the fear of God, nor dare swear, though we must bear and suffer so much on that account from the world."—Menno Simons.

(g) "God has instituted civil government for the punishment of the wicked and the protection of the pious, etc."

"Regarding revenge whereby we resist our enemies with the Sword, we believe and confess that the Lord Jesus has forbidden his disciples and followers all revenge and resistance and has thereby commanded them not to return evil for evil nor railing for railing; but to put up the sword into the sheath, or as the prophets foretold, beat them into plough shares, etc."

"Regarding the swearing of oaths we believe and confess that the Lord Jesus has dissuaded his followers from and forbidden the same; that is, that he commanded them to swear not at all; but that their "Yea" should be "yea," and their "Nay," "nay," etc.— Mennonite Confession of Faith, 1632.

(h) "And whereas many of us are now prisoners can not take the oath of allegiance because we can not swear at all."—Anabaptists of Kent County, England in a petition to Charles II, 1660, quoted in Tracts on Liberty of Conscience by Hansard Knollys Society, p. 307.

(i)
Error 104.
"That Poedobaptism is unlawful and anti-christian and 'tis as lawful to baptize a Cat, or a Dog, or a Chicken as to baptize the infants of believers."—Part II. 28.
Error 158.

In England, on the other hand, by the close of the seventeenth century the Quakers stood alone as exponents of the non-resistant doctrine. Here at the time when Pennsylvania was settled they had not yet gained any exemption from the oath. It was not until 1689 that any concessions were made to their

Struggles of Quakers for Exemption from the Oath

"'Tis unlawful for Christians to defend Religion with the Sword or to fight for it when men come with Sword to take it away, Religion will defend itself."—Part II. 34.
Error 159.
" 'Tis unlawful for Christians to fight, and take up arms for their laws and civil liberties."
Error 160.
" 'Tis unlawful to fight at all or to kill any of the creatures for our use, as a chicken or any on other occasion."
Error 168.
"That 'tis unlawful for a Christian to be a magistrate but upon turning Christian he should lay down his magistracie, neither do we read after Cornelius was baptized (though he were a Centurion before and a man in command and authority) that ever he meddled any more with his band called the Italian band." Part II. 35.
Error 40.
"That tis not lawful for Christians to take an oath, no not when they are called before authority and brought into court." Part III. 14.—These extracts are taken from "Edwards Gangrena", a "Treatise on the Sectaries of England and their Errors", published in London, 1647.
(j) "For as much as the consciences of sundry men, truly conscienable may scruple the giving or taking of an oath, and it would be noways suitable to the nature and constitution of our place (who profess ourselves to be men of different consciences and not willing to force another) to Debar such as can not do so, either from bearing office amongst us, or from giving in testimony in a case depending."
"Be it enacted by the authority of this present Assembly that a solemn profession or Testimony in a Court of Record, or before a Judge of Record shall be accounted, throughout the whole Colonie of as full force as an oath."—Rhode Island Colonial Records, I. 181. (1647).
(k) "For as much as experience hath plentyfully and often proved yet since ye first arising of ye Anabaptists, about a hundred years since they have been ye incendaries of Commonwealths, and

tender consciences. The Act of Toleration permitted a solemn promise and declaration to take the place of the oath of allegiance and abjuration. In 1696 Parliament passed an act providing a modified form of the affirmation, which however was still objectionable to the Quakers. This act was renewed frequently in later years and was given a wider application, but it was not until 1833 that the affirmation was made equal in every respect to the usual oath.

The law of 1696 was applied to Pennsylvania by Queen Anne but withdrawn again in 1705.[3] No provision was made in it for the Mennonites. The laws passed by the colony of Pennsylvania very early made it possible for those conscientiously opposed to the oath to substitute the affirmation. The laws of England discriminated in favor of the Quakers only, and it may be for this reason that the Mennonites in 1706 petitioned the Provincial Council[4] that

Pennsylvania Laws on the Oath

> ye infectors of persons in Maine matters of religion, and ye troublers of churches in all places where they have bene and yet they who have held ye baptizing of infants unlawful have usually held other errors or heresies together therewith, though they have (as other hereticks use to do) concealed ye same till they spied out a fit advantage and opportunity to vent them, by way of question or scruple and whereas divers of this kind have since our coming into New England, appeared amongst ourselves, some whereof have (as others before them) denied ye ordinance of magistracy, and ye lawfulness of making war, and others ye lawfulness of magistrates and their inspection into any breach of ye first table, which opinions, if they should be connived at by us, are like to be increased amongst us and so must necessarily bring guilt upon us, infection and trouble to ye churches, and hazard to ye whole community."—It is ordered and agreed etc."—Mass. Rec., II. 85. (1644).

3. Restored again 1725. See Proud, History of Pennsylvania. II. 190.
4. Col. Rec., II, 241.

ROHRERSTOWN CHURCH. Where the Lancaster conference meets each spring.

since they (with their predecessory for above 150 years past) could not for conscience sake take an oath, the same provision may be made for them by Law as is made for those called Quakers in this Province and that the said Law may be sent home with the rest passed by the late Assembly in order to obtain the Queens Royal approbation.

The Quakers who had control of the government of Pennsylvania had a tender regard for the religious scruples of the Mennonites and granted them all the religious liberty they themselves enjoyed. In 1717 the Council, alarmed at the large German immigration that seemed to threaten them, passed an ordinance to the effect that all newcomers should take an oath of allegiance to his Majesty and his Government. The Mennonites, however, "who can not for conscience sake take any oaths" are to be admitted "upon their giving any equivalent assurance in their own way and manner:"[5] This provision evidently did not apply to any of the non-resistant denominations except the Mennonites, for on November 4, 1742, a petition was received by the council from the Amish[6] demanding that the oath be changed in the naturalization laws, since they

though not Quakers, are conscientiously scrupulous to taking any oath, they can not as the Law now stands be naturalized.[7]

---

5. Col. Rec., III. 29.
6. Hazard, Register, VII. 151.
   Conyngham the author of this article says that this petition was written in 1718. Conyngham however is altogether unreliable in almost everything he says about the Amish. His statement here is not consistent with facts. It is altogether likely that this may be the 1742 petition referred to by Watson. See Watson, Annals, II. 109.
7. Without naturalization they could not bequeath their lands to their children.

The Assembly passed the desired legislation.[8] From this time on it appears that neither Mennonites nor Amish had any occasion to petition for further civil exemptions, until the time of the Revolution, after the control of the government had passed out of the hands of the Quakers and when all non-resistant sects found it difficult to maintain a strictly neutral attitude toward the war.

Maryland is the only state to mention the Mennonites by name in its constitution. Article 36 in the Declaration of Rights drawn up by the Constitutional Convention of 1776 declares that

Maryland Constitution Exempts Mennonites

the manner of administering an oath to any person ought to be such as those of the religious persuasion, profession or denomination of which such person is one generally esteem the most effectual confirmation, by the attestation of the Divine being, and that the people called Quakers and those called Dunkers, and those called Menonists holding it unlawful to take an oath on any occasion ought to be allowed to make their solemn affirmation in the manner that Quakers have been heretofore allowed to affirm and to be of the same avail as an oath in all such cases as the affirmation of Quakers has been allowed and accepted within this state instead of an oath. And further on such affirmation, warrants to search for stolen goods, or the apprehension or commitment of offenders, ought to be granted or security for the peace awarded and Quakers, Tunkers and Menonists ought also on their solemn affirmation as aforesaid to be admitted as witnesses in all criminal cases not capital.

---

3. Votes of Assembly, III. 505. The Records call them German Protestants. They were not Quakers but were scrupulous of taking any oath. Hazard calls them Omish (See Hazard Register V. 21) and I am inclined to think that this is the petition quoted in Hazard VII. 151.

In 1794 the General Assembly confirmed this article and further enacted that Quakers, Menonists and Tunkers when elected to any civil office might substitute a simple affirmation for the usual oath.[9] In 1797 a law was passed to the effect that before any of the above mentioned were to be admitted as a witness in a court of justice

the court shall be satisfied by such testimony as they may require, that such person is one of those who profess to be conscientiously scrupulous of taking an oath.

In Virginia there was less religious liberty before the Revolution than in Pennsylvania and Maryland.

Virginia Liberal toward Mennonite Scruples

Here there was an established state church which enjoyed many civil and religious privileges that were denied the other denominations. This church was supported out of the common funds, controlled very largely the education of the youth, and her priests alone could perform marriage rites. Other denominations by the time of the Revolution were generally permitted freedom of worship, but in addition to supporting themselves they were compelled to help keep up the established church.

The Shenandoah Valley, where the Mennonites were located, contained comparatively few Anglicans. Many of the early settlers were Dissenters, Baptists,

---

9. Kilty, Laws of Maryland, II. 1794, Ch. 49. See also Index under Menonist and Quaker.

Presbyterians, Mennonites, Quakers and Tunkers.[10] Here the established faith was especially unpopular, and in the struggle for religious liberty in Virginia the inhabitants of the Valley played a conspicuous role. All the dissenting churches maintained a vigorous fight for exemption from the payment of tithes, and for equal privileges to perform marriage rites among their own number. The Mennonites and Quakers furthermore were compelled to demand the additional exemption from the oath and military service.

The Mennonites, as we have seen, came into the Valley before the middle of the eighteenth century, but some were driven back into Pennsylvania again before 1758. They must have returned in considerable numbers again before the Revolution, for we find in the Records of the House of Burgesses for June 15, 1775, a petition

of the community of Christians called Menonists presented to the House and read, setting forth that the petitioners hold it to be contrary to the Word of God to swear in any matter whatever so that they can not become witnesses in matters of controversy depending in any court nor can execute the office of Executor of any Testament, nor undertake the administration of any intestate's estate whereby they suffer many inconveniences, and therefore praying that they may have the same liberty of affirming to the Truth of any matter as is indulged to the people called Quakers, whose religious persuasion that of the Petitioners nearly resemble.[11]

This petition was referred to the committee for

---

10. In 1780 a new marriage law making concessions to Quakers and Mennonites was passed. See Henning, X. 362.
   "There were not many church of England ministers in the Valley and they had to ride far and charged exhorbitant prices. Wedding parties often had to go to them."—Foote, Sketches of Virginia, 331.

11. Kennedy, Journal of the House of Burgesses, 217.

religion who were ordered to examine the matter and report the same with their opinion thereupon to the next house. Although there seems to be no record of any statute passed in consequence of this request it is likely that the Mennonites were granted the same privileges as the Quakers in this as in other matters of religious toleration.

The Mennonites were also among the first in the state of Virginia to secure legal exemption from the marriage laws. In 1780 the Assembly enacted that any Menonist or Quaker minister might legally celebrate the rites of matrimony and

> join together as man and wife those who may apply to them agreeable to the rules and usage of the respective societies to which the parties to be married respectively belong.[12]

The contracting parties were to secure marriage certificates from the proper civil authorities. Any clerk of a Mennonite or Quaker meeting who failed to return such certificate within three months was subject to a fine of five hundred pounds of tobacco. Only four ministers of each sect in each county were to be granted licenses by the judge or elder magistrate to perform marriage rites. This brought no hardship upon the Mennonites, however, since at this time there was only one settlement in the state and that a comparatively small one. The same act provided that no persons of other denominations were to be joined together in matrimony without a lawful license or thrice publication of bans in the respective parishes where the parties to be married resided in accordance with the provisions of an act passed in 1748.

---

12. Henning, X. 361, 363.

The three states mentioned were the only ones in which Mennonites were found before 1800. After 1800 they spread rapidly into other states but nowhere outside of Maryland, Virginia, or Pennsylvania, did they find it necessary to repeat the struggle for the right of affirmation. Many of the later states, influenced, no doubt, by the example of these older ones, made provision either in their constitutions or by statute for substituting a simple declaration or affirmation for the usual oath wherever such oath is required. The United States Constitution provides for the use of the affirmation in the Presidential and other oaths of office, an alternative which seems to have been inserted by the Convention without debate.[13]

In the struggle for exemption from military service the peace sects frequently encountered a more vigorous opposition than in their demand for the right of affirmation. The objection to the oath was a question which was of little interest to others, but the refusal to bear arms in time of war was a matter not so easily overlooked and often misunderstood by their neighbors and those in authority. In Pennsylvania so long as the Quaker regime lasted, the Mennonites found no difficulty in practicing their peace principles. In fact for the fifteen years immediately preceding the downfall of the Quaker government in 1756 these two denominations were forced to combine their strength in a common fight for the maintenance of their peace principles. These were the years of one of the Colonial

Exemption from Military Service

---

13. Elliot, Debates, V. 498.

wars and of Indian incursions. The Assembly, in which the Quakers were still in the majority, refused to declare war against the Indians or provide for the defense of the frontier. The larger part of the population, including among the leaders, Benjamin Franklin and Governor Thomas, were strenuously opposed to the peaceful measures of the Quaker Assembly.[14] The Quakers although representing a minority of the population yet were able to retain control of the Assembly largely through their political alliance with the German peace sects who shared the Quaker views on non-resistance. We learn from a letter written by Dr. William Smith in 1755 that the Quakers succeeded in manipulating the German vote in such a way as to elect assemblymen from the German counties who were committed to the Quaker principles of government. This was done largely through the influence of Christopher Sauer the Dunkard printer, who by means of his almanacs, newspapers and other German publications, had secured wide acquaintance among the Germans, and especially the non-resistant Germans—the Mennonites, Dunkards, Schwenkfelders and Moravians—in the frontier counties.[15] It was through fear of military conscription and heavy taxes that the German non-resistants were drawn to the side of the Quakers in the struggle for the maintenance of their peace policy. Just how generally and how effectively the German vote was cast for Quaker assemblymen it is difficult to tell, but the political broadsides printed by Sauer and still preserved in the library of the

---
14. Votes of Assembly, III. 364.
15. Sharpless, Quakerism and Politics, p. 131.

Pennsylvania State Historical Society leave no doubt as to the reality of the struggle between the peace and war parties for the support of the German non-resistants, who held the balance of power. Especially is it difficult to tell just how much the Mennonites contributed to the net result of this struggle. Documents are not available and perhaps not extant from which a conclusive judgment might be made. It is altogether likely, however, that the Mennonite vote in Lancaster county and perhaps in Bucks did much to keep the Quaker assembly in power long after it had fallen out of favor with the people at large.[16] The

---

16. The following letter written to a politician in Bucks county in 1765 shows that even after the downfall of the Quaker regime the Mennonites were still a local political factor that needed to be reckoned with.

"I went up lately to Bucks Court in order to concert measures for their (i. e some friends) election, in pursuance of which we have appointed a considerable meeting of Germans, Baptists and Presbyterians to be held next Monday at Neshaminy, where some of us, some Germans and Baptists of this place have appointed to attend, in order to attempt a general confederacy of the three societies in opposition to the ruling party. We have sent up emissaries among the Germans which I hope will bring them into this measure, and if it can be effected, will give us a great chance for carrying matters in that county. Could that be carried, it would infallibly secure our friends a majority in the House, and consequently enable them to recall our dangerous enemy, Franklin, with his petitions, which is the great object we have in view, and which should engage the endeavors of all our friends at the approaching election to make a spirited push for a majority in the Assembly, without which all our struggles here will prove of little service to the public interest..... If you knew thoroughly the methods Mr. Franklin is taking at home to blacken and stigmatize our society, you would perhaps judge with me that you never had more reason to exert yourselves in order to overset him, which we can only do by commanding a majority in the Assembly. I have seen a letter lately from a person of character, that advises us of his wicked designs against us. The little hopes of success, as well as the difficulty of engaging proper persons for the purpose, has discourged me from attempting a project recommended by some friends of sending up some Germans to work upon their country-

final break came, as we saw, in 1756, when the Quakers lost their majority in the Assembly and that body immediately voted to make war upon the Indians. From this time on until the Revolution the Mennonites were in constant fear lest they might be forced to violate their religious convictions.

> men. But that no probable means may fail, I have sent up some copies of a piece lately printed by Sowers of Germantown, to be dispersed, and which may possibly have some effect.
> As I understand the Mennonites have certainly resolved to turn out Isaac Saunders this year, though the only good member your county has, I would beg leave to offer you and other friends the following scheme, as the only probable chance, I think, you have to carry the election and keep Mr. Saunders. If the scheme is properly executed and can be conducted without danger of a riot, I think you could infallibly carry your ticket by it.
> Don't attempt to change any of your members save Webb. If you can run Dr. Kuhn, or any popular German, and can keep Mr. Saunders, you will do great things. As soon as your ticket is agreed on let it be spread through the country, that your party intend to come well armed to the election, and that you intend, if there's the least partiality in either sheriff, inspectors, or managers of the election that you will thrash the sheriff, every inspector, Quaker or Menonist to a jelly; and further I would report it, that not a Menonist nor German should be admitted to give in a ticket without being sworn that he is naturalized and worth 50 pounds and that he has voted already; and further, that if you discovered any person attempting to give in a vote without being naturalized, or voting twice, you would that moment deliver him up to the mob to chastise him. Let this report be industriously spread before the election which will certainly keep great numbers of the Mennonists at home. I would at the same time have all our friends warned to put on a bold face, to be every man provided with a shillelah, as if determined to put their threats in execution, though at the same time let them be solemnly charged to keep the greatest order and peace. Let our friends choose about two dozen of the most reputable men, magistrates, etc., who shall attend the inspectors, sheriffs and clerks during the whole election, to mount guard half at a time, and relieve one another at spells, to prevent all cheating and administer the oath to every suspicious person, and to commit to immediate punishment every one who offers to vote twice. I'll engage if you conduct the election in that manner, and our people turn out with spirit, you can't fail of carrying every man on your ticket, as I am well assured not a third of the Mennonists are naturalized, I would submit this to your consideration. If its well thought of,

During the early stages of the Revolution there was little of united action in preparing for the common defense. Each colony mustered its own militia, provided its own arms and ammunition and in general regulated its own affairs regardless of what other colonies or the Continental Congress were doing. Early in 1775 the Assembly of Pennsylvania recommended that all able-bodied white male inhabitants of the province "associate" for the common defence. Those who would not join such voluntary military organizations were called "non-associators." Remembering, however, that many of the people of Southeastern Pennsylvania were Quakers, Mennonites, Dunkards and of other non-resistant denominations, the Assembly on June 30, 1775, since

Associators during the Revolution

> many of the good People of this Province are conscientiously scrupulous of bearing arms further recommended to the associators for the defence of their county and others, that they bear a tenderly and brotherly Regard toward this class of their Fellow subjects and Countrymen.[17]

To these conscientious people on the other hand it was suggested that

> they cheerfully assist in proportion to their abilities such associators as can not spend their time and substance in the Public Service without great injury to themselves.

---

take your measures immediately, I beg no mention may be made of the author of this. I see no danger in the scheme but that of a riot, which would require great prudence to avoid." Samuel Purviance, Philadelphia, to Col. Burd, quoted by Thomas Balch, in Letters and Papers Relating chiefly to the Provincial History of Pennsylvania. (Phil 1885). 209. Quoted also in Hart's Source Book, p. 127.

17. Votes of Assembly, I. 594.

MENNONITES AND THE STATE 369

It will thus be seen that while the Mennonites were excused from military service it was suggested that they pay for the privilege.

There was much opposition from the various military associations to this lenient policy of the Assembly. Many petitions soon came in complaining that the people who were religiously scrupulous were few compared to those who "made conscience a convenience." A very considerable share of the property they said was in the hands of people professing tender conscience in military matters.[18] They were especially opposed to the arrangement by which the non-combatants were allowed to make voluntary contributions. The proportion each was to pay they said ought to be fixed. No doubt these contributions were not large, but the Quakers were out and out opposed to paying at all. They objected as conscientiously to the supporting of war by money as to the bearing of arms.[19] The Mennonites were less consistent. While they would not carry weapons themselves, they appear generally not to have objected to supporting the cause by their means.

As a result of these petitions the Assembly resolved on Nov. 7, 1775, that all non-associators contribute an equivalent to the time spent by the associators in acquiring military discipline.[20] Ministers and servants alone were excepted. In order that no one might escape paying his just portion it was further ordered on November 24, that the committee which was appointed to adjust the accounts of the various bat-

---
18. Votes of Assembly, I. (Sep. 27, 1775).
19. Votes, I. 635.
20. Votes, I. (Nov. 7, 1775).

talions of associators, be directed to make particular enquiry concerning the contributions made

by the people called Menonists, Amish Menonists and Sunday Baptists (possibly the Ephrata Dunkards in Lancaster county) in pursuance of the late House of Assembly on the thirtieth of June last, and report to this house at their next meeting how much of the said contributions has been paid.[21]

Mennonite and Dunkard Petition of 1775

The Mennonites fearing that their position might be misunderstood and that they might be forced to join the associators sent (in conjunction with the German Baptists) a petition to the Assembly in which they stated definitely that although they could not conscientiously take up arms in defence of their country, yet they had always thought it their duty to pay tribute. The petition was reported in the Assembly on November 7. In spite of its length it is given in full here in the hope that it may throw some light upon the subject under discussion.

An address or Declaration by divers persons in Behalf of the Societies of Mennonists and German Baptists in this Province was presented to the House and follows in these words, viz.,

In the first place we acknowledge us indebted to the most high God, who created Heaven and Earth, the only good Being to thank him for all His great Goodness and Manifold Mercies and Love through our Savior Jesus Christ who is come to save the souls of Men, having all Power in Heaven and on Earth. Further we find ourselves indebted to be thankful to our late worthy assembly for their giving so good an Advice in these troublesome Times to all Ranks of People

---

21. Votes, I. 653.

in Pennsylvania, particularly in allowing those, who, by the Doctrine of our Savior, Jesus Christ are persuaded in their consciences to love their enemies, and not to resist Evil, to enjoy the Liberty of their Consciences for which, as also for all the good Things we enjoyed under their Care, we heartily thank that worthy Body of Assembly and all high and low in office who have advised to such a peaceful measure hoping and confiding that they and all others entrusted with Power in this hitherto blessed Province, may be moved by the same spirit of Grace which animated the first Founder of this Province, our late worthy Proprietor William Penn to grant Liberty of Conscience to all its inhabitants that they may in the great and memorable Day of Judgment be put on the right Hand of that just Judge, who judgeth without Respect of Person and hear of him these blessed Words, "Come ye blessed of my Father, inherit the kingdom prepared for you, etc., what ye have done unto one of the least of these my Brethren ye have done unto me," among which number (i. e. the least of Christ's Brethren) we by his Grace hope to be ranked; and every Lenity and Favour shewn to such tender conscience, although weak, Followers of this our blessed Saviour will not be forgotten by him in that great Day.

The Advice to those who do not find Freedom of Conscience to take up Arms that they ought to be helpful to those who are in Need and distressed Circumstances we receive with Cheerfulness towards all Men of what Station they may be—it being our Principle to feed the Hungry and give the Thirsty Drink. We have dedicated ourselves to serve all Men in Every Thing that can be helpful to the Preservation of Men's Lives but we find no Freedom in giving or doing, or assisting, in anything by which Men's Lives are destroyed or hurt.—We beg the Patience of all those who believe we err on this Point. We are always ready, according to Christ's command to Peter, to pay the Tribute, that we may offend no Man, and so we are willing to pay Taxes, and so render unto Caesar those Things that are Caesar's and to Godd those Things that are God's. Although we think ourselves very weak to give God his due Honour he being a Spirit and Life, and we only Dust and Ashes. We are also willing to be subject to the higher Powers and give in the manner Paul directs us: for he beareth the Sword not in vain, for he is the Minister of God, a Revenger to execute wrath upon him that doeth Evil. This Testimony we lay down before our worthy Assembly and all other Persons in Government, letting them know that we are thankful as above mentioned and that we are not at Liberty in Conscience to take up Arms to conquer our Enemies but rather to pray to God, who has Power in Heaven and Earth, for us and them. We also crave the Patience of all the Inhabitants of this Country what they think to see clearer in the Doctrine of the blessed Jesus Christ, we will leave to them and God, finding ourselves very poor; for Faith is to proceed out of the Word of God, which is Life and Spirit, and a Power of God and our Conscience is to be instructed by the same, therefore we beg for Patience, our small Gift, which we have given, we gave to those who have power over us, that we may not offend them, as Christ taught us by the Tribute Penny. We heartily pray, that God would govern all Hearts of our Rulers, be they high or low, to meditate those good Things which pertain to our and their Happiness. (Ordered to lie on the table).[22]

As we have just seen, military exemption was granted by the Assembly to all non-resistants on the very day this petition was received. This provision obtained throughout the war and was re-enacted later. The Constitution of 1790 declared that "those who conscientiously scruple to bear arms shall not be compelled to bear arms but shall pay an equivalent for personal service." This article was preserved in later constitutions and is a part of the fundamental law of Pennsylvania today.

In Maryland there were comparatively few Mennonites before the Revolution. Their influence was much less than that of their Pennsylvania brethren and thus they met less opposition to their demands.

---

22. Votes of Assembly, I. 645.

But here, too, they had to resort to petition for all the exemptions they enjoyed. The petition for freedom from military service is not to be found anywhere in the published records, but a resolution recorded in the minutes of the Constitutional Convention of 1776 shows us what its contents must have been. Under date of July 6, the following entry occurs in the Journal on the reading of the petition of the "Society of Mennonites and German Baptists:"

Maryland Exempts on Payment of War Tax

> Resolved that the several committees of observation may at their discretion prolong the time or take security for the payment of any fine by them imposed for not enrolling in the militia and may remit the whole or any part of the fines by them assessed and it is recommended to the committees to pay particular attention and to make a difference between such persons as may refuse from religious principles or other motives.[23]

The Mennonites were exempted from militia duty but were under obligations during the war to pay a fine if the local committee of observation saw fit to collect it.

These same provisions were re-enacted later. The law of 1793 provided that "Quakers, Menonists and Tunkers and all others who are conscientiously scrupulous of bearing arms and who refuse to do militia duty shall pay a sum of three dollars annually." In 1811 a new act exempted Quakers, Menonists and Tunkers between 18 and 45 years of age on payment of five dollars annually. This would excuse them, however, only from the militia musters in time of peace. When called into active service all were com-

---

23. Am. Arch. 4th Ser., VI. 1504.

pelled to enlist. The law of 1834 says nothing about fines but declares that all Quakers, Menonists and Tunkers must submit to the commanding officer of the district a certificate from a licensed preacher in the Society who shall certify of their good standing in their respective churches. This legislation continued practically unchanged until the time of the Civil war.[24]

Virginia was exceedingly liberal in her militia laws at first. In 1766 the Quakers were granted entire exemption from all militia duty,[25] and in July, 1775, the same favorable terms were extended to the Mennonites.[26] During the Revolutionary war, however, there arose considerable opposition among those who lived in Mennonite communities to this liberal policy. The Committee of Observation in Frederick county presented a petition to the Constitutional Convention on June 19, 1776, in which they set forth that altogether they had a tender regard for the conscientious scruples of every religious society, they at the same time thought it an injustice to subject "one part of the community to the whole burden of government while others equally share the benefits of it." They suggested that all Quakers and Mennonites be compelled to pay a sum of money assessed by the

Virginia Liberal in Military Laws

Frederick County Objects. 1776

---

24. Kilty, Laws of Maryland, II. 1793, Ch. 53; Ibid, 1798, Ch. 100; Kilty, Harris and Watkins, Laws of Maryland, IV, 1811. Ch. 182. Sec. 12, 44. 18; Ibid, 1812, Ch. 9. Sec. 2.
Hughes, Laws of Maryland, (1835) 1834, Ch. 251. Sec. 1.
25. Hening, VIII. 242.
26. Hening, IX. 34; also IX. 139.

county court for failure to appear at the militia musters and that in case of active service they should be drafted in the same proportion as the other inhabitants of the county; if they refused to serve then they were to furnish a substitute.[27]

This petition evidently had some effect, for in October of the following year these suggestions were embodied in a new law. According to this act Mennonites when drafted were to be discharged, but were under obligation to furnish a substitute who was to be paid for by a levy on the membership of the entire church.[28] This law remained in force with practically few changes until the Civil war. The Code of Laws in force in 1860 made no direct mention of Mennonites, but provided for a minimum fine of seventy five cents on all privates who failed to attend militia musters or other meetings required by law. This fine of course the Mennonites paid each year. Virginia, however, under the pressure of the Civil war soon resorted to more severe measures. The militia act of 1862 exempted those who were prevented from bearing arms by the tenets of the church to which they belonged, only on the following conditions: (1) that they pay to the sheriff of the county the sum of $500, and the further sum of two per cent of the assessed value of all their taxable property; (2) that they take the oath or affirmation of allegiance to the Confederate government; (3) in case they refuse to pay the said fine then they shall be employed in the capacity of teamsters or in such other character

Militia Act During Civil War

---

27. Am. Arch. 4th Ser., VI. 1579.
28. Hening, IX. 345. See also X. 314, 261, 417; XI. 18; XII. 24.

as the service may need which does not require the actual bearing of arms; (4) and provided further that all persons thus exempted surrender all arms which they may own for the public use.[29] This law was soon succeeded and partially annulled by the Conscription Act of the Confederate government in October of the same year. The Constitution of 1870 finally provided for militia exemption on payment of a fine, but no musters are required in time of peace.

Many of the newer states, influenced either by the direct petitions of non-resistants or by the example of the three states already named, have since provided either in their constitutions or by statute for the conscientious scruples of those opposed to militia duty. Militia service, furthermore, is now practically everywhere placed on a voluntary basis and consequently there is no longer any military question in this country for the Mennonite. Even in the case of actual war it is not likely that conscription acts will be necessary as was true in the late rebellion.

Many States Exempt from Oath and Military Service

Thus far we have been concerned with the relation of the Mennonites to the colonial and state governments. The Civil war brought them into direct touch for the first time with national legislation. During the early years of the struggle the national government found comparatively little difficulty in keeping the armies supplied with men. After the first flush of enthusiasm and patriotic ardor had spent

Conscription Act of 1864

---

29. See Militia Act, March 29, 1862, in Acts of the General Assembly of Va. 1861-2. (Richmond, 1862) p. 50.

itself, however, and it was seen that the war was to be long and bloody, it became evident that the ranks could not be kept full by volunteers alone. On March 3, 1863, an act was passed for the enrolling of the national forces, one section of which provided for a draft if necessary. There is no reference whatever in this act to exemptions on religious grounds. On Feb. 24, 1864, a more stringent conscription act was passed. Section 17 of this measure exempts in general terms all the non-resistant denominations and reads as follows:

> And be it further enacted, that members of religious denominations who shall by oath or affirmation declare that they are conscientiously opposed to the bearing of arms and who are prohibited from doing so by the rules and articles of faith and practice of said religious denominations, shall when drafted into the military service be considered non-combatants, and shall be assigned by the Secretary of War to duty in hospitals or to the care of freedom, or shall pay the sum of $300 to such person as the Secretary of War shall designate, to be applied to the benefit of the sick and wounded soldiers: Provided, that no person shall be entitled to the benefit of the provisions of this section unless his declaration of conscientious scruples against bearing arms shall be supported by satisfactory evidence that his deportment has been uniformly consistant with such declaration.[30]

Although these provisions are worded in general terms, yet they are meant to apply to specific non-resistant denominations, all of which had been sending in petitions since the spring of 1863 asking for exemption from compulsory service. This section was as much debated in Congress as any other in the bill and every particular provision in it was the result of careful consideration both on the floor of the two

---

30. United States Stat. at Large, Vol. 13, Chap. XIII. Sec. 17.

houses and in the committee rooms. Without these various petitions section 17 would never have been a part of the act. The Quakers no doubt were the most influential in securing the exemption. They were better known than the other denominations, were the most vigorous petitioners, and had some influence among those in authority.[31] But the Mennonites deserve no little credit for the final result. They had in Thaddeus Stevens from Lancaster, who was then one of the most prominent members of the Lower House, a warm friend and staunch defender of their interests. Being from Lancaster he was thoroughly acquainted with their principles, and as a lawyer he did much of the legal business for the Mennonites of the county. These were usually Republican in their political beliefs and voted solidly for Stevens. As a part of his constituency he could not afford to lose their support. Stevens did not take a leading part in the debates on the floor of the House but in the committee room, where after all the most of the legislation is made, he was frequently consulted,[32] and no doubt had considerable to do in the outlining of the main features of the bill.

While this is not exclusively a Mennonite measure yet it became the act under which Mennonites all over the country were drafted into service in 1864. And since Mennonites were to a certain extent responsible for one section of the bill it may not be out of order here to recount briefly its history in Congress. An analysis

---

31. Senator Anthony and Secretary Stanton were of Quaker descent. See Cartland, Southern Heroes, p. 129.

32. Congressional Globe, 38 Cong. 1st. session, Part I. See Index under Army, bill (36).

of its history will help us also to understand what each
of the non-resistant denominations contributed to its
final form.

As early as December 16, 1863, a motion was
made to amend the army bill that had been passed the
previous spring.[33] The old bill contained a $300 com-
mutation clause in accordance with which one could
pay $300 in lieu of actual service when drafted. Ac-
cording to the new bill this clause was to be repealed.
It was this proposed repeal that brought in the petitions from the peace denominations. The first petition
to be introduced came on December 23, 1863, from the
Amana Society in Iowa. On January 6, 1864, a petition was read from the Quakers of Baltimore and New
York, who objected not only to the repeal of the clause
but to any exemption clause with a money fine attached. As in former years they objected just as
seriously to the payment of money for war purposes
as to actual military service. Other petitions were
soon sent in by the Mennonites, Dunkards, Shakers
and Moravians.

A new bill had finally been introduced in the
Senate on December 16. The first mention of an exemption clause appears on January 14, when Senator
Wilson moved that "all members of religious denominations conscientiously opposed to bearing arms, be
assigned to hospital service or pay $300." Harlan who
was afraid lest this might be made to cover many who
were not members of such denominations added the
clause "and are prohibited from doing so by the rules
and articles of faith of said religious denominations."
Doolittle then moved to amend by exempting "those

---

33. Congressional Globe, 38 Cong., 1st Sess. Part I. p. 37.

of good standing." The entire day was taken up in discussing this exemption clause and especially the Quakers' objection to the payment of money. In order to overcome these scruples it was proposed that this exemption money should be applied to the care of the sick and wounded. The bill was passed by the Senate on the 19th with the following exemption clause:

1. Those religiously opposed to military service are to be assigned by the Secretary of War to duty in the hospitals or to the care of freedmen.

2. If they refuse to serve then they are to pay the sum of $400 to be applied to the care of the sick and wounded.

3. Such persons are to be exempted from the draft during the time for which they have been drafted.

The bill was brought to the House, read and discussed. Stevens immediately moved to reduce the exemption money from $400 to $300. Schneck proposed that the clause referring to the disposition of the $300 be stricken out, whereupon Stevens spoke in behalf of the Quakers. "I do not think," he said, "that we ought to violate their religious belief." Mr. Denning, chairman of the committee which drafted the bill, explained the difficulty the committee had in agreeing on the details of the exemption clause. His statement contains several interesting facts and shows that others in addition to those who took part in the open debate in the House, were responsible for its final form. He said, the committee in drafting their amendment had before them petitions from Quakers, Society of Ebenezer, Amana Society, Dunker, Shaker, and Moravians.

There are also the Mennonites, he said, whose conscience

tells them to take no oath, to do violence to no man, to take
patiently the spoiling of their goods, to pray for their
enemies, and to feed and refresh them when hungry or
thirsty.[34] It was thought such a vast door would be opened
by admitting conscientious scruples as a ground of exemption
that the committee was in favor of rejecting it altogether.
From the best information we could get there are now about
500,000 non-resistants in this country, and if this principle is
once adopted there will be an active revival among all the
non-resistants soon and their ranks will be suddenly and fully
recruited, at least it was in view of the immense number that
might claim conscientious scruples as a ground of exemption
either truly or falsely, that induced the committee to oppose
conscientious scruples altogether.

Had it not been for Stevens and others who were supported by large non-resistant constituencies the clause might have been omitted altogether.

But, continues Denning, upon consultation with members
upon this floor, particularly members representing non-resistant constituencies we found that there is an earnest wish
so far as their respective districts are concerned, that some
amendment of this kind should be introduced into the bill.

The debate continued at intervals all through January and far into February. On the tenth of the latter month Creswell moved to amend the exemption clause which was now section 17 of the original army bill by the addition:

that no person shall be entitled to the benefits of the provisions of this section unless his declaration of conscientious
scruples against bearing arms shall be supported by satisfactory evidence that his deportment has been uniformly
consistent with such declaration.

---

34. Congressional Globe, 38 Cong. 1st Sess. Part I. p. 579.'

The bill finally passed the House, was slightly altered by the Senate, and with the exemption clause as stated in the beginning of this discussion, it was signed by the president on February 24, and thus became the law of the land. How the Mennonites fared under this law during the fall of 1864 is told in other chapters.

In the meantime the same subject had been up in the Congress of the Confederacy. During the summer of 1862 a new army bill was introduced. **Conscription Acts of the Confederacy** During August and September a number of the peace denominations of Virginia sent memorials to the Congress asking for exemption from service.[35] The bill which passed October 11, 1862, released from military duty all persons

> who have been and now are members of the Society of Friends, and the Association of Dunkards, Nazarenes, and Mennonists in regular membership in the respective denominations: Provided members of the Society of Friends, Nazarenes, Menonists and Dunkards shall furnish substitutes or pay a tax each of $500 into the public treasury.[36]

We saw that in 1860 the militia code of Virginia, the only state of the South in which Mennonites were found, exempted them from the militia musters on the payment of a minimum fine of seventy-five cents. When Virginia seceded, however, and war broke out this provision was annulled. In 1861 a draft was made and several Mennonites were forced into the service.

---

35. See Confederate Congress Journal. H. R., V. 336, 379, 460. Also Journal of Confederate Senate, 410. Both found in Senate Doc. V. 26. 58th Congress, Second Session.
36. Va. Stat. at Large, 77.

Many others were imprisoned in Richmond for refusing to serve.[37] It is said that Algernon A. Gray who was well acquainted with the Mennonites at Harrisonburg had much to do with the release of the prisoners and perhaps with the passage of the exemption clause in the act passed by the Confederate Congress in 1862.[38] The Mennonite Confession of Faith was placed in the hands of the Confederate officials for the purpose of explaining the Mennonite position on the question of war.

The law passed by the Congress in 1862 remained in force for about twenty months. But the war began to tell heavily on the ranks of the southern armies. Every effort was put forth to send men to the front. On December 8, 1863, President Davis suggested to the Confederate Congress that the list of exemptions be curtailed.[39] In accordance with this suggestion a new law was passed in the summer of 1864, removing all exemptions on religious grounds.[40] During the rest of the war the Mennonites of Virginia suffered many hardships.

With this exception, which must be explained on the ground of the desperate straits in which the Confederate government found itself toward the close of the war, the civil authorities in America have always been very considerate of the tender consciences of the Mennonites. It is true of course that frequently their motives were misunderstood and that in a few

---

37. See article by L. J. Heatwole in Hartzler and Kauffman's History of Mennonites, 210.
38. See Harrisonburg (Va.) Register for Aug. 13, 1885.
39. Senate Doc., Vol. 30. 38 Cong. Second Session. 594 Journal of Confed. Congress.
40. Va. Statutes at Large, 162.

cases they were rather severely dealt with in times of war by those lawless elements for which in such times no authority can be held responsible.

But before the law, when once their principles were comprehended, they have always had a hearing. They have many reasons to be thankful for free America. Few nations have granted them such free exercise of their religious faith. They have asked for much and have received much. Exemption from military service is the last privilege any nation is likely to grant but in America that right is now recognized. In Pennsylvania the Mennonites were fortunate in casting their lot with the Quakers and were granted equal privileges with them. In Maryland their religious tenets were recognized in the fundamental law of the state. In Virginia during the rule of the established church they were favored above all other dissenting bodies.[41] Today nearly every state in the union exempts them from bearing arms and from taking the oath.

But if the civil powers have been considerate of Mennonite scruples, the Mennonites on the other hand have not been undeserving of those favors. Although no people have less to do with the state than they, none are less of a burden to it. Practically none ever resort to a lawsuit, except in defense and for that purpose very seldom; few are ever brought before a criminal or civil court. Taken all in all, there are few people more industrious, frugal, thrifty, honest, peaceful and law-abiding than the Mennonites. Even though their direct influence upon the course of Amer-

---

41. See Foote, Sketches of Virginia, for objections of the Presbyterians to concessions made to the Mennonites in the education bill of 1784.

ican history may have been slight, yet they have been the very first of modern religious denominations to stand for an ideal that may be called distinctly American—complete separation of church and state, and universal peace. In conclusion we can not help quoting what Dr. Benjamin Rush, signer of the Declaration of Independence, said of the Lancaster County Mennonites over one hundred years ago, in his Manners of the German Inhabitants of Pennsylvania, "Perhaps those German sects of Christians who refuse to bear arms for the shedding of human blood may be preserved by Divine Providence as the center of a circle which shall gradually embrace all nations of the Earth in a perpetual treaty of friendship and peace."

CHAPTER XV

PRINCIPLES, CUSTOMS AND CULTURE

The Mennonites of today are the direct lineal as well as the spiritual descendants of the European Anabaptists of the sixteenth century. Most of them trace their ancestry through the centuries to the days of the early reformers. Mennonite names today are almost identical with the names of the Anabaptists of 1600. In faith, in doctrine, in religious practice and in their social spirit, they differ little from their ancestors. The Anabaptist doctrines of non-resistance, non-swearing of oaths, non-participation in civil government, and rejection of infant baptism and seclusion from the world are just as rigidly maintained by the main body of the Mennonites in America as ever they were by Grebel, Mantz, and Blaurock in the early sixteenth century.

Origin of Mennonite Doctrine and Practice

The significance and meaning of these religious tenets, as well as their influence upon the Quakers, Baptists, and Dunkards has been told elsewhere and needs no repetition here but it may not be out of order to remind the reader that in America, too, the Mennonites have been among the earliest, if not the very first of those who stood for two ideals which have been characteristic of American religious and political life, namely—complete separation of state and church, and universal peace.

In religious practices also as well as in doctrine, the Mennonites have perpetuated the teachings of the Anabaptists. Among the customs which **Feet-washing** the latter introduced into their religious worship was that of feet-washing, in connection with the communion service. This practice was common among some of the Anabaptists of Europe and was in vogue in some form also among other religious organizations. The pope still practices the observance on certain occasions of religious ceremony, as do also some of the church officials of the Greek Catholic church. The practice was also common at one time among some branches of the Baptist denomination as well as among other offspring of the Anabaptists. The "Primitive" Baptists still observe the custom.

Among the Mennonites of Europe there was no uniformity of practice. The custom was not observed everywhere in Holland, nor, as we have seen, in Switzerland. With the exception of the Mennonites of Germantown and Franconia, it was introduced by the early immigrants into America due perhaps partly to Amish influence. It is now still rigidly maintained among all Mennonites in America with the exception of the General Conference branch of the church.

Another religious custom which is now confined almost exclusively to the Dunkards and the Mennon-

ites is the wearing of the prayer head covering among the women of the church.[1] The prac-
Prayer Head-covering tice of wearing a covering of some sort on the head during religious worship was common among the Anabaptists, and if one may judge from the portraits of the women of past generations it was not unusual among later Protestant denominations. This covering which at first was perhaps some sort of veil finally developed into a small cap made of light material and just large enough to cover the head. The custom is common among most of the branches of the American Mennonite church, but has been discarded by the General Conference Mennonites and other of the more liberal elements of the denomination.

In their social spirit the Mennonites have ever been exclusive. This spirit also has been a bequest from their Anabaptist ancestors. It was
Social Spirit a development which resulted partly from the conception that the world was corrupt and the Christian must remove himself from it as much as possible, and partly from the persecutions, which they suffered during their early history. For centuries in Europe they were hounded from one hiding place to another, and it was but natural that they should develop the feeling that their rights in this world were few. These circumstances together with the fact that they came largely from the ranks of the common people engendered within them a humble and seclusive spirit. When they immigrated to America they always settled in comparatively new regions where it was possible for them to form small

---

1. Based on I Corinthians 11:2-16.

colonies and thus perpetuate their own religious and social environment. Disintegrating influences from without were guarded against by a rule of the church which forbade intermarriage with members of other denominations. And thus as a result of these various forces which have been operating for more than three centuries, the main body of the American Mennonites has been able to maintain and perpetuate not only the religious principles, but the customs, the language, the spirit and in a few cases almost the style of dress of their European ancestors of the sixteenth century. Nowhere else in America can one get so near to the spirit and the customs of the common people of Switzerland and Germany of three hundred years ago as among the Amish and some of the Mennonites of Pennsylvania.

Conservatism   This exclusive spirit engendered conservatism. The Mennonites have always been slow to change their habits and opinions. This tendency is manifested especially in their attitude toward the adoption of new forms of dress. They have always been among the last to discard old styles for the new. This has been due in part to a commendable desire to escape the changing whims and vanities of fashion, and in part to their conservative instincts which suspected everything "new" as worldly. Both men and women have always been exceedingly plain and modest in their style of dress. The significance attached to plain dress is well typified by the phrase "turned plain" which in Lancaster county always means to join church. In recent years a considerable change has taken place in many localities on the subject of dress restrictions.

Today with the exception of the most conservative branches of the church most of the restrictions regarding the style and cut of dress have been discarded so far as the men are concerned, but the women are still required to wear the cape in Lancaster county; and with the exception of several of the more liberal branches of the church they are still required to wear the bonnet instead of a hat.

Bonnet   The bonnet, once in common use among the Quakers, is a relic of a form of head dress which was once common among the wives and daughters of many of the pioneers of the country.

The first German immigrants were usually of the poorer people, and the women wore a sort of shawl or kerchief on their heads. This was soon replaced by the home made bonnet. The next stage in the evolution of woman's head dress was the hat which admitted of more ornament, but the majority of Mennonites never adopted that form of head gear.

Church Government   In church government the Mennonites have always followed the congregational type. Robert Brown, the Englishman, is often called the father of congregationalism, but long before Brown was born small bands of Anabaptists were found in the cities along the Rhine, in Germany and Holland and in Southeastern England. These communities were self-governing so far as religious matters were concerned, and claimed absolute independence both from the state and outside ecclesiastical organizations.

Conferences of these independent bodies, to be sure, were frequently held, not for the purpose, however, of passing regulations which were to be binding

PRINCIPLES, CUSTOMS AND CULTURE

Early Conferences

on individual congregations, but rather to unite upon some common statement of the principles and doctrines of their faith and to confer on other questions of common interest. One of the earliest of these meetings was held at Schleitheim, Germany, in 1527, when one of the earliest Anabaptist confessions of faith of which we have any record was drawn up. Among other meetings of a similar nature and for a similar purpose was the one called in 1632 at Dordrecht, Holland, at which was drawn up the confession which has since been adopted by most of the Mennonites of both America and Europe.

In America a conference was held of all the ministers in Pennsylvania in 1725 for the purpose of deciding on an English translation of their confession. Similar meetings no doubt were held more or less regularly for various purposes throughout the eighteenth century, although we have no record of any prior to the Revolutionary war. Finally several districts held regular conferences, the oldest of which were the Franconia and Lancaster districts. By 1844 Christian Herr wrote:—

The Mennonite congregations in Pennsylvania are divided into three general circuits, within each of which semi-annual conferences, consisting of bishops, elders or ministers, and deacons, are held for the purpose of consulting each other, and devising means to advance the spiritual prosperity of the members.

As new settlements developed, new conferences were organized. Thus the Canadian churches have met in conference since about 1820. Virginia did not establish one until 1835. During the last fifty years others have been established among all the western congregations, generally by states. The Amish churches did not favor such meetings, and it was not until 1862 that they held their first "Diener Versammlung" of all the American churches. These ministers' conferences were kept up annually until 1878 when they were abandoned. Since then the Amish Mennonite congregations have all organized themselves into conference districts, but the Old Order are still opposed to any departure from the old ways.

The purpose of these meetings in the early history of the church, both in Europe and America, as we saw, was merely advisory, with no thought **Their** of passing regulations binding on the vari- **Purpose** ous congregations. Each congregation had its own deacons, preachers and many of them their own elders commonly called bishops. In America, however, as the communities grew in number the jurisdiction of the bishops extended over a larger number of congregations. With the exception of the General Conference Mennonites and the Illinois (Stuckey) Conference, the Mennonites are drifting away from the earlier form of church government. The conferences are more and more assuming the authority to make regulations which shall be binding on all the congregations within the district. In some of the larger communities the government has been almost completely transformed from the congregational type to a rule by bishops. Lancaster county with a membership of over 8,000 is almost completely under the control of a few bishops. Much might be said both for and against this tendency. On the one hand the congregational system of self-government may prevent the church from acting unitedly and thus most effectively in any particular cause. But on the other hand the Episcopal form affords an opportunity for a few men of strong personality to dominate the conference and dictate the policy of the church. Uniformity and formality may thus be gained at the expense of individuality and spirituality.

One of the most interesting studies in the life of the Pennsylvania Mennonites as well as of all Pennsylvania Germans is the development of **Pennsylvania Dutch** their spoken dialect, the so-called "Pennsylvania Dutch" which is not Dutch at all, but German. This dialect is by no means confined to the Mennonites, but is common among all of the descendants of the original German settlers, including the Lutherans, Reformed, Dunkards, Schwenkfelders and Moravians. No history of the Mennonite people, however, can be complete without some reference to their language.

This dialect which is a strange mixture of English and German words, with many forms peculiar to itself, is the product of the close contact of the two tongues during the last two hundred years. The German immigrants maintained their own language when they first entered the colony. But they were surrounded by English Quakers and the official language of the state was English. From the very beginning the modification of the German speech began by the introduction of English words which were often attached to German forms. Pastorius himself, the founder of Germantown, was one of the first to yield to this tendency. Pennsylvania Dutch may be said to begin with an expression which he made very early in the history of Germantown. Speaking of certain lawyers' fees, he says, "Ich fand, dasz alle **lawyers gefeed** waren".

The first step in the development of the dialect was the introduction of many English nouns to replace the German names for the same object. The following extract taken from Armbruster's Almanac for 1760 illustrates this method of growth and also the stage which Pennsylvania Dutch had reached at that time.

Ein Gespräch zwischen zwei deutschen Leuten in Amerika, welches hier aufgeschrieben und an die Deutsche Gesellschaft auf der Universität zu Leipzig geschickt worden, um zu hören ob die Gelehrten in Deutschland solche Sprache verstehen können.

"Oh Andi du Hannes, **Servant** Kobes, hast du schon **gebrikfestet?**"

"O nein, Ich habe so viel **Trubble**, dasz ich jetz mit **Brikfest** nicht **meddlen** kan."

"Was is den die **Matter?**"

"Well der **Matter** is Ich schickte meinen **Serven** auf ein paar **Errants** eine meile von **Taun** und gab ihm meinen **Stallion** mit, aber der **Roock** geht mit ein paar **gut for nothing fellows** in ein **Tavern** und trinkt eine Mocke Krock. In des **worked** der **Stallion** den **Breidel** ab und lauft in Trint Yockels **meddos.** Yockel sagt er ist über die **Bort Fennse** von der **Orchard** gesprungen, und so durch die **Yard** in eine **Lane** bey Yockels **Barn** vorbey und längst den **Waal** von seinen **Flower Garten** über den Kleinen **Run** auf die **pastert** gekommen und hier ist er noch mals über die **Fensse** gesprungen. Aber mein **Serven** bube sagt es sind nur **Storys.** Die **gate** ist aufgestanden, und Yockels **journeymen** und seine zwei **Prinzisse** nebst noch einem **Carpenter** standen bey dem **Ditch** zwischen der **Roth** und der **Fenz** und sie hätten den **Stallion** wohl **ketchen** können."

Man hat in Deutschland von diesem bunten Gespräch geurteilet, dasz es nicht Deutsch sei und hat sich gewundert wies möglich ist, dasz man so viel Hauptwörter in English redet, dasz man nicht lieber die wenige deutsche Wörter, womit die vorigen verbunden sind auch Englisch macht. Alsdann könntens doch die Englischen verstehen. So aber verstehts niemand als die Deutschen in America.

In course of time, however, more marked changes took place, and the Pennsylvania Dutch of today is no longer a mixture of German verbs and English nouns, but a distinct compound made up of both, but unlike either. The following poem by H. Harbaugh, from a book of poems called "Harbaughs Harfe" serves as a fair example of the dialect as it is still heard in Bucks and Montgomery counties.

DIE NEIE SORT DSCHENT' LEIT

O heert, ihr liebe Leit, was sin des Zeite;
    Dass unser ens noch dess erlewe muss.
'N jeder Bauerbuh muss **Kärridsch reide,**
Un Baure-Mäd, die schleppe rum in Seide,
    Un Niemand nemmt an all dem Schtoltz Verdruss.

'N eegne **Boghie** hot 'n jeder Bauerbuh,
    'N schrier Gauel un G'scherr mit Silwerb'schlege druf,
Un **plenti** Zehrgeld ah im Sack,—do is kee' Ruh,
Am Samschdag gehn die **Dschent'** Leit 'm Schtedel zu
    Un schtelle dort am deirschte Wertshaus uf.

Wie is des junge Bauervolk doch ufge**dresst,**
    Wie heewe se die Kepp so schteif un hoch.
Wie dhun se in de schtolze **Fäsch'ns** renne,
M'r kann se nimme vun de Schtadtleit kenne,
    Sie mache all ihr Hochmuts Wege noch.

D'er Vatter denkt: Was hab ich schmärte Sehne,
    Die Mutter sagt: Mei Mäd die kumme raus.
So schteil kosst Geld. Ja well, m'r kann jo lehne.
Sell geht'n Weil, bass uf, du werscht's ball sehne,
    Der Vater "geht d'r Bungert Fens ball 'naus".

> Vor Alters war es en Sinn un Schand,
>   Meh' Schulde mache as m'r zahle kann;
> 'Sis net mehr so: m'r gebt **just Notice** dorch die **Editors**
>   M'r het **geclos't**, un dhut **cumpounde** mit de **Creditors,**
> Wer so betriegt, der is en **Dscherit'lmann.**
>
> Wie lebt m'r nau? Ich sehn dhu weescht noch nix.
>   M'r lebt **juscht** d'rvor: des **fixt** die **Lah.**
> M'r eegent nix—die Fraa hots all in Hand—
> M'r is ihr **Edschent, manedscht** Geld un Land
>   Un geht **nau** in die Koscht bei seiner Fraa.

This dialect in its different stages of development has been in common use in conversation among the Mennonites in Pennsylvania from the time of their first settlement in the colony almost up to the present. Their reading matter, however, was written in High German and thus the language of the pulpit was likely

How They Went to Church

to be more dignified than that used in ordinary conversation. It was far into the nineteenth century, however, before the English replaced the German even in religious services. At present the church worship is conducted in the English tongue everywhere except in Bucks county and among the more recent immigrants in the western states, where some form of German is spoken, and among the Old Order Amish, who still speak from the pulpit as well as in daily conversation in the dialect of their fathers.

Toward higher learning the American Mennonites have never until recently been well disposed. This was due in part to their inherited prejudices, **Attitude** in part to their form of occupation and in **Toward** part to their experience. The leaders of the **Learning** Anabaptists, Grebel, Hubmeir and Denk, and the early Mennonites, Menno Simons and Dirck Philip, were all men of learning. But the rank and file of their followers were of the common people, with little learning outside of a more or less thorough knowledge of the Bible. And even these leaders, although educated men themselves, taught that University training was not necessary for preaching the Gospel. As a consequence, after these early leaders had died, learning disappeared from among the Mennonites. It was not until the beginning of the eighteenth century that it was again revived in Europe and educated leaders once more began to direct the work of the church.

The early immigrants to Pennsylvania, being pioneer farmers, had neither opportunity nor inclination to devote any time to higher learning. The early pioneers of Germantown, many of whom were Hollanders, seemed an exception to the general rule, for here the Mennonites and Quakers together established in 1701 the Germantown Academy, with Pastorius as the first teacher. Here a number of the Mennonite youths of the community received their first school training.

But while opposed to higher learning, the Mennonites favored such elementary instruction as seemed practical to them. Consequently they established private subscription schools where reading, writing and some work in numbers were taught. In many cases the meeting house also served as a school house. By 1718 Christopher Dock[2] had begun a school in the Skippack settlement which was soon held alternately in the meeting houses of the Salford and Skippack congregations. Wickersham in his History of Education in Pennsylvania says that before 1740 the Mennonites had established schools in Upper Hanover, in Montgomery county, and in the church houses near Coopersburg, and Upper Milford in Lehigh county. The latter he says was built of "logs and divided into two apartments by a swinging partition suspended from the ceiling. One apartment was used for religious, the other for school purposes".[3] The early meeting houses in Lancaster county were made to serve a like purpose. Schools were kept during the eighteenth century in the houses at Willow Street, Mellingers, Strasburg, two in the north west part of Manheim township, three in Warwick, and one in Brecknock township.

When the free public school system was inaugurated in Pennsylvania in the early part of the nineteenth century, the Mennonites together with the other German sects, were at first opposed to the movement, because it would take the education of the youth out of the hands of the church and would substitute the English for the German language. But after they had

---

2. See Martin G. Brumbaugh. The Life and Works of Christopher Dock.
3. Page 165.

once adjusted themselves to the new system none supported it more heartily than they.

While Mennonites everywhere encouraged instruction in the elements of learning, none of them favored higher education until far into the nineteenth century. This does not mean that none of their young men ever wandered from the trodden paths, for occasionally one would find his way to some college or university where he invariably made a good record as a student. Scores of men who hold high positions in other churches, in colleges and in every walk of life claim a Mennonite ancestry. But these men at the end of their college career had been trained away from many of their earlier religious beliefs, and finding little inducement to return to the church under whose wing they had been brought up, drifted into other denominations. This only intensified the prejudice against such training, and at the same time robbed the church of the very element which ought to have helped it most to higher ideals of service and culture.

First Colleges

It finally began to dawn upon a few of the leaders of the denomination that if this process were to continue indefinitely, the Mennonites must ever play an insignificant role in the religious world. The first to awaken to this fact was the General Conference branch of the church, which in this as in several other lines of progress took the lead among the various branches of the denomination. J. H. Oberholtzer was one of the first to advocate a more thorough training for the ministry. His efforts were warmly seconded by Daniel Hoch of Canada, Daniel Krehbiel of Iowa, and Ephraim Hunsberger of Ohio. At the suggestion of Oberholtzer the first preliminary conference which was held in Iowa in 1860, discussed the need of a theological seminary.

The conference of 1863 decided to establish a school which was to be known as the "Christian Educational Institution of the Mennonite Denomination", and appointed a committee to collect funds and choose a suitable location. On January 2, 1868, the school was opened at Wadsworth, Ohio, with Christian Showalter of Iowa as the first principal, one other instructor, and twenty-four students. Its purpose was primarily to train young men and women for Christian work, although secular subjects were also taught. Most of the instruction was to be conducted in the German language. The school never prospered. The attendance scarcely ever went beyond that of the opening day. Although there were only three teachers, expenses could hardly be met. C. J. van der Smissen who had been called from Germany to the chair of theology did not always agree with Principal Showalter as to the management of the school. The latter finally resigned and the former was given entire control of the institution. Finally, the churches of the West and those of Pennsylvania fell into a quarrel over certain matters of policy. As a result of these conflicting interests, the institution had to be closed in 1878, just ten years after the first students entered its doors for instruction.

School at Wadsworth

There remained, however, still a demand especially among the western churches for a church school. In 1882 the Kansas conference which was made up almost exclusively of German immigrants from Russia

BLUFFTON COLLEGE

GOSHEN COLLEGE

and Prussia, established at Halstead, Kansas, the "Mennonite Seminary," with H. H. Ewert **Bethel** as the first principal. The instruction was **College** to be carried on in both the German and English languages. This institution has since enlarged its policy and offers regular collegiate courses. In 1893 it was removed to Newton, Kansas, and became known as Bethel College. The faculty in 1907, under the presidency of C. H. Wedel, consisted of ten instructors, and a total enrollment of 121 regular students. The patronage is largely from the local Kansas churches.

The Old Mennonites did not awaken to the need of a church school until within the last ten years and even then there was very little sentiment **Goshen** in favor of such an institution in the church **College** at large. Goshen College owes its existence to the efforts of a few of the more liberal minded leaders of both branches of the main body, who recognized that it was only through an educational institution controlled by the church that the young men of talent could be saved from casting their lot with other denominations. Among these men were John S. Coffman, Jonathan Kurtz, D. J. Johns, J. S. Hartzler, D. D. Miller, Herman Yoder, Lewis Kulp and J. F. Funk. All of these men were from near Elkhart, Indiana, which at the time was the religious and intellectual center of the main branch of the denomination.

In 1895 Dr. H. A. Mumaw established a private Normal and Business school in Elkhart under the name of Elkhart Institute. Soon after, the Elkhart Institute Association composed of most the above named men and a few others was formed for the purpose of developing this institution into a general church school. The next year a building was erected in which the school was held until 1902 when it was moved to Goshen, Indiana, at which time also its name was changed to Goshen College. This college which began thus as a private enterprise has since been placed under the management of the Mennonite Board of Education whose members are appointed by the conferences of both branches of the main body. Goshen College has grown steadily from the beginning. It has been fortunate in securing and maintaining a faculty under the presidency of Noah E. Byers, made up of young men and women every one of whom has had thorough training in the best universities in the land, and at the same time is conservative and sensible enough to retain the respect and confidence of the church at large. During the year which closed in 1908 the faculty was composed of twelve regular instructors and the enrollment was three hundred and six.

Goshen College has not yet passed through the experimental stage. While it has gained many friends especially among the more liberal minded and more influential men of the church, yet there are a number of communities especially in Pennsylvania which are not in favor of a church school. The college nevertheless has already exerted a marked influence upon the religious activities and ideals of culture within the church, and if it retains the confidence of its constituency as no doubt it will, it should do more than any other agency to transform the ideals and the policy of the entire body, and together with other Mennonite schools ought to do much to bring about a better understanding between, if not an entire unification of at least all the more progressive wings of the Mennonite denomination. In 1909 another Mennonite school was established at Hesston, Kansas. This school has just been organized with D. H. Bender as principal and T. M. Erb as business manager.

The awakening of the entire church to the need of educating its young people is only one of the evidences of renewed life. With this interest in education there sprang up also an interest in other lines of advancement, such as Sunday schools, missions, and evangelization.

Evangelization and Missions

Here again the General Conference branch was the first to catch hold of the spirit of progress. It was for the cause of evangelization and home mission work that Hoch and Oberholtzer urged a closer union among their congregations in the late fifties of the last century. Finally a missionary society was established for the purpose of supporting a foreign missionary. But it was some years before active work began. S. S. Haury a student at Wadsworth was the first volunteer, but the society was undecided where to begin work. Haury first visited Holland in the hope of enlisting his services with the Mennonite missionary society at Amsterdam, but he soon returned. After a visit to Alaska, he finally established an industrial and educational mission in 1880 among the Arrapahoe Indians in Indian Territory. Among other early missionaries to the Indians were C. H. Wedel, H. R. Voth, A. E. Funk, and O. S. Shultz.

The famine in India in 1897 turned the eyes of the church to that country as a promising mission field.

J. A. Penner and his wife now represent the General Conference Mennonites in a station located in Central Province.

Among the Old Mennonites and the Amish Mennonites the mission interest appeared a few years later. The general spiritual and intellectual awakening of these two wings of the denomination was due among other causes, very largely to the liberalizing influences of the Mennonite Publishing Company of Elkhart, Indiana. Here was concentrated the best talent and the most progressive congregation of the entire church. Here were published the Herald of Truth and numerous papers and religious books. Many of the brightest young men and women of other localities were employed in various capacities by the firm, all of whom helped to make the congregation at Elkhart the most progressive and cultured in the entire denomination. The influence of the Publishing house and the congregation was felt throughout the entire church. Among the men who dominated the spirit of the Elkhart church were J. F. Funk, president of the company, A. B. Kolb, editor of the Herald of Truth, and John S. Coffman, the pioneer Mennonite evangelist.

Of these Coffman who was a man of strong and pleasing personality, came into contact with the greatest number of young men of promise. In the course of his evangelistic visits throughout the country during the late eighties and early nineties, he brought new life to many congregations which had hitherto done little aggressive work, and inspired many young men to higher ideals of life. Among these men who have since gained a strong influence over the church were M. S. Steiner of Ohio, D. H. Bender of Maryland,

J. A. Ressler of Pennsylvania, A. D. Wenger of Iowa, C. K. Hostetler of Ohio, N. E. Byers of Illinois and Daniel Kauffman of Missouri. Coffman was ably assisted in his work of evangelization and the finding of young men of promise by such ministers as D. J. Johns, D. D. Miller, and J. S. Hartzler of Indiana; J. S. Shoemaker of Illinois; C. B. Brenneman and John Blosser of Ohio, and others.

The first important result of the work of these men was the organizing of a Sunday school conference which was to represent the entire church. The first session was held in 1892 at Middlebury, Indiana. For the first time now the younger men of the church were given an opportunity to discuss and organize various lines of aggressive Christian work. These conferences have since been divided into districts. They are largely conducted by the younger people and have done more than any other one agency to promote the missionary and educational interests of the church.

Among the questions discussed at the meeting at Middlebury was the question of establishing a mission in Chicago. The prime mover in the enterprise was M. S. Steiner, who has ever since been the leader in the missionary cause. At the next session of the Sunday school conference which was held at Bluffton, Ohio, Steiner was appointed Superintendent of a mission which was to be established in the city. This station, the first one established by the Old Mennonites and the Amish is at present in charge of A. H. Leaman.

Since the Chicago Mission was organized a number of others have been founded in other cities, including Philadelphia, Kansas City, Toronto, Canton, Ohio,

Fort Wayne, Indiana, and Lancaster, Pennsylvania.

The first foreign mission was located in India, in the wake of the famine of 1896-7. The tale of misery which came from that country touched the hearts of the Mennonites, and a "Home and Foreign Relief Commission" was organized at Elkhart for the purpose of sending them relief. This organization collected from all branches of the denomination a large supply of provisions and money and sent a shipload of grain to India in charge of George Lambert, well known in the church as a traveler through the Orient. Lambert, after his return aroused considerable interest among the various congregations in behalf of the natives of India.

A sentiment gradually began to spread among the leaders in the home mission cause that this act of mercy ought to be followed with an attempt to bring to the benighted people of India the message of the Gospel. Among the men most active in urging the cause were M. S. Steiner, Dr. W. B. Page, who as a student at Ada, Ohio, a few years before had volunteered as a foreign missionary, and J. A. Ressler of Pennsylvania. At a meeting held at Elkhart in November, 1898, at which these men and many of the leaders of the church were present, it was decided that J. A. Ressler and Dr. W. B. Page and his wife, be sent to India to open up a mission station in that country. This little party set sail the following spring and finally selected a site near Dhamtari, Central Province, for the proposed mission. Ressler has ever since retained the superintendency of the enterprise, but Dr. Page was soon obliged because of ill health to return home. A number of other devoted Christian young men and women have since dedicated their lives to the work. Some of these have also been obliged to return because of the unwholesome climate. Others have sacrificed their lives in the cause and lie buried near the scenes of their labors. But the broken ranks are continually being filled by those who are willing to sacrifice their all upon the altar of Christian duty and love for their fellow men. In 1907 the entire force consisted of eleven men and women.

All of these mission stations both home and foreign are now under the control of the Mennonite Board of Missions and Charities[4] of which organization M. S. Steiner is the president, and are supported by all branches of the denomination except the General Conference, the Defenseless Mennonites, and the Mennonite Brethren in Christ, all of which have mission stations of their own. The interest in missions has been growing rapidly, and there is at present considerable agitation in favor of another station in South America.

No sketch of the secular and religious life of the Mennonites would be complete without at least some reference to their habits of thrift and industry. Throughout their entire history they have everywhere been spoken of as an honest, industrious and prosperous people. Mosheim, the historian, says of the Mennonites of Holland in his day that they "owned the finest land, drove the finest equipages, lived in the best houses, and were in every way the most industrious people in Holland". This character-

Mennonite Virtues

---

4. This board also has control of an orphan home located at West Liberty, Ohio, and an old people's home in Wayne county, Ohio.

ization might be applied with just as much truth to almost any of the settlements in America. The Mennonites of Lancaster county, and the Amish of Woodford county, Illinois, have attained perhaps, to as high an average of material prosperity as any other farming community in the entire country.

With the other virtues which enter into the composition of true character the Mennonites as a whole are endowed to an unusual degree. While as a denomination they may fall behind others in their attainments in the world of culture, yet in the possession of the sounder virtues they are surpassed by none. They are sober, honest, industrious, peaceable and religious, —withal among the most useful citizens of the land.

CHAPTER XVI

LITERATURE AND HYMNOLOGY

The early Mennonite immigrants brought with them few books, although such as they had they knew well. In addition to their Bibles, prayer **Books Brought** books and confessions of faith, there **from Europe** may have been found scattered copies of the works of Menno Simons, Dirck Philip or of the Bloedig Toneel among the Hollanders, and of the Froschauer[1] Bible and the Ausbund among the Palatines. This slight stock, furthermore, was soon exhausted and since neither Dutch nor German religious books were to be had in America, the Germantown church as early as 1708 wrote to the church at Amsterdam, asking for a supply of Bibles, prayer books and catechisms.[2]

The first book published expressly for and at the

---

1. The so-called Froschauer Bible was issued by a well known publisher at Zurich, Switzerland, by the name of Froschauer. It was popular among the Swiss Anabaptists and was condemned by the civil and religious authorities of Berne and Zurich. Many old editions are still to be found among the Mennonites and Amish of Pennsylvania and Illinois.
2. See de Hoop Scheffer. Inventaris der Archiefstukken Berustende bij de Vereenigde Doopsgezinde Gemeende te Amsterdam.

Confession of Faith 1712

request of the Pennsylvania Mennonites was an English edition of their confession of faith which was printed at Amsterdam 1712.[3] This was one of the very first books to be printed anywhere for the Germans of America, and the only English edition of any of the standard Mennonite books for more than a century. The preface explains the demand at this time for an English translation of the confession.

Since among the Christians many controversies, divisions, quarrels and strife about many and several articles and things concerning the Christian religion have been raised inasmuch that every religious society hath given out and published their separate meaning and their own confession that so it might be known what they believe and what they do assert or not and that the Confession of Faith of the harmless and defenceless Christians called Menonists or Baptists is as yet but little known in many places without the United Provinces for the greatest part of the people doth not know what they believe and confess of the word of God and by reason of that ignorance can't speak and judge rightly of their confession nor the confessors themselves, nay through prejudice as a strange and unheard of thing do abhor them so as not to speak well but ofttimes ill of them. Therefore it hath been thought fit and needful to translate at the desire of some of our fellow believers in Pennsylvania our Confession of Faith into English so as for many years it hath been printed in the Dutch, German, and French languages, which Confession hath been well approved of both in the Low countries and in France by several eminent persons of the Reformed religion. And therefore it hath been thought worth while to turn it also into English, that those of that nation may become acquainted with it and so might have a better opinion thereof and of its possessors and not only so but every well meaning soul might enquire and try all things and keep that which is best.

---

3. A copy of this book can be found in the library of the Pennsylvania State Historical Society, at Philadelphia.

This edition evidently was soon exhausted, for in 1727 it was reissued, but this time it was printed on the press of A. Bradford, of Philadelphia, a well known printer of that day. This was the first book published in America for the Mennonites. After this there seemed to be no more demand for an English confession of faith until 1810, when the Mennonites of Virginia had an edition printed at New Market, Virginia. A few years later, in 1814, another edition was published at Doylestown, Pennsylvania, and in 1837 appeared the well known Burkholder confession, published at Winchester, Virginia. The first three were all translations of the Dort confession of 1632, but the last was a copy of the so-called "large" confession of thirty-three articles found in Martyrs Mirror, to which was added "Nine Reflections" by Bishop Peter Burkholder of Virginia, all written in the German language and translated into English by Joseph Funk. During recent years many English and German editions of the Dort confession have been printed at Elkhart, Indiana.

Later Editions

The next Mennonite book to be published was the old song book, Ausbund, printed by Christopher Sauer at Germantown in 1742. But since the book is described more fully elsewhere it is given merely a passing mention here.

The greatest literary undertaking with which the Mennonites of the Colonial period were connected was the translation from the Dutch into German, and the printing of their well known book of martyrs, now commonly called the Martyrs Mirror. The Martyrs Mirror, as its name suggests, is the record of the mar-

The Martyrs Mirror

tyrs of the Mennonite and kindred faiths, and is one of the sources of information on Mennonite history. It was not written by one man, but is a compilation made by a number of men during a period of nearly one hundred years. It had its inception in a small book, written in the Dutch language and printed in the Netherlands in 1562 under the title of "Het Offer des Herren," which contained a short history of the "Doopsgezinde." This book appeared in many editions during the next fifty years and was frequently burned at the stake with the Anabaptist martyrs by the Spanish inquisitors in the Netherlands.

In 1617 a large edition was compiled by two well known Mennonites, Hans de Ries and Jacques Outerman, and printed at Hoorn by Zacharias Cornelisz, under the title of "Historie der Warachtighe Getuygen Jesu Christi." In 1631 it was again enlarged at Haarlem by Hans Passchiers von Wesbrich, under the name "Martelaars Spiegel der Wereloose Christenen." The book was given its final form at Dortrecht in 1660 by a Mennonite theologian, Thielman Jansz van Bracht, with the title "Het Bloedig Toneel der Doopsgezinde en Wereloose Christenen." The same book was reproduced in 1685 with 104 copper plate engravings made by a well known artist of that time, Jan Luyken. This is the final form of the work from which all later translations have been made.[4] The title in full, translated reads as follows,— "The Bloody Theatre or Martyrs Mirror of the Defenseless Christians who baptized only upon confession of faith and who

---

4. For a full account of the history of the Martyrs Mirror see Historical and Biographical Sketches by S. W. Pennypacker.

suffered and died for the testimony of Jesus their Savior from the time of Christ to the year A. D. 1660. Compiled from various authentic chronicles, memorials and testimonials by Thielman J. van Bracht."

As can be seen by the title the author does not confine himself to the martyrs of the Mennonite faith, but includes all those who according to his judgment opposed infant baptism, war and the oath. In general this would mean the Anabaptists but van Bracht begins with the martyrdom of Jesus, John and Stephen, whom he includes among the defenseless martyrs, then traces the history of persecutions through the period of the Roman emperors, and then takes up often in harrowing detail the fate of various sects of the medieval and early modern age, including the Lyonists, Petrobrusians, Waldenses, Wycliffites, Hussites, Anabaptists and Mennonites. In this way the compiler of the Martyrs Mirror tries to trace the history, not of a distinct religious sect, but of several religious practices and beliefs which a number of the sects in spite of many differences held in common.

In addition to the detailed accounts of the martyrdom of numerous individuals, the book contains brief historical sketches of various non-resistant sects, together with numerous confessions of faith of the Anabaptists in different communities. Some of this information van Bracht secured from original documents to which he had access. The greater part of the work, however, is a compilation of what earlier historians had to say on the subjects which he discusses. In all, he consulted three hundred and fifty-six authorities in the preparation of the Martyrs Mirror.

Next to the Bible, this book was the one most highly prized by the Mennonites during and after the years of persecution. It told of the sufferings, courage and sublime faith, not only of those of their own religious belief, but often of those of their own blood. Many of the names found in the Martyrs Mirror, such as Kuster, Rhoads, Gotwalts, Landis, Meylin, Keyser, Brubaker, Zug, Bachman, Garber and others still sound familiar to one acquainted with the Mennonites of today, and explain in part why the book was so highly esteemed by them.

This book written in the Dutch language, several of the early immigrants brought with them to Pennsylvania. Although there were only a few copies in the settlement, and these written in a language understood by a comparatively small number, yet there did not seem to be much demand for more until about 1745 when the war between the English and French, and the danger of Indian incursions made the Mennonites who lived along the frontier in the border counties fear for the inviolability of their non-resistant principles. Feeling that their younger people needed some instruction in this direction they bethought themselves of the old Martyr book. There now began to be a general demand for a translation in the German language which could be read by all. Accordingly on October 19, 1745, Jacob Godschalk, of Germantown, Dielman Kolb of Salford, Michael Ziegler of Skippack, and Heinrich Funck of Indiantown wrote to the church at Amsterdam, asking for a German translation. The Hollanders, however, unwilling to undertake the work did not reply for four years, and then only to say that they could not grant the request of their American brethren. In the meantime the Pennsylvanians had undertaken the translation and printing of the book themselves. Under the supervision of Heinrich Funck and Dielman Kolb they had arranged with the Seventh Day Baptists of the Ephrata cloister, where a printing press had been established only a few years before, for an edition of 1300 copies. This was considered a great undertaking in those days, since the book was exceptionally large and all the paper to be used had first to be manufactured at the cloister. The entire work of making the paper and printing and binding consumed the time of fifteen men for three years. The translation was made from the Dutch edition of 1685 by Peter Miller the well known linguist of the cloister. The work was finally completed in 1749,[5] as a large folio volume of over 1200 pages with the title, "Der Blutige Schauplatz oder Märtyrer Spiegel," etc. S. W. Pennypacker, in speaking of this enterprise says:—

It was the most extensive outcome of the literature of the American colonies. The paper was made at Ephrata; the binding was done there; and there was nothing anywhere else in the colonies to compare with it as an illustration of literary and theological zeal.

In 1814 the second American edition was published by Joseph Ehrenfried of Lancaster, Pennsylvania which was authorized by a number of ministers of that day. The edition was sold by subscription and was

---

5. This edition is rare. Copies can be found in the libraries of John F. Funk, of Elkhart; S. W. Pennypacker, Philadelphia; John E. Roller, Harrisonburg, Virginia; The Mennonite Publishing House, Scottdale, Pennsylvania; and the Pennsylvania State Historical Society, Philadelphia.

largely a reprint of the Ephrata book. Shem Zook of Mifflin county, Pennsylvania, published a third edition in Philadelphia in 1849, which was reissued by John F. Funk and Brother of Elkhart, Indiana, in 1870. The first English translation was made by I. D. Rupp in 1837. The Hansard Knollys Society of London in 1857 printed the first English edition in Europe for the English Baptists. The last English edition in America was issued by the Mennonite Publishing Company of Elkhart, Indiana, in 1887. This is the last and perhaps the most reliable edition in America. It was translated by J. F. Sohm and John F. Funk from the Dutch edition of 1660.

Equally as well known as the Martyrs Mirror were the works of Menno Simons, the early leader of the Mennonite faith. Menno Simons found time amid the various duties of an unusually active life to write many letters to his brethren and to reply with his pen to many attacks made upon his religious views by his enemies. These controversial and polemical treatises on the doctrines of the Christian church as understood by himself and the Anabaptists in general constitute almost his entire literary efforts from his renunciation of the Roman church to his death.

Works of Menno Simons

Among the various subjects upon which he wrote during this period are baptism, the holy supper, magistracy, oaths, capital punishment, warfare and the ban. On all of these doctrines he practically held the views of the peaceful, non-resistant Anabaptists of that day. On the incarnation, however, he approached the opinions of Melchior Hoffman, who denied the true humanity of Christ. This view was repudiated by most of the Anabaptists of his time as well as by the Mennonites of the present.

In 1543 Menno became involved in a controversy with John a Lasco, a famous theologian of that time, on the question of the incarnation, hereditary sin, sanctification and the Christian ministry. This controversy culminated in a three days' public disputation proposed by a Lasco and agreed to by Menno. A misleading report of the event published by a Lasco drew from Menno the next year two written treatises. In 1553 he held a public disputation on the same general subjects with Martin Micronius, another well known theologian. This also resulted in a written defence by Menno. During the preceding year he had also written a defence against a bitter attack made upon the Anabaptists by Gellius Faber. Among the short treatises of Menno's are his "Renunciation of Rome," and his "Testimony against Jan van Leyden." The most important, however, of all his writings and the most complete exposition of his views is his "Foundation Book," first published in 1555. It was written as a consequence of the differences of opinion which existed at the time among the Anabaptists of the Netherlands with reference to the application of the practice of shunning to the conjugal relations. Menno who believed that the usual relations between husband and wife should be suspended in case either were excommunicated, wrote a vigorous defence of his position. The treatise does not confine itself, however, to this subject but contains the mature views of Menno on most the Anabaptist doctrines, and has since become a sort of confession of faith for his followers.[6]

These various treatises were frequently published during the seventeenth and eighteenth centuries, both singly and collectively in both the Dutch and the German languages. When the first American edition appeared I have not been able to determine, but as early as 1794, at least, the "Fundament Buch" containing 675 pages was published at Lancaster by Joseph Albrecht and Company. In 1833 Heinrich Kurtz of Osnaburgh, Ohio, translated from the Dutch, and published "Menno Simons' Sämtliche Schriften." Later incomplete editions in German were published by Johann Baer of Lancaster in 1835, and one at Skippack, Pennsylvania, in 1851. The first complete work was printed at Elkhart in 1876. John Herr about the middle of the century published an incomplete English edition as did also I. D. Rupp in 1863. The first and last complete Edition came from the press of John F. Funk and Brother of Elkhart in 1871.

After the Martyrs Mirror and the Works of Menno Simons, the next best known book among the early Mennonites was perhaps Dirck Philip's Enchiridion, or Handbook. Dirck Philip was a younger contemporary of Menno Simons and was also a Dutchman. At Embden the two were closely associated in their work of preaching the Gospel, and they maintained the most friendly relations throughout the life of Menno. The Enchiridion or "Handbüchlein," as it has been called in German, deals with the same subjects as do the writings of Menno and largely from the same point of view. The following table of contents reveals

Dirck Philip's Handbüchlein

---

6. See A. H. Newman. History of Antipedobaptism. P. 302.

the nature of the subject matter—"Baptism, Incarnation, New Birth, Shunning, The Spiritual Restitution, Sending of Preachers, The Church of God, etc." The book first appeared in the Dutch language printed at Haarlem in 1578. Since that date many German editions have appeared. It has never been translated into English. The first American edition was published in 1811 by Joseph Ehrenfried at Lancaster under the title "Enchiridion oder Handbüchlein." It was published the second time in 1857 by Christian Moser at New Berlin, Ohio, and a third time in 1872 at Elkhart. The book is still popular among the conservative Amish and especially among the Old Order branch, largely because Philip advocates a rigid observance of the practice of shunning, a custom still literally observed by this branch of the church.

Jacob Denner

There are two other Mennonite books with which the early Mennonites of Pennsylvania were more or less familiar—Jacob Denner's Sermons, and the works of Johann Deknatel. Jacob Denner (1659-1746) was a Mennonite preacher at Hamburg, Germany. It was while he was pastor here that he published a series of sermons under the title of "Christliche und Erbauliche Betrachtungen über die Sonn—und Festtags Evangelia des Ganzen Jahrs," in Altona, November, 1730. A special edition of five hundred copies of this book was published in Germany in 1792, under the supervision and at the expense of John Herstein and John Smutz of Schwenksville, Pennsylvania. These men brought the books from Germany and sold them to their brethren in Montgomery, Bucks, and

Lancaster counties.[7] An American edition was published in Philadelphia in 1860 under the direction of S. B. Musselman.

Johannes Deknatel was also a preacher at Amsterdam. His book, which in German bears the title "Acht Predigten über Wichtige Materien," **Johann Deknatel** was first printed in Dutch but later, in 1757, in German. It has never been printed in America except in fragments.

In addition to the books thus far described which were all written by Mennonite authors, and in the interests of their faith there were other **Non-Mennonite** works which were not always written **Works** by Mennonites nor especially for them, but yet popular among them during the early days. Among these may be mentioned "Güldene Äpfel in silbernen Schalen," first printed at Ephrata in 1745, at the request of several members of the Mennonite church; "Geistliches Blumen-Gärtlein Inniger Seelen," published for the eighth time in America in 1800; "Die Wandelnde Seele," written by a Dutch Mennonite preacher in Holland in the seventeenth century and published many times since in both English and German and still in print; and Gottfried Arnold's "Kirchen und Ketzer Historie," imported from Europe in 1785 but never printed in America.

As already seen, the Mennonites of America added very little of their own to their original store of liter-

---

7. N. B. Grubb, in Mennonite Year Book and Almanac, 1906.

ature during the first century of their settlement here. Few of them seemed to have literary talent and none the time to exercise such as they had. The building of homes in the wilderness and the establishing of churches left little time for anything else. And so although eager to supply themselves with such religious books as they could get from Europe, they produced nothing of their own until 1744 when Heinrich Funck published on the press of Christopher Sauer, his "Ein Spiegel der Taufe mit Geist, mit Wasser und mit Blut."

Books by American Authors

Heinrich Funck

This book, as is suggested in the title, is a dissertation on the subject of baptism. Sauer, who was a Dunkard and consequently held views different from Funck's on the subject, withheld his name from the publication. New editions of the book appeared in 1834, 1850 and in 1861. Bishop Funck also wrote another and larger work which was published in 1763 by Aaron Armbruster of Philadelphia under the title, "Eine Restitution oder Erklärung einiger Hauptpunkte des Gesetzes." This book was widely read among the Mennonites at that time, and was reprinted at Biel, Switzerland, in 1844, and again at Lancaster in 1862. It contains over 300 pages and gives "an explanation of some of the principal parts of the law, their fulfillment through Christ and their signification under the Gospel dispensation."[8]

Another book or pamphlet written about the same time as "Ein Spiegel der Taufe," although not distinct-

---

8. John F. Funk. The Mennonite Church and her Accusers, p. 63.

ively a Mennonite work in the sense that it deals with the doctrines or practices of the church, yet deserves mention here because it was written by a Mennonite and describes the methods of a pioneer Mennonite school teacher. The pamphlet in question, the first work on pedagogy published in America, is Christopher Dock's "Schulordnung", written about 1750 and printed in 1770 by Christopher Sauer, Jr., of Germantown.[9]

Christopher Dock's Schulordnung

Christopher Dock was one of the early immigrants to Pennsylvania, having arrived with his father in 1714. Not much is known of his early life, but by 1718 we find him teaching a subscription school among the Mennonites on the Skippack where he remained for ten years. At the expiration of that time he became a farmer for the following ten years, in the meantime, however, teaching for four summers at Germantown. In 1738 he again returned to his earlier profession, that of teaching, which he followed until his death in 1770. Most of his time was spent in two communities in Montgomery county—Salford and Skippack. Being a successful teacher he was invited by Christopher Sauer, the printer of Germantown to write and publish a treatise on his method of teaching, for the benefit of other teachers

to whom it is given to properly instruct their children, but who may not be so well gifted that they may find something therein to be helpful to them; as well as others who are unconcerned whether the children learn anything or not, just so they get their money, that they may be made ashamed

---

9. See S. W. Pennypacker. Historical and Biographical Sketches; also Martin G. Brumbaugh. The Life and Works of Christopher Dock.

when they see that the parents also know how a well ordered school should be conducted; and finally also to instruct the parents how to deal with children whom one desires to teach something good, since in this land the parents themselves must teach the children, and many others would rather do it than send the children to such teachers who are infected with an inconsistent life.

Dock wrote the pamphlet but modestly requested that its publication be deferred until after his death. And so it was not printed until twenty years later, after both Dock and the elder Sauer had died and the printing establishment had passed into the hands of Christopher Sauer, Jr., who had at one time been a pupil of Dock's. The full title of the pamphlet is, "Eine einfältige und gründlich abgefaszte Schulordnung, darinnen deutlich vorgestellt wird, auf welche Weise die Kinder nicht nur in denen in Schulen gewöhnlichen Lehren bestens aufgebracht, sondern auch in der Lehre Gottseligkeit wohl unterrichtet werden mögen aus Liebe zu dem menschlichen Geschlecht. Aufgesetzt durch den wohl erfahrenen und lang geübten Schulmeister Christoph Dock: Und durch einige Freinde des gemeinen bestens dem Druck übergeben. Germantown. Gedruckt und zu finden bey Christoph Sauer. 1770."

The Schulordnung consists of answers to a number of questions suggested by Sauer regarding Dock's methods of teaching, among others,—How he receives his children, How he teaches them their A,B,C's, How he maintains discipline, How he secures the love of the children, etc. In answer to the first question, the school master says he meets the children with a friendly handshake, and asks them whether they will be obedient children. He starts them out in their educational career by teaching them the A, B, C's. As soon as they have mastered this their first step they pass on to the Ab's. Dock believed in rewarding diligence, and industry, and in securing the co-operation of the parents in encouraging the child to learn. For as soon as it had reached this stage the father owed it a penny and the mother had to boil it two eggs. Very little time evidently was given for play during the day. Since many of the children came from a distance, not all would be present at the appointed time. While they were gathering in, those present would read from the New Testament for the first exercise, and when all had arrived the work of the day was begun with a song and the Lord's Prayer. One hour was given for dinner, but since children would be likely to misuse this time, the school master read to them from the Old Testament.

Dock believed in appealing to the pride of the children as an incentive to good work. The poorest reader in the New Testament class, which was the advanced reading class, had to go to the foot of the bench. The last one was always designated a "lazy" scholar. In the elementary classes the child that learned its lessons well received a cipher marked on the hand with chalk. This meant that it had failed in nothing. When one had three mistakes all cried out "faul" (lazy). "This", he says, "does more to make them study than a continual dread of the rod." If the child who had failed did not correct its mistakes before night the other children might carry the word "faul" home with them. If it corrected the mistakes the word "fleiszig" (industrious) was called out by all.

JOHN F. FUNK
(1835—)

JOSEPH STUCKEY
(1825-1902)

JOHN S. COFFMAN
(1848-1899)

J. H. OBERHOLTZER
(1809-1895)

In his methods of discipline Dock was perhaps typical of the school masters of his day, but yet he understood human nature well and realized the limitations of the rod as a corrective for all the sins of the children under his care. "A slap of the hand", he says, "and the birch rod may keep wickedness from manifesting itself but it cannot change the heart." Speaking of the prevailing bad habits among the children and the method of dealing with them he says,—

Concerning the means to prevent these evil growths from getting the upper hand, I see clearly that it is not in the power of man to destroy the root in the ground. God alone through the strength of His Holy Spirit must give us His blessing. Still it is the duty of the preacher and elders, and parents and school masters, first to themselves and neighbors and fellowmen and to the young to work as much as they are able through God's mercy, not only to make this stained coat hateful but that it may be taken off.

Among the faults common to the children of his day he mentions swearing and cursing, lying, which he calls "an old time sin since Adam", stealing, pride and quarreling. His remedy for swearing is to ask the boy (since this fault is confined to the boys) whether he understands what he says and whether he learned the words from some one else or not. Generally this is learned from some one else, Dock says. The boy is then instructed in the meaning of the words he uses and is told to instruct, in turn, the one from whom he learned them. For the first offence no other punishment is provided. For the second offence the boy is seated on the bench of punishment. If he promises to be more careful in the future, he is given several slaps with the hand. For later offences the penalty is made more severe. As to lying, it is not in man's power to root out the evil. Preachers and parents must help in destroying the habit. It is the teacher's duty to instruct the child and to quote appropriate verses of Scriptures.

Dock next tells how he maintains silence in the school room. Lessons in those days were studied in a whisper or in an audible tone, as was also the custom in the schools of England at that time. "I walk up and down the room," he says, "and when I think they have learned their lesson I order them to be quiet."

The last question which he discusses is, How to teach the children to love and fear their teacher. Here again Dock shows himself a natural born teacher. He says, "I have a great love for the children, a grace from God, otherwise it would be a great burden among the scholars."

The religious tone of this, as of all rural schools of the time in Pennsylvania was high. The Testament, Old and New, was used as a text book and was made the basis for both reading and writing. Although Dock was a Mennonite and taught in Mennonite meeting houses, yet he had many pupils from other denominations. Catechisms and creeds he could not teach, but this did not make his teaching any the less religious. He read to his pupils from the Bible, sang religious songs, and made lists of questions with answers taken from the Scriptures wherein they were taught "the fear of God."

In addition to this work on teaching, Dock composed many devotional songs for children and also wrote, "A Hundred Rules of Conduct for Children," in which he describes minutely what should be the behavior of children in all hours of the day under every circumstance,—in the morning, at bed time, at the table, in school and on the street.[10]

The "schulordnung" was put through a second edition the same year, and was issued a third time in 1861 by Bishop Jacob Nold of Ohio.[11] It was perhaps never widely read even among Mennonites, and is known today only by the antiquarian. It is given space here for its historical interest, since it was perhaps the first work on pedagogy or school teaching printed in this country. Today no history of education in America is complete without at least some reference to Christopher Dock, the pious schoolmaster on the Skippack, and for that reason too it is thought worthy of a place in this short sketch of the literature of the Mennonites.

The remainder of Mennonite literature throughout the eighteenth and nineteenth centuries is largely doctrinal and controversial in character, written for the most part by those who have headed the numerous schisms from the main body. Except to the various branches of the church founded by these writers the only interest attached to these works lies in the information they give to the student of Mennonite history.

The first of these justifications is Christian Funk's

---

10. Several of these rules may not be without interest to the reader.
    Rule 48. When you have had enough get up quietly, take your stool with you, wish a pleasant meal time and go to one side and wait what will be commanded you.
    Rule 49. Do not stick the remaining bread in your pocket, but let it lie on the table.
    Rule 34. The bones, or what remains over, do not throw under the table, do not put them under the table cloth, but let them lie on the edge of the plate.
11. A copy of this edition can be found in the library of John F. Funk, Elkhart, Indiana.

"Ein Aufsatz oder Vertheidigung von Christian Funk gegen seine Mit-Diener der Mennoniten Gemeinschaft," which was published by Liebert and Billmeyer of Germantown in 1785. It contains an account of the "Funk" schism of 1777 and is practically the only printed source of information on that period of Mennonite history. The work also appeared in English in 1809 under the title, "A Mirror for all Mankind," a reprint of which was made in 1814.

Christian Funk

Another author of several controversial pamphlets was John Herr, founder of the so-called "Herrite" or Reformed Mennonite faction. In 1816 he published a pamphlet, "The True and Blessed Way." In 1819 appeared "Eine Kurze und Apostolische Antwort von mir Johannes Herr auf den Brief von Abraham Reinke." His "Erläuterungs Spiegel, oder Eine Gründliche Erklärung von der Bergpredigt," was published at Lancaster in 1827. As already seen, in 1863 he edited and published an incomplete edition of the works of Menno Simons. In this edition he wrote a preface in which he compares Menno's teaching with his own and points out that in no way has he deviated from the path followed by that leader.

Writings of John Herr

The most able writer of the Reformed Mennonite church, and its historian, was Daniel Musser of Lancaster county, whose first literary effort was a pamphlet published in 1860 under the title, "A Comparison of the Present Nominal Church with the Scriptural Representation of the Church of Christ." This

Daniel Musser's History of the Reformed Mennonites

was followed by "Nonresistance Asserted", which was published near the close of the Civil war. Both of these pamphlets have appeared in the same volume with his larger and most important work, "The Reformed Mennonite Church, Its Rise and Progress, with its Principles and Doctrines," published at Lancaster in 1873.

The purpose of Musser's history is to justify Herr and his followers in the schism of 1812. Although decidedly biased in his judgments, he shows a wide range of knowledge in the general field of Mennonite history. He takes up the history of the old Mennonite church from the days of Menno Simons and tries to show that although it has since become spiritually dead, yet at that time it was a pure church. Soon after persecutions ceased, however, and the Mennonites were given religious liberty they began to forget God and to become corrupt. This corruption had probably already set in when the first settlement was made in America in 1683. But from this time on the church hastened rapidly to a complete corruption, so that by 1800 it was a dead institution. It was this condition of things, according to Musser, that caused Herr's followers to withdraw from the old body and organize what they considered a pure church. The major part of the book is taken up with an attempt to show from contemporary authority that the church was spiritually dead, and with a history of the early steps in the organization of the Reformed Mennonites.[12]

Another book similar in character and purpose to

---

12. The Mennonite Church and her Accusers by John F. Funk is a reply to Musser's book.

that of Musser's, was written in 1850 by Jacob Stauffer and published at Lancaster in 1855 under the title, "Ein Chronik oder Geschicht-Büchlein der Sogenannten Mennonisten Gemeinde." Stauffer, like Musser, covers briefly the early history of the church, but dwells chiefly upon his own personal experience in the church at the time he was expelled, and upon his efforts to build up an organization of his own.

The Stauffer Book

About this same time, in 1847, occured the Oberholtzer schism, which was also productive of several controversial pamphlets, the most important of which are two written by Oberholtzer himself. The first appeared in 1853 under the name, "Aufschlusz der Verfolgungen gegen Daniel Hoch von Canada." The second, "Verantwortung und Erläuterung," was published at Milford Square, Pennsylvania, in 1860.

Pamphlets by Oberholtzer

The most prolific writer among all the Mennonite schismatics was John Holdeman, of Wayne county, Ohio, founder of the so-called Holdeman branch of the church. In 1864 appeared, "A Reply to the Criticisms of I. W. Rosenborough," on the work entitled the "Old Foundation." The next year he published, "Eine Vertheidigung gegen die Verfälscher Unserer Schriften, wie auch eine Erklärung und Erläuterung der Absicht der Christlichen Taufe." This was followed in 1876 by, "A History of the Church of God", which is the chief printed source of information for the origin of this branch of the denomination. In 1878 appeared a comprehensive doctrinal work called

John Holdeman a Prolific Writer

"Ein Spiegel der Wahrheit." This was followed in 1890 by, "A Treatise on Redemption, Baptism and the Lord's Supper," and in 1891 by, "A Treatise on Magistracy, War, Millennium, Holiness and the Manifestation of Spirits."

One other book deserves mention in this short sketch of Mennonite literature, Benjamin Eby's "Kurzgefaszte Kirchen-Geschichte und Glaubenslehre der Taufgesinnten oder Mennoniten." This was practically the first unbiased historical sketch of the Mennonites that was writen by an American author. It was first printed in 1841 and was later reissued at Lancaster in 1853, since which time it has appeared in several editions.

The modern rage for writing books has not escaped the Mennonites. During recent years a considerable number of works of a doctrinal, historical or devotional character have appeared. These are too numerous to mention here, and whether any of them will live beyond their own short day time alone can tell. Among the best known of living writers on Mennonite subjects are J. F. Funk, M. S. Steiner, Daniel Kauffman and John Horsch among the Old Mennonites, and H. P. Krehbiel and N. B. Grubb among the General Conference Mennonites.

Hymnology
Turning now to the hymnology of the early Mennonites we find of course that they brought with them such hymnbooks as were in use among their brethren in their native land. The Hollanders no doubt brought the hymns sung among the Mennonites in the Netherlands, while the Palatines came with the well known Ausbund, or "Dicke Liederbuch" as it was popularly called in later

years. Since the settlement in Pennsylvania came to be almost entirely German, the Ausbund became the leading hymnbook in all the Mennonite churches. The Ausbund, the full title of which reads, "Ausbund; das ist etliche schöne Lieder, wie sie im Gefängnis zu Passau in dem Schloss von den Schweitzer Brüdern und anderen Rechtgläubigen Christen gedichtet worden," is a compilation of hymns, sung originally by the Schweizer brethren[13] who were imprisoned in the castle of Passau in Bavaria in 1527. To the hymns sung by these people, others were added from time to time until in its final form the Ausbund contained one hundred forty hymns, some with more than thirty long stanzas. The first edition was printed in Switzerland in 1571 where it soon became the popular song book of the Mennonites of that region. When later the Swiss were driven into the Palatinate, it was introduced into Germany. Several editions were printed during the seventeenth century, although it had to be done secretly. The first American edition was printed in 1742 by Christopher Sauer of Germantown, It was reprinted in 1751, 1767, 1785, 1815, and six times since, making eleven editions in all, the last of which appeared in 1905 at Elkhart, Indiana.

Ausbund

It was at first in common use among both branches of the Mennonite church, but before 1800 the Mennonites began to discard it for more modern hymns. The Amish, however, everywhere retained it, and it is still in use among the Old Order Amish.

The Ausbund is perhaps one of the oldest hymn-

---

13. For a short history of the Schweizer Brüder see Martyrs Mirror.

books in use anywhere among Protestant churches. It contains hymns written by the early martyrs, mostly Anabaptist, hymns reciting the story of the death of some of these men and women, and hymns expounding various church doctrines.

Among those of the first class is hymn five written by George Blaurock who was burned at the stake in 1527. Number six was written by Felix Mantz, while Michael Sattler, another early martyr wrote the seventh, and Hans Hut, the eighth. These men were the leading Anabaptists of their day and all died for their faith. Among hymns which were not written by Anabaptists is number thirty-eight of which John Huss is the author.

The eleventh hymn, still popular among the Amish, tells the story of the martyrdom of Jörg Wagner. The second verse illustrates the narrative character of many of the songs of this class.

> Also thät Jörg der Wagner auch
> Gen Himmel fuhr er in dem Rauch
> Durch Kreuz ward er bewähret
> Gleich wie man thut dem klaren Gold
> Von Herzen ers begehret.

Verse seven continues the story of his death,

> Der Henker führt ihn an ein'm strick
> Im Rathaus las man ihm vier stück
> Darauf stund ihm sein Leben
> Eh er eins widerrufen wollt
> In Tod thät er sich geben.

One of the best known of these hymns during the middle of the last century among the Amish, and still sung in some localities is the so-called Haszlibacher Lied, which tells of the faith and death of Hans Haszlibach. The first verse is introductory to the story which the following verses narrate.

> Was wend wir aber heben an
>   Zu singen von ein'm alten Mann
> Der war von Haszlibach.
>   Haszlibacher ward er genannt
> Aus der Kilchöri Summiswald.

This Haszlibach, being suspected of heresy, was taken into custody by the authorities of the State Church and cast into prison. Considering it their duty, however, to turn him from the error of his ways, the priests entered his cell one Friday morning for that purpose, but all of no avail.

> Der Haszlibacher auf der Statt
>   Sie über disputiret hat
> Da sprach er bald zu ihn'n
>   Von mein'm Glauben thu ich nicht abstan
> Eh will ich Leib und Leben lahn.

On Saturday night an angel visited him in prison and urged him to remain steadfast in his faith, promising to sustain him in the coming ordeal. On Monday night the priests again entered the prison to persuade tim to recant, but again in vain. The old man nobly determined to stand by his convictions.

> Von mein'm Glaub thu ich nicht abstahn
>   Das Göttlich Wort ich Selber kann
> Mein sach befehl ich Gott
>   Es ist mein'm Herz ein ringe Busz
> Wan ich unschuldig sterben musz.

He was finally put to death but before the deed had been done an angel had again appeared to him and had prophesied that three signs would appear at his beheading. These prophecies were fulfilled as the executioner severed the head from the body.

> Darnach man ihm sein Haupt abschlug
> Da sprang er wieder in sein' Hut.
> Die Zeichen hat man gesehen
> Die Sonne ward wie rothes Blut
> Der Stadel-Brunn that schwitzen Blut.

The executioner, witnessing these signs, became convinced that he had shed innocent blood and himself became a convert to the new faith.

This song with the moral at the end written by one who was a fellow prisoner of Haszlibach's is typical of many of the martyr songs in the book, with this exception, however, that few contain such a large element of superstition and show such a firm belief in the supernatural.

In addition to these martyr hymns, the book contains a few of a devotional nature and a larger number of a doctrinal character. Religion in those days was much more closely associated with doctrine than now, and hence we find that many of the songs of the time, instead of giving expression to the gratitude of the heart for favors bestowed or to some spiritual longing of the soul, contain an exposition of some Bible doctrine. Thus hymn number fifty-seven treats of love, and begins with, "Die Lieb ist kalt jetzt in der Welt." Number fifty bears the title, "Ein Ander Schön Lied von den Sieben Gaben des Heiligen Geistes." Hymn fifty-four discusses infant baptism. Eighty-one deals with the doctrine of the Trinity, and is a good illustration of this class of songs. The first verse reads as follows:

> Herr Gott Vater, zu dir ich schrey
> Ich bitt, dein Weisheit mir verley
> Dasz ich ein Lied mög singen
> Vom wesen deiner Einigkeit
> Das sich verlegt in die Dreyheit
> Herr Gott, lasz mir gelingen
> Dann je allein du warst und bist
> Ewig zu allen Zeiten.
>
> Die Dreyheit sollt du wohl verstahn
> Wie sie Johannes zeiget an
> Vater, Wort, Geist thut nennen
> Sie in dem Himmel Zeugen seyn.
> Die drei namen dienen in ein
> Ihr sollt es wohl vernehmen
> Des Vaters allmächtige Kraft
> Wird ersehen bei'n Geschöpfen
> Die er durch das Wort hat gemacht
> Sein Geist all's thut bekräften
> Wann er sich des würd unterstahn
> Den Geist in sich zu sammeln
> Müszt's all's wieder vergahn.

Then follow seventeen more stanzas of the same length and along the same strain.

These hymns have been sung in America for two hundred years, and in Switzerland for almost two hundred more, with scarcely any change either in melody or in words. The book has never been revised, merely reprinted. The Amish have always been opposed to the use of notes and so the melodies even within the last hundred years wherever the book is used, have been learned by ear and in this way transmitted from one generation to another.[a] These old hymns although pervaded by the somber and gloomy atmosphere of the times when they were written, and with no poetical merit and with very little of the true spirit of praise, yet have this decided superiority over many of our modern songs—they have the ring of sincerity in them. Many of them were composed by writers who were in prison waiting to be led to the stake or the executioner's block. And thus whatever else may be said about them, they at least express a real and sincere anguish or hope of the heart. It is this sincerity together with the simplicity of expression which has made these hymns hold their own for so many years.[14]

As already said, the Mennonites began to discard the Ausbund before the close of the eighteenth century. The first distinctively Mennonite hymnal after

---

[a.] The Amish never set their hymns to written music. For the two following songs I am indebted to Professor Joseph W. Yoder, director of music in the State Normal School of Lockhaven, Pennsylvania. The music attempts to reproduce as nearly as possible the exact melody of these two songs as they are still sung among the Amish of Pennsylvania and other states. Professor Yoder gives these instructions for reading music:

"All the notes between two consecutive bars are sung to one syllable. This necessitates slurring throughout the entire piece, and as slurring is one of the characteristics of these tunes, the marks indicating slurs are omitted, but understood. The whole notes represent a sustaining of the voice almost as long as a whole note in 2-2 time; the half note somewhat shorter and the quarter note a quick swing of the voice, a mere touch of the voice to that note; and the double notes represent a rather long sustaining of the voice. A slight stress of the voice on the first part of each syllable, is probably as near to the accent as we can come, as there is little if any accent."

[14.] Many of the editions of the Ausbund have an appendix containing the names of Swiss martyrs from 1635 to 1646. Many of these names sound familiar to American Mennonites and Amish. Among them are—Meyli, Frick, Gut, Kolb, Landis, Huber, Bachman, Heesz, Egly, Nüssly, Schnebly.

Weil nun die Zeit vorhanden ist.

Der Lobgesang.

the Ausbund was a book called "Die Kleine Geistliche Harfe," which consisted of four hundred and seventy-five psalms and hymns, for a few of which the music was printed with the words. The first edition was printed in 1803 on the Billmeyer press of Germantown, under the title of "Die Geistliche Harfe der Kinder Zions oder Auserlesene geistreiche Gesänge allen Heilsbegierigen; Insonderheit aber allen Christlichen Gemeinden des Herrn zum Dienst und Gebrauch mit Fleisz zusammen getragen und in gegenwärtige Form und Ordnung gestellt nebst einem dreyfachen Register. Auf Verordnung der Mennonisten Gemeinden." The purpose of the publishing of a new hymn book appears in the preface of this edition, which shows that for some time before the Ausbund had no longer been in common use. The preface reads,

Die Kleine Geistliche Harfe

Weil die Psalmen David's mehrenteils gebräuchlich waren in der Versammlung und man doch nicht überall solche bücher gehabt auch in mancher Versammlung zwei oder dreierley Gesangbücher waren so hat Man es dienlich angesehen ein Gesangbuch drucken zu lassen damit Man sich mit mehrer gleichförmigkeit in dem Lob und der Anbetung Gottes Unsers Heilandes Jesus Christus Vereinigen könnte.

Other editions of "Die Kleine Harfe" appeared in 1811, 1820, 1834, 1848 and several times since.

Another book which appeared about the same time and was in general use among the Mennonite churches during the first three quarters of the nineteenth century, was the "Unpartheiisches Gesangbuch." The first edition was printed by Johann Albrecht of Lancaster in 1804. The title page reads as follows, "Ein Unparteiisches Gesangbuch, enthaltend

Unparteiisches Gesangbuch

Geistreiche Lieder und Psalmen zum Allgemeinen Gebrauch des wahren Gottesdienstes. Auf Begehren der Brüderschaft der Mennonisten Gemeinen aus vielen Liederbüchern gesammelt mit einem dreifachen Register zum erstenmal ans Licht gestellt." This hymnal was reprinted in 1808, 1820, 1829, 1841 and several times since, and is still used in some parts of Pennsylvania. The "Allgemeine Lieder-Sammlung", popular among the German speaking Mennonites and the Amish, was first published by J. F. Funk and Brother, of Elkhart, in 1871.

The first English song book was compiled by a committee of Virginia Mennonites and published at Harrisonburg, Virginia, in 1847, under the title, "A Selection of Psalms, Hymns and Spiritual Songs." The book was reprinted five times by Joseph Funk on his hand press at Singers Glen, Virginia. He later sold his rights to J. F. Funk and Brother who have since printed several editions.

First English Hymnal—1847

Almost without exception these books thus far described were without notes, since both Mennonites and Amish regarded written music in the church hymnals as a worldly innovation. There was no objection, however, to learning new tunes for the old hymns from other note books. Joseph Funk in order to supply this need published in 1832 a note book of sacred melodies, "The Harmonia Sacra." This book soon became very popular among the Mennonites of Virginia and Pennsylvania, and was extensively used in singing schools and as a book of melodies for the hymnals

"Note" Books

Harmonia Sacra

which appeared later. It passed through seventeen editions, and was for many years the recognized compendium of church music in Virginia, Pennsylvania and other eastern states.

"The Philharmonia," compiled by Martin Wenger and first published by J. F. Funk and Brother in 1875,

Philharmonia was the successor to the Harmonia Sacra and fulfilled the same purpose. It is still in print.

During the past fifty years many hymnals have appeared among the various branches of the Mennonite church, but space can not be taken here to enumerate them. Neither is it necessary, since none of them have occupied an important place in the history of Mennonite church music. They have usually lasted for only a few years.

In addition to the various forms of religious literature thus far described there was another form of reading matter with which the Mennon-

German ites of Colonial times as well as other
Almanacs Germans of Southeastern Pennsylvania were familiar,—the well known Sauer Almanac, published first by Christopher Sauer, Sr., and later by his son, Christopher Sauer, Jr. This almanac which was printed annually for about three quarters of a century, together with perhaps a few books on medicine and household economy furnished practically all the secular reading matter found on the book shelves of that day. The Sauer Almanac was followed early in the nineteenth century by the Baer Almanac of Lancaster. This publication was found in nearly every Mennonite home in

LITERATURE AND HYMNOLOGY 443

Pennsylvania and other eastern states during the middle half of the century and is still in print. The first almanac published expressly for the Mennonite people was issued by J. F. Funk and Brother. It first appeared in 1870 and has since then acquired a wide circulation. It contained the names of all the ministers of the church and other church information of value. In addition to this almanac there have also appeared within recent years two year-books, one published by the Eastern Conference of the General Conference Mennonites, and the other by the Mennonite Board of Missions and Charities.

Early Printing Presses

No branch of the denomination until within recent years has owned or controlled a printing establishment. Such books as the church needed or as individuals desired to publish were printed by the early German printers of Pennsylvania, or during the nineteenth century, occasionally in other states. The best known of these early printers of Pennsylvania were Christopher Sauer of Germantown, and the Ephrata Brethren in Lancaster county. Nearly all of the Mennonite books of the eighteenth century were issued from these two establishments. These in turn were followed near the close of the century by the Billmeyer press of Germantown the successor to the establishment of Christopher Sauer, Jr., who in turn had succeeded his father. During the early part of the nineteenth century Joseph Ehrenfried of Philadelphia, printed an edition of the Martyrs Mirror, an edition of Dirck Philip's Handbüchlein and perhaps several other Mennonite books. The press, however, which occupied a position among the Mennonites and other

Germans of Pennsylvania during the early part of the nineteenth century similar to that of the Sauer press during the eighteenth, was that of Johann Baer and Son of Lancaster. None of these printers were Mennonites.

The first venture of the American Mennonites in the publication field was made by Henry Bertolet, a minister in the Skippack congregation, who published a paper called "Der Evangelische Botschafter" in July 1836. There was so much opposition to the movement, however, that only one issue was published.[15]

Mennonite Presses

In 1847 Joseph Funk of Virginia established in a small village, since called Singers Glen, in Rockingham county, a small hand press upon which for many years were printed the Harmonia Sacra, the Collection of Hymns and Songs, and other publications. Soon after this, in 1852, J. H. Oberholtzer set up a small press in Milford Square, Bucks county, Pennsylvania, upon which was printed the "Religiöser Botschafter", the predecessor of the "Christlicher Bundesbote," the German organ of the General Conference branch of the denomination. The largest and most important of the printing establishments devoted to the interests of the church was that of John F. Funk and Brother, first located in Chicago in 1864, but later removed to Elkhart, Indiana. This firm which has since become the Mennonite Publishing Company, for many years issued the Herald of Truth, the leading organ of the main branch of Mennonites, and a number of other religious papers, and has served as the official publish-

---

15. See article by Daniel Kauffman in Family Almanac, 1909. Scottdale, Pa.

ing house for a large part of the church. The most
recent private Mennonite publishing concern was the
Gospel Witness Company of Scottdale, Pennsylvania.
None of these enterprises were owned or controlled by
the church. In 1908 a publication board, appointed by
various Mennonite and Amish Conferences purchased
the periodicals of the Mennonite Publishing Company,
the Gospel Witness Company and the Mennonite Book
and Tract Society, and established The Mennonite
Publishing House, which is now located at Scottdale,
Pennsylvania. The new firm is now controlled by the
church and is the church publishing house of the Old
Mennonites and the Amish. The Herald of Truth
and the Gospel Witness have been merged into the
Gospel Herald. The House now publishes five weekly
papers in both the German and English languages, one
monthly and various church and Sunday school supplies. Other branches of the denomination also have
their church papers which are issued either by private
enterprises, or by church publishing houses.

CHAPTER XVII

THE PRESENT

It is the purpose here to present the reader with a brief summary of the present status of the various branches of the denomination. The names assumed by some of these divisions may be misleading to one not acquainted with the history of the church. The tendency among all is to use the term Mennonite. Even the Amish now speak of themselves as Amish-Mennonites, and two of the divisions of this branch have assumed the name Mennonite, without any reference to the prefix. The classification made here is based not upon the name used but upon the origin of the different branches. The two main divisions which existed at the beginning of their American history, and from which all later divisions have sprung are the Mennonites and the Amish. The largest of these is the Mennonite, which is further subdivided into the Old Mennonites, Reformed Mennonites (Herrites), "Wisler" Mennonites, General Conference Mennonites, Mennonite Brethren in Christ, Church of God in Christ (Holdemanite), and Brueder Gemeinde.

Branches of the Denomination

Of these the Old Mennonites embrace the largest membership. This is the parent body from which the others have sprung and is still conservative in spirit and religious practice. The term old is not an official part of the name, but is used here merely to distinguish the main body from the later divisions. It includes the following conferences, all of which are entirely independent of one another—Lancaster county, Franconia (composed of the churches in Montgomery, Bucks and Berks counties), Southwestern Pennsylvania, Washington county (Md.) and Franklin county (Pa.), Virginia, Ohio, Indiana-Michigan, Illinois, Iowa-Missouri, Kansas-Nebraska, Pacific coast, Nebraska-Minnesota (composed of Germans from Russia), Ontario, and Alberta-Saskatchewan. By far the largest of these is the Lancaster county conference. It is also the most conservative and is not altogether in sympathy with the progressive spirit of some of the western conferences.

Old Mennonites

The official church organ of the Old Mennonites is the Gospel Herald, published by the Mennonite Publishing House, at Scottdale, Pennsylvania. These conferences also support the Mennonite Board of Missions and Charities, which has established a foreign mission in India, and a number of home missions in various large cities, including Chicago, Philadelphia, Kansas City, Toronto, Ft. Wayne, Canton, and others. Some of the conferences also through the Mennonite Board of Education, control Goshen College and the school at Hesston, Kansas. Among the men still living, who have been most influential within recent years in the church are John F. Funk, founder of the

Herald of Truth and the Mennonite Publishing Company, author, publisher and preacher; Daniel Kauffman, writer, editor of the Gospel Herald, and evangelist; J. S. Shoemaker; Menno S. Steiner, author and preacher, and president of the Mennonite Board of Missions and Charities; Jacob N. Brubacher and Isaac Eby, bishops of Lancaster county; A. S. Mack, bishop in the Franconia district; A. D. Wenger, traveler and evangelist; J. A. Ressler, superintendent of the India Mission; Noah E. Byers, president of Goshen College; D. H. Bender, associate editor of the Gospel Herald and the first principal of the Hesston Mennonite school; A. H. Leaman, superintendent of the Chicago Mission; J. S. Hartzler, I. R. Detweiler, J. E. Hartzler, S. F. Coffman, Aaron Loucks, L. J. Heatwole, John Blosser, Noah Mack, George Lambert and others whom space does not permit to mention.

The General Conference Mennonites rank next with a constituency of about twelve thousand. In addition to the general conference which meets triennially, there are five district conferences—(1) the Eastern, composed of the congregations of eastern Pennsylvania, principally in Montgomery, Bucks and Berks counties; (2) the Middle district, composed of the scattered congregations in Ohio, Indiana, Iowa and Missouri; (3) the Western, which is made up largely of the churches in Kansas but also embraces several in Nebraska and Oklahoma; (4) the Northern, comprising several congregations in Minnesota and the Dakotas; and (5) the Pacific conference.

General Conference of Mennonites

The Mennonite Book Concern, located at Berne, Indiana, is the official publishing house, and the Bundesbote and the Mennonite, the leading papers of the church. The Western conference supports Bethel College, at Newton, Kansas; the Middle conference has established the Central Mennonite College at Bluffton, Ohio; while the Eastern conference is represented on the Board of Trustees of Perkiomen Seminary, a Schwenkfelder school, and sends many of its young men to that institution. Small local schools are also conducted among the Russian Mennonites in various localities. Mission stations are supported among the Arrapahoe Indians in Indian Territory, and in Central Province, India. Among the men still living who are doing most to enhance the interests of the church are Christian Krehbiel, pastor of the congregation at Halstead, Kansas; C. H. Wedel and David Goerz, of Bethel College; C. H. A. van der Smissen, of Summerfield, Illinois; H. P. Krehbiel, historian; N. B. Grubb, preacher and writer of Philadelphia; I. A. Sommer, editor, and J. J. Kliewer, pastor, both of Berne, Indiana; J. B. Baer, evangelist, of Bluffton, Ohio; and A. S. Shelley, of Pennsylvania.

Mennonite Brethren in Christ

The Mennonite Brethren in Christ have a membership of about six thousand or more and are divided into five conference districts,—Canada, Michigan,, Pennsylvania, Indiana-Ohio and Western. The official organ of the church is the Gospel Banner, which was formerly published in Berlin, Ontario, but since 1908 it is published by the Union Gospel Printing Company, of Cleveland, Ohio, under the editorship of C. H. Brunner. This church is imbued with a strong missionary spirit and supports stations in the Soudan, Chili, and Turkey.

The remaining branches of the Mennonite division of the church with several exceptions are too small to have separate publishing plants or mission stations and either read such religious papers as may suit their individual fancies, or such as are printed by the larger branches of the denomination.

Among the Amish the largest branch is the Amish-Mennonite, with a membership of a little over eight thousand. It comprises three confer-
Amish ence districts—(1) the Eastern, composed of the congregations in Pennsylvania, Ohio and Ontario; (2) Indiana; and (3) the Western district, which comprises the churches in all the states west of Indiana. The Amish-Mennonites have no church institutions of their own, but are officially represented on all the boards of the institutions of the Old Mennonites. These two churches are practically one in spirit, doctrine and religious practice, and act together in all church enterprises. Among the men who have recently done most to promote the interests of the body at large are Bishop Benjamin Gerig, and C. Z. Yoder of Wayne county, Ohio; D. D. Miller, evangelist and assistant editor of the Gospel Herald, and Bishop D. J. Johns of Indiana; S. H. Miller of Holmes county, Ohio; Bishop John Smith[1] of Illinois and Samuel Gerber of the same state; Levi Miller of Missouri; Bishop Sebastian Gerig of Iowa, and Bishop Joseph Schlegel of Nebraska.

The Old Order Amish with a membership of

---
1. Deceased, 1906.

THE PRESENT

about four thousand five hundred have no conferences, nor church institutions, but generally support the missionary enterprises of the Old Mennonites and Amish-Mennonites, and read the literature published by them.

Old Order

The Conservative Amish number a little over sixteen hundred in the United States and Canada. They differ little from the Old Order except that they worship in meeting houses and are less given to maintaining the old customs. They have no conferences. Each congregation is independent of all others.

The Illinois Conference of Mennonites is the name by which the so-called "Stuckey" Amish are known. The church is a branch of the Amish division, but it has assumed the simple name of Mennonite. It numbers about fifteen hundred members, principally in Illinois, but there are a few scattered congregations in Iowa and Nebraska. It maintains no separate church institutions, but supports the educational and missionary enterprises of the Old Mennonites and reads the literature of both publishing houses. The conference has no power to issue decrees that are binding on the congregations which compose it. It is merely an advisory body.

Illinois Conference of Mennonites

The Defenseless Mennonites, sometimes called "Egli" Amish, are likewise a branch of the Amish church. They have a membership of about one thousand principally in Illinois, Indiana and Ohio. C. R. Egli, one of the leading spirits, publishes at Gridley, Illinois, a paper in behalf of the church, called

Defenseless Mennonites

Heilsbote. The church also supports an orphans' home near Flanagan, Illinois, and several missionaries in Africa. It is also beginning to support many of the enterprises of the Old Mennonites and the Amish. The bond of sympathy between this branch of the denomination and the Amish and other divisions is growing.

These are the various divisions into which the Mennonite denomination is broken up. In addition to these there are still a number of independent congregations, especially among the immigrants from Russia in Manitoba and some of the Northern states which cannot be classified except according to their geographical location.

As to the number of Mennonites at present in America, accurate statistics are not at hand. The report of the United States census while not far out of the way, yet is not altogether accurate. The statistics for the Old Mennonites, Amish Mennonites and several others published in the Mennonite Year Book and Directory is fairly reliable. The official statistician of the General Conference Mennonites is H. P. Krehbiel. The following table compiled from several sources is meant to be only an approximate estimate, in round numbers, but it is not far from correct:

I. Old Mennonites.
1. Franconia 3,500
2. Lancaster 8,000
3. Washington and Franklin counties 800
4. Virginia 1,150
5. Southwestern Pennsylvania . . . 1,300
6. Ohio 1,300

THE PRESENT 453

7.	Indiana-Michigan	1,250
8.	Kansas-Nebraska	800
9.	Illinois	370
10.	Iowa-Missouri	565
11.	Pacific coast	150
12.	Nebraska-Minnesota	450
13.	Minnesota (independent)	500
14.	Alberta-Saskatchewan	150
15.	Ontario	1,500
II.	General Conference Mennonites	12,000
III.	Mennonite Brethren in Christ	6,000
IV.	Wisler Mennonites	1,900
V.	Reformed Mennonites	1,700
VI.	Brueder Gemeinde	700
VII.	Church of God in Christ (Holdeman)	600
VIII.	Mennonites in Manitoba (Russian)	8000
IX.	Amish Mennonite	
1.	Eastern district	3,800
2.	Indiana-Michigan	1,150
3.	Western district	3,150
X.	Amish-Mennonite (conservative)	1,650
XI.	Old Order Amish	4,500
XII.	Defenseless Mennonites	1,000
XIII.	Illinois Conference of Mennonites	1,500

Total 68,435

Total Number

In round numbers then the membership of the entire denomination in Canada and the United States counts up about 70,000. This includes only those who are actual members of the church. Since Mennonite families are on the average large, it may be safe to estimate the entire Mennonite population in America at about double the above number or about 150,000.

The Mennonites of all classes are still almost entirely a rural people. Very few congregations are found in the cities. Among the few exceptions are the churches in Philadelphia, Lancaster, Pennsylvania; Elkhart, Goshen and Berne, Indiana; Newton, Kansas, and several missions in the larger cities. There is a tendency, however, at present among the Mennonites as among all people, toward the towns and cities.

A Rural People

The different branches of the denomination have little religious intercourse with one another. As has already been indicated, the differences between them lies not in fundamental articles of faith, but in minor customs and practices, in several cases largely in customs of dress. There are, however, several centers from which radiate influences which are making for unification. As already seen the General Conference Mennonites aim at a final union of all branches, but they have not as yet made much headway except among scattered independent liberal congregations and among the more recent European immigrants. The Old Mennonites and Amish-Mennonites are practically one working body now, and have established a general conference in which these churches are represented. The Franconia and Lancaster conferences, however, do not as yet recognize the movement, and thus the influence of this conference is limited to the western congregations. The Defenseless Mennonites are also beginning to work in harmony with these two main branches of the denomination. But the time when all branches will unite again into one ecclesiastical body lies some distance in the future.

The Mennonite denomination is passing through a critical period of its history. The two questions of most vital importance to the future of the church are its relation to the unification movement, and to the question of a more liberal education for its young people. The denomination will never take the position which rightly belongs to it in the religious world until it passes favorably upon both of these questions.

Critical Period

CHAPTER XVIII

BIBLIOGRAPHY

Source material, either in print or manuscript, for the study of Mennonite history is meager. The Mennonites kept no church records and very often no family records. Hence our knowledge about them must be gleaned very largely from what their contemporaries incidentally said about them, from scattered letters here and there preserved either in family Bibles or some of the European church archives, or from such records as were kept by the civil authorities, of land entries, and Mennonite petitions from time to time for naturalization or for exemption from the oath and military service. The fact, however, that the Mennonites were pioneers both in Germantown and in Lancaster county makes it possible for us to know more about the early life of the first immigrants than would otherwise have been possible. They were in the very front of the great wave of German immigration which poured into Pennsylvania during the first half of the eighteenth century, and for this reason they have been given some general consideration by the students of the early Germans in America.

By far the most exhaustive and thorough work

done upon the subject of Pennsylvania Germans is that done by the Pennsylvania German Historical Society, the annual reports of which now cover seventeen large volumes (1891-1908). Separate volumes have been devoted to the Lutherans, Reformed, Schwenkfelders, Moravians, and Dunkards, but so far no complete treatise on the Mennonites has appeared. Many of the histories of these separate churches necessarily contain references to Mennonites which are of considerable value to the Mennonite historian, while volume nine is devoted almost entirely to biographical and historical sketches by Samuel W. Pennypacker, pertaining to the early history of the Germantown Mennonites. The chapter on the founding of Germantown has been written from information which Mr. Pennypacker has been gathering for years, and so far as it goes is perhaps the final word on the subject. Other works by Pennypacker, based largely on original sources and family history are "Hendrick Pennebecker," and "Annals of Phoenixville," both of which contain much of Mennonite family history.

Professor O. Seidensticker's "Bilder aus der Deutsch-Pennsylvanischen Geschichte" (1886) contains several chapters on the Germantown Mennonites which have hardly been excelled by Pennypacker. Two earlier sources for this subject which, however, need to be read critically and in some details discarded entirely, are the notices in Watson's Annals (1843), and in Hazard's Register (1828) and (1831). Volume XIV (1906) of the Pennsylvania German Society publications contains a chapter on Germantown which includes several letters and other matters of interest on the Germantown Mennonites. Morgan Edward's

"Material for a History of the American Baptists" (1770) contains a brief sketch of the Mennonites at the time and also gives a brief historical review of the Germantown church. The letterbook of James Claypool the original of which is in the library of the Pennsylvania Historical Society, and extracts from which appear in the Pennsylvania Magazine of History, Vol. X, gives a brief account of the sailing of the Concord in 1683. The Streiper papers in the library of the Pennsylvania Historical Society include a number of letters written by members of the Streiper family in Germantown to relatives in the Netherlands. The Pennsylvania Magazine of History, Vols. IV and V, contain several helpful sketches. Also suggestive are many of the family histories of the early Germantown families, including those of Konders, Shoemaker, Kassel, Keyser, Sauer and others. On the relation of the Quakers and Mennonites in Europe we must rely for our information on the journals of the Quaker missionaries themselves, including Fox's Journal, Sewell's "History of the Quakers," Story's Journal and Chalkley's Journal. The best general treatise on the subject is found in several chapters of Barclay's "The Inner Life of the Religious Societies of the Commonwealth," (London, 1876). The Pennsylvania Magazine of History, Vol. II, contains an article by Professor Seidensticker on "Penn's Travels in Germany and Holland in 1677." For the facts regarding the relation of the two denominations in Germantown we must rely largely on family histories and traditions, and on the records of the Abington Monthly Meeting, from which we can learn something of the religious activities of such of the

BIBLIOGRAPHY 459

early settlers as affiliated themselves with the Quakers in their religious work.

On the early settlement of Lancaster county, Rupp's "History of Lancaster County" (1844) is perhaps still the best authority. Alexander Harris's "Biographical History of Lancaster County" contains a great deal of biographical material, on the whole fairly reliable, of the early Mennonite families. The latest history of the county, by Ellis and Evans, has several articles on the Mennonites. The one written by E. K. Martin on the general field of Mennonite history is perhaps the best short treatise in English. The other is a short sketch of the early churches and ministers in the county written by Bishop J. N. Brubacher. All of these county histories contain much valuable information, but need to be critically examined, and the facts often need to be modified from other sources of information. De Hoop Scheffer's "Mennonite Emigration to Pennsylvania," translated from the Dutch by S. W. Pennypacker in the Pennsylvania Magazine, Vol. II, contains many facts on the European phase of the emigration to Lancaster county. Ernst Müller's "Geschichte der Bernischen Täufer" is also valuable for a comparison of European with Lancaster names. Pennsylvania Archives, Second series, Vol. XIX, contains many references to land entries made by early Mennonite immigrants. Of equal value are the records catalogued "'Old Rights, Lancaster County" in the office of the Secretary of the Interior at Harrisburg. Occasional notes can be found in Watson and Hazard, as well as in the various volumes of Pennsylvania Archives, and "Votes and Proceedings of the Assembly." For genealogical purposes much information can be gained from Egle's "Notes and Queries," and from Rupp's "Thirty Thousand Names," which contains a list of all the immigrants landed at Philadelphia from 1727 to 1776.

On the subject of the State and the Mennonites nothing has been written. The only sources of information are the occasional references to Mennonites found in the Pennsylvania Archives, Votes and Proceedings of the Assembly (Pa.), Journal of Burgesses (Va.), Constitutions and Statutes of Virginia, Maryland, and Pennsylvania, Colonial Records (Pa.), Congressional Globe and Journal of the Confederate Congress. On the Germantown experiment of self government the chief source of information is the original record book of the Court of Record, at present in the possession of the Pennsylvania State Historical Society.

On the subject of Anabaptists a large number of books have been written in the German language. Among the older works are Heinrich Bullinger's "Der Widertoufferen Ursprung, Fürgang, Sekten," etc. (1561); Sebastian Franck's "Chronika" (1578); and J. C. Fuesslin's "Beiträge zur Kirchengeschichte des Schweitzerlands" (1741). Among modern treatises are Ludwig Keller's "Wiedertäufer" (1880), "Die Reformation" (1885), and "Hans Denck" (1882); Emil Egli's "Aktensammlung zur Geschichte der Zürcher Reformation" (1879); and C. A. Cornelius' "Geschichte des Münsterschen Aufruhrs" (1855). In English not much has been written on the subject. Among the books that have appeared are Richard Heath's "Anabaptism—From its Rise at Zwickau to its Fall at Münster." (1905); and Belfort Bax's "Rise and Fall of the Anabaptists"; A. H. Newman's "A History of Antipedobaptism" contains an excellent bibliography on the subject.

On later American Mennonite history, printed and manuscript sources are also very meager. The historian must depend for his information largely on family histories, county and other local histories written during the past twenty-five years from information which is not always reliable. Two general histories of the Mennonites of America have been written, one by D. K. Cassel, and the other by Hartzler and Kauffman. Neither of these, however, are trustworthy except for such history as has been made during the present generation.

The best collection of Mennonite literature, which is largely polemical, however, and of little value to the historian, is to be found in the private library of John F. Funk, of Elkhart, Indiana. The Pennsylvania State Historical Society also has a number of books and pamphlets writen by Mennonite authors in its library in Philadelphia.

For the history of the church since 1865 the files of the Herald of Truth, of Elkhart, Indiana, furnish the most helpful source of information.

Many of these American sources mentioned in this brief sketch need to be accepted with extreme caution. To all this the student of Mennonite history needs to add such information as he has gained from personal observation in the localities named, special investigation into family histories, deed books and land surveys; and especially does he need to draw upon his personal knowledge of the manners, customs, habits, traditions, and characteristic names of the Mennonite people. All of these will often help him to settle points of fact which otherwise would remain subjects of doubt in his mind.

The following list practically exhausts the materials, secondary and original, on the American Mennonites and includes some of the most important works on the German and Swiss Anabaptists.

Asher, G. M. Historical Essay on Dutch Books and Pamphlets Relating to New Netherlands.

American Historical Review. Vol. IX.

American Archives, Fourth Series. Vol. VI.

Acts of the General Assembly of Virginia, 1861-2. Richmond, 1862.

Abington Records of Monthly Meetings of 1682-1746. Original records are in Friends Meeting House at Ogontz, Pa. A typewritten copy has been made for the Pennsylvania State Historical Society library in Philadelphia.

Augusta County (Va.) Records. From 1745 on.

Albert, G. D. History of Westmoreland County, Philadelphia, 1882.

Ausbund; das ist etliche schoene Lieder, wie Sie im Gefängniss zu Passau in dem Schloss von den Schweitzer Brüdern und andern recht gläubigen Christen gedichtet worden. Elkhart, Ind., 1905.

Barclay, Robert. The Inner Life of the Religious Societies of the Commonwealth. London, 1876.

Bean, T. W. History of Montgomery County. Philadelphia, 1884. The best history of the county.

Barton, William. Memoirs of the Life of David Rittenhouse, L. L. D., F. R. S. Philadelphia, 1813.

Burkholder, Peter. Eine Verhandlung von der äuszerlichen Wassertaufe und Erklärung einiger Irrthümer. Harrisonburg, Va., 1816. A copy of this pamphlet can be found in the private library of

Dr. John W. Wayland, of the University of Virginia.
────── Mennonite Confession of Faith, with nine reflections. Translated from the German by Joseph Funk. Winchester, Va., 1837.

Boehm, Henry. Reminiscences of Rev. Henry Boehm. New York, 1875.

Brumbaugh, Martin G. A. History of the German Baptist Brethren in Europe and America. Mount Morris, Ill., 1899.
────── The Life and Works of Christopher Dock. Philadelphia, 1908.

Brubacher, J. N. Brubaker Genealogy. Elkhart, Ind., 1884.

Bower, H. S. A Genealogical Record of the Descendants of Daniel Stauffer and Hans Bauer. Harleysville, Pa., 1897.

Balch, Thomas. Letters and Papers relating chiefly to the Provincial History of Pennsylvania. Philadelphia, 1855.

Brons, Anna. Ursprung, Entwickelung und Schicksale der Altevangelischen Taufgesinnten oder Mennoniten. Norden, 1891.

Brodhead, John R. History of New York, Harper Bros., 1853-1871. 2 Vol.

Borntreger, John E. Eine Geschichte der ersten Ansiedlung der Amischen Mennoniten und die Gründung ihrer ersten Gemeinde im Staate Indiana. Elkhart, Ind., 1907.

Bell, H. C. History of Leitersburg District. Leitersburg, Md., 1898.

Bartlaw, B. S. Centennial History of Butler County, Ohio, 1905.

Bullinger, Heinrich. Der Widertoufferen Ursprung, Fürgang, Sekten, etc. Zurich, 1561.

Bax, Belfort. Rise and Fall of the Anabaptists. London, 1903.

Beck, J. Die Geschichtsbücher der Wiedertäufer in Oesterreich-Ungarn. 1883.

Butler County, Ohio, History of. Western Pub. Co., 1882.

Cassel, D. K. Geschichte der Mennoniten. Philadelphia, 1890. This book consists largely of a compilation of sketches written by Pennypacker for other works, from various county histories, and several original articles on individual congregations. The work is not well arranged, is decidedly uncritical and fails to give proper credit for copied articles.

———— The Kulp Family. Norristown, Pa., 1895.

———— The Cassel Family. Norristown, Pa., 1896.

Chronicon Ephratense. Lancaster, Pa., 1889. This is a history of the community of Seventh Day Baptists at Ephrata. It is translated by J. Max Mark, D. D.

Bachman, Richard. Niclas Storch, 1880.

Colonial Records of Pennsylvania.

Cartland, F. C. Southern Heroes. Boston, 1895.

Congressional Globe, 38 Congress, Second session, Part I.

Conrad, Henry C. Thones Kunders and his Children. Wilmington, Del., 1891.

Chalkley, Thomas. Journal. Philadelphia, 1866.

Confession of Faith, Philadelphia, 1727. Printed by A. Bradford. Contains the names of the Mennonite ministers then living in Pennsylvania.

Claypool. Letter Book. Original in the library of the Pennsylvania State Historical Society.

Cox, W. W. History of Seward County, Nebraska. Lincoln, Neb., 1888.

Campbell, Douglas. Puritans in England, Netherlands and America. 1892.

Christianity Defined. A Manual of the New Testament Teaching. Hagerstown, Md., 1903. A doctrinal work published by the Reformed Mennonites.

Cornelius, C. A. Geschichte des Münsterschen Aufruhrs. 1855.

Day, Sherman. Historical Collections of the State of Pennsylvania. Philadelphia, 1843.

Davis, W. H. H. History of Bucks County. Doylestown, Pa., 1876. The best history of the county. Contains many local sketches on the Mennonites in the county.

Diffenderfer, F. R. The German Exodus to England in 1709. Lancaster, 1897. Published in Proceedings of Pennsylvania German Society, Vol. VII.

———— The Three Earls: An Historical Sketch. New Holland, Pa., 1876. A brief account of the settlement in Graffdale, Lancaster county, of Hans Graff in 1717.

———— Odds and Ends of Local History. Published in Proceedings of Lancaster County Historical Society, Vol. X. No. 6. Lancaster, 1906.

Dock, Christopher. Eine Einfältige und gründliche abgefaszte Schulordnung. Germantown, 1770.

Diekhoff, A. W. Die Waldenser im Mittelalter. Göttingen, 1851.

Döllinger, J. v. Beiträge zur Sekten Geschichte des Mittelalters. Munich, 1890.

Dexter, H. M. The True Story of John Smythe. 1881.

Egle, W. H. Notes and Queries, Historical and Genealogical. Harrisburg. From 1879 on.

Edwards, Morgan. Material for a History of the American Baptists. Philadelphia, 1770. Very rare. A copy in the library of the Pennsylvania State Historical Society.

Ellis and Evans. History of Lancaster County. Philadelphia, 1883. Contains article by E. K. Martin, on Mennonites and other material of value. But few of the articles are altogether reliable.

Egli, Emil. Die Zürcher Wiedertäufer. Zürich, 1878.

────── Akten Sammlung zur Geschichte der Zürcher Reformation. Zürich, 1879. 2 Vol.

────── Die St. Galler Täufer.

Eckhoff, A. In der neuen Heimath. New York, 1885.

Eby, A. Die Ansiedlung und Begründing der Gemeinschaft in Canada. Milford Square, Pa., 1872.

Eby, Ezra E. A Biographical History of Waterloo (Ont.) Township. Berlin, Ont., 1895. A detailed account of the earliest Mennonite settlements in Canada.

────── The Eby Family. Berlin, Ont., 1899.

Eby, Benjamin. Kurtzgefaszte Kirchengeschichte der Taufgesinnten oder Mennonisten. Elkhart, Ind., 1868.

Erbkam, H. W. Geschichte der Protestantischen Sekten. 1848.

Ellis, Franklin. History of Fayette County, Pa. 1882.

Fox, George. Journal.

Fretz, A. J. Wismer Family History. Elkhart, Ind., 1893.

────── Funk Family History, Elkhart, Ind.

Foote, W. H. Sketches of Virginia. Philadelphia, 1850.

Family Almanac. Mennonite Publishing Company, Elkhart, Ind. 1870-. Contains many short biographical sketches of early Mennonites.

Frederick County (Va.) Records. From 1743 on.

Funk, John F. The Mennonite Church and her Accusers. Elkhart, Ind., 1878.

Futhey and **Cope.** History of Chester County, Pennsylvania, 1881.

Ferris, Benjamin. Original Settlements on the Delaware.

Franck, Sebastian. Chronika. 1578.

Feestgave op Menno Simons (1892). Amsterdam, 1892.

Funck, Heinrich. Eine Spiegel der Taufe, mit Geist, mit Wasser, und mit Blut. Germantown, 1744.

Funk, Christian. Ein Auffsatz oder Vertheidigung von Christian Funk gegen seine mit-Diener der Mennoniten Gemeindschaft. Germantown, 1785.

——— A Mirror for all Mankind. Germantown, 1809.

Fernow, —. —. Documents Relating to the History of New York.

Fuesslin, J. C. Beiträge zur Kirchengeschichte des Schweitzerlandes. Zürich, 1741.

Grubb, N. S. The Mennonite Church of Germantown. Philadelphia, 1906.

Gibbons, Phoebe Earle. Pennsylvania Dutch, and Other Essays. Philadelphia, 1784. Largely descriptive, but one of the earliest books on the subject.

Growell, A. American Book Clubs.

Gnagey, Elias. The Gnaegi Family. Elkhart, Ind., 1897.

Glaubensbekenntnisz der neuen Deutchen Baptisten in den Vereinigten Staaten. Elkhart, Ind., 1877.

Gibson, John. History of York County. Chicago, 1886. The best history of the county.

Germantown Rath-buch, 1691 to 1706. The original is in the library of the Pennsylvania State Historical Society.

Griffis, W. E. Influence of the Netherlands upon England and America.

——— Brave Little Holland.

Hallesche Nachrichten. A translation. Philadelphia, 1881.

Heckler, James Y. History of Lower Salford Township. Harleysville, Pa., 1886.

Herald of Truth. Chicago and Elkhart, Indiana. From 1864 to 1908.

Hening, W. W. Statutes at Large (Va.), 1619-1822. 13 volumes.

Hazard, Samuel. The Register of Pennsylvania. Philadelphia, 1828-1832. Volumes I and VII contain many notices on early Mennonites. These are not reliable. The article in Vol. I on the Amish is altogether untrustworthy as to dates and most of the facts.

Hartzler, J. S. and Kauffman, D. Mennonite Church History. Scottdale, Pa., 1905. Contains a great deal of valuable material never printed before on the last fifty years of the history of the church, but not reliable on the earlier events.

Hartzler, Sr., John. Hertzler Genealogy. Elkhart, Ind., 1885.

Holcomb, W. P. Germantown, its Origin and Form of Government. Johns Hopkins Studies, Vol. IV.

Hess, John H. Genealogy of the Hess Family. Lititz, Pa., 1896.

Harris, Alexander. Biographical History of Lancaster County. Lancaster, Pa., 1872.

Holdeman, John. History of the Church of God. Lancaster, 1876.

———— Ein Spiegel der Wahrheit. Lancaster, 1878.

Hunsicker, Abraham. Das Religions, Kirchen und Schulwesen der Mennoniten. Milford Square, Pa., 1862.

Henry and Fulton Counties, Ohio, History of. D. Mason & Co., Syracuse, N. Y., 1888.

Herr, John. The True and Blessed Way. Lancaster, 1816.

———— Eine Kurtze und Apostolische Antwort. Lancaster, 1819.

———— Erläuterungs Spiegel. Lancaster, 1827.

BIBLIOGRAPHY

Heath, Richard. Anabaptism—From its Rise at Zwickau to its Fall at Münster. London, 1905.

Jenkins, C. P. The Guide Book to Historic Germantown. Germantown, 1904.

Jones, H. P. The Rittenhouse Paper Mill. Manuscript in the library of the Pennsylvania State Historical Society.

———— The Levering Family. Philadelphia, 1858.

Keyser, Charles S. The Keyser Family. Philadelphia, 1889.

Kalm, Peter. Travels in North America. London, 1812.

Kennedy, J. P. Journal of the House (Va.) of Burgesses, 1773-1776. Richmond, 1905.

Kilty, W. Laws of Maryland. Annapolis, 1800. 2 Vol.

Kilty, Harris, and Watkins. Laws of Maryland, 1799-1818. Annapolis, 1818. 4 Vol.

Kercheval, Samuel. A History of the Valley of Virginia. Woodstock, Va., 1850.

Kuhns, Oscar. The German and Swiss Settlements of Colonial Pennsylvania. New York, 1901.

King, Henry M. Religious Liberty. Providence, 1903.

Keller, Ludwig. Hans Denck. 1882.

———— Wiedertäufer. 1880.

———— Die Reformation. 1885.

———— Die Waldenser. 1886.

Klaasen, M. Geschichte der Taufgesinnten. 1873.

Kennedy, Robert P. Historical Review of Logan County, Ohio. Chicago, 1903. Has a good article on Amish of Logan county, by Bishop David Plank.

Krehbiel, H. P. History of the General Conference of Mennonites of America. St. Louis, 1898.

Locke, Mary Stoughton. Antislavery in America, Radcliffe College Monographs. Boston, 1901.

Le Fevre, Ralph. History of New Paltz. Albany, N. Y., 1903.

Landis, D. B. The Landis Family. Lancaster, 1888.

Laws of Maryland. (Hughes), 1834. Annapolis, 1835.

Müller, Ernst. Geschichte der Bernischen Täufer. Frauenfeld, 1895. This book contains many original letters and lists of names of Bernese Mennonites at about the time of the emigration to Pennsylvania. It is the best source for the European background of the emigration to Lancaster county.

Mombert, J. I. An Authentic History of Lancaster County. Lancaster, 1869. Contains good lists of early settlers.

Moser, Johannes. Eine Verantwortung gegen Daniel Musser's Meidungs Erklärung. Lancaster, 1876. A small pamphlet on the Ammansch-Mennonite controversy in Berne, 1693-1711. It contains many original letters with names of men who later came to Lancaster county.

Mittelberger, Gottlieb. Journey to Pennsylvania in the year 1750, and return to Germany in the year 1754. Translated by C. T. Eben. Philadelphia, 1898.

Menno Simons' Complete Works. Translated from the Dutch by J. F. Funk. Elkhart, Ind., 1871.

Minute Book of the Board of Property. Pennsylvania Archives, Second Series. Vol. XIX. Contains many notices regarding lands taken up by early settlers in Southeastern Pennsylvania.

Murphy, H. C. Anthology of New Netherland.

Mennonite Year Book and Directory. Published by the Mennonite Board of Missions and Charities. Scottdale, Pa., 1905-.

Montgomery, M. L. History of Berks County. Philadelphia, 1886.

BIBLIOGRAPHY 471

Mennonite Conferences of the Valley of Virginia, 1835-1884, Proceedings of. Elkhart, Ind., 1884.

Matthews and Hungerford, History of Lehigh County. Philadelphia, 1884.

Martyrs Mirror, by Tielman van Bracht. Translated by J. F. Sohm from the Dutch. Elkhart, 1887.

Musser, Daniel. The Reformed Mennonite Church; Its Rise and Progress with its Principles and Doctrines. Lancaster, 1873

Merx, Otto. Thomas Münzer und Heinrich Pfeiffer. 1889.

Mifflin County (Pa.) Records. From 1789 on.

New York Historical Society Collections. Second series. Vol. 3. Part 1. Appleton and Co., N. Y., 1857.

Newman, A. H. A History of Antipedobaptism. Philadelphia, 1897. Contains an excellent bibliography on the Anabaptists.

Nitsche, Richard. Geschichte der Wiedertäufer in der Schweiz. 1885.

Old Rights, Lancaster County. A manuscript collection of surveys, warrants, and deeds of early tracts of lands in the county. Found in the office of the Secretary of the Interior at Harrisburg.

Old South Leaflets, No. 95. A translation of part of Pastorius' description of Pennsylvania, with an introduction to the "Pennsylvania Pilgrim" by John Greenlief Whittier.

O'Callahan, E. B. History of New Netherlands. D. Appleton, 1855. 2 Vol.
——— Documentary History of New York. 4 Vol. Albany, 1850.

Oberholtzer, John H. Aufschlusz der Verfolgungen gegen Daniel Hoch von Canada. 1853.

―――― Verantwortung und Erläuterung. Milford Square, Pa., 1860.

Osiander, Lucas. Eine Predigt von dem Wiedertauf. 1582.

Pennylvania German Society, Proceedings. Published by the Society. 18 Vol. Lancaster, 1891―.

Pennsylvania Archives. Philadelphia and Harrisburg, 1852-1902. Four Series.

Pastorius, Franz Daniel. Beschreibung von Pennsylvanien, 1700. This work is edited with an introduction by Frederick Kapp, and published at Crefeld, 1884.

Pennypacker, Samuel W. Historical and Biographical Sketches. Philadelphia, 1883. Includes the Settlement of Germantown, Christopher Dock, Der Blutige Schau Platz, David Rittenhouse, etc.

―――― Annals of Phoenixville. Philadelphia, 1872.

―――― Hendrick Pennebecker. Philadelphia, 1894.

―――― The Pennypacker Reunion. Philadelphia, 1877.

―――― Bebbers Township and the Dutch Patroons of Pennsylvania. Published in the Pennsylvania Magazine of History, Jan., 1907.

―――― Pennsylvania German Society, Proceedings. Vol. IX. Contains a revised reprint of the sketches in Historical and Biographical Sketches, with additional articles on Mennonites.

Philip, Dirck. Enchiridion oder Handbüchlein. Lancaster, 1811.

Peachey, S. M. Memorial History of Peter Bitche. Lancaster, 1892.

Poore, B. F. Charters and Constitutions. Washington, 1878.

Penn-Logan Correspondence. Published by the Pennsylvania Historical Society. 1872. 2 Vol.

Perkiomen Region. The Past and Present. Edited by H. S. Dotterer. Issued periodically. Philadelphia, 1895—.

Proud, Robert. The History of Pennsylvania in North America. Philadelphia, 1797. 2 Vol.

Pennsylvania Magazine of History and Biography. Published by the Pennsylvania State Historical Society. Philadelphia. Vol's. 1-22.

Quack, H. P. G. "Plockhoy's Social Planen," in Beelden en Groepen. Amsterdam, 1892.

Rockingham Register, Harrisonburg, Va., for June 14, and July 26, 1895. Contains good sketches of Virginia Mennonites by L. J. Heatwole.

Rupp, I. D. History of Lancaster County. Lancaster, 1844. For many things still the source of all later histories of the county.

———— A Collection of Upwards of Thirty Thousand Names of German, Swiss, Dutch, French and other Immigrants to Pennsylvania (1727-1776). Of great value to the genealogist. The same list with index is found in Pennsylvania Archives. Second series. Vol. XVII.

———— The Religious Denominations of the United States. Philadelphia, 1844.

Ruoff, Ph. D., H. W. History of Montgomery County. Philadelphia, 1895.

Regier, Peter. Kurtzgefaszte Geschichte der Mennoniten Brüder Gemeinde. Berne, Ind., 1901.

Reiswick und Wadzek. Beiträge zur Kenntnis der Mennoniten Gemeinde. Berlin, 1821.

Rockingham County (Va.) Records. From 1777 on.

Runk & Co. Biographical Encyclopedia of Juniata County, Pennsylvania. Chambersburg, Pa., 1897.

Sewell, William. History of the Quakers.

Story, Thomas. Journal. Newcastle on Tyne, 1747.

Seidensticker, Oswald. Bilder aus der Deutsch-Pennsylvanischen Geschichte. New York, 1886.

———— First Century of German Printing in America, from 1728 to 1830.

Sachse, Julius F. The German Sectarians of Pennsylvania. Philadelphia, 1899.

———— The German Pietists of Provincial Pennsylvania. Philadelphia, 1896.

———— Letters Relating to the Settlement of Germantown. Philadelphia, 1903.

Strieper Papers. In Manuscript in the Bucks county collection in the library of the Pennsylvania State Historical Society. They include a number of letters writen by the early Striepers of Germantown to their friends in Holland.

Sharpless, Isaac. Quakerism and Politics. Philadelphia, 1905.

———— A Quaker Experiment in Government. Philadelphia, 1898.

Shoemaker, B. H. The Shoemaker Family of Cheltenham. Philadelphia, 1903.

Scheffer, Hoop de J. G. Inventaris der Archief Stukken Berustende bij de Vereenigde Doopsgezinde Gemeente to Amsterdam. A catalogue of documents and books in the Mennonite church in Amsterdam. It contains the titles and often the substance of many letters that were written from Switzerland and other parts of Europe to the Mennonites in Amsterdam and also several letters written from Pennsylvania.

———— The Mennonite Emigration to Pennsylvania. Translated from the Dutch by S. W. Pennypacker in Pennsylvania Magazine of History. Vol. 2.

———— Geschichte der Reformation in den Niederlanden.

Schmidt, C. B. Reminiscences of Foreign Immigration Work. An address at the Fourth Annual Convention of the Colorado State Realty Association. Held at Colorado Springs, June 20-23, 1905.

Stuckey, Joseph. Eine Begebenheit die sich in der Mennoniten Gemeinde in Deutschland und in der Schweitz von 1693 bis 1700 zugetragen hat. Elkhart, Ind., 1883.

Suderman, Leonard. Eine Deputations Reise von Russland nach America. Elkhart, 1897.

Stemen, C. B. History of the Stemen Family. Fort Wayne, Ind., 1881.

Souder, ——. History of Franconia Township. Harleysville, Pa., 1896.

Stockwell, A. P. History of Gravesend, Long Island.

Scott, Harvey. History of Fairfield County, Ohio. 1887. See article by Joseph Kurtz on the Amish settlements of the county.

Stapleton, A. Memorial of Huguenots in America. Carlisle, Pa., 1901.

Stauffer, Jacob. Eine Chronik oder Geschicht-Büchlein von der so genannten Mennonisten Gemeinde. Lancaster, 1855.

Schyn, H. Historia Mennonitorium. Amsterdam, 1723.

Starck, J. A. Geschichte der Taufe und Taufgesinnten. Leipzig, 1789.

Senate Document V. 26, 58. Cong., Second session.

Statutes at Large of the Confederate States of America. Ed. by Matthews. Richmond, 1864. 2 Vol.

Statutes at Large of Pennsylvania, 1682-1801. Harrisburg, 1897. 4 Vol.

Taylor Papers. Land surveys in Lancaster county before 1734. In collection of manuscripts in library of Pennsylvania State Historical Society.

Troyer, David A. Eine Unpartheischer Bericht von den Hauptumständen welche sich ereigneten in den so-genannten Alt Amischen Gemeinden in Ohio vom Jahr 1850 bis ungefähr 1861 wodurch endlich eine vollkommene Spaltung entstand.

The Christian Confession of Faith of the harmless Christians in the Netherlands known as Mennonists. First printed in English at Amsterdam in 1712. Reprinted by A. Bradford, Philadelphia,

1727. Very rare. A copy in the library of the Pennsylvania Historical Society.

Ten Cate, Bl. Geschiedenis der Doopsgezinden in Groningen, Overyssel, en Friesland. 1842.

United States Statutes at Large, 13 Vol.

Votes and Proceedings of the House of Representatives of the Province of Pennsylvania. Philadelphia, 1776. 6 Vol.

Wayland, Ph. D., John W. The German Element of the Shenandoah Valley of Virginia. Charlottesville, Va., 1907. Contains many references to the Mennonites of Virginia.

Woolman, John. Journal. Philadelphia, 1864.

Watson, J. F. Annals of Philadelphia and Pennsylvania in the Olden Time. Philadelphia, 1891. 3 Vol.

Wedel, C. H. Abrisz der Geschichte der Mennoniten. Newton, Kansas, 1904. A good brief summary of the whole field of Mennonite history.

Wing, Conway P. History of Cumberland County, Pa. Philadelphia, 1879.

Warner Beers & Co., History of Franklin County, Pa. Chicago, 1887.

Wickersham, J. P. History of Education in Pennsylvania. Lancaster, 1886.

Weingarten, Herman. Die Revolutions Kirchen Englands. Leipzig, 1868.

Zook, Shem. Eine wahre Darstellung von dem welches uns das Evangelium in der Reinheit lehrt, so wie auch ein unpartheischer Bericht von den Haupt Umständen welche sich in underschiedlichen Gemeinden ereigneten woraus endlich die unchristlichen Spaltungen entstanden sind. Mattawana, Pa., 1880.

zur Linden, Otto Friedrich. Melchior Hoffman, ein Prophet der Wiedertäufer. 1885.

INDEX

Allebach, Christian 184
Alstädt 28
A Lasco, John 60, 417
Albrecht, Joseph and Company 418
Amish 160
  Canada 226
  Doctrine and practice 234
  Diener Versammlung 239
  Early Life 213
  Egli defection 247
  First in America 210
  In Ohio 216
  In Indiana 221
  In Illinois 228
  In Nebraska 233
  In Missouri 233
  In Kansas 234
  In Iowa 223
  Immigration from 1820 to 1850 225
  New York 227
  New Amish 243
  Origin 208
  Old Order 241
  The Stuckey congregations 248
Anabaptists 17
Arets, Lenart 101
Armbruster, Aaron 421
Arnold, Gottfried 420
Augsburger, Christian 218
Ausbund 431, 432

Baer, Martin 177
Baer, J. B. 449
Baer Almanac 442
Baer, Johann 418, 444
Ban 49
Baptists, Seventh Day 180, 415
Baptism, infant 20
Basel 32
Bechtley, Jacob 186
Beissel, Conrad 180
Bender, D. H. 404, 448
Berne 32
Bergey, Hans Ulrich 184
Bethel College 401, 449
Blauch, Christian 196, 214
Blauch, Jacob 196
Blaurock, George 19, 40, 433
Blosser, John 405, 448
Bluffton College 449
Bowman, Wendal 146, 169
Bowman, Johannes 177
Boehm, Martin 177, 181, 216
Bouwens, Leonard 53
Bonnet 390
Brenneman, Daniel 308, 311
Brethren 22, 31
Brödli, Hass 22, 23
Brechbühl, B. 140, 142
Brunner, C. H. 449
Brubacher, J. N. 448
Brueder Gemeinde 341
Burghaltzer, Hans 177
Burkhart, Christian 198
Burchi, Hans 140, 142
Bullinger, Heinrich 41, 49
Byers, N. E. 402, 448

Castelberger 22
Charter of Paul I 325

Church Government 390
Chiliasm 37
Christlicher Bundesbote 444
Church of God 305
Civil government 48
Clemmer, Velte 184
Conestoga wagon 163
Collegiants 68
Coffman, J. S. 274
Community of goods 22, 50
Conferences 390
Confession of faith 410
Conscription Act of 1864 376
Confederate Conscription Acts 382
Coffman, S. F. 448
Crefeld 101
Cumberland valley 193
Customs 386
Culture 386

Danner, Michael 193
Denk, Hans 33, 37, 40
Der Lobgesang 439
Der Evangelische Botschafter 444
Detweiler, I. R. 448
Denner, Jacob 419
Deknatel, Johann 419, 420
Diener Versammlung 239
Die Kleine Geistliche Harfe 440
Die Frohe Botschaft 249
Die Wandelnde Seele 420
Doctrines of early Anabaptists 22
Dock, Christopher 422, 423, 427

Eby, Hans 270
Eby Benjamin 431
Ebersole, Abraham 159
Eby Isaac 448
Eckerlin, Michael 181
Egli defection 246
Egli C. R. 451
Ehrenfried, Joseph 415, 479, 443
Ein Spiegel der Taufe 421
Ein Spiegel der Wahrheit 431

Eicher, Johannes 160
Eicher church 225
Elkhart Institute 401
Engle, Christian 229
Enchiridion 418
Ephrata 181
Erläuterungs Spiegel 428

Faber, Gellius 417
Fairfax controversy 203
Feet-washing 387
Franconia 183
  Bucks county 185
  Berks county 186
  Chester county 187
  Every day life 189
  Literary activity 190
  Skippack region 183
Frick, Conrad 159
Frank Sebastian 32, 36
Friesland 39
Funk, Christian 427
Funk, Hans 159, 168
Funk, Henry 184
Funk, Heinrich 415, 421
Funk, J. F. 329, 401, 404, 416, 431, 447
Fundament Buch 418
Funk, Joseph 441

Gerber, Samuel 450
Gerig, Sebastian 450
Gerig, Benj. 450
Geistliches Blumen Gärtlein 420
Germantown 94
Germans in Virginia 199
Godshalk, Herman 184
Graybil, John 196
Good Jacob 198
Gnaegi, Christian 214
Goshen College 401
Gospel Herald 447
Gospel Witness 445
Goerz, David 449
Gospel Banner 449
Graff, Hans 146, 155
Grubb, N. B. 431, 449
Grebel, Conrad 19, 30, 31, 40
Güldene Aepfel 420

INDEX 481

Halteman, Hans 159
Haury, S. S. 403
Haszlibach, Hans 434
Hartzler, J. E. 448
Haszlibacher Lied 434
Hartzler, J. S. 401, 405, 448
Harmonia Sacra 441, 444
Herr, Christian 173, 177
Hessians 231
Heatwole, L. J. 315, 448
Herald of Truth 445
Heilsbote 452
Hershey, Benedict 169
Herr, Hans 168, 146
Herr, John 292, 418, 428
Herstein, John 419
Hetzer, Ludwig 32
Hirschi, Benedict 177
Hostater, Jacob 210
Hostetler, Oswald 159
Horekill 82
Hoffman, Melchior 33, 38, 40, 47
Horsch, John 431
Holdeman, John 305, 430
Hostetler, C. K. 405
Hoch, Daniel 344
Hocking valley 275
Hubmeir, Balthasar 31, 33, 35
Hut, Hans 33, 34, 37, 47
Hungary 38
Huss, John 433

Illinois Conference of Mennonites 248
Ingolstadt 36
Indian Creek 184
Indian Raids 202

Jansen, Peter 340
Jotter, Christian 160
Johns, D. J. 401, 405, 450
Juniata 196

Kauffman, Daniel 431
Kendigh, Martin 159

Kendig, Martin 146, 168
Keller, Ludwig 20
Keyser, Dirck 109
Kishacoquillas valley 215
Kistler, Michael 231
King, Joseph 252
Kindig, Benjamin 254
Kirchmeyer 36
Kliewer, J. J. 449
Kolb, A. B. 404
Kolb, Jacob 184
Kolb, Dielman 184, 159, 415
Kolb, Martin 184
Krehbiel, J. C. 345
Krehbiel, Christian 330, 449
Krehbiel, H. P. 350, 431, 449
Krehbiel, Daniel 399
Kurtz, Heinrich 418
Kurzgefaszte Kirchen-Geschichte 431
Kunders, Thones 101

Landis, Benjamin 177
Lambert, George 406, 448
Lantz, Lee 252
Leyden, John of 41, 50, 60, 406, 417, 448
Leaman, A. H. 448
Lensen, Jan 101
Lincoln county 266
Linville valley 204
Longacre, Christian 159
Longeneker, Daniel 186
Logan county 220
Loucks, Aaron 448

Mack, A. S. 448
Mack, Noah H. 448
Manitoba 336
Manz, Felix 19, 30, 31, 433
Matthys, Jan 40
Martyrs Mirror 411
Maryland 198
Meilin, Martin 169, 146
Mennonite Printing Presses
Mennonite Board of Guardians 334
Mennonite Executive Aid Committe 334

Mennonite Publishing Company 404, 416
Mennonites
  And the State 352
  Attitude toward civil government 352
  Attitude toward Learning 397
  As Pioneers 290
  During the Civil War 315
  Exemptions from the Oath 357
  Exemptions from military service 365
  First use of name 65
  First in America 81
  General Conference 343
  In Ontario 265
  In Prussia 78
  In Switzerland 74
  In the Palatinate 76
  In Netherlands 66
  Literature and Hymnology 409
  Mennonite Brethren in Christ 310
  Origin of Doctrine 386
  Protest Against Slavery 120
  Relation to English Separatists 71
  Reformed 292
  Swiss in America 277, 282
  Virtues 406
  Wisler 307
Menno Simons
  Birth 53
  Beliefs 58
  Controversial writings 56
  Death 62
  Influence 64
  Public disputations 61
  Price set on his head 61
  Renunciation of Rome 55
  Works of 416
Missions 403
Miller, D. D. 401, 405, 450
Miller, Jacob 216
Miller, Levi 450
Miller, Peter 415

Miller, S. H. 450
Moseman, Michael 230, 247
Molotschna 325
Micronius, Martin 417
Mirror for all Mankind 428
Millenarianism 37, 40
Münzer, Thomas 24, 25, 26, 37
Musser, Daniel 428 444
Münster 40
Mühlhausen 38

Nageli, Rudolf 180
Naffziger, Christian 226
Newcomer, Christian 159
Neus, Hans 110
New Amish 242
Netherlands 41
Non-resistance 40
Nold, Jacob 427

Oberholtzer, J. H. 298, 343, 430, 444
Op den Graff, Abraham 101
Op den Graff, Dirck 101
Overholts, Martin 146

Pastorius, Franz Daniel 102
Page, W. B. 406
Pennsylvania Dutch 393
Pennebeker, Hendrick 110
Peters, Isaac 342
Penner, J. A. 404
Persecution 31, 36, 98
Perkiomen creek, 184
Pequea colony
  Early Preachers 177
  Church Buildings 173
  Not Proselyters 181
  Naturalization 166
  Relation to Indians 164
  Redemptioners 171
  Relation to Dunkards 178
  Settlement 134
  Secular life 161
Pennypacker, S. W. 415
Philharmonia 442
Philip, Obbe 53

INDEX 483

Philip, Dirck 53, 418
Pingjum 53
Pitscha, Ulrich 159
Plank, Melchior 172
Plockhoy, Pieter Cornelisz 81
Principles, 386
Prayer Head-covering 388
Putnam county 230

Ramsauer, Heinrich 159
Reiff, John 198
Revolutionary War 253
Religiöser Botschafter 324, 444
Ressler, J. A. 405, 448
Reublin, William 19, 31, 35
Rebaptism 23
Rink, Melchior 39
Rittinghuysen, Willem 109, 117
Root, Ulrich 159
Ropp, Andrew 230
Ropp, Christian 230, 250
Ruth, Henry 184
Russian Immigration 324
Rupp, I. D. 416

Sauer, Christopher 422, 442
Schleitheim Confession 22, 42
Schantz, J. Y. 329
Schertz David 234
Schlegel, Joseph 234, 450
Schaffhausen 31, 35
Schantz, Peter 252
Schisms 291
Schellenberger, Peter 159
Schantz, Ben 177
Schulordnung 427
Showalter, Christian 346, 400
Shoemaker, J. S. 405, 448
Shelley, A. S. 449
Skippack 119
Slavery 206
Smith, John 450
Smutz, John 419
Snyder, Sicke 54
Somerset county 214

Sohm, J. F. 416
Sommer, I. A. 449
Sprunger, S. F. 349
Stauffer Jacob 304
Storch, Niclas 24
Steiner, M. S. 404, 406, 431,
Stutzman, Jacob 159
Stumpf, Simon 18, 50
St. Gallen 32
Strasburg 39, 40 438
Strickler, Abraham 199, 161
Strickler, Jacob 200
Stuckey, Joseph 240, 248
Strubhar, Valentine 252

Tazewell county 229
Telner, Jacob 100
Tithes 50
Troyer, Emanuel 252
Tuscarawas county 216
Tyson, Reynier 101

Van Bebber, Isaac Jacob 109
Van der Smissen, C. H. A. 449
Van der Smissen, C. J. 400
Verantwortung und Erläuterung 430
Virginia 199
Von Todtleben 331

War, Civil 314
  Revolutionary 253
Warkentin, Bernard 334
Waldenses 17, 24, 39
Waldshut 28, 31, 35
Wadsworth school 400
Wayne county 218
War taxes 254
Waterloo county 267
Wagner, Jörg 433
West Point 345
Wenger, Christian 159
Wedel, C. H. 401, 449
Wenger, A. D. 405, 448
Westmoreland county 196
West Point Colony 223

Weil nun die zeit Vorhanden ist 438
Wenger, Martin 442
Webersthal 156
Wesley City 228
Witmarsum 53
Wilmot Township 227
Wisler, Jacob 307
Woodford county 229

Yoder, Jacob 160

York county 193
Yoder, J. K. 240
Yoder, C. Z. 450

Zooks, 160
Zook, Moritz 160, 211
Zook, Shem 240, 416
Zook, Abe 242
Zug, Peter 159
Zurich 18
Zwickau Prophets 25

www.ingramcontent.com/pod-product-compliance
Lightning Source LLC
Chambersburg PA
CBHW071220290426
44108CB00013B/1236